Readings in Psychological and Educational Testing

edited by

LEWIS R. AIKEN, Jr.

Dana Professor of Psychology
Guilford College
Greensboro, North Carolina

Allyn and Bacon, Inc.   Boston

Library of Congress Catalog Card No.: 72-93072

**Readings in Psychological
and Educational Testing**

Table of Contents

Preface

Readings in Psychological and Educational Testing is designed for undergraduate and beginning graduate courses in psychological testing and for educational measurement and evaluation classes taught with some emphasis on the psychological foundations of testing. The selections comprise a representative sample of the available literature, including a mixture of theoretical and empirical readings on a wide range of problems and issues. The majority of the readings were written by recognized authorities in the field of psychological and educational measurement, but particular authors are not overly represented. An attempt has been made to strike a balance between a purely psychological emphasis and an educational measurement approach, although the stress on basic issues has resulted in the volume having a definite psychological flavor. In deciding what selections to include, attention was given to readability as well as significance, timeliness, and comprehensiveness. Consequently, several of the selections may appear rather long for a book of readings; the majority, however, are of medium length. Since developments in the field of testing have been rapid during recent years, a preference has also been shown for more recently published articles.

The four or five articles constituting each of the nine sections of the volume are closely tied to the majority of current textbooks on psychological and educational testing (Ahmann and Glock, 1971; Aiken, 1971; Anastasi, 1968; Brown, 1970; Cronbach, 1970; Karmel, 1970; Nunnally, 1970; Thorndike and Hagen, 1969). A table showing which articles are most appropriate for particular chapters in each of these textbooks has not been included, because many of the selections fit equally well in several contexts. Appropriate choices should be fairly obvious from a comparison of the table of contents of this volume with that of a particular textbook. Also, many of the readings may be used independently of a standard textbook, for example, in units on testing in general, educational, and industrial psychology courses, or classes in the psychology of personality.

None of the readings have been altered beyond changing the form of the references and citations to a uniform style and omitting certain unessential footnotes. The editor feels that abbreviating or excerpting important papers too often affects their meaning and fails to give the student a sufficiently detailed understanding of the research or theoretical issues involved. In any event, an important criterion in selecting the articles was that they should contain a minimum of redundancy, presenting their points directly but readably. Also, the reader of this volume will not be overwhelmed with complex statistical formulations; almost all of the statistical symbolism is fairly elementary. Books of readings having a more technical, statistical orientation (e.g., Jackson and Messick, 1967; Mehrens and Ebel, 1967) are readily available for instructors and students desiring that emphasis.

In surveying the selections contained in this volume, the reader may notice that none of them deal exclusively with response styles, the "Jensen controversy," testing and job discrimination, and several other contemporary issues in educational and psychological measurement. However, these topics have certainly not been avoided; they are considered in some detail, along with other issues, as a part of more comprehensive readings.

Each of the nine sections of the book is preceded by an introductory overview which briefly summarizes the articles, clarifies more complicated terminology, and attempts to bring the major ideas and issues discussed in that section into clearer focus. In addition, the reader will observe that the articles in each section, and the sections themselves, are arranged in a logical order, sometimes chronological, but mainly in terms of the progressive development of concepts and procedures. One of the unique features of this volume is the series of papers (Section VI) on individual and group differences in mental abilities. These papers are particularly appropriate as parallel readings for Chapter 6 of the editor's *Psychological and Educational Testing* (Aiken, 1971) and in courses or units concerned with individual differences. Another feature of *Readings in Psychological and Educational Testing* is the placement of the references for all 43 articles in a comprehensive bibliography at the back of the book. Also included is an index of the most important terms used in the readings, all of which are defined briefly in the readings themselves or in the section introductions. For more comprehensive definitions and discussion, the student should consult a textbook or glossary on psychological testing (see Appendix A of Aiken, 1971).

The editor of any book of readings owes his greatest debt to the authors who have kindly permitted him to reprint their work, in the majority of instances without remuneration to themselves. In addition, valuable assistance in the clerical tasks involved in preparing this volume was given by two of my students, Janet Corpening of Wake Forest University and Nita French of Guilford College, and by my constant companion Dorothy Aiken.

Lewis R. Aiken, Jr.
Urbana, Illinois

Readings in Psychological
and Educational Testing

Educational Achievement
and Test Design

It is appropriate that the lead section of this book of readings on psychological testing should deal with educational achievement tests. These are the oldest and most extensively used of all psychological tests. Although the design and analysis of other kinds of tests (aptitude, personality, interest, etc.) entail procedures that are rarely taught to nonpsychologists, the construction of educational achievement tests is a task shared by thousands of teachers and others whose primary concern is not psychological measurement. Since more teacher-made and standardized tests of scholastic achievement are constructed and administered every day than all other tests combined, psychologists and educators have continually sought to improve the effectiveness of these tests in evaluating and motivating students. The five articles in this section reflect that concern.

The first two articles focus on procedures and principles that have proven useful in constructing classroom tests. Julian Stanley stresses the importance of specifying educational objectives and designing tests to measure the attainment of those objectives. The uses and limitations of essay and objective questions, together with advice on how to write both kinds of items, are also considered. In the second article, Robert Ebel lists and discusses ten measurement principles for improving classroom tests. Especially noteworthy are principles 3-5: 3) Every important outcome of education can be measured; 4) The most important educational achievement is command of useful knowledge;[1] 5) Written tests are well suited to measure the student's command of useful knowledge. These three principles should provide material for lively debate among instructors and students.

[1] By command of "useful" or "substantive" knowledge, Ebel means understanding, i.e. seeing the relationships among aspects of verbal information, the imparting of which he views as the principal function of formal education (see Ebel, 1965, pp. 38-45). This definition of knowledge is more restrictive than that of Bloom, Hastings and Madaus (1971).

The third article, also by Robert Ebel, deals with the uses and limitations of standardized achievement tests. Four misconceptions about standardized testing are discussed: 1) that the most important outcomes of education are too subtle, complex and subjective to be measured effectively; 2) that testing is an unfriendly, threatening, anxiety-generating process from which the child should be shielded; 3) that the objectives of particular teachers or schools are uniquely different from those for which the standardized test was built; 4) that test-makers will dictate the curriculum.

The fourth article, by Ralph Tyler, considers seven by-products of the National Assessment of Educational Progress (NAEP), a long-term national survey of the knowledge, skills, understandings and attitudes of groups of American children and adults. The content areas selected for this nationwide census are: reading, writing, literature, social studies, science, mathematics, music, art, citizenship, career and occupational development. Two of these ten areas are assessed every year in a cyclical arrangement, repeating an area every five years, terminating in 1979. The results are expressed as percentages of examinees who give particular answers to items in each of the ten content areas. In the paper reprinted in this section, Tyler contrasts the primary objective of NAEP—to provide information on what groups of pupils have learned—with the "sorting, normative" approach of traditional standardized achievement testing.[2] One important distinction is that National Assessment gives information on all sections of the school population, providing a more rational basis for educational decision-making by parents, educators and legislators.

The last article in this section, by Alice Gustav, is the report of an empirical investigation concerned with college students' preferences for true-false, multiple-choice and essay tests, and the relationships of their preferences to study habits and test scores. The findings that true-false items were liked least and that students tended to study less and memorize details more for objective tests than for essay tests are, of course, serious criticisms of the objective test format. Also, in spite of attaining higher grades on objective tests, a greater percentage of students in this study actually preferred essay tests. These results and others point to the need for test designers to balance more effective sampling of content and greater ease and objectivity of scoring, which are features of an objective test, against students' attitudes toward different item formats and the positive educational consequences of having examinees organize and write their answers to essay items.

[2] In this context, see the articles by Hieronymus (no. 40), Ebel (no. 41) and Block (no. 42) in Section IX for a distinction between *normative testing* and the *criterion-referenced testing* of National Assessment.

1 | The ABC's of Test Construction*

Julian C. Stanley

Constructing a good test is one of the teacher's most difficult duties. Good tests do not just happen. Actual test construction, therefore, requires much thought and careful planning.

Planning the Test

A well-planned test will provide the means for evaluating progress toward the expected outcomes of instruction, as expressed in the educational philosophy of the particular school and as defined in the objectives of the particular course.

If the school hopes to produce "good citizens" with "integrated personalities," for example, tests must measure the development of good social attitudes and a widening range of significant interests.

For any given course, instructional objectives must be expressed in terms of the specific changes in pupil behavior or growth which the teacher hopes to bring about.

A teacher, for instance, should be conscious that such an objective as the development of an appreciation of literature may express itself in various forms of student reaction. He sets out then to phrase test questions which will determine whether a particular piece of writing gave individual students a sense of satisfaction and enthusiasm, made them want to read more by the same author, stimulated their own creative expression.

The well-planned test will reflect the relative amount of emphasis each objective has received in the actual teaching of the course. The same test might not be equally valid for two teachers of general science if one has emphasized the memorizing of isolated facts, while the other was more concerned with the interrelation of facts. Each teacher would be helped by

*From *National Education Association Journal,* 1958, **47**, 224-226. Copyright 1958 by the National Education Association of the United States. Reprinted by permission of the author and publisher.

drawing up in outline form a kind of table of specifications to indicate not only the objectives of the course, but also the relative amount of time spent on each.

The content of the test should show a similar proportion in regard to the *number* of items to be included but not the *type,* for the type of item depends upon the nature of the objective to be measured.

The well-planned test must be designed to accomplish the purpose it is to serve. If the purpose is to give the basis for school marks or classification, it will attempt to rank the pupils in order of their total achievement. But if the purpose is diagnosis, its value will depend upon its ability to reveal specific weaknesses in the achievement of individual pupils.

Diagnostic tests would cover a limited scope, but in much greater detail than a test of general achievement, and would be arranged to give scores on the separate parts. The range of difficulty of items is relatively less important, also, in diagnostic tests. This is true, too, of mastery tests administered at the end of a teaching unit to see whether minimum essentials have been achieved.

The well-planned test will also fit the conditions under which it is to be administered, such as the time available for testing, facilities for duplicating the test copies, and cost of materials, as well as the age and experience of the pupils being tested.

Preparing the Test

In actual construction of a test, these suggestions have helped:

1. Prepare a rough draft of the test as soon as possible. Many teachers jot down items day by day for possible inclusion to help ensure that no important points will be omitted, particularly those appearing in supplementary material that might be overlooked if the textbook itself is the chief basis of the test.

2. Do not make the test items too easy. Many teacher-constructed tests fail to make the items difficult enough. This, no doubt, is due in part to the influence of the "70% should be the passing grade" tradition. However, the test that is too easy is not an efficient instrument for measuring pupil progress.

3. Include more items in the first draft than will be needed in the final form. This will permit culling out of weak items and those not needed to produce proper balance.

4. Subject the test to critical revision some time after it is drafted by checking items against the table of specifications to see if they show the desired emphasis on various topics. If tests are submitted for criticism to

other teachers of the subject, points of doubtful importance can be weeded out and ambiguous wording corrected.

5. Include more than one type of item in the test. A variety of test types is more interesting to students. The test situation may also require that three or four forms of objective items be used, or that these be combined with discussion or essay-type questions.

6. Place all items of one kind together in the test. Sometimes completion, true-false, and multiple-choice questions are thrown together in random order. This arrangement is rarely, if ever, desirable. When like items are grouped, the pupil can take full advantage of the mind-set imposed by a particular form, and the teacher will find scoring and interpretation of scores easier.

7. Arrange test items in an ascending order of difficulty. The placing of very difficult items at the beginning is likely to produce needless discouragement for the average or below-average student.

8. Avoid a regular sequence in the pattern of responses. If items are arranged alternately true and false, or two true and two false, pupils are likely to catch on and answer correctly without considering the content of the item at all.

9. Make directions to the pupil clear, concise, and complete. Instructions should be so clear that the weakest pupil knows what he is expected to do, tho he may be unable to do it.

It is better to tell young children to "draw a line under" than to "underline." In lower grades, teachers find it helpful to read instructions aloud while the class follows silently the written instructions. If the form of the test is unfamiliar or complicated, a generous use of samples correctly marked, or practice tests, is recommended.

Regardless of how carefully a test is planned and edited, it is impossible to know solely by inspection exactly how good it is, or which are the weak items. If possible, therefore, the test should be given some advance tryout which will approximate the conditions under which the real test will be given, show the actual length of time it will require, and indicate what scoring difficulties may result.

Because various studies have shown that a majority of teachers, especially at the high-school level, use a combination of essay and objective questions, the uses and limitations of both will be briefly examined here.

The Essay Test

The essay test has both unique advantages and serious disadvantages. Some authorities claim that it calls forth less than half the knowledge the average pupil possesses on a subject, compared with results from an objective test, and takes twice the time to do it; that it overrates the importance of knowing how to say a thing and underrates the importance of having something to say; and that the score resulting from an essay test depends more upon *who* reads it and *when* than upon the student who wrote it.

Offsetting the serious scoring difficulties connected with essay tests and their frequently low degrees of validity, reliability, and usability, there is much to indicate that such tests have a legitimate place in the modern school.

Specifically, they are useful for measuring functional information, certain aspects of thinking, study skill and work habits, and an active social philosophy. These are educational objectives which emphasize the *functioning* of knowledge rather than its mere possession.

Such tests are especially valuable in courses in English composition and journalism, where the student's ability to express himself is a major instructional objective, and in advanced courses in other subjects where critical evaluation and the ability to assimilate and organize large amounts of material are important.

Essay tests have at least one other general merit: When pupils expect the test to be of that type, in whole or in part, they seem more likely to employ such desirable study techniques as outlining and summarizing, and to make a greater effort to recognize trends and relationships.

Despite popular opinion to the contrary, a high-quality essay test is more difficult to construct than is a good objective test. These three rules, however, should be helpful in improving the construction and use of essay tests:

1. Restrict such a test to those functions for which it is best adapted.

2. Increase the number of questions asked and decrease the amount of discussion required for each.

3. Make definite provisions for teaching pupils how to take such examinations.

Types of Objective Tests

The simple *recall test* item employs a direct question, a stimulus word or phrase, or a specific direction to elicit from the pupil a response based on his previous experience. The typical response is short—hence its other name, the short-answer question.

The main problem is to phrase these test items so that they will call forth responses from a higher level than mere memory, and so that they can be readily scored.

Example: Eight is what percent of 64?

The *completion test* consists of a series of sentences in which certain important words or phrases have been replaced by blanks to be filled in by the students. This test has wide applicability, but unless very carefully prepared, it is likely to measure rote memory rather than real understanding, or to measure general intelligence or linguistic aptitude rather than school achievement.

Scoring is also more subjective, and complicated by the fact that the missing words are written in blanks scattered all over the page, rather than in a column. This difficulty can be avoided by a form such as this:

1. The man who headed the first expedition to circumnavigate the globe was _____.

2. The Articles of Confederation were in force from 1781 to _____.

An *alternative-response test* is made of items each of which permits only two possible responses. The usual form is the familiar true-false item and its cousins, the right-wrong, yes-no, same-opposite, and multiple-choice questions.

While the true-false type of question is popularly considered easy to prepare, experienced test-makers point out that this type of test requires great skill, and care must be taken in wording so that the *content* rather than the *form* of the statement will determine the response. The following suggestions may be useful in constructing such tests.

1. Avoid specific determiners, that is, strongly worded statements containing words such as "always," "all," or "none," which may indicate to pupils that the statement is likely to be false.

2. Avoid using the exact language of the textbook, with only minor changes to give the true-false pattern, because this puts too great a premium on rote memory.

3. Avoid trick statements which appear to be true but which are really false because of some inconspicuous word or phrase, such as "The Battle of Hastings was fought in 1066 BC."

4. Avoid "double-headed" statements, especially if partly true and partly false, as in this sentence: "Poe wrote *The Gold Bug and The Scarlet Letter.*"

5. Avoid double negatives lest pupils versed in grammer conclude that two negatives equal an affirmative, while others think such statements are emphatic negatives.

6. Avoid unfamiliar, figurative, or literary language and long statements with complex sentence structure—for reasons which should be obvious.

7. Avoid words that may have different meanings for different students. "Often" may mean once a week to one child; three times a year to another.

A *multiple choice test* is composed of items which require the student to select a correct or definitely better response from two or more alternatives (at least four whenever possible). This is one of the most useful test forms. It may be used to ascertain the ability to give definitions, identify purposes and causes, similarities and differences, or to ask many other varieties of questions.

In phrasing multiple-choice questions, it is essential to avoid giving irrelevant or superficial clues, and to assure that the question measures more than memory. The diagnostic value of this type of item depends as much on the skillful wording of the incorrect choices presented as upon correct statements of the right choice.

Scoring may be facilitated by arranging the items in groups, putting together all items with the same number of choices, and requiring the simplest possible method of recording the response.

Other useful rules are:

1. Make all responses grammatically consistent. For example, if the verb is singular, avoid plural responses.

2. Use direct questions rather than incomplete statements whenever possible. This helps eliminate irrelevant clues.

3. Arrange the responses so that the correct choice occurs about equally in all positions, and do not consistently make the correct answer longer or shorter than the others.

4. Make all the responses plausible, and when testing at higher levels, increase the similarity in the choices under each item in order to better test the powers of discrimination.

A *matching test* involves the association of two things in the mind of the learner by requiring him to pair the items in two columns: events and dates, events and persons, terms and definitions, laws and illustrations, and the like. Matching exercises are well adapted to testing in *who, what, where,* and *when* areas but not to measuring understanding as distinguished from mere memory.

Since most of the tests used in classrooms are teacher-made, it is highly important that teachers develop proficiency in the building of tests by discriminating use of what is now known, by keeping themselves informed on new studies of testing techniques and methods, and by careful evaluation of their own testing, day by day.

2 | Measurement and the Teacher*

Robert L. Ebel

The principles of measurement of educational achievement presented in this article are based on the experience and research of a great many people who have been working to improve classroom testing. The particular principles discussed here were selected on the basis of their relevance to the questions and problems which arise most often when tests of educational achievement are being considered, prepared and used. While some of the principles may seem open to question, we believe a case can be made in support of each one.

1. *The measurement of educational achievement is essential to effective education.*

Learning is a natural, inevitable result of human living. Some learning would occur even if no special provision were made for it in schools, or no special effort were taken to facilitate it. Yet efficient learning of complex achievements, such as reading, understanding of science, or literary appreciation, requires special motivation, guidance and assistance. Efforts must be directed toward the attainment of specific goals. Students, teachers and others involved in the process of education must know to what degree the goals have been achieved. The measurement of educational achievement can contribute to these activities.

It is occasionally suggested that schools could get along without tests, or indeed that they might even do a better job if testing were prohibited. It is seldom if ever suggested, though, that education can be carried on effectively by teachers and students who have no particular goals in view, or who do not care what or how much is being learned. If tests are outlawed, some other means of assessing educational achievement would have to be used in their place.

*From *Educational Leadership,* 1962, **20,** 20-24. Reprinted by permission of the Association for Supervision and Curriculum Development and Robert L. Ebel. Copyright © 1962 by the Association for Supervision and Curriculum Development.

2. *An educational test is no more or less than a device for facilitating, extending and refining a teacher's observations of student achievement.*

In spite of the Biblical injunction, most of us find ourselves quite often passing judgments on our fellow men. Is candidate A more deserving of our vote than candidate B? Is C a better physician than D? Is employee E entitled to a raise or a promotion on his merits? Should student F be given a failing mark? Should student L be selected in preference to student M for the leading role in the class play?

Those charged with making such judgments often feel they must do so on the basis of quite inadequate evidence. The characteristics on which the decision should be based may not have been clearly defined. The performances of the various candidates may not have been observed extensively, or under comparable conditions. Instead of recorded data, the judge may have to trust his fallible memory, supplemented with hearsay evidence.

Somewhat similar problems are faced by teachers, as they attempt to assess the achievements of their students. In an effort to solve these problems, tests have been developed. Oral examinations and objective examinations are means for making it easier for the teacher to observe a more extensive sample of student behavior under more carefully controlled conditions.

The price that must be paid for a test's advantages of efficiency and control in the observation of student achievements is some loss in the naturalness of the behavior involved. In tests which attempt to measure the student's typical behavior, especially those aspects of behavior which depend heavily on his interests, attitudes, values or emotional reactions, the artificiality of the test situation may seriously distort the measurements obtained. But this problem is much less serious in tests intended to measure how much the student knows, and what he can do with his knowledge. What is gained in efficiency and precision of measurement usually far outweighs what may be lost due to artificiality of the situation in which the student's behavior is observed.

3. *Every important outcome of education can be measured.*

In order for an outcome of education to be important, it must make a difference. The behavior of a person who has more of a particular outcome must be observably different from that of a person who has less. Perhaps one can imagine some result of education which is so deeply personal that it does not ever affect in any way what he says or does, or how he spends his time. But it is difficult to find any grounds for arguing that such a well concealed achievement is important.

If the achievement does make a difference in what a person can do or does do, then it is measurable. For the most elementary type of measurement requires nothing more than the possibility of making a verifiable observation that person or object X has more of some defined characteristic than person or object Y.

To say that any important educational outcome is measurable is not to say that satisfactory methods of measurement now exist. Certainly it is not to say that every important educational outcome can be measured by means of a paper and pencil test. But it is to reject the claim that some important educational outcomes are too complex or too intangible to be measured. Importance and measurability are logically inseparable.

4. *The most important educational achievement is command of useful knowledge.*

If the importance of an educational outcome may be judged on the basis of what teachers and students spend most of their time doing, it is obvious that acquisition of a command of useful knowledge is a highly important outcome. Or if one asks how the other objectives are to be attained—objectives of self-realization, of human relationship, of economic efficiency, of civic responsibility—it is obvious again that command of useful knowledge is the principal means.

How effectively a person can think about a problem depends largely on how effectively he can command the knowledge that is relevant to the problem. Command of knowledge does not guarantee success, or happiness, or righteousness, but it is difficult to think of anything else a school can attempt to develop which is half as likely to lead to these objectives.

If we give students command of knowledge, if we develop their ability to think, we make them intellectually free and independent. This does not assure us that they will work hard to maintain the status quo, that they will adopt all of our beliefs and accept all of our values. Yet it can make them free men and women in the area in which freedom is most important. We should be wary of an educational program which seeks to change or control student behavior on any other basis than rational self-determination, the basis that command of knowledge provides.

5. *Written tests are well suited to measure the student's command of useful knowledge.*

All knowledge can be expressed in propositions. Propositions are statements that can be judged to be true or false. Scholars, scientists, research workers—all those concerned with adding to our store of knowledge, spend most of their time formulating and verifying propositions.

Implicit in every true-false or multiple-choice test item is a proposition, or several propositions. Essay tests also require a student to demonstrate his command of knowledge.

Some elements of novelty are essential in any question intended to test a student's command of knowledge. He should not be allowed to respond successfully simply on the basis of rote learning or verbal association. He should not be asked a stereotyped question to which a pat answer probably has been committed to memory.

6. *The classroom teacher should prepare most of the tests used to measure educational achievement in the classroom.*

Many published tests are available for classroom use in measuring educational aptitude or achievement in broad areas of knowledge. But there are very few which are specifically appropriate for measuring the achievement of the objectives of a particular unit of work or of a particular period of instruction. Publishers of textbooks sometimes supply booklets of test questions to accompany their texts. These can be useful, although all too often the test questions supplied are of inferior quality—hastily written, unreviewed, untested, and subject to correct response on the basis of rote learning as well as on the basis of understanding.

Even if good ready-made tests were generally available, a case could still be made for teacher-prepared tests; the chief reason being that the process of test development can help the teacher define his objectives. This process can result in tests that are more highly relevant than any external tests are likely to be. It can make the process of measuring educational achievement an integral part of the whole process of instruction, as it should be.

7. *To measure achievement effectively the classroom teacher must be (a) a master of the knowledge or skill to be tested and (b) a master of the practical arts of testing.*

No courses in educational measurement, no books or articles on the improvement of classroom tests, are likely to enable a poor teacher to make good tests. A teacher's command of the knowledge he is trying to teach, his understanding of common misconceptions regarding this content, his ability to invent novel questions and problems, and his ability to express these clearly and concisely; all these are crucial to his success in test construction. It is unfortunately true that some people who have certificates to teach lack one or more of these prerequisites to good teaching and good testing.

However, there are also some tricks of the trade of test construction. A course in educational measurement, or a book or article on classroom testing can teach these things. Such a course may also serve to shake a teacher's faith—constructively and wholesomely—in some of the popular misconceptions about the processes of testing educational achievement. Among these misconceptions are the belief that only essay tests are useful for measuring the development of a student's higher mental processes; that a test score should indicate what proportion a student does know of what he ought to know; that mistakes in scoring are the main source of error in test scores.

8. *The quality of a classroom test depends on the relevance of the tasks included in it, on the representativeness of its sampling of all aspects of instruction, and on the reliability of the scores it yields.*

If a test question presents a problem like those the student may expect to encounter in his later life outside the classroom, and if the course in which his achievement is being tested did in fact try to teach him how to deal with such problems, then the question is relevant. If the test questions involve, in proportion to their importance, all aspects of achievement the course undertakes to develop, it samples representatively. If the scores students receive on a test agree closely with those they would receive on an independent, equivalent test, then the test yields reliable scores.

Relevance, representativeness and reliability are all matters of degree. Procedures and formulas for calculating estimates of test reliability are well developed, and are described in most books on educational measurement. Estimates of representativeness and relevance are more subjective, less quantitative. Yet this does not mean that relevance and representativeness are any less important than reliability. The more a test has of each the better. While it is possible to have an irrelevant and unrepresentative but highly reliable test, it is seldom necessary and never desirable to sacrifice any one of the three for the others.

Either essay or objective test forms can be used to present relevant tasks to the examinees. Ordinarily, the greater the novelty of a test question, that is, the smaller the probability that the student has encountered the same question before, or been taught a pat answer to it, the greater its relevance. Because of the greater number of questions involved, it is sometimes easier to include a representative sample of tasks in an objective than in an essay test. For the same reason, and also because of greater uniformity in scoring, objective tests are likely to yield somewhat more reliable scores than are essay tests.

9. *The more variable the scores from a test designed to have a certain maximum possible score, the higher the expected reliability of those scores.*

Reliability is sometimes defined as the proportion of the total variability among the test scores which is not attributable to errors of measurement. The size of the errors of measurement depends on the nature of the test—the kind and the number of items in it. Hence for a particular test, any increase in the total variability of the scores is likely to increase the proportion which is not due to errors of measurement, and hence to increase the reliability of the test.

Figure 1 shows some hypothetical score distributions for three tests. The essay test consists of 10 questions worth 10 points each, scored by a teacher who regards 75 as a passing score on such a test. The true-false test consists of 100 items, each of which is worth one point if correctly answered, with no subtraction for wrong answers. The multiple-choice test also includes 100 items, each of which offers four alternative answer options. It, too, is scored only for the number of correct answers given, with no "correction for guessing."

Note, in the data at the bottom of Figure 1, the differences among the tests in average score (mean), in variability (standard deviation), in effective

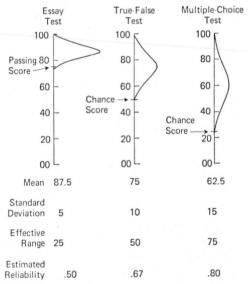

Figure 1. Hypothetical Score Distributions for Three Tests

range and in estimated reliability. While these are hypothetical data, derived from calculations based on certain assumptions, they are probably reasonably representative of the results most teachers achieve in using tests of these types.

It is possible to obtain scores whose reliability is above .90 using 100 multiple-choice items, but it is not easy to do, and classroom teachers seldom do it in the tests they construct. It is also possible to handle 100-point essay tests and 100-item true-false tests so that their reliability will equal that of a 100-item multiple-choice test. But again, it is not easy to do and classroom teachers seldom succeed in doing it.

10. *The reliability of a test can be increased by increasing the number of questions (or independent points to be scored) and by sharpening the power of individual questions to discriminate between students of high and low achievement.*

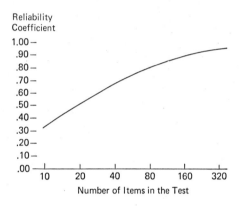

Figure 2. Relation of Test Reliability to Test Length

Figure 2 illustrates the increases of test reliability which can be expected as a result of increasing the number of items (or independent points to be scored) in a test. Doubling the length of a 10-item test whose reliability coefficient is .33 increases the reliability to .50. Doubling again brings it up to .67, and so on. These estimates are based on the Spearman-Brown formula for predicting the reliability of a lengthened test. While the formula requires assumptions which may not be justified in all cases, its predictions are usually quite accurate.

Figure 3 shows how the maximum discriminating power of an item is related to its level of difficulty. These discrimination indices are simply differences between the proportions of correct responses from good and poor students. Good students are those whose total test scores fall among the top 27 percent of the students tested. Poor students are those whose scores make up the bottom 27 percent. An item of 50 percent difficulty does not necessarily have (and usually will not have) an index of discrimination of 1.00. Its discriminating power may be zero, or even negative. But items of middle difficulty have higher ceilings on their discriminating power. What is more important, they not only can have, but usually do have, greater discriminating power than very easy or very difficult items. An item that no one answers correctly, or that everyone answers correctly, cannot discriminate at all. Such an item adds nothing to the reliability of a test.

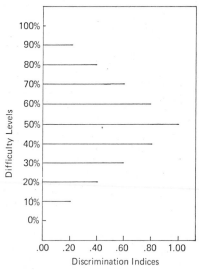

Figure 3. Maximum Discrimination Attainable
with Items at Different Levels of Difficulty

In summary, the ten principles stated and discussed in this article represent only a sample of the important things classroom teachers need to know about educational measurement. These principles, and the brief discussion of each presented here, may serve to call into question some common practices in classroom testing, or to suggest some ways in which classroom tests might be improved. They are not likely, and are not intended, to say all that needs to be said or do all that needs to be done to improve educational measurement in the classroom. It is our sincere belief, however, that a teacher whose classroom testing reflects an understanding of these principles will do a better than average job of measuring student achievement.

3 | Standardized Achievement Tests: Uses and Limitations*

Robert L. Ebel

Standardized tests of educational achievement are essential educational tools, especially in the elementary school. They can be used to improve the effectiveness of the competent teacher or school administrator. They can help motivate and reward the child. They can provide a basis for constructive cooperation between parents and teachers in guiding the child's educational development. They can help the school staff and the community it serves assess the effectiveness of the school program.

A demonstration of how standardized tests can focus public attention on an educational need occurred recently in New York City. Results of a city-wide standardized reading test showed that the average reading ability of school children in New York was below the national average. A few years before, it had been above the national norm. While these findings were doubted, discounted, and rationalized by experts and spokesmen inside the schools and out, there was almost universal support for the vigorous action taken by the Board of Education to strengthen the program of reading instruction. Among other things, the number of specialists in remedial reading on the school staff was sharply increased.

This use of standardized tests as a basis for judging the effectiveness of a school program has been criticized by some educators. They point out that half the pupils or schools *have* to be below the norm and that remedial programs can never alter this situation. Further, they say, it is unreasonable and unfair to expect the same levels of achievement of all pupils and all schools. A pupil ranking well above average may, in fact, have less reason for self-satisfaction and complacency than a pupil ranking below average, if the high ranking pupil had educational advantages the other lacked.

There is merit in both these criticisms, perhaps more in the second than in the first, but it would be dangerous to accept them completely. No pupil, no

*From *National Elementary Principal,* 1961, **41**(1), 29-32. Copyright © 1961, National Association of Elementary School Principals, National Education Association. All rights reserved.

teacher, no schoolboard, no community should be continuously satisfied with their educational achievements, and few are. Information provided by standardized tests of achievement helps them focus their dissatisfactions more purposefully and take remedial action more constructively.

The second criticism is sometimes used in general terms as a rationalization for below average performance. It contains enough truth to be a persuasive argument for unsound interpretations of test results and for inaction when action is needed. On the basis of intelligence tests and other measures, we know it is unreasonable to expect the same achievement of all pupils and all schools. Unfortunately, the usual effort to obtain a standard of reasonable expectancy of achievement from intelligence test scores is based, I think, on some misconceptions about intelligence, achievement, and the educational process.

The important point to remember is that most pupils and many schools could achieve considerably more than they have achieved. Further, it is probably true that the pupils and schools which are below average in achievement have both the greatest need and the greatest opportunity to improve.

Understanding the causes of inferior achievement is an important prelude to effective remedial action. No child's potential and no school's potential for educational achievement is unlimited. But this should never be used as an excuse for inaction.

If standardized tests are valuable tools, why do many schools lag in using them effectively? Lack of full awareness of the potential value of test information and lack of training in how to use that information may be partly responsible. But there are also three common misconceptions about educational testing which may account for much of the skepticism about the value of tests and the reluctance to use them more extensively.

Importance of Tangible Outcomes

The first of these misconceptions is the belief that the most important outcomes of education are too subtle, too complex, too subjective to be measured effectively. Elementary school teachers are less guilty on this score than some college professors who take off on flights of fancy when discussing intangible but supposedly essential outcomes of education.

Teachers of young children know that the development of skills in the tool subjects and the establishment of solid foundations for understanding and interest in the major fields of human knowledge are concrete, specific, important objectives. But some of them may feel that tests, especially objective standardized tests, fail "to get at" the real essentials of achievement in these skill and foundation subjects. This mystical devotion to a hidden reality of achievement which is more essential than overt ability to perform has never satisfied the research worker. He wants to know the nature of this hidden reality and what evidence there is that it is important.

Danger of Overemphasis on Adjustment

The second misconception about educational testing arises from over-concern with the child's immediate happiness and self-satisfaction. Extreme supporters of this view often regard testing as an unfriendly, threatening, anxiety-generating process. They would shield the child from its stress and possible pain. I demur, and call as a first witness the physician.

Most of us learn to adjust to the physician's prescriptions, whether they are bad-tasting medicines, disinfectants that sting, shots that hurt, or even surgery. There is some emotional stress and discomfort, but the end result is usually increased health. To do what must be done a doctor needs courage, but this implies no lack of sympathy. What it does imply is farsighted concern for the ultimate welfare of the patient.

I have been appalled by the lack of this farsighted attitude among some advocates of child-centered education. They talk as if the teacher's primary responsibility were to guard the child's ego against any bruises whatsoever. Let him achieve as much as he can without strain, they say, but be careful not to ask too much of him. Their excess of concern for protection of the child's present "security" may, however, encourage neglect of needed small readjustments until they accumulate into a crisis of major proportions.

Take the case of Sharon which illustrates a problem all too many schools and families have become unhappily acquainted with in recent years. Sharon was the third of four children in an upper middle-class family. Her early years at school were uneventful. Periodic descriptive reports indicated that she was adjusting well and making progress. If any standardized tests were given, the significance of the results was not reported to the parents.

Midway through the third grade, trouble developed. Sharon began to say she hated school and to seek escape by feigning illness. Investigation showed that the basic problem was that Sharon couldn't read, at least not nearly as well as her classmates. They were beginning to refer to her as "dumb." The parents proposed that Sharon attend the reading clinic of a nearby university and perhaps get special individual instruction. The school staff counselled against such a step, arguing that they could provide all the special help needed, now that the problem had been identified. Further, they said, much harm could be done if too much attention were paid to the problem. Better to treat it as casually and quietly as possible, they said.

Despite some misgivings, Sharon's parents agreed. For a while, things seemed to improve. Sharon was happier in school. She brought home reports of small triumphs, of special recognitions and opportunities. The school reports, still couched in general, unthreatening phrases, indicated generally satisfactory progress. Then, near the end of Sharon's eighth-grade year, trouble developed again. Her teacher recommended that she repeat the grade because of her serious reading disability. The special attention she had received had apparently taught her to learn by listening, but she had not learned effective self-direction in reading.

After some plain-speaking conferences between teacher and parents, Sharon did not fail. She did go to summer reading camps. She went on to high school and took five years to finish college instead of four.

If the school had had a systematic program of standardized testing and had reported the results regularly, Sharon's reading disability would probably have been identified before it was translated into an emotional and social problem. And once the difficulty was identified, if the school had been more concerned with Sharon's future welfare than her current happiness, the problem might well have been corrected before it affected her subsequent schooling. In education, as in medicine and justice, an excess of present sympathy can postpone or even defeat the procedures necessary for an individual's future welfare.

Limited Value of Purely Local Objectives

The third misconception about standardized educational achievement tests results in their avoidance or de-emphasis on the ground that this teacher's objectives or that school's objectives are uniquely different from those for which the standardized test was presumably built.

We all recognize that it is desirable for both teachers and schools to have freedom to experiment with new materials and methods and that it is unwise for them to be bound tightly to a rigidly prescribed curriculum. It is good that they can capitalize on their own unique talents and opportunities. But it is also necessary that they recognize their responsibilities to develop the same basic skills and fundamental understandings which other teachers and other schools are seeking to develop.

What constitutes a good elementary education today in Bangor, Maine, is not radically different from what constitutes a good elementary education in

Los Angeles, California. Even if the ideal elementary education in one locality should differ from the ideal in another, it would be unwise to build an educational program around only the local needs. For it is certainly true that many of those educated in one place will spend most of their lives in some other.

One of the essential values of a well-constructed standardized test is its reflection of expert consensus on nationwide objectives of achievement. Instead of asking how well the standardized test fits local objectives, the test selector should ask with how much competence the test constructors can speak concerning the common objectives of all schools. A teacher should not ask a standardized test to provide evidence on how well she has taught all the things she has tried to teach, but only on the things that all teachers ought to have taught. For those achievements which are truly and rightly unique to a particular school or teacher, locally constructed tests are the best answer.

Will the Test-Makers Dictate Curriculum?

Many of those who mistrust the nationally developed standardized tests of achievement frequently express fear that the test-makers will dictate the curriculum. There is some basis for this belief, but it should not be a source of anxiety. If the standardized test is taken seriously, it will certainly exert some influence on teaching. But if the test is constructed by competent experts, that influence should be more beneficial than harmful.

The content and emphasis of textbooks, courses of study, teaching methods, and tests of achievement should all be sanctioned by the same kind of authority—a consensus of expert judgements. If the test-makers try, as many of them do, to catch and reflect in their tests a consensus of the judgement of curriculum specialists, it seems unreasonable to charge them with attempting to dictate curricular developments. If standardized tests of achievement are supplemented by locally constructed tests, there is slight danger that the use of standardized tests will result in undesirable uniformity in curricula.

Expert Test Construction

A well-constructed standardized achievement test provides an independent, broadly based definition of *desirable goals* of achievement in *all* schools. This is one of its primary values. Two others are related to it. The first is expert, painstaking test construction. The second is independent, broadly based norms of achievement.

Those who prepare standardized tests, in consultation with subject-matter experts, usually are skilled in writing items. In addition, they pre-test the items to identify those which are too difficult or too easy or which fail to discriminate clearly between high and low achievers. Careful attention is also given to the balance of the test among content areas and item types.

The result of the expertness and care applied to the construction of a standard test of educational achievement is usually a technically better test than a local teacher or group would be likely to create. The tasks it presents are those the pupils should be able to handle. The scores it yields discriminate reliably different levels of achievement. It is usually convenient to administer and score and is efficient and economical in its yield of useful information.

The provision of national, regional, or statewide norms for score interpretation is a third valuable contribution of the standardized achievement test. To secure accurate norms for clearly defined and widely appropriate reference groups is not a simple matter. It is even more difficult to present these norms so that they will be easy to use and to interpret properly.

These norms enable the user of a standardized test to obtain an external, broadly based standard for judging the achievements of pupils. Norms are not universal standards. Nor are they self interpreting. An oversimplified approach to test norms can rob them of much of their potential usefulness. After the comparison of local achievements with external norms has been made and the difference noted, one must still ask, "Is this good or bad?" and "Why do we seem to do so well, or poorly?" and "Under the circumstances, what should we do about the situation?" Standardized tests and their norms will not provide any automatic answers, but they can provide the basis for wise planning and for more reasonable decisions.

Schools exist to educate pupils, but it is the exceptional classroom teacher or school administrator who can report very precisely how much learning the pupils have acquired. Enrollment, attendance, and per-pupil cost can be specified accurately and in detail, but the acquisition of skills, knowledge, and attitudes is not readily stated in statistical terms. Educational achievement is not easy to measure, and existing tests leave much to be desired. But relatively few schools and teachers are obtaining and using even a small fraction of the information on educational achievement that existing tests could provide. I am persuaded that competent teachers and school systems can improve their effectiveness rapidly by making good use of existing standardized tests of educational achievement. Combined with other efforts, the systematic and skillful use of standardized tests should move any school toward higher levels of achievement.

4 | National Assessment—Some Valuable By-Products for Schools*

Ralph W. Tyler

A major purpose of the national assessment program is to provide the lay public with census-like data on the educational achievements of our children, youth, and adults—data which will furnish a dependable background of information about our educational attainments, the progress we are making, and the problems we still face in achieving our educational aspirations.

As the assessment program has developed, however, some interesting and valuable by-products, not contemplated or foreseen in the early stages, have appeared. This article will deal with these by-products and their potential value for schools and for principals.

It came as a surprise to some of us to discover that the testing programs commonly conducted in the schools do not furnish information about what our pupils have learned. Instead, they indicate 1) how far a student is above or below the average score of the group with which he is compared, and 2) how far the average score of a classroom or school is above or below the average of the group with which it is compared. From present test results we cannot obtain such useful information as what percent of our 13-year-old children can read and comprehend a simple newspaper paragraph, or what percent of 17-year-old youth have acquired one or more marketable skills.

Why haven't traditional tests been designed to find out what individuals or groups have learned? Why have they been constructed to report only relative achievements in relation to other individuals or groups?

The approach commonly used in test development in the past can largely be attributed to the assumption that testing is primarily a sorting process. Tests are employed to sort people for courses, for curricular tracks, for admission to college, and the like. They measure individual differences and relative performances of groups; they do not appraise individual and group progress in learning. Using these tests, the schools, then, are largely sorting and selecting agents rather than educational agents.

*From *National Elementary Principal,* 1969, **48**(6), 42-48. Copyright ©1969, National Association of Elementary School Principals, National Education Association. All rights reserved.

It was in a society in which most people were unskilled laborers and relatively few people were among the professional, social, and political elite that such a concept of testing developed. Now, however, our society is quite different. Science and technology have freed people from being "hewers of wood and drawers of water." Only 5 percent of the labor force is unskilled. Opportunities for employment in technical, professional, managerial, and service occupations have increased more than 300 percent in one generation. Our society is now seeking to identify potential talents of many sorts and to furnish opportunities for these talents to be developed through education.

Research on the brain and in behavioral genetics indicates that the learning requirements in our schools and colleges place no strain on the basic potential of the vast majority of human beings. Schools can be designed and redesigned to help all students learn. From the standpoint of any student, the way to judge whether or not an institution is an educational one is to find out whether the student gains a wider range of alternatives in his life choices with each year of schooling. An educational institution is one in which a human being is aided to find new doors of opportunity—not trained ever more narrowly to fit into a niche in society. In such a school, new kinds of tests can serve in various ways to promote and guide the development of the student.

One valuable by-product of the national assessment project, therefore, is the clarification of the difference between testing for sorting and testing that can help substantially in the education and guidance of individuals.

A second by-product, useful to the principal, is the demonstration that the educational objectives of a school can be formulated and agreed upon in a way that involves parents, laymen, and school staff members. This greatly increases the common understanding of what schools are trying to do. Because a major purpose of the assessment project is to provide helpful information about the progress of education that can be understood and accepted by lay citizens, the procedures used in the construction of assessment exercises involved laymen. In each field, scholars, teachers, and curriculum specialists formulated statements of the objectives which they believe faithfully reflect the contribution of that field and which the schools are seriously seeking to attain. For each of these major objectives, prototype exercises were then constructed. These were exercises which, in the opinion of scholars and teachers, give students an opportunity to demonstrate the behavior implied by the objective. The lists of objectives and the prototype exercises which help to define them were then reviewed by a series of panels of citizens living in various parts of the country in cities, towns, and villages. The laymen who participated were nominated by national organizations in response to a request for the names of persons interested in education who resided in various sections of the country—in rural, urban, and suburban communities.

Each panel spent two days reviewing the material and making a judgment about each objective. The judgment was made in terms of two questions: "Is this something important for people to learn today? Is it something I would like to have my children learn?"

This process resulted in some revisions of the original listing of objectives and a few eliminations. The procedure was designed to insure that every objective being assessed is: 1) considered important by scholars, 2) accepted as an educational task by the school, and 3) deemed desirable by leading lay citizens. This should help to eliminate the criticism frequently encountered with current tests in which some item is attacked by the scholar as representing shoddy scholarship, or criticized by school people as something not in the curriculum, or labeled by prominent laymen as being unimportant.

This review of objectives by lay panels was useful in constructing assessment exercises; it was also an educational experience for panel members—an experience which they found enlightening and rewarding. A number of the lay panelists reported that these review sessions gave them a much clearer understanding of the purposes of the schools than they had had before.

The sessions also furnished an opportunity for discussing and clarifying some of the common causes of public misunderstanding about such objectives as those in the areas of citizenship, vocational education, biology, social studies, and mathematics. At the request of their local school officials, some of the laymen had earlier participated in formulating objectives for the school or had served on committees to review and criticize the stated educational objectives. They reported that they had not found these experiences fruitful. The difference between the earlier tasks and the work they undertook in the assessment project was largely due to the use of prototype assessment exercises to help clarify the meaning of each statement of objectives. For example, in the field of writing, the material presented to the panels included statements of objectives and prototype exercises such as the following:

Objective: *Write to communicate adequately in a social situation.*

This was defined by such exercises as:

a) Invite your parents to the PTA meeting next Monday at 7:00 p.m. (age 9)

b) Thank your aunt for the gift she sent you. (age 13)

c) Write directions for adding cream cheese and other ingredients to make a special treat from a prepared cake mix. (age 17)

d) Prepare written directions which tell a friend how to get to your home from the nearest highway exit. (adult)

Objective: *Write to communicate adequately in school situations.*

This was defined by such exercises as:

a) Announce the results of the election of crossing guards. (age 9)

b) Take notes of names, addresses, dates, books, etc., mentioned in a 5-minute taped lecture. (age 17)

Objective: *Write to communicate adequately in a business or vocational situation.*

This was defined by such exercises as:

a) Fill out an application for a driver's license. (age 17)

b) Write a letter of reference for a neighbor seeking employment. (adult)

Objective: *Appreciate the value of writing.*

This was defined by responses to such questions as the following:

a) Have you written anything during the past week? What was it? Do you think it was worth doing? (age 9)

b) When you have spare time, do you use some of it to write something? What do you write? Do you do this often? Did you write anything this week? (ages 13 and 17)

When the objectives are defined in this way by prototype exercises, they are likely to be understood by the layman. Abstract statements alone are often so general that they are meaningless, or they use trite and hallowed terms, like "citizenship," which are commonly approved but mean different things to different people. Discussions of objectives, when guided by examples of this sort, are more easily focused on real issues regarding the aims of the school.

Typically, the public has understood only in very general terms the objectives of a modern educational program. Many people have not really thought of today's objectives as different from those which they perceived when they were children. One result of this limited or distorted perception is evident when we fail to obtain the necessary public support for some of our important educational tasks. The list of objectives developed by the procedure used in the assessment—a procedure involving parents, laymen, and school personnel—should greatly increase public understanding of what the schools are trying to do and gain further appreciation of the importance of these aims. Educators may well find this form of discussion a helpful way to clarify or to modify some of their own views.

A third useful by-product of the assessment project is the demonstration that appraisal exercises can be constructed to provide information about the progress of the entire range of school children, not merely data about the so-called "average" child.

The traditional achievement test is constructed to measure individual differences and to furnish reliable average scores for grades or schools. The test items, therefore, are concentrated on those which are typical of average performance. Exercises which all children or nearly all children can do, as well as those which only a very few can do, are eliminated from such tests.

In reviewing current tests to see whether they could be used in the national assessment, we found that more than 80 percent of the items in the most widely used achievement tests fell between the 40 percent and 60 percent level of difficulty. Only about 5 percent of the items were exercises which could be answered by students in the lower third of the class, and another 5 percent represented tasks appropriate for the upper third. For assessing the progress of education, and for informing teachers, principals, and parents in local schools about the achievements of their children, we need to know what *all* children are learning—the disadvantaged or "slow" learners, the most advanced, and the middle or "average." The construction of exercises appropriate for these purposes has been a challenge and a new venture for test constructors. It required the development of exercises in which approximately one-third of the test items represent achievements characteristic of the lower third at that age level, one-third represent achievements characteristic of the middle third at that age level, and one-third represent achievements of the top third.

The contractors found these requirements difficult to meet because their previous experience had not involved appraising the achievements of the upper and lower thirds. In the initial try-outs, we found that many of the exercises made for the lower third used language that could not be understood by the pupils. They did not know what they were being asked to do. It is *extremely* important to distinguish between failure on an exercise *because the child doesn't understand what he is asked to do* and failure *because he is unable to do the task.* In a number of cases, we found that simplification of the instructions opened the way for "slow" learners to demonstrate what they had learned.

A second defect in the first attempt of the contractors to assess the progress of the lower third was the failure to include examples of achievements that represent earlier or lower stages of progress in learning. By consulting with teachers in Head Start programs and with those who had much experience in working with disadvantaged children, the staff was able to construct a sample of exercises appropriate for appraising the progress in learning of "slow" learners. The later tryouts indicate that the final battery of assessment exercises furnishes information about the achievements of the total range of children.

Now that the contractors have learned how to construct batteries of this sort, it should be possible for schools to get tests and other appraisal instruments that will enable teachers, principals, and parents to obtain information about the progress of the entire range of children in the school. This will help to focus attention on 1) the successful efforts of the school, and 2) the problems being encountered that require added efforts or different efforts. This then is a third by-product of the national assessment.

A fourth by-product is the demonstration of the feasibility of using a variety of appraisal techniques rather than being limited to the use of paper-and-pencil tests. We have long recognized that many important kinds of educational achievements are not validly indicated by pupil responses on group tests. This is true, for example, of intellectual and aesthetic interests, habits and practices in the areas of citizenship, social attitudes, occupational skills. Experimental projects in evaluation have shown that valid evidence about these kinds of achievements can be obtained by using a variety of devices such as questionnaires, interviews, observation, and performance tests.

These devices have not been considered feasible for use in schools generally, largely because it has been assumed that their use would require too much time. This view of the great amount of time required to make appraisals by means other than paper-and-pencil tests derives from the notion that every pupil must be given every appraisal exercise. Where the purpose is to assess the achievements of groups and subgroups of pupils, sampling methods can be employed as they are in the national assessment. The total battery given this spring is divided into 14 parts, and no one pupil takes more than 1/14th of the total. Some pupils take paper-and-pencil tests; some answer questions about their interests and habits; some show their skills by actual performance tests; and some are involved in a group project where some of their citizenship practices can be observed. By using carefully designed sampling procedures, it is possible to estimate the achievements of a total pupil group from the reactions obtained in the samples of pupils. A single elementary school will probably not have a large enough enrollment to permit dividing the total into 14 samples and still have a sufficient number in each sample to give reliable estimates. But if there were a small number, such as 64 in each grade for example, four samples could be formed and each sample could be given one-fourth of the total list of appraisal exercises. This would permit the use of devices for assessing interests, attitudes, practices, and skills, as well as paper-and-pencil tests. A more comprehensive and useful evaluation of educational progress could thus be conducted.

A fifth by-product of national assessment is the clear indication that appraisal exercises can be constructed to aid teachers in their daily work. At least four kinds of tests or other devices would be helpful to teachers in the classroom:

1. *Placement tests* that help the pupil identify the extent of his progress

in each area of instruction and thus indicate in what section of a sequential program he can fruitfully begin his learning. The appropriate section for him to begin would be one in which he can learn things he does not already know and in which his present background should afford an adequate basis for further study. Tests of this sort can be constructed when basic objectives and prototype exercises for different age levels have been formulated, reviewed, and agreed upon. This appraisal does not give the same results as the grade equivalents obtained from traditional tests.

2. *Diagnostic tests* which are based on "work samples" of learning exercises that 1) utilize various appropriate modes of presentation, of problem solving, or practicing, and 2) employ various sensory modalities. Such tests furnish representative samples of the different modes of learning that can be used by the student and enable him to test himself on auditory, visual, and tactile presentations and reactions. These tests should help the pupil to select, at least initially, the means of learning he will find most effective in his own development in this area of the curriculum.

3. *Mastery tests* that sample the pupil's comprehension of basic concepts and his ability to utilize the essential skills that are required to proceed to the next unit in the sequential educational program. The purpose of such tests is not to place him on a scale with relation to his peers but to identify the readiness of the student to move on in his educational development. All, or nearly all, pupils will attain the level of essential mastery; otherwise, the educational program is inappropriate for the students enrolled. The exercises will not be concentrated at the 50 percent level of difficulty as those in current achievement tests are; each exercise will be an example of the desired skill, knowledge, or the like, at the level in which it is commonly used. Every pupil is expected to perform satisfactorily practically all of the exercises as an indication of mastery. In present experimental and developmental programs, "practically all" is defined as 85 percent of them. Such mastery tests enable the student to recognize when he is ready to move on to the next unit or set of educational experiences.

4. *Tests of generalization* that enable the pupil to determine the extent to which he is able to apply what he has learned in the educational program to the many other situations in his life in which this learning is relevant. These tests will consist of exercises that have not been used in his training but that represent new illustrations of the concepts and skills he has been seeking to master. The tests will include not only simulation and "description of situations" but also actual samples of the situations in other courses, on the playground, and in the wider community where the learning has significant application. The purpose of education is to enable the pupil to gain the

competencies he needs in order to continue developing throughout his life—not just the competencies that enable him to get along in school. The student, therefore, needs to appraise his effectiveness in using what he is learning.

Since the beginning of the development of educational achievement tests, educators have recognized the potential value of tests as aids to teaching, but the potential has not been fully realized and the expectations have not been largely fulfilled. We now recognize that there have been two major obstacles: 1) the failure to produce tests that could be effectively used in planning and conducting the instructional program; and 2) the lack of a feasible procedure for incorporating a system of testing into the normal classroom activities. We now can see the elimination of both of these obstacles. Appraisal exercises useful to the teacher can be constructed, and there are practical procedures for their use in normal classroom situations.

A sixth by-product of the national assessment project is the development of ways of reporting the results of educational evaluation that can readily be understood by children, parents, and interested citizens. The results of the national assessment will not be presented in terms of test scores. The following form will be used in reporting: (The statistics are, of course, hypothetical at this point.)

For the sample of 13-year-old boys of higher socio-economic status from rural and small-town areas of the Midwest region, it was found that:

94 percent could read a typical newspaper paragraph like the following: (Note: such a paragraph will be included in the report.)

68 percent could write an acceptable letter ordering several items from a store. (Note: a sample letter will be included.)

57 percent took a responsible part in working with other children in playground and community activities like the following: (A specific illustration will be included.)

You will note that the report presents the actual exercise and gives the percent of each population group that answered the question or performed the task indicated. In the case of writing, samples of what the children have written will be shown, along with the percent of pupils whose compositions were at least as adequate as the samples reproduced.

Parents and other laymen responded enthusiastically to this form of reporting. They believed that seeing the actual examples of the exercises gave them a much clearer idea of the achievements that were being assessed than they got from a test title alone. They also felt that reporting in terms of the "percent" of the group who were able to perform the task indicated was a more understandable figure than a test score or some other abstract measure such as standard scores, percentile ranks, and the like.

The reaction of laymen to this way of reporting the national assessment suggests to me that they would also find this type of reporting results of local school appraisals to be more understandable and thus more helpful than reports presented to the local community in terms of scores. The concrete character of the reports would permit the school administrator to discuss both progress and problems. This results from the fact that the report would not give simply a *single* index of school achievement but would report on different tasks. Some of these would be tasks which most students may have mastered; others would be tasks that might show considerable variation in the proportion of persons who have learned to do them.

Finally, one of the most significant by-products of the national assessment project is to be found in the suggestions it provides for monitoring and studying the outcomes of the school's educational program. At present, the prevailing procedure followed by principals in monitoring the effectiveness of the school programs is the use of standardized tests, comparing the mean test scores in each major subject with similar scores in previous years and with national norms or mean scores of other comparison groups.

When the school population is relatively homogeneous or when the chief community concern is with the education of the "average" child, mean scores on present tests are useful indications of the outcomes of the program. However, as I have pointed out earlier, present tests do not furnish a reliable indication of the achievements of children in the upper and lower parts of the distribution. One may, therefore, be misled by the consistency of mean scores over the year to believe that the school program is continuing to produce desired results when in fact a considerable part of the school population is achieving very differently. Or, conversely, we may be dismayed to note that mean scores are lower when, as a matter of fact, the children in the lower third or the upper third are making greater achievements while the "average" child is achieving somewhat less. Tests which furnish information about the achievements of *all* sections of the school population provide a more helpful basis for focusing efforts toward improvement of learning for all children.

Incidentally, our previous preoccupation with means and with the performance of the "average" child may partly account for the common tendency in our schools to seek *the method, the test, the instructional aids* for each subject field rather than conceiving of the school population as composed of children with different backgrounds, different attitudes, different skills in learning. It is fruitful to view the learning situation as one in which the majority of children will be successful in learning, whatever methods or materials are used. But we must not forget that there are minority groups requiring special attention—children who need procedures and materials geared to their background, their skills, their particular ways of learning.

This appears to be a major conclusion of Jeanne Chall's (1967) comprehensive review of research in the teaching of reading. Most children learn to read, whatever method may be used with them, but there are some children who do not successfully cope with the reading tasks. These require special study and the development of or the selection of procedures and materials that are helpful to them in their efforts to learn. As long as present tests are used and a cross section of the school population is involved, the findings regarding reading achievements will continue to show relatively minor differences in the results achieved by different reading methods.

As he monitors the educational program of his school, the principal can obtain data that will furnish more help in recording and analyzing progress and problems by using tests and other assessment exercises designed to indicate what is being learned by the entire range of pupils. By identifying problem areas he can *focus* efforts to improve, rather than scatter energies indiscriminately.

The Exploratory Committee on Assessing the Progress of Education and its successor, the Committee on Assessing the Progress of Education, have reported in some detail the anticipated values to education and educators that are likely to come from the assessment project itself. This article, as indicated earlier, is intended to suggest some things that were not contemplated or foreseen in the original planning of the project. The seven by-products mentioned seem to me to be significant for the school principal and the staff. And as the assessment data are analyzed and reported, we hope that there may be still other ways in which the project will prove helpful to administrators, teachers, and children.

5 | Students' Preferences for Test Format in Relation to Their Test Scores*

Alice Gustav

A. Introduction

At present there are trends toward greater use of objective, rather than essay, questions for classroom examinations. In large part, this has occurred because the former are assumed to be more independent of subjective factors. This view has been supported by a considerable body of research on the effects of conscious and unconscious distortion of test responses due to students' feelings about the content of questions. However, little work has been reported concerning their preferences for test format and the relationship of such attitudes to test grades. The present study describes an investigation of these problems.

B. Subjects and Procedure

One hundred and two students in three undergraduate psychology classes were used as subjects. In the first week of the term the students filled out a questionnaire in which they indicated (*a*) whether they liked or disliked true-false, multiple-choice, and essay questions; (*b*) their reasons for such likes or dislikes; (*c*) whether they studied differently if they knew in advance that an examination would be of a specific type; (*d*) if so, how they varied their study techniques; and (*e*) whether, despite any preferences, they believed that they did equally well on all types of tests.

Each class was given two examinations during the semester, plus a final examination. Other assignments were used as partial bases for final grades in the courses, but are not relevant to this study. Each of the first two examinations was constructed so that one-half contained a combination of true-false and multiple-choice items, and one-half contained essay questions. Each half

*From *Journal of Psychology*, 1964, **57**, 159-164. Copyright 1964 by The Journal Press. Reprinted with permission of the author and publisher.

was scored separately. The final examinations were completely objective. Thus, for most students, there were three sets of objective and two sets of essay questions. A few students missed one of the first two examinations. After the term was over, the students' responses to the questionnaire were tabulated and then compared with their test scores.

C. Results

Table 1 shows the number and per cent of freshmen, sophomores, juniors, and seniors who answered the questionnaire items affirmatively. The negative replies can be obtained by subtracting the affirmative figures from the totals: e.g., 16 (43 per cent) of the 37 freshmen said they liked TF items; therefore, 21 (57 per cent) had replied negatively. It can be seen from Table 1 that

TABLE 1   *Preferences For Test Format Compared with Year Level*

	Freshmen (N = 37)		Sophomores (N = 35)		Juniors (N = 14)		Seniors (N = 16)	
	N	%	N	%	N	%	N	%
Like TF	16	43	17	49	6	43	4	25
Like MC	30	81	27	77	8	57	9	56
Like essay	27	73	23	66	10	71	14	88
Do study differently	31	84	26	74	12	86	12	75
Believe they do equally well on all tests	21	57	20	57	8	57	10	63

expressed preferences are much the same at all stages of academic maturity. In each year level, TF is the type of item liked least, a large per cent of the group does study differently in anticipation of particular types of exminations, and slightly more than half believe that they do equally well on various types of tests despite any preferences they may have. With advanced standing, there is a decrease in the per cent who like MC.

The reasons given by these students for liking and disliking the various types of questions fell into several distinct categories. TF items were disliked because, it was said, they require guessing, involve trivial details, do not reveal creative ability, may fail to show a student's full amount of knowledge, and do not inspire motivation to study. On the other hand, when TF was liked, it was because a higher score is sometimes possible on the basis of guessing or recognition, and students with poor handwriting are not penalized.

MC shared the dislikes of TF, though to a lesser degree. Favorable views laid heavy emphasis on the possibility of recognition of correct responses, since several alternatives are offered in each question and because of the need to think more than on TF.

Essay questions were disliked primarily because grades might be lowered due to poor grammar, poor organization of known material, or possible teacher prejudice in grading. However, essays were enthusiastically liked as, in them, the students felt they were not limited to trivial details, they could present material in their own fashion, they could expand and defend their answers, and they could show what they had learned, which made their study seem worthwhile. A few students found essays easier by reason of the ability to build up a small amount of knowledge by writing around the topic.

Those who studied differently overwhelmingly stated that they memorized details in preparation for TF and MC, whereas they attempted to understand general principles for essays. A small group reported that they did not even bother to memorize anything for TF and MC, but simply depended upon their skill in recognition after having some slight exposure to the material. In preparation for essay tests, a few students admitted to memorizing selected details in order to be able to back up their answers.

We turn now to the second phase of the study: i.e., the relationship between expressed preferences and actual test scores. For each student, grades on the objective parts of the first two examinations and the total grade on the final examination—which was entirely objective—were compared with his replies to the questionnaire. The same was done for the essay parts of the first two examinations. Table 2, which summarizes these data, is read as follows: 37 per cent of the students who received grades of A and B, 35 per

TABLE 2   *Preferences for Test Format Compared with Test Grades*

	A and B		C		D and F	
	N	%	N	%	N	%
	Three objective tests combined					
	(N = 131)		(N = 97)		(N = 60)	
Like TF and MC	49	37	34	35	23	38
Do study differently	105	80	74	77	46	77
Believe they do equally well on all tests	85	65	58	60	24	40
	Two essay tests combined					
	(N = 75)		(N = 28)		(N = 85)	
Like essay	53	71	17	61	64	75
Do study differently	60	80	19	68	69	81
Believe they do equally well on all tests	50	67	17	61	42	49

cent of those who received C, and 38 per cent of those who received D and F on the objective tests said they liked TF and MC items, etc. As can be seen from Table 2, the per cent of students who like a given type of test item, and the per cent who vary their study techniques for different types of tests, remain much the same among above-average, average, and below-average students. There is a slight trend for a smaller percentage of below-average students to believe they do equally well on all types of tests, regardless of their preferences.

Since the final examinations and the objective halves of the first two examinations consisted of both TF and MC items, questionnaire reponses concerning both TF and MC were included in the above results. As an additional step, the final examinations were rescored, so that two grades were available for each student, one on the TF and one on the MC questions. Table 3 presents a comparison of these separate scores with the questionnaire responses. The findings are very similar to the previous data. TF remains the

TABLE 3   *Preferences for Test Format Compared with Grades on Separate Halves of Final Examinations*

	A and B		C		D and F	
	N	%	N	%	N	%
	TF part of final examinations					
	(N = 58)		(N = 31)		(N = 13)	
Like TF	28	48	11	35	5	38
Like MC	41	71	22	71	11	85
Do study differently	47	81	26	84	8	62
Believe they do equally well on all tests	39	67	16	52	4	31
	MC part of final examinations					
	(N = 27)		(N = 36)		(N = 39)	
Like TF	11	41	18	50	15	38
Like MC	17	63	29	81	28	72
Do study differently	24	89	28	78	29	74
Believe they do equally well on all tests	17	63	23	64	19	49

least-liked item, even by those who do well on it. Other percentages stay relatively constant for all grade-level students, with one exception: i.e., the lower-scoring students do not believe as strongly as the average and above-average students that they do equally well on all types of tests.

The next point concerns the relationship between relative quality of performance on objective and essay items versus students' beliefs that they do, or do not do, equally well on different test formats. Each paper on the first two examinations was examined to determine whether the person had obtained a higher score on the objective or essay half, or had done equally well on both halves. This was compared with his questionnaire response. Of those who said they felt they did equally well on all types, 53 per cent actually obtained higher scores on the objective half, 9 per cent did equally well on both parts, and 38 per cent did better on the essay. Of those who said they did not do equally well on all kinds of tests, 54 per cent had higher scores on the objective part, 15 per cent did equally well on both, and 31 per cent did better on the essay part. Obviously, as a group, regardless of beliefs, they perform in much the same manner.

D. Discussion

A general conclusion which can be reached from the results is that, for this group, a weak relationship exists between test grades and expressed preferences for test format. As noted in the last paragraph, only about one-third of the group actually obtained higher scores on essay questions; yet we find from 66 per cent to 88 per cent of the students (Table 1) preferring them. This raises an interesting question. Presumably, during the interval from freshman to senior year, these students should learn quite dramatically that they favor a condition which does not accrue to their practical benefit. Why, then, do they persist throughout their college career in such attitudes? Granted, this study is cross-sectional, not longitudinal, and therefore might conceal the possibility that given individuals change their preferences as they progress through college. Nevertheless, the consistency of responses, no matter how they are examined, makes that dubious. A clue to the answer may be obtained from a closer look at the phrasing of the students' responses. Mere enumeration of categories of reasons for liking different formats fails to yield the flavor and intensity of the statements, which reveal strikingly the subjective feelings of the students.

The students who prefer essay examinations appear to experience considerable frustration on objective tests because they feel blocked by not being permitted to display material in just the exact way they have learned it. They therefore complain that on objective tests they cannot show what they have learned. Student after student made some comment concerning essay tests such as: "You may say what you feel in your own words and explain everything you want made clear." The irrational elements here are that (*a*) objective tests cover far more material than essay tests, which enables the student to exhibit more knowledge on the former; and (*b*) the large number of students who do less well on essay tests are obviously not making things clear.

It is noteworthy, also, that many of the responses linked preferences for test format to amount of—and motivation for—study. Numerous students said they study less if they anticipate an objective test than if they expect an essay test. One frequently given reason contains a serious criticism of objective tests, which teachers ought to keep in mind. This is exemplified by statements such as: "I don't study as thoroughly (for objective) as for essay because recall isn't taxed as heavily," and "I usually find myself studying for a shorter period (for objective) and ignore much of the background material on each subject."

Another reason which students report creates greater incentive to study for essay tests is the satisfaction of being able to display what one has learned—e.g., "Because I can tell what I've learned, my study seems worthwhile." Learning for itself is not valued; students require that there be teacher approbation to make learning seem worthwhile. The irrational element noted above is pertinent here, too (i.e., they do not realize they are showing more knowledge on objective tests).

Further evidence of their need for outside pressure to encourage study is exhibited by responses which indicated awareness of the essay test as an instrument of learning: e.g., "You can develop the concept more fully and show exactly what you know and what you don't know. It also gives an opportunity to organize the material in your own mind and may itself be more enlightening than the original learning of the material." One might expect that a student sophisticated enough to utilize a test as a learning process would do this kind of study himself at home, and not wait for the examination. Apparently, the self-discipline is lacking.

It should be noted that not all who liked essays were prompted by a desire to improve their learning. There were those who frankly considered essays easier than objective tests because, on essays, as one student said: "A little knowledge goes a long way."

E. Summary

Responses to a questionnaire concerning methods of study and preferences for true-false, multiple-choice and essay questions were compared with actual test scores for 102 students in three undergraduate psychology classes. TF items were liked least, a large per cent of the group reported they studied differently in expectation of particular types of examinations, and slightly more than half believed they do equally well on all types of tests despite any preferences. These results were very similar for students of all four year levels in college and for those with above-average, average, and below-average test grades. The reasons students gave for such preferences illuminate personality characteristics which affect study habits.

Item Analysis, Norms and Interpretation of Test Scores

After a test is constructed and administered, it must be scored, improved if possible, and the results interpreted with respect to some meaningful frame of reference. Many papers and textbooks deal at length with the question of how to score test items, e.g., whether to "correct" for guessing and whether to assign different numerical weights to different items or responses.[1] In the case of essay tests, the usual recommendation is to give the same numerical weight to items having the same assigned length (half page or whole page). In regard to objective classroom tests, so-called "correction for guessing" formulas are not generally recommended. An appropriate raw score on multiple-choice, true-false, completion and matching items is simply the number of items that the examinee answers correctly.

But the test-constructor's task does not end when the test has been scored. He must now analyze each item to determine whether it contributes to the test as a whole in measuring whatever the test was designed to measure. The usual item analysis procedure begins by dividing examinees' total test scores or criterion scores into upper and lower groups (upper 27% and lower 27% of scores). Then an *item difficulty index*, defined as the percent of examinees in both the upper and lower groups who pass the item, is calculated. Next, an *item discrimination* (*item validity*) *index*, defined as the relationship between total test (or total criterion) scores and passing vs. failing the item, is computed. After the difficulty and discrimination indices of all items have been computed, individual items are retained or rejected in accordance with whether these two indices fall within desirable ranges.

[1] An initial version of this book included an article by Julian Stanley and Marilyn Wang (1970) on weighting test items and test-item options. Since the technical level of that paper is somewhat higher than that assumed for readers of this volume, it was decided to omit it. However, students with adequate backgrounds in statistics will not find a better summary of the topic than that given by Stanley and Wang.

The first article in this section, by John Flanagan, discusses these two indices or criteria of item effectiveness. Secondary criteria of item effectiveness, such as item intercorrelations, length of time required for a response, objectivity of scoring, "face validity" and defensibility or authoritativeness of correct answers, are also considered. Flanagan points out that information on both the difficulty and discriminating power of test items is needed, since item discriminating power (item validity) is affected by the interaction between item difficulties and item intercorrelations. Finally, a chart is presented for approximate computation of the product-moment correlation corresponding to given proportions of examinees in the upper and lower 27% groups who answer an item correctly.

The second article in this section, by Lange, Lehmann and Mehrens, illustrates how item analysis data can be used not only in selecting test items but also for improving items. The authors maintain that item revision is frequently a more economical procedure than attempting to write entirely new items to replace those with low discriminatory power. In reading this article, the student will find the following formulas for the item difficulty (p) and item discrimination (D) indices helpful: $p = (U_i + L_i)/(U + L)$, $D = (U_i - L_i)/U$, where U = number of examinees in the upper group on the total test score (upper 27%), L = number of examinees in the lower group on the total test score (lower 27%), U_i = number of examinees in the upper group who pass item i, and L_i = number of examinees in the lower group who pass item i.

An examinee's score on a standardized test becomes more meaningful when compared with norms computed on a representative sample of individuals for whom the test is intended. The articles by Harold Seashore and Eric Gardner clarify this point through discussions of various types of norms. The Seashore article includes a useful normal curve chart showing the relationships among percentile norms and various types of standard scores. In addition to describing the virtues of normative standard scores, Gardner lists four possible characteristics of test items that would aid in scaling and interpretation. These characteristics would make test scores more meaningful, but they are difficult or impossible to realize in actual practice.[2] Gardner maintains that although test-constructors should build as much meaning as possible into test scores themselves, normative data on the scores are also valuable.[3] In reading this article, the student should note the distinctions among different

[2] The article by Andrew Comrey in Section III (no. 11) gives more details on scaling and efforts to make psychological measurement more fundamental and precise.

[3] The distinction between *normative* and *criterion-referenced* tests, an important aspect of test interpretation, is dealt with in articles 40-42 of this volume.

scales of measurement (ordinal, interval, ratio). The scores on most psychological tests represent ordinal measurement rather than interval or ratio measurement scales. In contrast to an *ordinal scale,* where the numbers are merely designations of rank orders, on an *interval scale* equal arithmetical differences in scores imply equal differences in whatever psychological characteristic the test purports to measure. Finally, a *ratio scale* of measurement is an interval scale that has an *absolute zero*—signifying zero amount of the characteristic in question.

In the last article of this section, James Ricks begins with the two principles that 1) parents have a right to know whatever the school knows about the abilities, performance and problems of their children, and 2) the school has an obligation to communicate understandable and usable knowledge. Certainly few people would quarrel with the first principle, but its meaning is clarified by the second one. Thus, Ricks feels that parents and students should be told the results of tests, but in a language which they understand. For example, if numbers are to be used in communicating test results to parents, percentiles are usually more meaningful than IQs or standard scores. The counselor or teacher would be wise to begin his explanation with, "You score like people who . . ." or, "Your child scores like students who . . ." The statement would then be completed with usable information on the relationship of the examinee's score to the subsequent behavior of other students who have taken the test.

6 | General Considerations in the Selection of Test Items and a Short Method of Estimating the Product-Moment Coefficient from Data at the Tails of the Distribution*

John C. Flanagan

This paper is essentially a progress report concerning a series of studies of the procedures for the selection of test items. The present discussion will review briefly the arguments for the use of statistical criteria in the selection of test items, point out fallacies in previous studies and discussions of these statistical considerations, and present a short method of obtaining validity coefficients.

Unless the author of a number of test items writes only items of an entirely uniform degree of excellence, in which case, of course, no improvement by any method of selection would be possible, the refinement and improvement of a test usually requires the use of empirically obtained statistical indices of the characteristics of the item. The importance of such statistical indices may be illustrated by quoting from a previous report by the present writer (Flanagan, 1937) " . . . the reliability coefficient of a test composed of one hundred items having item intercorrelations of .15 would be .95. If another group of one hundred items having intercorrelations of .03 and measuring the same general function are added to this test, the reliability coefficient for the total test composed of two hundred items is slightly less than the previous value." A table is being prepared which will provide a simple means of determining which ones of a group of experimental items should be included in the final form to obtain the maximum reliability coefficient for the finished test. The proportion of items which should be used would depend on the degree of excellence and heterogeneity of the original items. It appears quite obvious that some published tests would have been improved had half of the items not been included. The resulting increase in efficiency appears very desirable at the present time when so many demands are being made on the students' time.

*From *Journal of Educational Psychology*, 1939, **30**, 674-680. Reprinted with permission of the author.

In selecting items, there are two primary considerations: First, "Is the item valid?" That is, does it discriminate between persons having much of the quality being measured and persons having only a relatively small amount of this quality? This question is usually answered in terms of some statistical index of the validity of the test item. The second consideration is, "Is the difficulty level of the item suited to the group for which it is intended?" It has frequently been pointed out that items which either all students or no students get correct are performing no measuring function in the test.

Although much time and energy have been spent on empirical studies in an effort to discover the most satisfactory procedure for selecting the best items for inclusion in a final form of a particular test, these studies have produced conflicting results, and have conspicuously failed to settle the issue. A favorite type of empirical study has been the comparison of several methods of obtaining validity coefficients. Most of these studies are of little practical value because the experimenters have failed to control the effect of item difficulty on test validity. It should be emphasized that these are two separate considerations. As will be mentioned later, items of fifty per cent difficulty tend in certain situations to provide the most valid test. Therefore, a method which combines a rough measure of validity or discriminating value with a device which will favor items of fifty per cent difficulty will tend to appear to be superior to a method which provides a more valid index of item validity unaffected by difficulty. Obviously, in a practical situation, these two factors or item validity and item difficulty should be given separate consideration, and an index which obscures the estimate of validity by combining it with a difficutly characteristic is to be avoided. Similarly, empirical studies of the effect on test validity of item difficulty have neglected the factor of item validity.

In addition to these empirical studies, there have been several logical discussions of statistical criteria for selecting test items. Several investigators have brought forth logical proofs to show that a test should be composed of items of fifty per cent difficulty. Here, again, the proofs are based on assumptions which are artificial and fallacious in representing typical conditions. It can easily be shown that, to obtain the maximum amount of discrimination between the individuals in a particular group, a test should be composed of items all of which are of fifty per cent difficulty for that group, provided the intercorrelations of all the items are zero. This situation obviously never exists. It can also be shown that a rectangular distribution of item difficulties extending from the level of ability of the highest individual in a group to the level of the lowest individual in the group is necessary to obtain maximum discrimination among the members of the group, provided the intercorrelations between all of the items are unity. This situation also must be regarded as a purely hypothetical one. The practical situation is one which is intermediate between these extremes. Therefore, we may dismiss the notion that all items should be of fifty percent difficulty as one based on a hypothetical situation which is contrary to fact. The decision concerning the most desirable distribution of item difficulties for a particular test should be based on the accuracy of measurement desired at various levels and the intercorrelations of the items affecting scores at these levels.

Although the two factors which have been mentioned are usually regarded as the primary considerations in the selection of test items, they are by no means the only considerations. For example, item intercorrelations, although shown to be of only minor importance for certain types of tests, may, in particular situations, be of paramount importance. Some statistical methods have been devised for taking item intercorrelations into account, such as the approximation procedures devised by the present writer in 1934 and 1936. (Flanagan, 1935, 1936) However, the typical method of controlling item intercorrelations has been some relatively crude method such as the selection of items with respect to various logical categories. This procedure is commonly known as one of obtaining adequate sampling.

Two other considerations of importance in particular situations are length of time required per item, and objectivity of scoring. It need hardly be said that a test of one hundred items requiring only twenty minutes of testing time would, in general, be definitely superior to one of fifty items requiring the same amount of testing time, even though the average of the item validities in the first case was somewhat lower. Objectivity of scoring is almost entirely a practical consideration, but becomes of great importance in certain situations.

The final pair of criteria which will be mentioned are illustrated by such competitive examinations as those given by Civil Service Commissions. These criteria are "face-validity" and defensibility or authoritativeness of the correct answer. By "face-validity" is meant the requirement that examinations appear to measure what is popularly understood from the title. By defensibility or authoritativeness is meant the ability of the examiners to convince interested parties that the answer given by the examiners is the correct answer. Although these are definitely secondary considerations from the measurement point of view, they frequently are of great practical importance.

Although it is clear that these secondary considerations can rarely be neglected, the major considerations in most situations remain those considered above; namely, item validity and item difficulty.

It follows from the definition given above for item validity that the best index of validity is one which provides an index of the extent to which an item will predict the criterion. Such an index is provided by the product-moment correlation coefficient and its various modifications. The most common situation is one in which the biserial correlation coefficient applies. These coefficients have been widely used and various procedures have been developed for reducing the relatively large amount of time and effort required for their computation. Even though these procedures have materially decreased the labor involved, many individuals feel that the time expended in obtaining these coefficients is frequently not justifiable. Such individuals have made considerable use of the upper- and lower-groups method. T. L. Kelley reported a number of years ago that, if upper and lower groups were to be used, the certainty with which the means of the upper and lower groups are differentiated is a maximum when the two tails of the normal distribution each contain twenty-seven per cent of the cases. Kelley (1939) has recently amplified this statement showing that in certain situations a slightly smaller proportion of all cases appears desirable. He concludes, however, that "Upper and lower groups consisting of twenty-seven per cent from the extremes of the criterion score distribution are optimal for the study of test items, provided the differences in criterion scores among the members of each group are not utilized." (Kelley, 1939, p. 24)

The upper- and lower-groups method has been quite extensively used in connection with a chart which provides a graphic indication of the separation, in terms of quarter-sigma units, of the means of the upper and lower groups on the particular item. In many situations, it appears advantageous to have the index in terms of the degree of relationship shown between the item and the criterion. For example, such coefficients facilitate thinking in terms of the relation between item validity and test validity. The writer, therefore, has prepared a chart based on Tables VIII and IX in *Tables for Statisticians and Biometricians,* Part II, edited by Karl Pearson. Pearson's tables give volumes of the normal bivariate surface included in any cell whose lower limit is 0.0, 0.1, 0.2, ... 2.6 standard deviations, and whose upper limit runs to infinity, for specified correlations at intervals of .05 from −1.00 to +1.00.

The derived chart (Fig. 1) shows the values of the product-moment coefficient of correlation corresponding to given proportions of success in the upper and lower twenty-seven per cent of the criterion group.

A project to determine the standard error of a correlation coefficient obtained by the use of this and similar charts is now in progress. It is clear that such a chart, utilizing as it does the information from only about half of the cases and lumping these cases together into only two groups, will give much less accurate results than does the more usual biserial correlation coefficient. However, the results obtained from this chart have been found to be satisfactory approximations to the biserial coefficients in the comparisons which have been made by the writer.

In practice, it appears that frequently it is satisfactory to use the values obtained from this chart together with an index of difficulty found by averaging the difficulties for the upper and lower groups.

In conclusion, it should be mentioned that such a procedure as that just

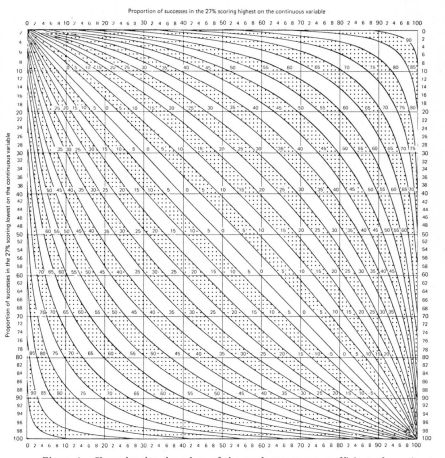

Figure 1. Chart showing the values of the product-moment coefficient of correlation in a normal bivariate population corresponding to given proportions of successes.

Example: The correlation coefficient between the continuous variable and an item on which 56% of the group achieving scores in the highest 27% for the continuous variable succeed and on which 23% of the group achieving scores in the lowest 27% for the continuous variable succeed is .35.

described provides a very rapid method of obtaining difficulty and validity indices for items when the test have been administered with answer sheets for the International test-scoring machine. The item analysis unit tabulates the number of correct responses to ninety items for a group of one hundred papers in about fifteen minutes. Thus a simple item analysis of the type herein described for about four hundred cases on a one hundred fifty item test would require only a couple of hours after the tests had been scored. The scoring itself should require a little more than an hour under these circumstances.

Summary

Most recent discussions of the various techniques which have been proposed for the selection of test items have contained major fallacies. Empirical studies have, in general, overlooked the fact that there are *two* very important considerations involved in any selection of test items. The first consideration is item validity or discriminating power, and the second one is item difficulty. The empirical selection of items by means of a single index of item validity overlooks the necessity for separate consideration of these two criteria, and any comparison of methods on this basis is, therefore, of only trivial value.

Logical discussions concerning the optimum distribution of item difficulties have invariably overlooked the very important bearing of item validities on this function. Therefore, these discussions may also be regarded as having little practical significance.

In certain special situations, secondary considerations such as item intercorrelations, length of time required for a response, objectivity of scoring, "face-validity," and defensibility or authoritativeness are important factors in determining which items should be chosen.

A short method of obtaining item validity and item difficulty indices was presented. The chart utilized in this procedure was based on Kelley's finding that upper and lower groups containing twenty-seven per cent of the cases were optimum for certain related estimations. Pearson's *Tables for Statisticians and Biometricians* was used in obtaining the charted values.

Though the method does not in any way depend on any particular type of item or method of scoring, its brevity is probably best illustrated by stating that within three or four hours of the time four hundred tests of one hundred fifty items are received in the office, a simple item analysis including the necessary scoring and checking may be obtained if the International test-scoring machine is used.

7 | Using Item Analysis to Improve Tests*

Allan Lange, Irvin J. Lehmann and William A. Mehrens

Every major textbook in measurement discusses the improvement of a test through the use of item statistics. Most students taking a course in test construction remember that item analysis can be useful in item selection decisions. Unfortunately, they tend to forget that item analyses can also be useful for item revision. Too frequently a person doing an item analysis of a multiple-choice test fails to go beyond computing the item difficulty and discrimination indices. When only this superficial analysis is completed, reasons underlying any item failures can not be discerned and item revision is difficult. It is when the responses to each of the foils[1] have been examined that item revision can be accomplished most effectively.

The purpose of this paper is to study the value of using a complete item analysis in rewriting items that have been shown to lack appropriate discrimination power. The researchers were interested in seeing whether it was more efficient to rewrite "poor" items than to write new items to improve the discrimination power of a test.

Method

About 600-700 students take an introductory educational psychology course at Michigan State University each term. For many years, a part of the evaluation procedure has been multiple-choice examinations. The tests are revised each quarter. Past revision have been conducted primarily by taking previous exam questions that have discriminated well and are still of appropriate content. These were used together with new items written by the instructors. Seldom were individual items rewritten through revision of the foils and even when that was done, no systematic follow-up of these rewritten items was undertaken to determine whether their discriminating powers improved.

*From *Journal of Educational Measurement*, 1967, 4, 65-68. Copyright 1967 by the National Council on Measurement in Education. Reprinted with permission of the senior author and publisher.

[1] A "foil" is a distractor or incorrect option in a multiple-choice item [Editor's note].

An instructor familiar with the course content was asked to review a 60-item test given the previous quarter, and select items that were appropriate in content for the test being prepared. A complete item analysis had been conducted on this test showing the difficulty and discrimination indices, as well as the percent of people in the upper and lower 27% who responded to each alternative.[2] Thirty-two items in this test were found to be still appropriate in content. These 32 items were then examined and 18 were found to be acceptable for use without revision, 14 being in need of revision. These 14 items were revised by an instructor. The major revisions were accomplished by looking at the item analysis data on the foils and revising those foils which were not pulling in the proper direction, that is, those which were not more attractive to the lower group than the upper group. The total time needed for revision was about 1 hour. Examples of the type of revision that was done and the consequences are shown in the following items.

Original Form

Motivation is an internal state. Yet we continually talk as though it were a tangible, measurable quality. As a teacher you would most likely be able to best judge the motivation of a particular student by

1. giving him an intelligence test.
2. having his mother in for a parent-teacher conference.
*3. observing his behavior in the classroom and drawing your own conclusions.
4. McClelland's tests of internal motivation.
5. reviewing his past and present academic record.

Item Analysis:

	1	2	3	4	5	OMIT	N = 615
U	0	10	63	5	21	1	DIFF 58
L	2	9	52	11	26	0	DISC 11

Revised Form

Motivation is an internal state. Yet we continually talk as though it were a tangible, measurable quality. As a teacher you would most likely be able to best judge the motivation of a particular student by

1. giving him an interest inventory.
2. having him write an autobiography.
*3 observing his behavior in the classroom and drawing your own conclusions.
4. McClelland's tests of internal motivation.
5. reviewing his past and present academic record.

Item Analysis:

	1	2	3	4	5	OMIT	N = 560
U	3	21	53	3	20	0	DIFF 43
L	5	27	32	9	26	0	DISC 21

---

[2] The discrimination index used was the "D" index. See Findley (1956) and Englehart (1965) for a more thorough discussion.

Of the 14 revised items, 10 considered to have the best chance of showing an improvement were chosen and placed in the new exam along with the 18 good items and 32 new items. Construction of the new items took approximately five times as long per item as the item revisions.

Results

Table 1 shows the item discrimination indices on the 18 items used without revision (control items) and the 10 revised items on both the old and new test. Every one of the 10 revised items showed an improvement in discrimination, the lowest increase being 3 points and the greatest being 28. Nine of the 18 control items improved in discrimination, 8 decreased in discrimination.

Table 2 shows the average discrimination of the control and revised items for both the old and new test as well as the average discrimination of the new items on the new test.[3] The average discrimination of the control items was 2.3 points lower in the new test while the average discrimination of the revised items was 10.3 points higher. The revised items had a higher average discrimination than the new items written specifically for the exam.

TABLE 1   *Item Discrimination*

Control Items		Revised Items	
Old Test	*New Test*	*Old Test*	*New Test*
18	21	17	24
29	22	17	31
26	31	11	16
30	9	22	25
30	19	16	20
34	28	11	21
33	36	18	46
27	27	23	30
26	14	21	29
48	43	5	22
27	26		
29	31		
28	29		
32	33		
28	16		
40	41		
24	34		
22	30		

[3] The average difficulty did not change much between the old and new test for either control or revised items. The items in both the control and revised groups seemed to be slightly easier for those students taking the new test, but the change was very slight indeed.

TABLE 2   *Average Item Discrimination*

	Old Test	New Test
Control Items	29.5	27.2
Revised Items	16.1	26.4
New Items	....	23.6

Conclusions

The results of this study show that items can be improved, without too much effort, through use of a complete item analysis. The study suggests that revising poor items may be a more economical process for obtaining good items for future tests than by discarding those items and attempting to replace them with new items. In this study it took about 5 times as long to develop a new item as it did to revise an old one, and the discrimination of the new items averaged 2.8 points less than the average of the revised items. While some new items must always be written to preserve the validity of a test, there is strong evidence in this study for using the complete item analysis information to revise existing poor items. Far too often, item analysis is used only for item selection. Item revision accomplished through examination of the information concerning the individual distractors can be a valuable, efficient method of improving tests.

8 | Methods of Expressing Test Scores*

Harold G. Seashore

An individual's test score acquires meaning when it can be compared with the scores of well-identified groups of people. Manuals for tests provide tables of norms to make it easy to compare individuals and groups. Several systems for deriving more meaningful "standard scores" from raw scores have been widely adopted. All of them reveal the relative status of individuals within a group.

The fundamental equivalence of the most popular standard score systems is illustrated in the chart on the next page. We hope the chart and the accompanying description will be useful to counselors, personnel officers, clinical diagnosticians and others in helping them to show the uninitiated the essential simplicity of standard score systems, percentile equivalents, and their relation to the ideal normal distribution.

Sooner or later, every textbook discussion of test scores introduces the bell-shaped normal curve. The student of testing soon learns that many of the methods of deriving meaningful scores are anchored to the dimensions and characteristics of this curve. And he learns by observation of actual test score distributions that the ideal mathematical curve is a reasonably good approximation of many practical cases. He learns to use the standardized properties of the ideal curve as a model.

Let us look first at the curve itself. Notice that there are no raw scores printed along the baseline. The graph is generalized; it describes an idealized distribution of scores of any group on any test. We are free to use any numerical scale we like. For any particular set of scores, we can be arbitrary and call the average score zero. In technical terms we "equate" the mean raw score to zero. Similarly we can choose any convenient number, say 1.00, to represent the scale distance of one standard deviation.[1] Thus, if a distribution

*From *Test Service Bulletin, No. 48,* New York: The Psychological Corporation, 1955. Copyright, ©, 1955 by The Psychological Corporation. Reprinted by permission of the publisher.

[1] The mathematical symbol for the standard deviation is the lower case Greek letter sigma or σ. These items are used interchangeably in this article.

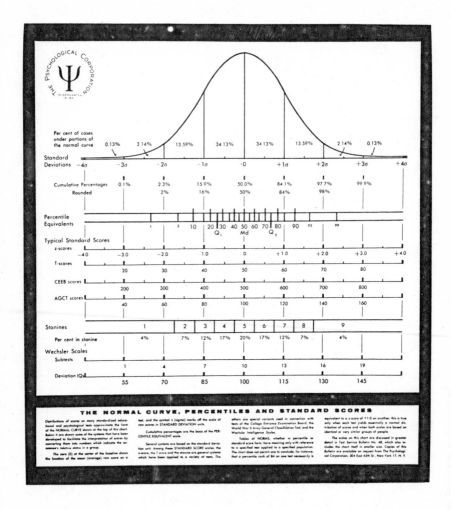

NOTE: This chart cannot be used to equate scores on one test to scores on another test. For example, both 600 on the CEEB and 120 on the AGCT are one standard deviation above their respective means, but they do not represent "equal" standings because the scores were obtained from different groups.

of scores on a particular test has a mean of 36 and a standard deviation of 4, the zero point on the baseline of our curve would be equivalent to an original score of 36; one unit to the right, $+1\sigma$ would be equivalent to 40, $(36 + 4)$; and one unit to the left, -1σ, would be equivalent to 32, $(36 - 4)$.

The total area under the curve represents the total number of scores in the distribution. Vertical lines have been drawn through the score scale (the baseline) at zero and at 1, 2, 3, and 4 sigma units to the right and left. These lines mark off subareas of the total area under the curve. The numbers printed in these subareas are per cents—*percentages of the total number of people.* Thus, 34.13 per cent of all cases in a normal distribution have scores falling between 0 and -1σ. For practical purposes we rarely need to deal with standard deviation units below -3 or above $+3$; the percentage of cases with scores beyond $\pm 3\sigma$ is negligible.

The fact that 68.26 per cent fall between $\pm 1\sigma$ gives rise to the common statement that in a normal distribution roughly two-thirds of all cases lie between plus and minus one sigma. This is a rule of thumb every test user should keep in mind. It is very near to the theoretical value and is a useful approximation.

Below the row of deviations expressed in sigma units is a row of per cents; these show *cumulatively* the percentage of people which is included *to the left* of each of the sigma points. Thus, starting from the left, when we reach the line erected above -2σ, we have included the lowest 2.3 per cent of cases. These percentages have been rounded in the next row.

Note some other relationships: the area between the $\pm 1\sigma$ points includes the scores which lie above the 16th percentile (-1σ) and below the 84th percentile $(+1\sigma)$—two major reference points all test users should know. When we find that an individual has a score 1σ above the mean, we conclude that his score ranks at the 84th percentile in the group of persons on whom the test was normed. (This conclusion is good provided we also add this clause, at least subvocally: *if this particular group reasonably approximates the ideal normal model.*)

The simplest facts to memorize about the normal distribution and the relation of the *percentile* system to deviations from the average in sigma units are seen in the chart. They are

Deviation from the mean	-2σ	-1σ	0	$+1\sigma$	$+2\sigma$
Percentile equivalent	2	16	50	84	98

To avoid cluttering the graph reference lines have not been drawn, but we could mark off ten per cent sections of area under the normal curve by drawing lines vertically from the indicated decile points (10, 20, . . . 80, 90) up through the graph. The reader might do this lightly with a colored pencil.

We can readily see that ten per cent of the area (people) at the middle of the distribution embraces a smaller *distance* on the baseline of the curve than ten per cent of the area (people) at the ends of the range of scores, for the simple reason that the curve is much higher at the middle. A person who is at the 95th percentile is farther away from a person at the 85th percentile in units of *test score* than a person at the 55th percentile is from one at the 45th percentile.

The remainder of the chart, that is the several scoring scales drawn parallel to the baseline, illustrates variations of the *deviation score* principle. As a class these are called *standard scores.*

First, there are the *z-scores.* These are the same *numbers* as shown on the baseline of the graph; the only difference is that the expression, σ, has been omitted. These scores run, in practical terms, from -3.0 to $+3.0$. One can compute them to more decimal places if one wishes, although computing to a single decimal place is usually sufficient. One can compute z-scores by equating the mean to 0.00 and the standard deviation to 1.00 for a distribution of any shape, but the relationships shown in this figure between the z-score equivalents of raw scores and percentile equivalents of raw scores are correct only for normal distributions. The interpretation of standard score systems derives from the idea of using the normal curve as a model.

As can be seen, T-scores are directly related to z-scores. The mean of the raw scores is equated to 50, and the standard deviation of the raw scores is equated to 10. Thus a z-score of $+1.5$ means the same as a T-score of 65. T-scores are usually expressed in whole numbers from about 20 to 80. The T-score plan eliminates negative numbers and thus facilitates many computations.[2]

The College Entrance Examination Board uses a plan in which both decimals and negative numbers are avoided by setting the arbitrary mean at 500 points and the arbitrary sigma at another convenient unit, namely, 100 points. The experienced tester or counselor who hears of a College Board SAT-V score of 550 at once thinks, "Half a sigma (50 points) above average (500 points) on the CEEB basic norms." And when he hears of a score of 725 on SAT-N, he can interpret, "Plus $2\frac{1}{4}\sigma$. Therefore, better than the 98th percentile."

---

[2] T-scores and percentiles both have 50 as the main reference point, an occasional source of confusion to those who do not insist on careful labelling of data and of scores of individuals in their records.

During World War II the Navy used the T-score plan of reporting test status. The Army used still another system with a mean of 100 and a standard deviation of 20 points.

Another derivative of the general standard score system is the *stanine* plan, developed by psychologists in the Air Force during the war. The plan divides the norm population into nine groups, hence, "standard nines." Except for stanine 9, the top, and stanine 1, the bottom, these groups are spaced in half-sigma units. Thus, stanine 5 is defined as including the people who are within $\pm 0.25\sigma$ of the mean. Stanine 6 is the group defined by the half-sigma distance on the baseline between $+0.25\sigma$ and $+0.75\sigma$. Stanines 1 and 9 include all persons who are below -1.75σ and above $+1.75\sigma$, respectively. The result is a distribution in which the mean is 5.0 and the standard deviation is 2.0.

Just below the line showing the demarcation of the nine groups in the stanine system there is a row of percentages which indicates the per cent of the total population in each of the stanines. Thus 7 per cent of the population will be in stanine 2, and 20 per cent in the middle group, stanine 5.

Interpretation of the Wechsler scales (W-B I, W-B II, WISC, and WAIS) depends on a knowledge of standard scores. A subject's raw score *on each of the subtests* in these scales is converted, by appropriate norms tables, to a standard score, based on a mean of 10 and a standard deviation of 3. The sums of standard scores on the Verbal Scale, the Performance Scale, and the Full Scale are then converted into IQs. These IQs are based on a standard score mean of 100, the conventional number for representing the IQ of the average person in a given age group. The standard deviation of the IQs is set at 15 points. In practical terms, then, roughly two-thirds of the IQs are between 85 and 115, that is, $\pm 1\sigma$.[3] IQs of the type used in the Wechsler scales have come to be known as *deviation IQs,* as contrasted with the IQs developed from scales in which a derived mental age is divided by chronological age.

Users of the Wechsler scales should establish clearly in their minds the relationship of subtest scaled scores and the deviation IQs to the other stan-

---

[3] Every once in a while we receive a letter from someone who suggests that the Wechsler scales ought to generate a wider range of IQs. The reply is very simple. If we want a wider range of IQs all we have to do is to choose a *larger arbitrary* standard deviation, say, 20 or 25. Under the present system, $\pm 3\sigma$ gives IQs of 55 to 145, with a few rare cases below and a few cases above. If we used 20 as the standard deviation, we would *arbitrarily* increase the $\pm 3\sigma$ range of IQs from 55-145 to 40-160. This *is* a wider range of numbers! But, test users should never forget that adaptations of this kind do not change the responses of the people who took the test, do not change the order of the persons in relation to each other, and do not change the psychological meaning attached to an IQ.

dard score systems, to the ordinary percentile rank interpretation, and to the deviation units on the baseline of the normal curve. For example, every Wechsler examiner should recognize that an IQ of 130 is a score equivalent to a deviation of $+2\sigma$, and that this IQ score delimits approximately the upper two per cent of the population. If a clinician wants to evaluate a Wechsler IQ of 85 along with percentile ranks on several other tests given in school, he can mentally convert the IQ of 85 to a percentile rank of about 16, this being the percentile equal to a deviation from the mean of -1σ. Of course he should also consider the appropriateness and comparability of norms.

Efficiency in interpreting test scores in counseling, in clinical diagnosis, and in personnel selection depends, in part, on facility in thinking in terms of the major interrelated plans by which meaningful scores are derived from raw scores. It is hoped that this graphic presentation will be helpful to all who in their daily work must help others understand the information conveyed by numerical test scores.

9 | Normative Standard Scores*

Eric F. Gardner

A single isolated test score is of little or no value. For a score to have meaning and be of social or scientific utility, some sort of frame of reference is needed. A number of different frames of reference have been proposed and have been found to have value.

One possible frame of reference is the content of the test itself. Among derived scores one of the earliest was the per cent of a defined sample of tasks which an individual has completed satisfactorily. The deficiencies inherent in these kinds of scores have been discussed so many times in the literature no attempt will be made here to go into detail again. A few of the issues are the lack of comparability of per cent scores on the same test for different people, the lack of comparability from test to test, and the lack of algebraic utility. The following comments illustrate these points. John and Jane might each have scores of 60 per cent on the same test but have answered correctly very different items. A score of 80 per cent on a hard test is obviously not comparable to a score of 80 per cent on an easy test. For algebraic utility, equal units throughout the scale are desirable. It is not reasonable to assume that the difference between scores of 60 per cent and 70 per cent represent the same difference in ability as that between 90 per cent and 100 per cent. Such scores ignore differences between items of the test in representativeness, difficulty and importance. Also it is obvious that the meaning of such scores is entirely dependent upon the particular sample of items included.

The content provided by the items of a test yields scores which may be directly related to standards set by the examiner who prepared the test. He may regard a score as good or poor on the basis of his judgments of the difficulties of the items and the expected performance of those taking the examination. Such judgments are difficult to make and frequently are not related to the realities of the situation. For example, when teachers or examining boards discover that very large proportions of those examined have fallen below the standard they originally built into the examination, they generally revise their judgments about the test and re-evaluate the test results. Thus the content or "absolute" frame of reference is supplemented by a relative frame of reference based upon knowledge of the performance of the group of examinees.

The inadequacy of the content frame of reference led to a consideration of additional approaches. One of the most commonly used frames of reference is the performance of some well-defined group of examinees. The College Board score scale, with a mean of 500 and a standard deviation of 100 for a group of examinees on which it was established some years ago, is one type of normative standard score. The I.Q. and grade scores are different types of basically normative standard scores.

This type of score provides a meaningful report of the examinee's performance in relation to those of members of a defined reference group. For example, it may be more useful to know how an examinee's performance on a particular test compares with those of his peers, than to know how it compares with the standards of the examiners. For many purposes, such as selection, placement and prediction, it is useful to know the location of a given score with respect to a particular frequency distribution of scores. For example, a grade score of 6.5 incorporates in it the information that the subject has obtained a score that is the same as the average of the normative group of sixth-graders who have been half a year in school. An I.Q. of 100 indicates that on the particular intelligence test the subject performed at the same level as the average of the normative group. A standard score of 600 indicates performance which is one standard deviation above the mean of the normative group.

In most cases the test user is concerned about frames of reference based on both content and group performance. He is interested in having knowledge about the specific responses of the individual to the items of the test and also knowledge about the performance of the individual relative to that of other individuals.

If we ignore practical considerations and concern ourselves with characteristics of items that would aid in scaling and test interpretation, there are a number of desirable properties that can be mentioned. Some of these are difficult or impossible to obtain; while others, if obtained, would almost certainly prevent our achieving more important characteristics. Considering each specific issue in isolation and simultaneously assuming that all other necessary requirements for a good test are met, we could argue the following properties would be desirable:

1. *The test consists of items which constitute a representative sample of the domain tested.* It should be a sample of behaviors that represent the objectives which have previously been defined.

2. *The items in the test form a Guttman Scale.* This property implies that the items selected can be ranked in the same order of difficulty for each individual. Once the items have been so ranked, any examinee will answer correctly all those items of less difficulty and incorrectly all those of greater difficulty. Thus a score of 17 means that the person answered correctly the first seventeen items and incorrectly all others. Such an arrangement of items permits an unambiguous interpretation of the score 17 in that all people who score 17 have answered correctly the same items.

3. *The items in the test can be arranged along a continuum of the variable under consideration in such a way that the raw scores constitute an interval scale.* The items included in such a test would have the property of representing equal differences in ability between adjacent items. For example, the difference in ability represented by scores of 53 and 54 would be the same as that represented by scores of 85 and 86.

4. *The items are of such nature that a zero score on the test represents zero amount of the ability being tested.* If the condition specified in property 3 is now added, the scale becomes a ratio scale which is amenable to all four arithmetic operations.

5. *The items provide a scale unit which is meaningful.* There are advantages in having the size of unit related to the standard error of measurement in such a way that a user has some idea as to the likelihood of a difference being entirely due to error.

A test possessing the properties just enumerated (that is, consisting of items which 1) adequately represent the domain to be tested and 2) can be ranked in order of difficulty, and starting with an absolute zero will provide successively equal increments of knowledge) provides a raw score scale with very desirable characteristics. Unfortunately these properties, although desirable, are difficult to achieve and in many practical situations the achievement of one results in less success in achieving another. For example, I would argue that property 1 is paramount for any achievement test. That is—a good achievement test should itself define the objectives measured. These objectives are set up by those agents of society who are responsible for decisions concerning educational objectives, and the test constructor must attempt to incorporate that definition in the building of the examination. This point of view implies that the method of scaling an educational achievement test should not be permitted to determine the content of the test or to alter the definition of objectives implied in the test. It is most probable that an attempt to select items so that the raw score scale produced has properties 2 and 3 (an interval Guttman Scale) would eliminate from the test sample important concepts and skills.

Sampling from Populations of Items and Examinees

This discussion so far has suggested that the interpretation of achievement test scores requires one to consider two very different types of frames of reference, each associated with a particular sampling problem.

The first problem is concerned with an acceptable sample of items. For a test score to be meaningful the particular variable under consideration must be defined, and the user must have knowledge about the adequacy of the items to sample this domain. Hence, specific knowledge of the field and of the items included in the test is necessary for the adequate interpretation of a raw score.

The second problem is concerned with a sample of examinees. Information about such things as item or test difficulty, functioning of decoys, norms and predictive effectiveness is dependent upon empirical data. To be meaningful these indices must be derived from an acceptable sample of people obtained from a well-defined population. A difficulty index for a reading item obtained from a typical fourth grade obviously does not have the same meaning as one obtained from a typical sixth grade. A person scoring at the eighty-fourth percentile, or obtaining a T-score of 60 in an arithmetic test where the score is calculated from a typical seventh grade sample, is not performing at the same level as one whose standing at the eighty-fourth percentile on the same test is calculated from a below-average seventh grade. Likewise a pupil with a vocabulary grade score of 6.2 obtained from a representative sample of fifth graders, in say, Mississippi, is certainly not comparable to a pupil making a score of 6.2 based on a national representative sample. By the same token, one would hardly expect a set of decoys for an arithmetic multiple-choice item to function in the same fashion in both a fifth and ninth grade. The importance of the particular reference population which is used cannot be overemphasized.

Current Practice

In the construction of an achievement test, the issue of the sampling of the items is considered under the concept of validity—usually content validity. Appropriate objectives are defined, tables of specifications are established, and trial items are constructed to sample the variable described.

Data are then obtained to give information about the statistical characteristics of the items. In the light of this additional information, the test is assembled in such a way that the items will sample both content defined by the objectives and the ability of the examinees for which it is designed.

Attempts are then made by scaling procedures to approximate some of the other desirable properties which the test does not acquire solely through the relationship of the items to each other. Current methods of scaling educational achievement tests are based upon the statistical properties of the test, or of the individual items constituting the test with reference to a particular population of examinees. That is, such scales are derived from normative data.

Raw scores on some educational achievement tests are meaningful in themselves in terms of content of the test. For example, a score of 30 on a test built of 50 basic addition combinations gives some information about the particular student without regard for the performance of any other person. However, groups of such items arranged with reference to such a meaning do not constitute scales. You cannot compare 30 out of these 50 basic addition facts with 30 out of a different set, or six out of 15 rules of grammar, or with a possible number of vocabulary items in Russian. Some frame of reference is needed so that performance from person to person and group to group can be compared. The scaling job still remains to be done.

Any added meanings of scaled scores is due entirely to the contribution of the normative data, and that meaning applies, strictly speaking, only to the particular reference population involved in the scaling process. This statement holds whether the scale is based solely upon item statistics or upon some operations on the total score. Normative standard scores are dependent upon the sample of subjects selected (Gardner, 1953, pp. 13-21).

Let us consider the role of the population in several common scaling procedures. A familiar frame of reference is provided by the performance of individuals in a single well-defined group on a particular test at a particular time. Two commonly used scales have been derived within such a frame of reference. The simplest are ordinal scales, such as percentile scores, in which the scale number describes relative position in the group. The second type are interval scales where an effort has been made to obtain algebraic utility by definition. The T-score of McCall represent an interval scale where equal units have been defined as equal distances along the abscissa of a postulated normal population frequency distribution. A variation is the College Entrance Examination Board scores with a mean of 500 and standard deviation of 100 for the parent normally distributed population.

A second type of frame of reference is provided by the test performance of individuals belonging to well-defined subgroups where the subgroups have a specific relationship to each other within the composite group.

Within this frame of reference both ordinal and interval scales have been derived. Initially the basic problem is to obtain ordinally related subgroups such as grades 1 to 9 or age groups from a specific population for the scaling operation. Age scores and grade scores provide ordinal scales which have had wide utility in the elementary grades. Attempts have been made to obtain the merits of an algebraically manipulatable scale by utilizing ordinal relationship of subgroups but introducing restrictions in terms of the shape of frequency distributions. Efforts to obtain interval scales within such frames of reference have been made by Flanagan (1939) in the development of Scaled Scores of the Cooperative Tests and by Gardner (1950) in the development of K-Scores.

Test scores are used by administrators, teachers and research workers to make comparisons in terms of rank, level of development, growth and trait differences among both individuals and groups. Hence many types of scales and norms have been developed depending upon the intended use. Each is consistent within itself but the properties of the scales are not completely consistent from one type of scale to another. For example, a grade scale is not appropriate for measuring growth in a function unless one is willing to accept the assumption that growth is linearly related to grade. The scaling of the Binet items involves the assumption of a linear relationship between Mental Age and Chronological Age. As valuable and useful as the Binet Scale has been for the purpose for which it was designed, it has obvious limitations when we try to infer the "true" nature of intellectual growth.

It should be emphasized that the adoption of any one of the scales available does not exclude the use of any of the others. In fact, most situations require the test user to utilize more than one type of scale or norm for an adequate interpretation of test results.

Conclusion

Normative standard scores are measures obtained from scales having certain specific properties, and they incorporate in the numerical values certain information about the normative group used. They are obtained by statistically manipulating the raw score responses of a defined group of people on a defined sample of content. It is desirable to facilitate the interpretation of test scores by giving them as much direct meaning as possible. As Flanagan (1951) has said "... if much information is built into the score itself, continual use makes its interpretation more and more direct and immediate. It is also of great assistance if such fundamental built-in meanings can be as constant from one test to the next as possible." However, the amount of meaning that can be built into any single reference scale will constitute only a very small part of the total amount of meaning to be desired by all of the test users from those results. It is almost always necessary to supplement the knowledge inherent in the scores with other normative data. Norms based on a variety of different groups have considerable merit. Different types of norms such as grade scores, percentile scores and various types of standard scores all have their place. The case for all normative standard scores stands or falls on their ability to provide additional and more useful information than can be obtained from the raw scores from which they were derived.

10 | On Telling Parents About Test Results*

James H. Ricks, Jr.

Like any other organization dealing with people, a school has many confidences to keep. School administrators, teachers, and especially guidance workers inevitably come to know items of private information. A gossip who carelessly passes such information around abuses his position and his relationship with his students. It is both right and important that some kinds of information be kept in confidence.

What about test results? Do they belong in the category of secrets, to be seen only by professional eyes and mentioned only in whispers? Or is their proper function best served when they become common knowledge in the school and its community? (In some towns, names and scores have been listed in the local newspaper, much like the results of an athletic contest.)

We think neither extreme is a good rule. Sometimes there is a reason to make group data—figures such as the average and the range from high to low—generally public. Seldom should individual results be published except for the happy announcement of a prize won, a scholarship awarded, and the like. But short of general publication, school guidance workers face a particularly important question: Should parents be told their children's test results?

Hard questions, often, are hard because they deal with genuinely complicated problems. Simple "solutions" to such questions are likely to be a trap rather than an aid if their effect is to divert our attention from the difficulties we truly face. Simple rules or principles, on the other hand, can be of real help as one tackles complex problems and situations. This article will present some rules that we have found useful in facing questions such as—

"What should I say when a mother wants to know her son's IQ?" "Should we send aptitude test profiles home with the children?" "We feel that parents in our school ought to know the results of the achievement tests we give, but then it's hard to explain the discrepancies between these and the teachers' grades."

No single procedure, obviously, can be appropriate for every kind of test. Nor for every kind of parent. To Mr. Jones, a well-adjusted and well-educated father, a report of his daughter's test scores may enhance his understanding of her capacities and of what the school has been giving her. To Mr. Green, a somewhat insecure and less knowledgeable man, the identical information may spark an explosion damaging to both child and school. And the counselor or teacher often has no sure way of knowing which kind of person he will be reporting to.

Two principles and one verbal technique seem to us to provide a sound basis for communicating the information obtained from testing. The two "commandments" are absolutely interdependent—without the second the first is empty, and without the first the second is pointless.

The first: *Parents have the right to know whatever the school knows about the abilities, the performance, and the problems of their children.*

The second: *The school has the obligation to see that it communicates understandable and usable knowledge.* Whether by written report or by individual conference, the school must make sure it is giving *real* information—not just the illusion of information that bare numbers or canned interpretations often afford. And the information must be in terms that parents can absorb and use.

Few educators will dispute the first principle. It is in parents that the final responsibility for the upbringing and education of the children must lie. The responsibility requires access to all available information bearing on educational and vocational decisions to be made for and by the child. The school is the agent to which parents have delegated part of the educational process—but the responsibility has been delegated, not abdicated. Thoughtful parents do not take these responsibilities and rights lightly.

The parents' right to know, then, we regard as indisputable. But, to know what?

Suppose that, as a result of judicious testings, the school knows that Sally has mastered social studies and general science better than many in her ninth grade class, but that few do as poorly as she in math. In English usage she stands about in the middle, but her reading level is barely up to the lower border of the students who successfully complete college preparatory work in her high school. The best prediction that can be made of her probable scores on the College Boards three years hence is that they will fall in the range which makes her eligible for the two-year community college, but not for the university. She grasps mechanical concepts better than most boys, far better than most girls. Looking over the test results and her records, her experienced teacher recognizes that good habits and neatness of work have earned Sally grades somewhat better than would be expected from her test scores.

All of these things Sally's parents should know. Will they know them if they are given the numbers—Sally's IQ score, percentiles for two reading scores, percentiles on another set of norms for several aptitude tests, and grade-placement figures on an achievement battery?[1]

Telling someone something he does not understand does not increase his knowledge (at least not his correct and usable knowledge—we are reminded of the guide's observation about the tenderfoot, "It ain't so much what he don't know, it's what he knows that ain't so that gits him in trouble"). Transmitting genuine knowledge requires attention to content, language, and audience. We have already referred to some of the characteristics of parents as an audience. Let's look at the other two elements.

Content means that to begin with *we* must ourselves know what we are trying to get across.

We need to know just what evidence there is to show that the test results deserve any consideration at all. We need equally to know the margins and probabilities of error in predictions based on tests. If we don't know *both* what the scores mean *and* how much confidence may properly be placed in them, we are in trouble at the start—neither our own use of the information nor our transmission of it to others will be very good.

Content—what we are going to say—and *language*—how we are going to put it—are inseparable when we undertake to tell somebody something. In giving information about test results, we need to think about the general content and language we shall use and also about the specific terms we shall use.

To illustrate the general content-and-language planning: a guidance director may decide that he wants first to get across a sense of both the values and the weaknesses of test scores. One excellent device for his purpose would be an expectancy table or chart. Such a chart can make it clear to persons without training in statistics that test results are useful predictors *and* that the predictions will not always be precise. Local studies in one's own school or community are of greatest interest. But the guidance director who lacks local data may still find illustrative tables from other places helpful in preparing parents and students to use test results in a sensible way. (An example is given in Figure 1, with references to others that may be found elsewhere.)

Specific terms used in expressing test results vary considerably in the problems they pose. Consider, for example, the different kinds of numbers in which test results may be reported.

---

[1] The implied "No" answer to this question does not, of course, refer to those few parents trained in psychometrics—perhaps even to a point beyond the training of the school staff. Parents include all kinds of people.

Figure 1. The guidance director found, in the classes of 1953 and 1954, 101 boys and 85 girls who had taken the *Differential Aptitude Tests* (including Verbal Reasoning and Numerical Ability) in their Tenth Grade years and the *Scholastic Aptitude Test* of the College Entrance Examination Board as Seniors. Since the CEEB reports two scores—Verbal and Math—there were four sets of data: Boys—Verbal, Boys—Math, Girls—Verbal, and Girls—Math. The chart for the boys' CEEB Verbal results looked like this:

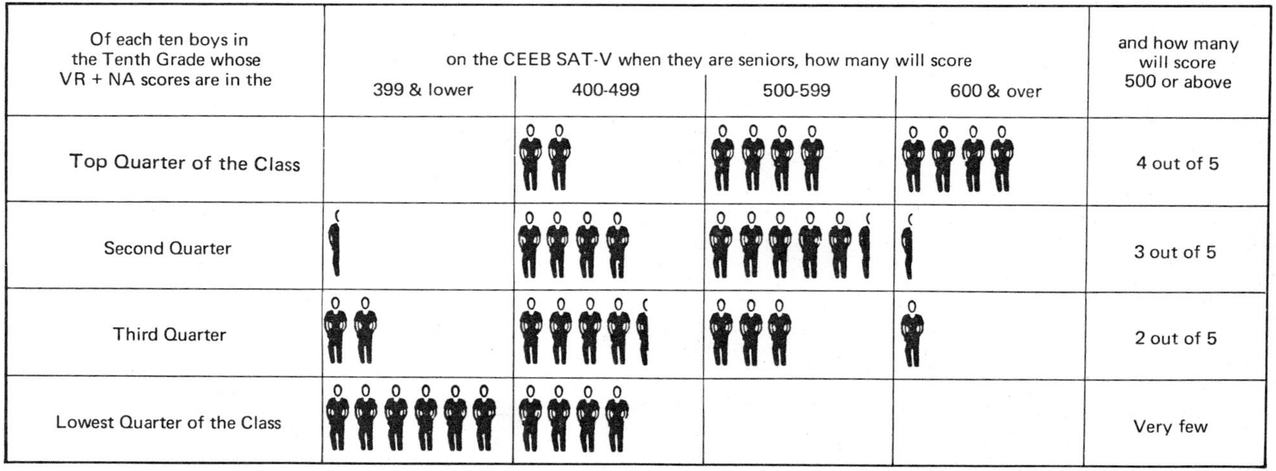

Of each ten boys in the Tenth Grade whose VR + NA scores are in the	on the CEEB SAT-V when they are seniors, how many will score					and how many will score 500 or above
	399 & lower	400-499	500-599	600 & over		
Top Quarter of the Class						4 out of 5
Second Quarter						3 out of 5
Third Quarter						2 out of 5
Lowest Quarter of the Class						Very few

The other three charts were similar in appearance. For additional illustrations of expectancy charts and tables, see TEST SERVICE BULLETINS 38 and 53; the *Differential Aptitude Tests Manual*, 3rd Edition, pages 62-64; and the *Modern Language Aptitude Test Manual*, 1959 Edition, pages 15 and 16.

IQ's are regarded as numbers that should rarely if ever be reported as such to students or to their parents. The reason is that an IQ is likely to be seen as a fixed characteristic of the person tested, as somehow something more than the test score it really represents. The effect, too often, is that of a final conclusion about the individual rather than that of a piece of information useful in further thinking and planning. Few things interfere more effectively with real understanding than indiscriminate reporting of IQ scores to parents.

Grade placement scores or **standard scores** of various kinds are less likely to cause trouble than IQ scores are. Still, they may substitute an illusion of communication for real communication. Standard scores have no more meaning to most parents than raw scores unless there is opportunity for extensive explanations. Grade placements *seem* so simple and straightforward that serious misunderstandings may result from their use. As noted in a very helpful pamphlet, (Katz, 1958) a sixth-grade pupil with grade-placement scores of 10.0 for reading and 8.5 for arithmetic does not necessarily rank higher in reading than he does in arithmetic when compared to the other sixth-graders. (Both scores may be at the 95th percentile for his class—arithmetic progress much more than reading progress tends to be dependent on what has been taught, and thus to spread over a narrower range at any one grade.)

Percentiles probably are the safest and most informative numbers to use Provided their two essential characteristics are made clear: (1) that they refer not to per cent of questions answered correctly but to per cent of people whose performance the student has equalled or surpassed, and (2) who, specifically, are the people with whom the student is being compared. The second point—a definite description of the comparison or "norm" group—is especially important in making the meaning of test results clear.

Much more can be said about the kinds of numbers used to convey test score information. Good discussions can be found in a number of textbooks. But a more fundamental question remains—*are any numbers necessary?*

We intend nothing so foolish as suggesting a ban on the use of numbers in reporting test results. But we have been struck repeatedly by the fact that some of the very best counselors and many of the best written reports present numerical data only incidentally or not at all.

Along with the two "commandments" at the beginning of this article, we mentioned a verbal technique. Generally, we dislike formulas for writing or speaking. This one, however, seems to have advantages that outweigh the risks attending its suggestion. It's just a few words:

"You score like people who . . ." Or, to a parent, "Your son (or daughter) scores like students who . . ."

The sentence, of course, requires completion. The completion depends on the test or other instrument, the reason for testing, and the person to whom the report is being given. Some sample completions:

"... people who are pretty good at office work, fast and accurate enough to hold a job and do it well."

"... people who don't find selling insurance a very satisfactory choice. Three out of four who score as you do and become insurance salesmen leave the job for something else in less than a year."

"... students who find getting into liberal arts college and getting a B.A. degree something they can attain only with extra hard work. On the other hand, they find a year or two of technical school interesting and they probably do well in the jobs to which that leads."

"... students who are disappointed later if they don't begin a language in the ninth grade and plan to take some more math and science. It's easier to head toward business later if you still want to than to go from the commercial course into a good college."

"... students who don't often—only about one out of four—manage to earn a C average their freshman year at State."

"... students who have more than average difficulty passing in arithmetic—you [*or, to a parent,* he] may need some extra help on this in the next few years."

Many more samples will come readily to mind. The most important thing to note is that a satisfactory report combines two kinds of information:

1) the test results of the individual person, and
2) something known about the test or battery and its relationship to the subsequent performance of others who have taken it.

Also, a satisfactory completion puts the school or the counselor out on a limb, at least a little. Some variant of "That's not so!" or, more politely, "How do you know?" will be the reaction in some cases, probably less frequently voiced than it is felt.

Well, let's face it. The decision to use a test at all is a step out on a limb. Some limbs are broad and solid and the climber need feel little or no anxiety. Some are so frail that they offer only hazard, with the bait of an improbable reward. We climb out on some limbs of medium safety because there is evidence of a real chance that they will help us, and those whom we test, toward a worthwhile goal.

The words of the formula need not actually be used in each case. Sometimes percentiles, grade placement scores, or a profile may be what the parents should receive. But it is well to try first mentally stating the meaning of the results in the language suggested above. If this proves difficult or discomforting, a warning signal is on—reporting the numbers is likely not to be constructive in the case at hand!

The audience of parents to which our test-based information is to be transmitted includes an enormous range and variety of minds and emotions. Some are ready and able to absorb what we have to say. Reaching others may be as hopeless as reaching TV watchers with an AM radio broadcast. Still others may hear what we say, but clothe the message with their own special needs, ideas, and predilections.

The habit of using the formula, and of thinking a bit about what answer to give if the response is a challenging or doubting one, puts the interpreter of test scores in the strongest position he can occupy. In the case of achievement tests, it requires him to understand why and how the particular test or battery was chosen as appropriate for his school and his purpose. In the case of aptitude (including scholastic aptitude or intelligence) tests, it requires him to examine the evidence offered in the test manual and research studies to back up the test's claim to usefulness. And it reminds him always that it is in the end *his* thinking, *his* weighing of the evidence, *his* soundness and helpfulness as an educator or counselor that is exposed for judgment—not the sometimes wistful ideas of the test author or publisher.

The school—or the counselor—*is* exposed for judgment when telling parents about the abilities and performances of their children. The parents have the right to know. And knowledge in terms they can understand and absorb is what the school must give.

Mental Measurement and Reliability

Discussions and arguments concerning the nature and precision of mental measurements have filled many volumes since the time of G. T. Fechner and J. F. Herbart. In the opinion of many physical scientists and mathematicians, test scores and other numbers obtained from psychological and educational investigations are not really measurement at all—at least not in the fundamental sense in which the term is used in the more exact sciences. This allegation has stimulated psychometricians and educational measurers to exert a great deal of effort in attempting to make their measurements more fundamental and precise. In the first article of this section, Andrew Comrey discusses some of the issues that have attended these efforts. One issue is the question of the nature of the scale unit, i.e., the distinctions among *ordinal, interval* and *ratio* scales of measurement. Comrey's main conclusion is that fundamental measurement in psychology is impossible until a great deal more is known about the physiological basis of behavior. Therefore, rather than setting as their major goal the attainment of fundamental measurement, Comrey suggests that mental testers should expend most of their energies on improving the practical utility or predictive validity of tests.

The other four articles in this section deal with test *reliability,* the accuracy or dependability of test scores. Reliability may also be defined as relative freedom from errors of measurement, and, as the *Standards for Educational and Psychological Tests and Manuals* (APA, 1966) indicate, different methods of determining reliability take different sources of error into account. Therefore, as recommended by the *Standards,* for every reliability study the method and sources of error variance accounted for in the test scores need to be carefully described. Traditional methods of obtaining information on test reliability have included studies of comparable forms, internal consistency, and comparisons over time, a reliability coefficient being computed as the end result of a particular study. The articles by Wesman, Richardson and Kuder, and Doppelt consider various aspects of the traditional or classical approach to reliability. The final article, by Thorndike, compares the classical approach with *generalizability theory* and cites other recent developments concerning the dependability of behavioral measurements.

Alexander Wesman presents an overview of the reasons for needing information on a test's reliability and procedures for estimating it. It is noted that the required magnitude of a reliability coefficient depends on the kind of decision (e.g., group vs. individual) that is to be made on the basis of test scores. But the size of the obtained coefficient depends on many factors: 1) type of coefficient computed (*internal consistency, test-retest, equivalent forms*), 2) range of ability in the group, 3) interval of time between testings, 4) whether or not the test is speeded. Wesman points out that internal consistency formulas (Spearman-Brown, Kuder-Richardson) are not accurate with speeded tests, and that the ideal type of reliability information is based on retesting with an equivalent form of the test. Other matters of interest discussed in this article are interscorer reliability, the reliability of part scores, and the importance of a reliability coefficient being based on a group that is representative of the population of examinees for whom the test is intended.

The article by M. W. Richardson and G. F. Kuder is reprinted here because of its clear exposition of formulas derived in the earlier classical paper on test reliability written by these same two men (Kuder & Richardson, 1937). Empirical comparisons of four different formulas with each other and with the older Spearman-Brown split-half procedure are made. Conditions under which these four formulas are appropriate, together with the facts that they give underestimates of "true" reliability and are not appropriate with speeded tests, are discussed. Formulas 20 and 21 of this article are the ones most frequently cited in later literature as the Kuder-Richardson reliability formulas. Another form of formula 21, $r_{tt} = \frac{n}{n-1} \left[1 - \frac{\overline{X}(n - \overline{X})}{n\sigma^2} \right]$, where $\overline{X}$ is the arithmetic mean of total test scores,[1] is given more frequently in textbooks on psychological and educational testing. The student in the 1970s may regard as quaint the emphasis that these writers place on computational efficiency. However, he should remember that the year 1939, when most calculations were done by desk calculator, was before the age of electronic computers. The student with a better background in algebra than that required for this article should also read the classical theoretical paper by Kuder and Richardson (1937).

Although reliability is defined as relative freedom from errors of measurement, some error of measurement is reflected in every test score. Thus, in classical reliability theory, an examinee's obtained test score (X) is defined as the sum of his true score (T) on the test plus error of measurement (E), i.e.,

[1] The other symbols in this formula are defined in the article by Richardson and Kuder (no. 13).

X = T + E. The more reliable the test, the larger will be the true score component and the smaller the error component of the obtained score. Since the tester would obviously like to know the examinee's true score uncluttered by errors of measurement, a technique which allows one to estimate the error component is required. In the classical theory, as explained in Doppelt's article, this is done by means of the standard error of measurement. The *standard error of measurement* (SE_M) is an estimate of the standard deviation of the hypothetical normal distribution of scores which an examinee would obtain if he took the test an infinite number of times. From the definition $SE_M = SD \sqrt{1 - r_{tt}}$, where SD is the standard deviation of obtained test scores and r_{tt} the reliability coefficient, the student will note that SE_M varies inversely with the size of the reliability coefficient. Doppelt clarifies the use of SE_M in defining limits around the observed score within which we can be fairly confident that a person's true score falls. He also points out that, since probability statements involving the SE_M statistic are properly made only with reference to the limits within which the true scores of a certain percentage of examinees having a given obtained score could be expected to fall, SE_M should be used only in an approximate sense in defining limits for the true score of a single examinee.

In the final article of this section, Robert Thorndike compares the newer statistical sampling conceptualizations of test reliability with classical "true score" theory. The newer formulations of *generalizability theory* (Cronbach, Rajaratnam & Gleser, 1963) conceive of reliability (or *generalizability*) as the precision with which a test score (the "sample") represents a hypothetical "universe" value. Thorndike notes that analysis of variance and intraclass correlation models may be employed to assess the reliability of scores by selecting not only a random sample of persons, but also a sample of situations in which the test is administered and different samples of test items. These procedures lead to a variety of reliability formulas, of which the Kuder-Richardson formulas are merely a special case. Since 1963, when the Thorndike article was written, a great deal of theoretical and empirical work on statistical sampling models of test scores has been done. Students with substantial training in statistics are encouraged to consult the volumes by Lord and Novick (1968) and by Cronbach *et al.* (1970) for a thorough discussion of issues and procedures related to this topic. However, it is important to temper one's enthusiasm for statistical theories of mental test scores with the realization that, as concurred upon by Comrey and Thorndike, first priority in constructing tests should be given to the prediction of events that have some social utility. Thus, sometimes it is necessary to sacrifice more precise measurement (i.e., greater reliability) for validity of wider scope.

11 | Mental Testing and the Logic of Measurement*

Andrew L. Comrey

By comparison with measurement in the physical sciences, psychological measurement has always enjoyed a somewhat unsavory reputation and has even been called by some the "queen of the inexact sciences."[1] Many writers have pointed out deficiences in the techniques employed in psychology, and some (Ferguson *et al.,* 1938; Gage, 1934; Johnson, 1936; Smith, 1938; Thomas, 1942) have based their criticisms upon alleged violations of the traditional "laws of measurement." In a previous article (Comrey, 1950) certain implications of the logic behind measurement were given some attention. The traditional requirements were stated, criticisms of psychological measurement were discussed, and an interpretation of the position of psychological measurement with respect to these requirements was offered.

In the present paper, some of the general problems of psychological measurement will be discussed as they apply to the mental-test field. A brief review of the requirements of fundamental measurement will be given, together with a discussion of some difficulties in applying this model to mental testing. Some of the consequences of these difficulties for measurement practice will be mentioned and, finally, some suggestions regarding criteria for evaluating mental-test methods will be made which depart from the customary criteria of conformity to the pattern of fundamental measurement. The point of view will be expressed that the excellence of measurement methods in mental testing may be judged by the practical validity of those methods for the purposes at hand, in addition to comparing them with the model of measurement in the physical sciences. Reasons for giving greater emphasis to the former criterion will be offered.

Criticisms of Mental Testing

Perhaps the most comprehensive treatment of the requirements for fundamental measurement has been given by Campbell (1920, 1928). Some of the

*From *Educational and Psychological Measurement,* 1951, **11,** 323-334. Copyright 1951 by G. Frederic Kuder. Reprinted with permission of the author and publisher.
[1] The writer wishes to express his appreciation to Drs. J. P. Guilford, L. L. McQuitty and L. J. Cronbach for critical comments on some of the ideas presented in this paper.

more important requirements will be summarized with respect to ordinal characteristics, the relation of equality, and the operation of addition. The requirements for order specify that a class of elements must be defined unambiguously such that the elements vary with respect to some particular property. To be measurable with respect to that property, the elements must vary only in degree, not in kind. Furthermore, a relation, "greater," which is transitive and asymmetrical, must be physically defined. That is, if stimulus A is greater than stimulus B, and B is greater than C, then A should be greater than C; also, if A is greater than B, B cannot be greater than A.

To satisfy the requirements for equality, a physical definition of the relation, "equals," is needed. This definition must be such that physical equality is transitive and symmetrical, i.e., if A = B, and B = C, then A = C; also if A = B, then B = A. And, finally, the requirements for addition state, among other things, that some experimental operation must be found whereby two elements possessing the measurable property can be added together to get an element containing an amount of this property greater than that of either element added. For properties which satisfy these requirements, a complete, or *fundamental* measurement is possible. Numbers assigned to elements of such classes of measurables can be manipulated in accordance with the rule of arithmetic. Furthermore, such measurements are made on scales with equal-unit and ratio properties. A few properties so measurable are weight, length, period of time, and electrical resistance.

It is fairly well known that certain difficulties are involved in trying to apply the model of fundamental measurement to the mental-test area. One of the first criticisms laid at the doorstep of mental testing is that classes of measurables are not even defined, i.e., the class of degrees of some property supposedly indicated by different scores on some test do not represent merely differences in degree but differences in kind as well. A gestalt interpretation of mental organization would tend to contradict the notion that merely a quantitative difference is reflected by different test scores. Furthermore, the relation of equality does not meet the necessary conditions. It is stated that equal test scores do not mean identity with respect to some ability. Individuals may get the same test scores by solving correctly different combinations of items. Furthermore, by this line of reasoning, if A = B (i.e., equal test scores), and B = C, there is no reason to suppose that the underlying ability organizations of A and C are the same, even though their numerical test scores are identical.

Interesting as these objections may be, the psychologist can minimize their importance on operational grounds. He can state that by the only measuring instrument available to him, i.e., the test, A = B if they have the same test score. Aside from the question of difference in kind represented by different test scores, no contradiction in the actual numbers assigned can occur with respect to the relations, "greater," and "equals." The fact that different combinations of items add up to the same score does not bother him too much because he feels that if the items themselves are of the same sort, the total score should be fairly indicative of the person's level of achievement.

That mental testing has no suitable operation of addition is quite apparent, and critics have not failed to mention this point. There seems to be no way to add physically one psychological magnitude to another to get a third even greater in amount. With fundamentally measurable variables, such as weight, length, resistance, and so on, this can be accomplished easily and, from such an operation, numbers can be assigned such that differences and ratios are endowed with the desired experimental meaning. The fact that the operation of addition is not defined in mental testing leads to considerable difficulty, since this operation is employed in fundamental measurement to endow measurement scales with equal-unit and ratio properties. Thus, it would appear that mental-test workers may not be able to develop test scales with equal units and ratio properties.

Let us consider, for a moment, two opposed points of view which might be adopted with respect to the nature of measurement involved in a mental test. First, it might be assumed that the human mind is composed of an undetermined number of abilities. A test may tap, so to speak, a few of these abilities which inhere basically in the physiological structure of the organism, but the test can be only an indirect measurement in terms of certain behavioral manifestations. A direct measurement is out of the question, at the present state of our knowledge of physiology, for there is no way that variations in these abilities can be directly observed. Behavioral products represent the only available indicators of such underlying variables at the present time.

Taking a simple case, suppose there were such an underlying ability and a test which measured this variable alone, plus some error variance. What is the functional relationship between the performance variable and the underlying ability? If a performance variable is to be used to yield a measure of ability in this sense, it is obvious that such functional relationships must either be determined experimentally, or assumed to follow a certain form. This functional relationship must be known before the task of securing equal-unit scales, with respect to the underlying variable, can be accomplished, for the equality of units must be in terms of the underlying ability, not the performance.

Unfortunately, it is not now possible to determine the nature of such functional relationships. An independent measure of the underlying ability would be necessary before the relationship of such measures to scores on the performance test could be found. Since no independent measurements (e.g., physiological determinations) for the underlying variable can be taken, this method of proceeding is impractical. It should be mentioned at this point that an approach to this problem can be made through the use of certain types of judgments. Reese (1943) employed fractionation and equal-appearing-interval methods for the scaling of the subjective difficulty of digit series and words in a vocabulary test. These methods do not comprise an experimental verification of unit equality on an underlying mental-ability variable, however. They do allow an operational meaning to be attached to unit differences on the subjective scale, but such units do not represent those of a fundamental type for the underlying variable.

From this analysis, it appears evident that one cannot *prove* that a performance or behavior test yields equal units along the scale of some basic underlying ability which in itself is not directly observable. It should be emphasized that the task of disproving an assumption of equal units in such cases is equally difficult, for this, too, would require experimental checks of the relationship between the performance variable and independent measurements of the underlying ability.

An opposite position which might be assumed by some persons with respect to the nature of measurement involved in a mental test is the point of view that a test measures a variable of some kind, or variables, and these behavioral products themselves are what concern us. It amounts to a behavioristic approach, so to speak, which denies the necessity of dealing in terms of concepts which have no basis in observation. The extreme behaviorist might ask, "What is the point of assuming an underlying ability which cannot be measured, observed, or proved to exist?"

If the second approach is taken, what are the consequences? First, the matter of a functional relationship between the behavior variable and a hypothetical underlying variable is no longer of importance. The behavior itself is the variable, as determined by the performance on some test. The emphasis with this approach is switched from a consideration of whether the test measures the underlying variable properly to that of whether the variable measured is a useful one. It is assumed that the measures obtained from a test represent some variable in a one-to-one fashion. Since the variable is defined by the test scores, there can be no question as to whether the units on such a test are equal, because that is implicit in the assumptions. It follows from the general approach involved that the units of such tests are equal by definition. It is not the intention of the writer to advance either of these positions as his own. These points of view are considered as representing opposed positions which may flank most observers rather than represent them. The point of importance in this discussion is merely that *regardless* of what systematic position one adopts, we do not have equal units of the fundamental type with any mental test and we will not have them until means are devised for direct observation of underlying physiological phenomena.

Some Possible Consequences of the Difficulties

It has already been suggested that the objections raised against mental-test methods with respect to the requirements for order and equality are probably not crucial. The issues raised by the failure to achieve an operational definition of addition in mental testing are more serious, however. Since equal-unit and ratio properties of measurement scales are based upon addition, mental testing faces the the task of evaluating the effects of this deficiency.

The most obvious conclusion which might be drawn is that measurement in this area is confined to the ordinal level. That is, numbers assigned by means of mental tests can indicate only the rank-order positions of performances to which those numbers have been given. This is the sort of conclusion which is often made by critics of psychological measurement. Smith (1938, pp. 141-2), in particular, states that equal units can be derived only through a process of addition. It would follow that ratio properties would also demand such a process.

Now, it is quite clear that many of the statistical procedures which are applied to mental-test results demand something in the way of a unit of measurement (Boring, 1920). Means, standard deviations, product-moment correlations, and all the statistical procedures based upon these must necessarily depend upon interval sizes along the scale of measurement. This is no less true of the rank-difference correlation method, which is derived from the product-moment formula, and hence involves the same concepts. (Ratio characteristics of measurement scales do not constitute as much of a loss to mental testing as the lack of equal units, for most purposes, since the typical statistical treatments need not involve such relations between test scores.)

These considerations suggest that one of two courses of action must be taken by those attempting to use mental tests for measurement purposes. First, they may show that using methods involving unit assumptions do not introduce serious errors or that certain procedures can be employed to minimize such error in spite of the absence of fundamentally-equal units. Secondly, they may avoid the use of methods of analysis which depend upon interval interpretations. The multiple-cutting-score methods, for example, do not demand such assumptions. Further, non-parametric methods may be used for statistical tests of hypotheses.

It is likely that further development of measurement techniques in mental testing will proceed along both these lines. Certainly, there is a vast unexplored territory in the area of the second procedures suggested above. With respect to the first program, it can be stated that insufficient attention has been given to the problem of determining the degree and kind of error introduced into the results of measurement by virtue of the fact that such measurements lack certain characteristics they are presumed to have. In the next section, criteria for judging the work of measurement methods will be treated in the light of the discussion to this point.

Criteria for Evaluating Mental Test Methods

The fundamental-measurement model has typically been used as a criterion by which measurement procedures should be evaluated. Those procedures which fit this scheme are termed "good" methods, and procedures which fail to do so are held to be primitive and unsatisfactory as scientific instruments. Mental tests fall in this latter category, for they certainly fail in at least one important respect to fit the fundamental-measurement model, namely, in their defection with respect to the operation of addition. Are there other criteria by which mental tests can be evaluated which may be more useful? Under the first criterion mentioned above, all mental tests are unsatisfactory, and no discrimination among them is provided. Certainly, some tests are better and more useful than others.

The obvious answer to this question is that other criteria *are* available for judging the value of procedures in mental testing. These criteria are to be found in the validity of such instruments for the practical purposes of assessing and predicting status under a variety of conditions. Lest some misunderstanding on this point arise, it should be hastily added that the logic of fundamental measurement should not be forgotten or ignored. It is a good thing to know where one's methods fail to meet this more exacting pattern in order to avoid the errors which are likely to occur in the absence of this knowledge. The fact that mental-test methods do not satisfy such criteria need not blind us to the possibility and usefulness of evaluation in terms of these other more practical criteria.

Whereas many difficulties are involved in the use of mental tests for the purpose of establishing scientific laws (Thomas, 1942), there seems to be little doubt as to their value for certain practical purposes. It seems reasonable to assert that mental testing is and will be for some time essentially an empirical science with certain rather well-defined practical objectives rather than primarily a theoretical scientific enterprise. At least, in terms of relative proportion of activity in this area, such a position could scarcely be questioned. Some individuals may object to this point of view, since personal preferences in matters of emphasis are involved. Be that as it may, this position will be adopted with respect to the objectives of mental testing.

These considerations lead to certain conclusions regarding the attitude which practical mental-test workers should adopt toward the logic of measurement. In the first place, they should abandon attempts to manipulate their test scores *for the purpose* of making their measurements approximate fundamental measurement. It is quite clear that such objectives can never be attained in this manner. This is the case because these objectives can be attained only through experimental operations upon the underlying physiological determiners of behavior. The practical test worker is not in a position to engage in the type of research activity which might conceivably succeed in reaching such ends. This fact would be evident to anyone familiar with the logic of fundamental measurement so that mental-test workers should by all means be acquainted with measurement theory.

It should be pointed out in this connection that scaling procedures which are apparently designed for obtaining measurement properties beyond rank order are not necessarily bad. What is not defensible is to assume that such procedures can stand on their own because they *appear* to resemble, in the end result, measurement in the physical sciences. Whether such methods are good or bad can be assessed in terms of their capacity to help achieve the practical objectives of mental tests. Ultimately, methods may become available for checking the claims of such procedures with respect to measurement properties beyond rank-order but, for the present, such claims must rest upon assumptions for which there is insufficient experimental evidence.

Attempts to improve quantification techniques in mental testing should not be confined to the pattern of fundamental measurement but should be spread over a much wider area. Any and all techniques should be explored which might conceivably lead to better predictions or assessments of status, *even though* such techniques do not appear to have any possibility of making mental-test measurement more like fundamental measurement.

As a matter of fact, some such successful techniques may appear to be in contradiction to a goal in terms of the fundamental-measurement pattern. An article by Richardson (1936), for example, emphasizes the importance of considering the effects of test difficulty on validity. Richardson states that the validity of a test depends in large measure upon whether the test is properly tailored to the job with respect to difficulty. He states:

> Suppose, for example, that a test of clerical aptitude is meant to sort out the best 15 percent of all applicants. This is on the assumption that the labor market is such

that one hundred persons will apply for 15 positions. It is then clear that the optimal difficulty of test elements should be in the neighborhood of plus 1 sigma and that easier tasks would give us discriminations between individuals in whom we are not interested.

. . . Under any circumstances involving educational or psychological measurement, the distribution of difficulty of the elements or tasks can be arranged to fulfill more accurately the purposes of measurement.

If, by some procedure, it were possible to develop a test of clerical aptitude which would represent truly a fundamental-measurement scale with a given number of items, the scale would be the same whether 15 per cent or 85 per cent of the applicants were being selected. Under conditions where error variance is not present in the test, success would probably be equal for any cutting score. However, under the conditions of testing existing, this fixed scale could not do the measuring job at a given level as well as a test tailored for that level, although this fixed scale might conceivably be the best general-purpose scale. Thus, the approach to better measurement through meeting the requirements for fundamental measurement, were it possible, would not necessarily give the best practical methods, since it ignores at least one of the important factors affecting test validity.

The methods to be employed in mental testing, then, have a definite purpose and they can be evaluated in terms of that purpose. From the standpoint of the ideas presented here, the primary value of item analysis and factor analysis, for example, lies in the possibility of using such techniques to increase predictive efficiency. Developing batteries of pure tests to predict some criterion through factor analysis of tests and criteria constitutes a method the value of which can definitely be assessed in terms of higher validity coefficients. The same criteria can be applied to other methods introduced into the mental-test field. Where such good means are available for evaluating measurement methods, it seems inappropriate to rely principally on comparisons with abstract logical criteria that were designed for a different context.

Summary

1. Many difficulties lie in the path of securing for mental-test measurement the type of rigor found in the fundamental type of measurement. Among these, one of the most serious is the impossibility of obtaining equal units without independent physiological assessment of the variables under consideration.

2. This failure brings up many important problems with respect to the treatment of mental-test data by statistical methods, since many of these

methods presume that a unit of measurement has been established. Some justification for the use of such methods should be offered.

3. It would be desirable to attain a fundamental type of measurement for mental testing but, at present, such a goal seems out of reach. If fundamental measurement is made the sole yardstick by which the excellence of measurement procedures are to be judged, mental-test methods are automatically classed as primitive and virtually without prospect of substantial improvement.

4. The objectives of mental testing are held to be primarily empirical in nature. Testing techniques are designed mainly for the prediction and assessment of status. These objectives provide additional criteria by which mental-test methods can be judged, namely, the practical validity determinations for the purposes at hand.

5. Mental-test workers should certainly be aware of what is involved in fundamental measurement, but they should devote their major efforts toward developing measurement techniques which give some hope for better satisfying the practical validity criteria rather than the fundamental-measurement criteria. This position is taken because a) the fundamental-measurement criteria cannot be attained by the methods available to the mental-test worker, if at all, and b) the practical-validity criteria and the fundamental-measurement criteria may sometimes be contradictory objectives in the practical situation.

12 | Reliability and Confidence*

Alexander G. Wesman

The chief purpose of testing is to permit us to arrive at judgments concerning the people being tested. If those judgments are to have any real merit, they must be based on dependable scores—which, in turn, must be earned on dependable tests. If our measuring instrument is unreliable, any judgments based on it are necessarily of doubtful worth. No one would consider relying on a thermometer which gave readings varying from 96° to 104° for persons known to have normal temperatures. Nor would any of us place confidence in measurements of length based on an elastic ruler. While few tests are capable of yielding scores which are as dependable as careful measurements of length obtained by use of a well-marked (and rigid!) ruler, we seek in tests some satisfactory amount of dependability— of "rely-ability."

It is a statistical and logical fact that no test can be valid unless it is reliable; knowing the reliability of a test in a particular situation, we know the limits beyond which validity in that situation cannot rise. Knowing reliability, we know also how large a band of error surrounds a test score—how precisely or loosely that score can be interpreted. In view of the importance of the concept of reliability, it is unfortunate that so many inadequacies in the reporting and use of reliability coefficients are to be found in the literature. This article is intended to clarify some aspects of this very fundamental characteristic of tests.

Reliability coefficients are designed to provide estimates of the consistency or precision of measurements. When used with psychological tests, the coefficients may serve one or both of two purposes: 1) to estimate the precision of the test itself as a measuring instrument, or 2) to estimate the consistency of the examinees' performances on the test. The second kind of reliability obviously embraces the first. We can have unreliable behavior by the examinee on a relatively reliable test, but we cannot have reliable performance on an unreliable instrument. A student or applicant suffering a severe

*From *Test Service Bulletin, No. 44.* New York: The Psychological Corporation, 1952. Copyright, ©, 1952 by The Psychological Corporation. Reprinted by permission of the publisher.

headache may give an uncharacteristic performance on a well-built test; the test may be reliable, but the subject's performance is not typical of him. If, however, the test items are ambiguous, the directions are unclear, or the pictures are so poorly reproduced as to be unintelligible—if, in short, the test materials are themselves inadequate—the subject is prevented from performing reliably, however propitious his mental and physical condition.

This two-fold purpose of reliability coefficients is reflected in the several methods which have been developed for estimating reliability. Methods which provide estimates based on a single sitting offer evidence as to the precision of the test itself; these include internal consistency estimates, such as those obtained by use of the split-half and Kuder-Richardson techniques when the test is given only once, as well as estimates based on immediate retesting, whether with the same form or an equivalent one. When a time interval of one or more days is introduced, so that day-to-day variability in the person taking the test is allowed to have an effect, we have evidence concerning the stability of the trait and of the examinee as well as of the test. It is important to recognize whether a reliability coefficient describes only the test, or whether it describes the stability of the examinees' performances as well.

How High Should a Reliability Coefficient Be?

We should naturally like to have as much consistency in our measuring instruments as the physicist and the chemist achieve. However, the complexities of human personality and other practical considerations often place limits on the accuracy with which we measure and we accept reliability coefficients of different sizes depending on various purposes and situations. Perhaps the most important of these considerations is the gravity of the decision to be made on the basis of the test score. The psychologist who has to recommend whether or not a person is to be committed to an institution is obligated to seek the most reliable instruments he can obtain. The counselor inquiring as to whether a student is likely to do better in one curriculum or another may settle for a slightly less reliable instrument, but his demands should still be high. A survey of parents' attitudes towards school practices needs only moderate reliability, since only the *average* or group figures need to be highly dependable and not the specific responses of individual parents. Test constructors experimenting with ideas for tests may accept rather low reliability in the early stages of experimentation—those tests which show promise can then be built up into more reliable instruments before publication.

It is much like the question of how confident we wish to be about decisions in other areas of living. The industrial organization about to hire a top executive (whose decisions may seriously affect the entire business) will usually spend large sums of time and money to obtain reliable evidence concerning a candidate's qualifications for the job. The same firm will devote far less time or money to the hiring of a clerk or office boy, whose errors are of lesser consequence. In buying a house, we want to have as much confidence in our decision as we can reasonably get. In buying a package of razor blades, slim evidence is sufficient since we lose little if we have to throw away the entire package or replace it sooner than expected. The principle is simply stated: the more important the decision to be reached, the greater is our need for confidence in the precision of the test and the higher is the required reliability coefficient.

Two Factors Affecting the Interpretation of Reliability Coefficients

Actually, there is no such thing as *the* reliability coefficient for a test. Like validity, reliability is specific to the group on which it is estimated. The reliability coefficient will be higher in one situation than in another according to circumstances which may or may not reflect real differences in the precision of measurement. Among these factors are the range of ability in the group and the interval of time between testings.

Range of Talent

If a reliability estimate is based on a group which has a small spread in the ability measured by the test, the coefficient will be relatively low. If the group is one which has a wide range in that particular talent, the coefficient will be higher. That is, the reliability coefficient will vary with the range of talent in the group, even though the accuracy of measurement is unchanged. The following example may illustrate how this comes about. For simplicity, we have used small numbers of cases; ordinarily, far larger groups would be required to ensure a coefficient in which we could have confidence.

In Table I are shown the raw scores and rankings of twenty students on two forms of an arithmetic test. Looking at the two sets of rankings, we see that changes in rank from one form to the other are minor; the ranks shift a little, but not importantly. A coefficient computed from these data would be fairly high.

TABLE I *Raw Scores and Ranks of Students on Two Forms of an Arithmetic Test*

Student	Form X		Form Y	
	Score	Rank	Score	Rank
A	90	1	88	2
B	87	2	89	1
C	83	3	76	5
D	78	4	77	4
E	72	5	80	3
F	70	6	65	7
G	68	7	64	8
H	65	8	67	6
I	60	9	53	10
J	54	10	57	9
K	51	11	49	11
L	47	12	45	14
M	46	13	48	12
N	43	14	47	13
O	39	15	44	15
P	38	16	42	16
Q	32	17	39	17
R	30	18	34	20
S	29	19	37	18
T	25	20	36	19

Now, however, let us examine only the rankings of the five top students. Though for these five students the shifts in rank are the same as before, the importance of the shifts is greatly emphasized. Whereas in the larger group student C's change in rank from third to fifth represented only a ten per cent shift (two places out of twenty), his shift of two places in rank in the smaller top group is a forty per cent change (two places out of five). When the entire twenty represent the group on which we estimate the reliability of the arithmetic test, going from third on form X to fifth on form Y still leaves the student as one of the best in this population. If, on the other hand, reliability is being estimated only on the group consisting of the top five students, going from third to fifth means dropping from the middle to the bottom of this population—a radical change. A coefficient, if computed for just these five cases, would be quite low.

Note that it is not the smaller number of cases which brings about the lower coefficient. It is the narrower range of talent which is responsible. A coefficient based on five cases as widespread as the twenty (e.g., pupils A, E, J, O, and T, who rank first, fifth, tenth, fifteenth, and twentieth respectively on form X), would be at least as large as the coefficient based on all twenty students.

This example shows why the reliability coefficient may vary even though the test questions and the stability of the students' performances are unchanged. A test may discriminate with satisfactory precision among students with wide ranges of talent but not discriminate equally well in a narrow range of talent. A yardstick is unsatisfactory if we must differentiate objects varying in length from 35.994 to 36.008 inches. Reliability coefficients reflect this fact, which holds regardless of the kind of reliability coefficient computed. It should be obvious, then, that *no reliability coefficient can be properly interpreted without information as to the spread of ability in the group on which it is based.* A reliability coefficient of .65 based on a narrow range of talent is fully as good as a coefficient of .90 based on a group with twice that spread of scores. Reliability coefficients are very much a function of the range of talent in the group.

Interval Between Testings

When two forms of a test are taken at a single sitting, the reliability coefficient computed by correlating the two forms is likely to overestimate somewhat the real accuracy of the test. This is so because factors such as mental set, physical condition of examinees, conditions of test administration, etc.—factors which are irrelevant to the test itself—are likely to operate equally on both forms, thus making each person's pair of scores more similar than they otherwise would be. The same type of overestimate may be expected when reliability is computed by split-half or other internal consistency techniques which are based on a single test administration. Coefficients such as these describe the accuracy of the test, but exaggerate the practical accuracy of the results by the extent to which the examinees and the testing situation may normally be expected to fluctuate. As indicated above, coefficients based on a single sitting do not describe the stability of the subjects' performances.

When we set out to investigate how stable the test results are likely to be from day to day or week to week, we are likely to underestimate the test's accuracy, though we may succeed in obtaining a realistic estimate of stability of the examinees' performances on the test. The underestimation of the test's accuracy depends on the extent to which changes in the examinees have taken place between testings. The same influences mentioned above—mental set, physical condition of examinees, and the like—which *increase* coefficients based on a single sitting are likely to *decrease* coefficients when testing is done on different days. It is unlikely for example, that the same persons who had headaches the first day will also have headaches on the day of the second testing.

Changes in the persons tested may also be of a kind directly related to the content of the particular test. If a month has elapsed between two administrations of an arithmetic test, different pupils may have learned different amounts of arithmetic during the interval. The second testing should then show greater score increases for those who learned more than for those who learned less. The correlation coefficient under these conditions will reflect the test's accuracy *minus* the effect of differential learning; it will not really be a reliability coefficient.

For most educational and industrial purposes, the reliability coefficient which reflects *stability of performance* over a relatively short time is the more important. Usually, we wish to know whether the student or job applicant would have achieved a similar score if he had been tested on some other day, or whether he might have shown up quite differently. It would be unfortunate and unfair to make inportant decisions on the basis of test results which might have been quite different had the person been tested the day before or a day later. We want an estimate of reliability which takes into account accidental changes in day-to-day ability of the individual, but which has not been affected by real learning between testings. Such a reliability coefficient would be based on two sittings, separated by one or more days so that day-to-day changes are reflected in the scores, but not separated by so much time that permanent changes, or learning, have occurred. Two forms of a test, administered a day to a week apart, would usually satisfy these conditions. If the same form of a test is used in both sittings, the intervening time should be long enough to minimize the role of memory from the first to the second administrations.

Ideally, then, our reliability coefficient would ordinarily be based on two different but equivalent forms of the test, administered to a group on two separate occasions. However, it is often not feasible to meet these conditions: there may be only one form of the test available, or the group may be available for only one day, or the test may be one which is itself a learning experience. We are then forced to rely on coefficients based on a single administration. Fortunately, when such coefficients are properly used they usually provide close approximations to the estimates which would have been obtained with alternate forms administered at different times.

Some Common Misconceptions

Reliability of Speed Tests

Although estimates of reliability based on one administration of the test are often satisfactory, there are some circumstances in which *only* retest methods are proper. Most notable is the case in which we are dealing with an easy test given under speed conditions. If the test is composed of items which almost anyone can answer correctly given enough time but which most people tested cannot finish in the time allowed, the test is largely a measure of speed. Many clerical and simple arithmetic tests used with adults are examples of speed tests. Internal consistency methods, whether they are of the Kuder-Richardson or of the split-half type, provide false and often grossly exaggerated estimates of the reliability of such tests. To demonstrate this problem, two forms of a simple but speed-laden clerical test were given to a group. For *each* form the odd-even (split-half) reliability coefficient was found to be over .99. However, when scores on Form A were correlated with scores on Form B, the coefficient was .88. This latter value is a more accurate estimate of the reliability of the test. Many equally dramatic illustrations of how spurious an inappropriate coefficient can be may be found readily, even in manuals for professionally made tests.

If a test is somewhat dependent on speed, but the items range in difficulty from easy to hard, internal consistency estimates will not be as seriously misleading as when the test items are simple and the test is highly speeded. As the importance of speed diminishes, these estimates will be less different from the coefficients which would be obtained by retest methods. It is difficult to guess how far wrong an inappropriate coefficient for a speeded test is. *Whenever there is evidence that speed is important in test performance, the safest course is to insist on an estimate of reliability based on test-and-retest,* if necessary with the same but preferably with an alternate form of the test.

Part vs. Total Reliability

Some of the tests we use are composed of several parts which are individually scored and the part scores are then added to yield a total score. Often, reliability is reported only for the total score, with no information given as to the reliability of the scores on the individual parts. This may lead to seriously mistaken assumptions regarding the reliability of the part scores—and, thus, of the confidence we may place in judgments based on the part scores. The longer a test is, other things being equal, the more reliable it is; the shorter the test, the lower is its reliability likely to be. A part score based on only a portion of the items in a test can hardly be expected to be as reliable as the total score; if we treat the part score as though it has the reliability of the total score, we misplace our confidence—sometimes quite seriously.

As an example, we may look at the Wechsler Intelligence Scale for Children, one of the most important instruments of its kind. Five subtests are combined to yield a total Verbal Score for this test. The reliability coefficient for the Verbal Score, based on 200 representative ten-year-olds, is .96—high enough to warrant considerable confidence in the accuracy of measurement for these youngsters. For the same population, however, a single subtest (General Comprehension) yields a reliability coefficient of only .73—a far less impressive figure. If we allow ourselves to act as though the total test reliability coefficient of .96 represents the consistency of measurement we can expect from the Comprehension subtest, we are likely to encounter unpleasant surprises on future retests. More importantly, any clinical judgments which ignore the relatively poor reliability of the part score are dangerous. Test users should consider it a basic rule that *if evidence of adequate reliability for part scores is missing, the part scores should not be used.*

Reliability for What Group?

This question may be considered as a special case under the principles discussed above with respect to range of talent. It is worth special consideration because it is so often ignored. Even the best documented of test manuals present only limited numbers of reliability coefficients; in too many manuals a single coefficient is all that is made available. On what group should a reliability coefficient be based?

Each of us is a member of many groups

When we interpret an individual's test score, the most meaningful reliability coefficient is one based on the group with which the individual is competing. Stated otherwise, the most appropriate group is that in which the counselor, clinician or employment manager is trying to make decisions as to the relative ability of the individuals on the trait being measured. Any one person is, of course, a member of many groups. An applicant for a job may also be classified as a high school or college graduate, an experienced or inexperienced salesman or bookkeeper, a local or out-of-state person, a member of one political party or another, below or above age thirty, etc. A high school student is a boy or girl; a member of an academic, trade or commercial school group; a member of an English class, a geometry class, or a woodworking or cooking class; a freshman or a junior; a future engineer or nurse or garage mechanic. Obviously, it would be impossible for a test manual to offer reliability for *all* the groups of which any one individual is a member.

The appropriate group is represented by the individual's present competition. If we are testing applicants for clerical work, the most meaningful reliability coefficient is one based on applicants for clerical work. Coefficients based on employed clerical workers are somewhat less useful, those based on high school graduates are still less useful; as we go on to *more general* groups—e.g., all high school students or all adults—the coefficients become less and less meaningful. Similarly, as we go to *less relevant* groups (even though they may be quite specific) the reliability coefficients are also less relevant and less meaningful. The reliability of a test calculated on the basis of mechanical apprentices, college sophomores, or junior executives reveals little of importance when we are concerned with clerical applicants. What we need to know is how well the test discriminates among applicants for clerical work. If we can define the population with even greater specificity and relevance—e.g., female applicants for filing jobs—so much the better. *The closer the resemblance between the group on which the reliability coefficient is based and the group of individuals about whose relative ability we need to decide, the more meaningful is that coefficient of reliability.*

Test Reliability vs. Scorer Reliability

Some tests are not entirely objective as to scoring method; the scorer is required to make a judgment as to the correctness or quality of the response. This is frequently true in individually-administered tests (Wechsler or Binet for example), projective techniques in personality measurement (Rorschach, Sentence Completion, etc.) and many other tests in which the subject is asked to supply the answer, rather than to select one of several stated choices. For tests such as these, it is important to know the extent of agreement between the persons who score them. Test manuals usually report the amount of agreement by means of a coefficient of correlation between scores assigned to a set of test papers by two or more independent scorers.

Such a correlation coefficient yields important information—it tells us how objectively the test can be scored. It even contributes some evidence of reliability, since objectivity of scoring is a factor which makes for test reliability. Such a coefficient should not, however, be considered a reliability coefficient for the test; it is only an estimate of *scoring* reliability—a statement of how much confidence we may have that two scorers will arrive at similar scores for a given test paper. Moreover, it is possible for a test to be quite unreliable as a measuring instrument, yet have high scoring objectivity. We should remember that many objective tests—those in which the person selects one of several stated options—are not very reliable, yet the scoring is by definition objective. A short personality inventory may have a retest reliability coefficient of .20; but if it is the usual paper-and-pencil set of questions with a clear scoring key, two scorers should agree perfectly, except for clerical errors, in assigning scores to the test. The coefficient of correlation between their sets of scores might well be 1.00.

In short, information as to scorer agreement is important but not sufficient. The crucial question—How precisely is the test measuring the individual?—is not answered by scorer agreement; a real reliability coefficient is required.

A Practical Check-list

When reading a test manual, the test user would do well to apply a mental check-list to the reliability section, raising at least the following questions for each reliability coefficient:

1. What does the coefficient measure?
   a. Precision of the test—coefficient based on single sitting?
   b. Stability of examinees' test performances—coefficient based on test-and-retest with a few days intervening?

2. Is it more than a reliability coefficient? . . . . does it also measure constancy of the trait? . . . . is the coefficient based on test-and-retest with enough intervening time for learning or similar changes to have occurred?

3. Do scores on the test depend largely on how rapidly the examinees can answer the questions? If so, is the reliability coefficient based on a test-and-retest study?

4. Are there part scores intended for consideration separately? If so, is each part score reliable enough to warrant my confidence?

5. Is the group on which this coefficient is based appropriate to my purpose? Does it consist of people similar to those with whom I shall be using the test?

6. Since a reliability coefficient, like any other statistic, requires a reasonable number of cases to be itself dependable, how large is the group on which the coefficient is based?

If, and *only* if, the coefficients can be accepted as meeting the above standards, one may ask:

7. In view of the importance of the judgments I shall make, is the correlation coefficient large enough to warrant my use of the test?

A reliability coefficient is a statistic—simply a number which summarizes a relationship. Before it takes on meaning, its reader must understand the logic of the study from which the coefficient was derived, the nature of the coefficient and the forces which affect it. Statistics may reveal or conceal—what they do depends to a very large extent on the logical ability and awareness the reader brings to them. Figures do lie, to those who don't or won't understand them.

13 | The Calculation of Test Reliability Coefficients Based on the Method of Rational Equivalence*

M. W. Richardson and G. F. Kuder

The authors have previously published a theoretical paper in which several new formulas for the estimation of test reliability were derived.[1] The present paper is partly in response to suggestions from various persons that the actual computations be explicitly outlined. In this way it may be possible to show that at least three of the four formulas are feasible in ordinary testing practice. One of the more precise formulas requires less time than does the Spearman-Brown split-test technique which has become almost a ritual among testers. Finally, this paper gives us an opportunity to present further results. Such empirical results cannot, however, furnish proof or disproof of the theoretical bases of the formulas. They do help to describe the operation of the formulas on tests which do not meet the assumptions fully.

Perhaps it should be said at the outset that the lack of satisfaction by a test of the special assumptions basic to the theory is not peculiar to these formulas, nor to test theory, for that matter. For example, the split-test Spearman-Brown technique assumes equal standard deviations of the two halves, and also implicitly assumes that the correlation coefficient between the two halves is representative of the many different coefficients that could be obtained if the test were halved in different ways. The particular way of splitting the test that is adopted in any given situation determines the value of the reliability coefficient that will be obtained. The particular split may not select a representative value from the many different estimates possible. The lack of uniqueness of a split-test estimate, plus the fact that the standard deviations of the two half-tests are not often equal, operate to make the method rather unsatisfactory in practice.[2]

*From *Journal of Educational Psychology,* 1939, **30,** 681-687. Reproduced with permission of the junior author.

[1] Kuder, G. F., and Richardson, M. W.: "The Theory of the Estimation of Test Reliability." *Psychometrika,* Vol. II, 1937, pp. 151-160.

[2] It should be noted that, in the authors' opinion, these formulas apply no better to time-limit tests than does the split-test Spearman-Brown method.

Although the theory of the new reliability formulas will not be repeated here, it is desirable to state that the reliability coefficient is defined as the coefficient of correlation between one experimental form of a test and a hypothetically equivalent form. Equivalence is precisely defined in terms of the items or elements of the test. The departures from exact equivalence are rationally defined, and are not dependent upon the experimenter's inevitable failure to construct two test forms which are closely equivalent.

The more exact formulas require more information than is ordinarily provided in the analysis of a test score distribution. None of the methods requires a rescoring of the test by halves or otherwise. All of them require the computation of the test-score variance (square of the standard deviation). In any event, the standard deviation (and variance) and the mean are always computed as a part of the description of the tested population.

The four formulas listed below are assigned numbers to correspond to those in the original paper. They are, in order of their theoretical exactness:

$$r_{tt} = \frac{\sigma_t^2 - \Sigma pq}{2\sigma_t^2} + \sqrt{\frac{\Sigma r^2_{it} pq}{\sigma_t^2} + \left(\frac{\sigma_t^2 - \Sigma pq}{2\sigma_t^2}\right)^2}; \tag{8}$$

$$r_{tt} = \frac{\sigma_t^2 - \Sigma pq}{(\Sigma\sqrt{pq})^2 - \Sigma pq} \cdot \frac{(\Sigma\sqrt{pq})^2}{\sigma_t^2}; \tag{14}$$

$$r_{tt} = \frac{n}{n-1} \cdot \frac{\sigma_t^2 - \Sigma pq}{\sigma_t^2}; \tag{20}$$

$$r_{tt} = \frac{n}{n-1} \cdot \frac{\sigma_t^2 - n\overline{pq}}{\sigma_t^2}. \tag{21}$$

Explanation of symbols:

r_{tt} is the reliability coefficient of test t.

σ_t^2 is the variance (square of the standard deviation of the scores on test t).

p is the percentage of correct answers given to a test item.

$q = 1 - p$ = percentage of incorrect answers given to the test item.

pq is the variance of a single item.

Σpq means the sum of the item variances, or sum of the products of p and q, for all the test items.

r_{it} is the coefficient of correlation between any item i and the test t.

$\Sigma r^2_{it} pq$ means the sum of the products of the square of each item-test coefficient by the corresponding item variance, the summation being made over the items.

$\Sigma\sqrt{pq}$ means the sum of the standard deviations of the n items.

n is the number of items.

$\bar{p}$ is the average percentage of correct answers given to an item, as computed by dividing the mean by the number of items.

It should be noted that Formula (8) requires an item analysis which provides an item-test coefficient for each item and the percentage of correct answers on each item. Formulas (14) and (20) require only the percentage of correct answers on each item, in addition to the standard deviation. Formula (21) requires only the mean, standard deviation, and the number of items. It is to be noted that Formulas (14), (20), and (21) do not require the computation of correlation coefficients between two sets of scores.

It may be instructive to indicate in a table the requirements of the various methods of estimating reliability coefficients. The cross denotes that the operation is required by, or implicit in, the method. The analysis furnished by Table I is pertinent to the question of the amount of labor involved in making an estimate of the reliability coefficient, neglecting for the moment differences in accuracy of the estimate. The problem of efficiency in getting the estimate then resolves itself into the relative time spent in operations 1 to 8 respectively. Some conclusions emerge from an inspection of the table and from experience common to test technicians. One of them is that Formula (8) requires more computational labor than any other in the list. A conclusion from the experience of the authors is that the results given by Formula (8) are so closely approximated by Formulas (14) and (20) that the additional labor is not justified in the normal situation. It is, of course, recognized that additional labor may be expended if it is sufficiently important for the purpose of the investigation that an extremely high order of accuracy be obtained. The formulas used in the Method of Rational Equivalence tend to give slight underestimates of the "true" value of the reliability coefficient. The authors believe that it is better to overestimate the relative amount of measurement error than to underestimate it. This is equivalent to preferring an underestimate to a fluctuating estimate of the reliability coefficient.

The latter requirement of setting the upper limit of the relative amount of error present in a test score distribution is met by Formula (21). This formula will in most cases underestimate, and will never overestimate, the reliability coefficient; *i.e.*, it will overestimate the percentage of variance which is error. Moreover the computation of this coefficient requires little labor. The minimum possible parameters used in the description of a test group provide all the data needed. Formula (21) may be regarded as a foot-rule method of setting the lower limit of the reliability coefficient, or the upper limit of error.

TABLE I

Number	Operation required, description	Formula				Split-test Spearman-Brown	Equivalent forms method
		8	14	20	21		
1	Construction of an equivalent form	..	..	..	..	..	X
2	Computation of mean score	1	1	1	X	X	X
3	Computation of standard deviation of test scores	X	X	X	X	X	X
4	Computation of coefficient of correlation between each item and the total test	X					
5	Computation of percentage of correct answers on each item	X	X	X			
6	Rescoring split halves of a test	..	..	..	..	X	
7	Substitution in a special formula, after other operations are performed	X	X	X	X	X	
8	Computation of a coefficient of correlation between two sets of scores	..	..	..	..	X	X

[1] Incidentally computed, but not used directly in the formula.

With the understanding that Formula (21) ordinarily furnishes an underestimate of the reliability coefficient, it becomes pertinent to inquire into the matter of the relative amount of labor involved in the application of Formulas (14) or (20) and the usual techniques. Comparing either of these formulas against the split-test technique, it is apparent from the table of necessary operations that the computation of the percentage of correct answers for n items must be compared with the rescoring of the halves of the split test and the computation of the coefficient of correlation between the scores on the halves. The authors have made only preliminary accountings of the time required for each, but are nevertheless of the opinion that the straightforward applications of Formulas (14) or (20) will in many cases require less time than does the traditional split-test Spearman-Brown technique. The cardinal fact about a single estimate by the split-test technique is that no one (not even the investigator) can be sure of the direction in which the estimate errs; it is commonly assumed that it overestimates the reliability of a test.

TABLE II

A Item number	B r_{it}	C r^2_{it}	D $r^2_{it}pq$	E p	F pq	G $\sqrt{pq}$
1	0.235	.0552	.0036	.930	.0651	.2551
2	0.312	.0973	.0144	.820	.1476	.3842
3	0.175	.0306	.0025	.910	.0819	.2862
4	0.116	.0135	.0020	.815	.1508	.3883
.	.	.	.	.	.	.
.	.	.	.	.	.	.
90	0.057	.0032	.0004	.860	.1204	.3470
	. . . . .	. . . . .	1.3678	. . . .	17.7914	39.6092

Considerations which are pertinent to the amount of labor involved in computing the value of p for each item, as required in Formulas (14) and (21) are (*a*) that the latest machine scoring methods[1] provide easy methods of counting the percentage of correct answers for each item, and (*b*) that facilitating tables are available for the computation of $\sqrt{pq}$, and pq.[2]

Table II illustrates in abbreviated form the method of calculating the reliability coefficient by Formulas (8), (14), and (20). The entire table must be filled out for Formula (8). Only certain selected columns, as indicated below, need be obtained for Formulas (14) and (20). The footings of the table are the sums of the respective columns. The data comprise a ninety-item test of aptitude for the physical sciences. As computed by the usual methods, $M_t = 50.820$ and $\sigma_t^2 = 148.0276$.

To solve by means of Formula (8) we use the sum of columns D and F with σ_t^2. By this formula

$$r_{tt} = \frac{148.0276 - 17.7914}{2 \times 148.0276} + \sqrt{\frac{1.3678}{148.0276} + \left(\frac{148.0276 - 17.7914}{2 \times 148.0276}\right)^2}$$

The result is 0.890, given here to three decimal places for sake of comparison.

---

[1] The reference here is to the International Business Machines 1939 model of their scoring machine.
[2] Facilitating tables and nomographs suitable for the new formulas have been prepared by Max D. Engelhart and Hugh Lewis.

To solve by means of Formula (14), we use the sums of columns F and G only, with σ_t^2. By this formula,

$$r_{tt} = \frac{148.0276 - 17.7914}{(39.6092)^2 - 17.7914} \cdot \frac{(39.6092)^2}{148.0276} = 0.890.$$

To solve by means of Formula (20), we use only the sum of column F, together with σ_t^2 and n. Substituting these values, we have

$$r_{tt} = \frac{90}{89} \cdot \frac{148.0276 - 17.7914}{148.0276} = 0.890.$$

The solution according to Formula (21) does not require any of the data in Table II, but only n, M_t, and σ_t^2. We have

$$\bar{p} = \frac{M_t}{n} = \frac{50.82}{90} = .5647.$$

Hence

$$r_{tt} = \frac{90}{89} \cdot \frac{148.0276 - 90(0.5647) \cdot (1.0000 - 0.5647)}{148.0276},$$

which equals 0.860. This estimate is less by 0.03 than that given by the more exact formulas. Although this reliability coefficient may be computed in five minutes of time from the mean, standard deviation, and the number of items, its accuracy is often high enough for practical purposes.

Reliability coefficients of the same test computed by the split-test Spearman-Brown method are here presented with the results obtained from the four formulas above, for purposes of comparison.

Odd *versus* even items, as printed	0.908
Halves with balanced difficulty	0.902
Random halves	0.894
Formula 8	0.890
Formula 14	0.890
Formula 20	0.890
Formula 21	0.860

The following estimates of reliability obtained by use of the various formulas from reading tests administered in the Chicago schools to children in Grades II, III, and IV have been kindly furnished by Dr. Max D. Engelhart:

	Reliability
Formula 8	.987
Formula 14	.977
Formula 20	.977
Formula 21	.966

The results obtained for the two tests reported here bear out the conclusion drawn from the data presented in the earlier paper, *i.e.*, that Formula (20) is adequate for most situations, producing a figure which is the same or slightly lower than that to be obtained by use of the most rigorous formula (Formula 8).

Summary

1) An analysis of the computational operations required for the reliability formulas by the Method of Rational Equivalence shows that the recommended formula (Formula 20) requires not more, and perhaps less, computational labor than does the split-test Spearman-Brown method.

2) Further empirical results show that the values computed by the recommended formula are close approximations to those computed by the more rigorous formulas.

3) For situations in which the investigator is satisifed with an underestimate of reliability, the formula which utilizes the mean, standard deviation, and number of items is ordinarily sufficient.

14 | How Accurate Is a Test Score?*

Jerome E. Doppelt

Every user of test scores knows that no test is perfectly accurate. The score on a test is determined principally by the ability or knowledge of the person who takes it, but the score is also affected by the inaccuracy of the test itself.

It would be helpful if we could know each time we see a score whether it is higher or lower than it should be, and by how much. Unfortunately, no one has ever figured out a practical way to determine the precise amount of error in an individual case. Statistics have been developed, however, for estimating the margin of error we should allow for in test scores. One of the most useful of these is the *standard error of measurement* (SE_M).

At this point, the reader may want to ask, "Doesn't the reliability coefficient tell us how accurate a test is?" The reliability coefficient does, of course, reflect the test's accuracy, but it has two drawbacks: (1) its numerical value depends, to a great extent, on the spread of scores in the group of people tested,[1] and (2) it does not help us directly in evaluating the scores earned by individual applicants and counselees. The SE_M avoids these two disadvantages. Later in this article, we will show how to compute the SE_M and present a table for estimating it for most tests.

Let us consider a practical situation in which it would be useful to have a measure of the accuracy of a test score. Suppose we have an opening for a junior executive in our company. We have a large number of applicants and among them is Henry Smith. He looks good on most counts, but he has a score of 28 on a test of administrative knowledge. The test norms show that a score of 32 would place an applicant within the upper half of all executive applicants and we desire to make our choice from the upper half. Since Smith looks promising in other ways we begin to wonder about his test placement.

If we could test him again, would he get 28 or some other score? Just what is Smith's *true* score on his test? Before we can make sense in talking

---

*From *Test Service Bulletin*, No. 50. New York: The Psychological Corporation. Copyright, ©, 1956 by the Psychological Corporation. Reprinted by permission of the publisher.
[1] For an illustration, see Wesman, Alexander G. Reliability and Confidence. *Test Service Bulletin*, No. 44, May, 1952.

about the difference between the *true* score and the *observed* or *obtained* score, we need to specify what we mean by *true* score.

Imagine that we have a very large number of comparable forms of our test. (We need not go into the statistics of comparable forms here; let us simply agree that comparable forms are interchangeable. That is, if we had to choose only one form to measure administrative knowledge, we would be equally happy with any one of the forms.) Now suppose we were able to corner Henry Smith and test him with all our tremendous number of equivalent forms. We would find that our hero does not always get the same score. As the number of forms administered gets larger and larger, we would discover that the distribution of Smith's scores begins to resemble the familiar "normal" curve. In this situation, we can reasonably decide that the average of the large number of scores is characteristic of Smith's performance on our test, and we will call this his *true* score.

At the beginning of the article we pointed out that the score on a test reflects primarily what the person tested brings to the task, but partly error of measurement in the test. The true score measures the performance that is characteristic of the person tested; the variations, plus and minus, around the true score describe a characteristic of the test.

When we use the standard deviation as a measure of the variation of observed scores around the true score, the result is called the *standard error of measurement*. Since this statistic has direct interpretable meaning in relation to the "normal" curve, we are in a position to make this statement:

> If we could know both an individual's exact true score and the SE_M which is characteristic of the test, we would know that about 68% of the scores the individual obtained on the vast number of comparable forms fall within one SE_M of his true score. A band stretching two standard errors above and below his true score would include about 95% of his obtained scores, and within three standard errors of the true score would lie over 99% of his scores on the many forms of the test.

Obviously it is useful to be able to say, putting it a little differently, that for about two thirds of all people tested, the observed scores lie within one SE_M of the true scores—and that for nineteen out of twenty cases the observed score will not be more than two standard errors away from the true score.

As explained in the Note at the end of this article, we must be quite careful how we make statements like the foregoing. It is not correct to say of an individual with a certain *observed* score that the odds are two out of three that his *true* score is within one SE_M of the score he got. But in the practical instance, we can use the SE_M in defining limits around the observed score within which we would be *reasonably sure* to find the true score. Whether the "reasonable limits" (as Professor Guilliksen (1950) has called them) will be one, two, or three times the SE_M will depend on the level of confidence the test user desires. The surer he wants to be of not making a mistake in locating the true score, the broader the margin of error he must allow for and therefore the less definite and precise will be the indication given by the test. The broader the score band we allow for each job applicant, for example, the greater the likelihood that his true score will be within it, but the harder it will be to tell the applicants apart.

Coming back to the case of Henry Smith, let us suppose that the test manual reveals that the SE_M is 3 points. If we establish "reasonable limits" of one SE_M on either side of the observed score, the band for Smith would extend over the score range 25-31. And since a score of 32 is needed before a person may be considered as belonging to the top half of executive trainees, we may decide that Smith does not belong in the top half of the group. We are not willing to act as if his true score is 32.

We could have established wider "reasonable limits," say 2 or 3 SE_M on either side of the observed score. We would then have greater confidence that our location of the true score *within the band* is correct. This extra confidence costs us something. We pay for it by having more people to be considered as possibilities. When there are many applicants, we usually want to reduce the number of eligible candidates even though we increase the possibility of making a wrong decision about the true score of some of them.

Since in practice we cannot give a large number of equivalent forms of a test in order to find the characteristic standard error of measurement, how *do* we determine it? The answer to this takes us back to the *reliability coefficient.*

As measured by the reliability coefficient, reliability means consistency of measurement. If the individuals of a group remain in about the same relative positions or ranks after successive testings, the test is "reliable" *for that group.* It is unfortunately true that a test will have different reliability coefficients depending on the groups of people tested: higher coefficients for groups with a wide spread of scores and lower ones for groups with scores bunched more closely together.

The SE_M is less subject to this variation; the formula for computing it takes into account both the reliability coefficient *and* the standard deviation for each group. The formula is simple:

$$SE_M = SD\sqrt{1 - r_{tt}}$$

where SD is the standard deviation of the obtained scores of a group and r_{tt} is the reliability coefficient computed for the same group.[2]

---

[2] We cannot automatically say that the more accurate or reliable of two tests is the one which has the lower value for its SE_M. As may be seen from the computing formula, the

Standard Errors of Measurement for Given Values of Reliability Coefficient and Standard Deviation

SD	Reliability Coefficient					
	.95	.90	.85	.80	.75	.70
30	6.7	9.5	11.6	13.4	15.0	16.4
28	6.3	8.9	10.8	12.5	14.0	15.3
26	5.8	8.2	10.1	11.6	13.0	14.2
24	5.4	7.6	9.3	10.7	12.0	13.1
22	4.9	7.0	8.5	9.8	11.0	12.0
20	4.5	6.3	7.7	8.9	10.0	11.0
18	4.0	5.7	7.0	8.0	9.0	9.9
16	3.6	5.1	6.2	7.2	8.0	8.8
14	3.1	4.4	5.4	6.3	7.0	7.7
12	2.7	3.8	4.6	5.4	6.0	6.6
10	2.2	3.2	3.9	4.5	5.0	5.5
8	1.8	2.5	3.1	3.6	4.0	4.4
6	1.3	1.9	2.3	2.7	3.0	3.3
4	.9	1.3	1.5	1.8	2.0	2.2
2	.4	.6	.8	.9	1.0	1.1

This table is based on the formula $SE_M = SD \sqrt{1 - r_{tt}}$. For most purposes the result will be sufficiently accurate if the table is entered with the reliability and standard deviation values nearest those given in the test manual. Be sure the standard deviation and the reliability coefficient are for the same group of people.

Like a true score for an individual, the SE_M for a test should be just one definite number if it is really a characteristic of the test rather than of the people tested. But if we look in a test manual, we may see that there appear to be differences among standard errors of measurement computed for different groups. For example, the SE_M is reported for each of the nine groups on the Numerical Test in the *Personnel Tests for Industry* series. The values range from 1.7 to 2.4. The explanation is that we have no way of computing the exact value of the SE_M—the formula merely provides an *estimate* of the SE_M. Estimates, of course, can be expected to differ. In any situation where we cannot obtain the true value of a statistic, it is advisable to have as many estimates of that value as practical. In the case of PTI-Numerical, we can be comfortable with the conclusion that the SE_M is about 2 points.

SE_M is tied in with the score units in which the standard deviation is expressed. A test with a standard deviation of 16 points may have the same reliability as a test with a standard deviation of 8 points. However, the SE_M of the first test will be numerically twice that of the second.

Many test manuals give both reliability coefficients and standard errors of measurement for the convenience of the user. When the SE_M is not given, it can be estimated readily by use of the reliability coefficient, provided the manual also states the standard deviation of the particular group of people on which the reliability coefficient is based. It is well worth the test user's time to make this computation; the table on page 107 permits an approximation to be made easily without any figuring.

If, as is too often the case, the manual does not present the standard deviation of the group for which the reliability coefficient is reported, it would be advisable for the user to write a letter to the test author.

NOTE: As textbooks usually point out, it is correct to make a statement of probability (such as "68% of the scores" or "two out of three times") *only* when the SE_M is applied to the *true* score. If a test has a standard error of 5.5, it is not correct to say of a person who obtains a score of 48 that the chances are two out of three that his true score is between 42.5 and 53.5. This person's true score is a definite number, although we do not know what it is. The statement that his true score lies between 42.5 and 53.5 is either true or false. Intermediate probabilities like "two out of three" or "one out of twenty" cannot properly be attached to it. The "reasonable limits" idea simply helps us to avoid making a mathematical statement of probability which would be technically inaccurate. Precise statements of probability in relation to confidence intervals are possible but lie outside the scope of this article.

15 | Reliability*

Robert L. Thorndike

The issues of test reliability may be approached, it has seemed to me, at three levels. The first of these is the verbal level of formulation and definition of the concept. A second level is that of mathematical model-building, leading to specification of a set of formulas and computational procedures by which the parameters specified in the model are to be estimated. A third level is that of experimental data-gathering procedures, under which certain tests are given to certain subjects at certain times and treated in certain ways to yield scores that are the raw materials to which we apply our formulas and computational procedures.

Developments in the past seventeen years appear to have been primarily at the first two of these levels. In fact, Oscar Buros, addressing the American Educational Research Association last year, expressed the view that the last thirty-five years have been retrogressive, so far as our empirical procedures for appraising reliability are concerned. He exhorted us to return to the virtuous ways of our forefathers and stick to the operation of testing the individual with two or more experimentally independent tests, in order to get the data which permit generalizations about precision of measurement over occasions as well as over test items, and to this I can only say "Amen." He urged us not to backslide from the high standards of precision that Truman Kelley laid down for us in 1927, and to this I would comment, "It all depends." But my point is that I am not aware of any distinctive proposals for new patterns of data-gathering that call for our special attention today, though it is always well that we be aware of the limitations of the methods we are using.

Turning now to verbal formulation, perhaps the major trend has been toward increasingly explicit formulation of the concept that performance on a test should be thought of as a sample from a defined universe of events, and that reliability is concerned with the precision with which the test score, that is, the sample, represents the universe. I shall not try to be a historian, but will merely note that this idea has been made fairly explicit by Buros, by Cronbach, by Tryon, and probably by others.

What we may call the "classical" approach to reliability tended to be conceptualized in terms of some unobservable underlying "true score" distorted in a given measurement by an equally unobservable "error of measurement." The corresponding mathematical models and computational routines were procedures for estimating the magnitude, absolute or relative, of this measurement error. The formulation in terms of sampling does away in one lightning stoke with the mystical "true score," somehow enshrined far above the mundane world of scores and data, and replaces it with the less austere "expected value" of the score in the population of values from which the sample score was drawn.

Now what are the implications, the advantages, and possibly the limitations of this "sampling" conception over the classic "true score and error" conception?

For myself, I cannot say that the advantage lies in simplication and clarification. This notion of a "universe of possible scores" is in many ways a puzzling and somewhat confusing one. Of what is this universe composed? Suppose we have given Form A of the XYZ Reading Test to the fifth graders in our school and gotten a score for each pupil. Of what universe of scores are these scores a sample—of all possible scores that we might have gotten by giving Form A on that day? Of all possible scores that we might have gotten by giving Form A sometime that month? Of all possible scores that might have been gotten by giving Forms A or B or C or other forms up to a still-unwritten Form K on that day? Of scores on these same numerous and presumably "parallel" forms—and we shall have to ask what "parallel" means under a sampling conception of reliability—at some unspecified date within the month? Of scores on the whole array of different reading tests produced by different authors over the past twenty-five years? Of scores on tests of some aspect of educational achievement not further specified?

As soon as we try to conceptualize a test score as a sample from some universe, we are brought face to face with the very knotty problem of defining the universe from which we are sampling. But I suppose this very difficulty may be in one sense a blessing. The experimental data-gathering phase of estimating reliability has *always* implied a universe to which those data corresponded. Split-half procedures refer only to a universe of behaviors produced at one single point in time, retest procedures to a universe of responses to a specific set of items, and so forth. Perhaps one of the advantages of the sampling formulation is that it makes us more explicitly aware of the need to define the universe in which we are interested, or to acknowledge the universe to which our data apply. Certainly, over the past thirty years, all of us who have written for students and for the test-using public have insistently harped upon the nonequivalence of different operations for estimating reliability, and emphasized the different universes to which different procedures referred.

The notion of a random sample from a universe of responses seems most satisfying and clear-cut when we are dealing with some unitary act of behavior, which we score in some way. Examples would be distance jumped in a broad jump, time to run 100 yards, speed of response on a trial with a reaction time device, or number of trials to learn a series of nonsense syllables to a specified level of mastery. In these cases, the experimental specification of the task is fairly complete. Thus, for the 100-yard run, we specify a smooth, straight, well-packed cinder track, a certain type of starting blocks, certain limitations on the shoes to be worn, a certain pattern of preparatory and starting signals, and a certain procedure for recording time. A universe could then be the universe of times for a given runner, over a certain span of days, weeks, or months of his running career. Data from two or more trials under these conditions would give us some basis for generalizing about the consistency of this behavior for this defined universe. We could also extend the universe if we wished—to include wooden indoor tracks for example, or to include running on grass, or running in sneakers instead of track shoes—and sample randomly from this more varied universe. As conditions were varied, we might expect typical performance to vary more widely and precision to be decreased.

We are usually interested in estimating precision for each of a population of persons, rather than just for some one specific person, and so we are likely to have a sampling from some population of persons. The nature of that population will also influence estimates of precision, and so it will be important that the population be specified as well as the conditions. Precision of estimating time to run 100 yards is probably much greater for college track stars than for middle-aged professors—for whom one might occasionally get scores approaching infinity. But it would be possible to specify the population of individuals fairly satisfactorily, as well as the population of behaviors for a given person. Within this at least two-dimensional universe, we could sample in a presumably random fashion, and we could then analyze our sample of observations to yield estimates of the relative precision with which a person could be located within the group or the absolute precision with which his time could be estimated in seconds.

When we are dealing with the typical aptitude or achievement test, however, in which the score is some type of summation of scores upon single items, the conception of the universe from which we have drawn a sample becomes a little more fuzzy. Here, fairly clearly, we are concerned with a sampling not only of responses to a given situation but also of situations to be responded to. How shall we define that universe? The classical approach to reliability tended to deal with this issue by postulating a universe of equivalent or parallel tests and by limiting the universe from which our sample is drawn to this universe of parallel tests. Parallel tests may be defined statistically as those having equal means, standard deviations, and correlations with each other and with other variables. But they may also be defined in terms of the operations of construction, as tests built by the same procedures to the same specifications. If we adopt the second definition, statistical characteristics will not be identical, but the tests will vary in their statistical attributes to the extent that different samples of items all chosen to conform to a uniform blueprint or test plan will produce tests with somewhat differing statistical values.

But some of the recent discussions seem to imply a random sampling of tests from some rather loosely and broadly defined domain—the domain of scholastic aptitude tests, or the domain of reading comprehension tests, or the domain of personal adjustment inventories. Clearly, these are very vague and ill-defined domains. A sampling expert would be hard put to delimit the universe or to propose any meaningful set of operations for sampling from it. And in the realm of practical politics, I question whether anyone has ever seriously undertaken to carry out such a sampling operation. One might argue that the data appearing in the manual of the XYZ Reading Test, showing its correlations with other published reading tests, are an approximation of such a domain sampling. But how truly does the set of tests, taken collectively, represent a random sampling from the whole domain of reading tests? One suspects that the tests selected for correlating were chosen by the author or publisher on some systematic and nonrandom basis—because they were widely used tests, because data with respect to them were readily available, or for some other nonrandom reason.

We note, further, that as we broaden our conception of the universe being sampled from that of all tests made to a certain uniform set of specifications to all tests of a certain ability or personality domain, we begin to face the issue of whether we are still getting evidence on reliability or whether we are now getting evidence on some aspect of construct validity. But, once again, perhaps we should consider it a contribution of the sampling approach that it makes explicit to us and heightens our awareness of the continuity from reliability to validity. Cronbach offers the single term "generalizability" to cover the whole gamut of relationships from those within the most restricted universe of near-exact replications to those extending over the most general and broadly defined domain, and develops a common statistical framework which he applies to the whole gamut. Recognition that the same pattern of statistical analysis can be used whether one is dealing with the little central core, or with all the layers of the whole onion, may be useful. On the other hand, we may perhaps question whether this approach helps to clarify our meaning of "reliability" as a distinctive concept.

A third context in which the random sampling notion has been applied to the conceptulization of reliability has been the context of the single test item. That is, one can conceive of a certain universe of test items—let us say the universe of vocabulary items, for example. A given test may be considered to represent a random sampling drawn from this item universe. This conception provides the foundation for the estimation of test reliability from the inter-relations of the items of the sample, and thus to a somewhat more generalized and less restrictive form of the Kuder-Richardson reliability estimates.

But here, again, we encounter certain difficulties. These center on the one hand upon the definition of the universe and on the other upon the notion of randomness in sampling. In the first place, there are very definite constraints upon the items which make up our operational, as opposed to a purely hypothetical, universe. If we take the domain of vocabulary items as our example, we can specify what some of the constraints might be in an actual case. First, there is typically a constraint upon the format of the item—most often to a five-choice multiple-choice form. Second, there are constraints imposed by editorial policy—exemplified by the decision to exclude proper names or specialized technical terms, or by a requirement that the options call for gross rather than fine discriminations of shade of meaning. Third, there are the constraints that arise out of the particular idiosyncrasies of the item writers: their tendencies to favor particular types of words, or particular tricks of distracter construction. Finally, there are the constraints imposed by the item selection procedures—selection to provide a predetermined spread of item difficulties and to eliminate items failing to discriminate at a designated level. Thus, the universe is considerably restricted, is hard to define, and the sampling from it is hardly to be considered random.

Presumably we could elaborate and delimit more fully the definition of the universe of items. Certainly, we could replace the concept of random sampling with one of stratified sampling, and indeed Cronbach has proposed that the sampling concept be extended to one of stratified sampling. But we may find that a really adequate definition of the universe from which we have sampled will become so involved as to be meaningless. We will almost certainly find that in proportion as we provide detailed specifications for stratification of our universe of items, and carry out our sampling within such strata, we are once again getting very close to a bill of particulars for equivalent tests. Just as random sampling is less efficient than stratified sampling in opinion surveys or demographic studies when stratification is upon relevant variables, so also random sampling of test items is less efficient than stratified sampling in making equivalent tests. Analytical techniques developed on the basis of random sampling assumptions will make a test appear less precise than it is as a representation of a population of tests which sample in a uniform way from different strata of the universe of items. It is partly in this sense that the Kuder-Richardson Formula 20 and the other formulas that try to estimate test reliability from item data, or from such test statistics as means and variances (which grow out of item data), are lower-bound estimates of reliability. They treat the sampling of items as random rather than stratified. They assume that differences in the factor composition of items either do not exist, or are only such as arise by chance.

Sometimes the facts suggest that this may be approximately the case. Thus, Cronbach (1951) compared the values that he obtained for tests divided into random halves and those divided into judgmentally equivalent halves for a mechanical reasoning test, and found an average value of .810 for random splits and .820 for parallel splits. For a short morale scale the corresponding values were .715 and .737. But frequently a test is fairly sharply stratified—by difficulty level, by area of content, by intellectual process. When this is true, correlation estimates based on random sampling concepts may seriously underestimate those that would be obtained between two parallel forms of the test, and consequently the precision with which a given test represents the stratified universe.

These reactions to random sampling as applied to tests and test items were stimulated in part by Jane Loevinger's presidential address to Division 5 at the recent American Psychological Association meetings (Loevinger, 1963), and I gladly acknowledge the indebtedness, without holding her responsible for anything silly that I have said.

The shift in verbal formulation to a sampling formulation is compatible with a shift in mathematical models of reliability to analysis of variance and intraclass correlation models. These models have, of course, been proposed for more than twenty years, but they have been more systematically and completely expressed in the past decade.

The most comprehensive and systematic elaboration of this formulation of which I am aware is the one distributed in hectographed form by Oscar Buros (1963), and available for $1.00 from the Gryphon Press. I confess my own limitation when I say that I find this presentation pretty hard to follow. I hope that others of you will be either more familiar with or more facile at picking up the notation that Buros has used, and will be able to pick from the host of formulas that are offered the one that is appropriate to the specific data with which you are faced.

One great virtue of analysis of variance models is their built-in versatility. They can handle item responses that are scored 0 or 1, trial scores that yield scores with some type of continuous distribution, or, where more than one test has been given to each individual, scores for total tests. They can deal with the situation in which the data for each individual are generated by the same test or the same rater, and also the situation in which test or rater vary from person to person. This latter situation is one of very real importance in many practical circumstances. How shall we judge the precision of a reported IQ when we do not know which of two or more forms of a test was given? How shall we appraise the repeatability of a course grade when the grade may be given by any one of the several different instructors who handle a course? If we have more than a single score for each individual, even though the scores are based on different tests or raters for each individual, we can get an estimate of within-persons variation. And whenever we have an estimate of within-persons variation we have a basis for judging the precision of a score or rating as describing a person. Clearly, with only two or three or four scores per person, the estimate of within-persons variance is very crude for a single individual. We must be willing to assume that the within-persons variance is sufficiently uniform from person to person for a pooling of data over persons to give us a usable common estimate of variance from test to test for each single individual. Having such an estimate, we can express reliability either as the precision of a score for an individual stated in absolute terms or as the precision of placement of an individual relative to his fellows.

As various writers have shown, the conventional Kuder-Richardson formulas emerge as special cases of the more general variance analysis approach. Likewise, the adjustment of correlational measures of reliability for test length are derivable from general variance analysis formulas.

I shall not try to recite to you a set of formulas today, because this would serve no good purpose. Rather, let me direct you to Tryon's 1957 article in the *Psychological Bulletin*, Buros' available if unpublished material (1963), and Cronbach's article in the *British Journal of Statistical Psychology* (Cronbach *et al.*, 1963). These, plus Horst's (1949) and Ebel's (1951) articles in *Psychometrika* should give you all the formulas you can use.

In closing, let me raise with you the question of how much you are willing to pay for precision in a given measurement. The cost is partly one of time and expense. But, given some fixed limit on time and expense, the cost can then be a cost in scope and comprehensiveness. We can usually make gains in precision by increasing the redundance and repetitiveness of successive observations. The more narrowly a universe is defined, the more adequately a given length of test sample can represent it. With all due respect to the error of measurement, we must recognize that it is often the error of estimate that we are really interested in. To maximize prediction of socially useful events, it may be advantageous to sacrifice a little precision in order to gain a greater amount of scope. Precision and high reliability are, after all, a means rather than an end.

Test Validity

Reliability is a necessary but not a sufficient condition for a good test. In addition to being reliable, a test needs to measure something of practical or theoretical value, that is, it must have *validity* for some purpose. The *Standards for Educational and Psychological Tests and Manuals* (APA, 1966, p. 12) lists three uses or aims of testing:

1. The test user wishes to determine how an individual performs at present in a universe of situations that the test situation is claimed to represent.
2. The test user wishes to forecast an individual's future standing or to estimate an individual's present standing on some variable of particular significance that is different from the test.
3. The test user wishes to infer the degree to which the individual possesses some hypothetical trait or quality (construct) presumed to be reflected in the test performance.

The *Standards* refer to the aspects of validity corresponding to these three uses of tests as *content validity, criterion-related validity* and *construct validity,* respectively. These three aspects of validity, together with other matters pertaining to the concept, are treated in the five articles of this section.

The first article, by Roger Lennon, is a comprehensive discussion of *content validity*—the extent to which examinees' responses to the items comprising a test are representative of their responses to a universe of situations of interest to the tester. Although an analysis of content validity occurs more frequently in connection with achievement tests, where an external criterion is either unavailable or inappropriate, certain authorities have also applied the notion of content validity to aptitude, interest and personality measurement. Lennon states that both the content of test questions and the processes which examinees employ in arriving at their answers to the questions must be taken into account in appraising a test's content validity. This suggestion is consistent with the recommendation that the first step in designing an achievement test should be the construction of a *table of specifications.* On the rows of such a table are listed the behavioral objectives, and on the columns the content (topical) objectives to be measured by the test; the descriptions of specific items are given in the body of the table.

Lennon elaborates on three assumptions that underlie the use of content validity: 1) the area of concern to the tester can be conceived as a meaningful, definable universe of responses; 2) a sample can be drawn from the universe in some purposeful, meaningful fashion; 3) the sample and the sampling process can be defined with sufficient precision to enable the test user to judge how adequately the sample performance typifies performance on the universe. Unfortunately, primarily because of the difficulty of defining and specifying objectives, these assumptions are never adequately met. An emphasis on specifying objectives and the recognition that a test score is only a sample of behavior, however, is important in reinforcing the fact that the validity of a test is specific to the purpose for which it is used and the examinees to whom it is administered.

The next two articles in this section, by Julian Stanley and Robert Thorndike, respectively, are concerned with *criterion-related validity,* or, more specifically, *predictive validity.* The predictive validity of a test pertains to the ability of the test to predict standings on academic, vocational or other criteria. Although Stanley mentions "life success," or long-term, criteria, he focuses on the more short-term criteria of grades and persistence in college. Stanley reviews a number of studies concerned with the predictive validity of aptitude and achievement test scores, as well as high school grades or rank in class and other measures, as predictors of success in college. Comparisons are made between the validity of these predictors for educationally disadvantaged and educationally advantaged students, his conclusion being that they predict about equally well for one group as for the other. Furthermore, Stanley maintains that nontest predictors such as teachers' ratings, principals' ratings and socioeconomic status may add something to the prediction of college grades and persistence, but they are no substitute for scores on standardized tests of ability or achievement.

Stanley's discussion of various political, social and emotional factors involved in college admissions and the pros and cons of special programs and open admissions deals with matters of great current concern. Consequently, the student may wish to reread this article in the context of Section VIII, where the social impact of testing and issues such as the cultural fairness or biasness of psychological and educational testing are considered in more detail. Obviously, the question of the differential validity of tests for the advantaged as compared to the disadvantaged, or for whites as compared to blacks, needs to be examined very carefully. But research that takes into account all of the variables pertaining to this question is difficult, especially in a rapidly changing society where ability differences among various social and ethnic groups have significant political and social implications.

The criteria employed in Thorndike's investigation—occupational membership and success within occupations 12 years after the predictor tests were administered—are more long-term, and consequently more difficult to predict, than grade-point averages or persistence in school. Thorndike found that, although the mean test scores of men who went into different occupations were significantly different, the intraoccupational variability of the test scores was almost as great as their interoccupational variability. Also, the correlations between test scores and measures of later occupational success averaged around zero. Thorndike discusses a number of plausible explanations for the negative results of this investigation: similarities among the occupational groups, failure to include adequate measures of interest, temperament and ability; the wide range of occupations within occupational groups; differences between variables important in training programs and those important on the actual jobs; the vague meaning of success in occupations where pay and promotion are institutionalized; contingency or "incidental" factors. The last four items in this list are considered to be the most critical in interpreting the findings.

The results of Thorndike's investigation highlight some of the difficulties in attempting to predict long-term criteria. Of special interest are contingency or "incidental" factors such as the nature of the situation in which an individual finds himself. As Mischel (1968) and others have documented at length, measures of the psychological characteristics of individuals are often less efficient in predicting their behavior in specific situations than the environmental or situational variables themselves. Certainly academic and vocational counselors need to be aware of the limitations of tests, especially as predictors of long-term criteria, and to learn to speak in terms of probabilities of certain behaviors in certain situations. In any event, situations or environments can also be "measured," and a number of interesting instruments designed to assess certain kinds of environments have been designed in the past several years (see Aiken, 1971, p. 304).

In the fourth article, Anne Anastasi discusses construct validity and other recent developments pertaining to test validity: decision theory, moderator variables, synthetic validity and response styles. The concept of *construct validity* refers to the extent to which scores on a test that is supposed to measure a certain construct ("trait") are related to measures of behavior in situations where that construct is felt to be an important variable. Related to construct validity is the *multitrait-multimethod matrix* of Campbell and Fiske

(1959) and the associated procedure for demonstrating construct validity by showing that a test has high correlations with measures with which it should correlate (*convergent validation*) but low correlations with measures with which it should not correlate (*discriminant validation*). Anastasi notes that the book on *decision theory* by Cronbach and Gleser (1957, 1965) called attention to the interactions among various factors that affect selection and placement. Among these factors are the selection ratio, the cost of administering the testing program, whether the tests measure aspects of the criterion not covered by other predictors and procedures for evaluating outcomes. Also, research on *moderator variables* has revealed that the predictive validity of a test may vary with the characteristics of a particular group and, as later research in educational contexts has demonstrated (see Cronbach, 1967), with the particular type of treatment or training program employed.

The next topic discussed by Anastasi is *synthetic validity,* in which the validity of a test in a new situation is estimated by determining the elements of that particular job and noting which of these elements have been shown by previous studies to have appreciable correlations with the test. Finally, the topic of *response styles,* social desirability and acquiescence in particular, is considered. In addition to the "two stages" of research on response styles referred to by Anastasi, there has subsequently been a "third stage." Research findings during this last stage have demonstrated that such stylistic variables do not appear to affect test scores as much as was originally believed (see Block, 1965).

In the last article of this section, Lee Sechrest proposes that, in addition to demonstrating the discriminant and convergent validities of tests used in applied, predictive contexts, evidence should be obtained for a test's incremental validity. *Incremental validity* refers to the extent to which the test increases the validity of predictions made on the basis of information that is already available. The suggestion that tests should be judged in terms of their contributions over and above that contributed by other information (e.g., school grades, interviews, biographical data) has been made previously (see Cronbach & Gleser, 1965). But Sechrest proposes that the correlations among predictor variables be corrected for attenuation[1] in order to determine whether an observed increase in the multiple or partial correlations between predictors and criterion is due merely to an increase in the reliability of the predictor variables rather than any independent contribution made by the test.

[1] The "attenuation" referred to is the decrease in the correlation between predictor variables caused by unreliability in one or both of them. A formula that "corrects for attenuation" gives an estimate of what the correlation would be if both variables were perfectly reliable: $r_{12} = r_{12} / (\sqrt{r_{11}} \sqrt{r_{22}})$, where r_{12} is the obtained correlation between variables 1 and 2, r_{11} and r_{22} their obtained reliabilities, and r_{12} the estimated correlation between 1 and 2 if both variables were perfectly reliable.

16 | Assumptions Underlying the Use of Content Validity*

Roger T. Lennon

The concept of *validity* of educational and psychological tests and diagnostic aids has been the subject of increasingly penetrating and sophisticated analysis, as befits its central position in test theory. While it cannot yet be asserted that our notions of validity are as fully elaborated, or even as generally agreed upon, as might be desired, we have assuredly come a long way from the time when the classic definition of validity as "the extent to which a test measures whatever it purports to measure" could be regarded as adequate.

Kinds of Validity

A reflection of the present stage of refinement of the validity concept is to be found in the *Technical Recommendations for Psychological Tests,* produced by the APA Committee on Test Standards (American Psychological Association, 1954). This Committee found it useful to distinguish four senses in which the term *validity* may be used, or four aspects of validity, namely, content validity, predictive validity, concurrent validity, and construct validity. Differentiation of the validity concept in this wise stems from a recognition of the various uses made of tests and psychological aids, and of the consequent variations in the kinds of evidence appropriate for judging their probable goodness or usefulness.

Content Validity: a Definition

Our present concern is with the first of the above named aspects of validity, namely, content validity. The term *content validity* is not defined in the text of APA's Technical Recommendations, but the meaning intended

---

*From *Educational and Psychological Measurement,* 1956, **16,** 294-304. Copyright 1956 by G. Frederic Kuder. Reprinted with permission of the author and publisher.

may readily be inferred from such statements in the report as these:

> Content validity is evaluated by showing how well the content of the test samples the class of situations or subject matter about which conclusions are to be drawn.

and again

> Content validity is indicated by a description of the universe of items from which selection was made, including a description of the selection process.

The *Technical Recommendations for Achievement Tests* produced by a joint committee of the American Educational Research Association and the National Council on Measurements Used in Education (1955) adopted the APA committee's usage. The AERA report similarly offers no formal definition of the term "content validity," stating merely that "content validity is concerned with the sampling of a specified universe of content."

We propose in this paper to use the term *content validity* in the sense in which we believe it is intended in the APA Test Standards, namely, to denote *the extent to which a subject's responses to the items of a test may be considered to be a representative sample of his responses to a real or hypothetical universe of situations which together constitute the area of concern to the person interpreting the test.*

Although the term *content validity* has only in recent years achieved currency in testing literature, the concept has readily identifiable forebears. Early analyses of validity commonly recognized two meanings of the term, often labeled *empirical* or *statistical,* on the one hand, and *logical,* or, for educational tests, *curricular,* on the other; and content validity is a lineal descendant of this second branch of the family. Like many terms, it does not yet have a universally accepted meaning. Anastasi (1961), for example, seems to equate content validity with *logical validity,* or *validity by definition,* even remarking that content validity has occasionally been used to denote a subspecies of *face validity.* In Cureton's usage (Cureton, 1951) content validity (at least for educational achievement tests) is synonymous with what he terms *curricular relevance* or *curricular validity*; and he is at some pains to distinguish it from what he calls *formal relevance* and *face validity.* Hence the need for specifying the sense in which we use the term.

Let it be noted particularly that in the definition proposed above, content validity is ascribed to the subject's responses rather than to the test questions themselves. This is to underscore the point that appraisal of content validity must take into account not only the *content* of the questions but also the *process* presumably employed by the subject in arriving at his response. Since the test user wishes to make inferences about a behavioral universe, the sample must also be a sample of behaviors; and the behaviors are the examinee's modes of response and the responses themselves. Hence content validity inheres in the responses, rather than exclusively in the items themselves. A given item may function as a measure of reasoning or generalization for one examinee, but measure merely recall for another. Zimmerman (1954), in a discussion of the nature of the spatial factors, observes that "A problem which would be solved spatially by one might evoke Visualization for another, or might be so simple for still another that he would depend more upon Perceptual Speed." Insofar as the items of a test lend themselves to response via different processes for various examinees, the possibility exists that its content validity differs from one examinee to another, even though the test questions are identical for all subjects.

Measurement of Content Validity

In speaking of "the *extent*" to which test matches universe, it is clearly implied that some tests possess this property to a greater extent than others. It is not to be inferred, however, that it is possible to express this degree of agreement in any precise quantitative terms. Indeed, as the Test Standards report makes clear, in most classes of situations measured by tests, quantitative evidence of content validity is not obtainable. We have no scale for measuring the representativeness of a sample. Content validity, as the Standards point out, is ordinarily to be established deductively, by defining a universe and sampling systematically within the universe. Approaches such as internal consistency analyses, factorial analyses, and Gulliksen's suggestions for appraising *intrinsic validity* are helpful in clarification and definition of the universe, and hence not without merit in evaluating content validity; but they cannot be considered sufficient bases for its appraisal.

Justification for Use of Content Validity

Some may be prompted to inquire why it is ever necessary or desirable to rely on content analysis as the basis for appraisal of validity, rather than on an empirical-quantitative approach involving correlation with criterion measures. The answer lies in the fact that in many testing situations (of which achievement testing forms the largest class) there is not available or readily accessible any dependable criterion variable, against which the "validity" of the test may be measured; and secondly, in the fact that there are certain uses of tests for which correlations with either contemporary or subsequent criteria are not meaningful as indicators of validity. When a test is intended to serve as the basis for determining how well an individual would perform at the present time on some universe of situations, and when circumstances do not permit measurement of the responses to the entire universe, then it is clear that the test user must rely upon correspondence between test sample and universe in deciding what confidence he may have in the inferences made on the basis of the test.

To appreciate more fully the types of tests or of testing situations in which the concept of content validity may appropriately be used, it is helpful to recall Goodenough's distinction between tests as *samples* and tests as *signs* (Goodenough, 1949). In the case of tests considered as samples, the tester is concerned with the type of behavior manifested in the test performance in its own right; the criterion, as Goodenough puts it, is intrinsic, and the question of the goodness of the test is a question of the representativeness and adequacy of the sample—a question, that is, of content validity. In the case of tests regarded as *signs*—aptitude tests, for example—the tester is not concerned with the test behavior as such, but only in its relation to some extrinsic criterion; for such tests, predictive and concurrent validity will ordinarily be of major interest.

The American Psychological Association Standards Committee conceives of content validity as appropriate for ability tests, achievement tests, personality inventories, and interest inventories, though not, of course, to the exclusion of evidence on other types of validity. Not all test theorists share the committee's views on the usefulness of a content validity approach for all these types of tests. Anastasi, for example, takes the position that "the use of content validity in the evaluation of aptitude or personality tests has little to commend it," (Anastasi, 1961) on the grounds that a given test may measure different functions in different groups, so that it is impossible to determine the functions measured by the test from an inspection of the content. In the final analysis, the appropriateness of a content validity approach depends on the types of inferences or interpretations to be made of the test results; or conversely, the soundness of various interpretations depends on the varieties of validity evidence at hand.

Assumptions Underlying the Use of Content Validity

Having in mind the definition of content validity offered above, and the types of tests in connection with which we are considering this concept, let us turn to a consideration of certain of the assumptions underlying the notion.

Three of these assumptions are singled out here for comment, as follows:

1) The area of concern to the tester can be conceived as a meaningful, definable universe of responses.
2) A sample can be drawn from this universe in some purposive, meaningful fashion.
3) The sample and the sampling process can be defined with sufficient precision to enable the test user to judge how adequately performance on the sample typifies performance on the universe.

Assumption 1. **The Area of Concern to the Tester Can Be Conceived as a Meaningful, Definable Universe of Responses.** Test theory has consistently held to the view that a test is a sample of behavior from which inferences may be made to a universe of behaviors. Even in the case of tests functioning as signs, to revert for a moment to Goodenough's term, the test behavior is nevertheless only a sample of the many behaviors which might be chosen to function as signs; and even in the case of tests which in effect duplicate the criterion behavior, the test is still a sample in the sense that it represents the behavior at a particular time, under particular circumstances, whereas the criterion is not so restricted. This sample-universe view is, of course, the heart of the notion of content validity.

In some ways this part of test theory may represent a too-facile analogy with statistical theory. In sampling theory, a *universe* is defined as a set or group of individuals having a common character or characteristic. It is essential that the universe be uniform in some meaningful sense—that it possess internal coherence. A universe should constitute a set or class sufficiently well defined so that it is possible to say of any given element that it either does or does not belong in the universe.

We may well inquire how frequently it happens that we can conceive of or define a "universe," in this sense of the word, for test-development purposes or, perhaps more to the point, how often we do it even when it is possible. In achievement testing, we can, to be sure, readily cite certain situations in which the universe can be identified and rigorously defined. The ability to handle correctly the hundred possible addition facts is the often-used illustration of a domain which can be specified with exactness. More often, however, particularly in fields other than achievement, the area of concern to the tester is vastly more complex, multidimensional, and resistant to precise definition. The test-maker's task is made no easier by the unhappy circumstance that the domain which he is attempting to define may be in many respects *terra incognita*.

Let us consider an ability such as "critical thinking." Is it possible to define a domain of critical thinking—to conceive of an exhaustive listing of all the situations in which there might be behavioral manifestations of an ability that is properly termed critical thinking? Again, is it possible to define a universe consisting of all the responses which might properly be designated manifestations of "introversion," or of "emotional stability," or of "ascendancy?" The very asking of these questions calls to mind the many assumptions, value judgments, problems of definition and other difficulties that stand in the way. These difficulties seemed so formidable to Goodenough as to cause her to conclude that in dealing with behavioral matters, we are, as a rule, unable to set precise boundaries for the forms of behavior to which trait names are applied. In her words, "we cannot say, 'Up to this exact point the universe which we call *intelligence* runs, but no further.' "

The difficulty of defining a universe in the realm of educational achievement is inextricably bound up with the difficulty of defining and specifying objectives. Cureton (1951) has furnished an analysis of an area of educational achievement, indicating that an adequate definition of the "universe" in this case must specify at least the following dimensions:

a. the acts or operations of which it is composed
b. the materials acted upon
c. the situations in which the acts or operations properly take place
d. the results or products of these acts or operations
e. the particular aspects of *a* through *d* which are relevant to the purposes at hand

Similar analyses of the universe (or domain or criterion behavior) with which we are concerned in the case of personality or interest inventories, or attitude questionnaires, reveal the complicated, often multidimensional character of these universes. Pursuit of this topic leads quickly into the realm of construct validity, and the types of issues so well set forth in the Cronbach-Meehl analysis of this latter concept (Cronbach & Meehl, 1955).

More often than not we find it desirable to sample from some universe other than the universe in which we are genuinely concerned, either because the universe of concern is unavailable or because in some other respects it is unsuitable as the source of test exercises. In the case of personality inventories, for example, we substitute a universe of responses to verbal situations for the universe of behaviors in which we are really interested. Some even seek to escape the difficulties of defining a universe by asserting that a test is a valid measure of only that hypothetical universe of which its items do constitute a representative sample. This procedure may be logically satisfying;

but it still remains to be demonstrated that such a hypothetical universe corresponds to the area or domain in which the test user is genuinely interested.

Assumption 2. **A Sample Can Be Drawn from the Universe in Some Purposive, Meaningful Fashion.** Let us assume that, difficult as it may be, we have succeeded in identifying and defining a universe adequately, for practical purposes. How are we to draw a sample from this universe in such a way that we may with confidence generalize from it to the universe? The success with which this is done is the measure of content validity.

Very, very rarely will the test constitute a *random* sample of the universe. In the first place, it is the exceptional test-building situation in which there exists a complete listing of all possible test items—i.e. a catalog of the universe—from which such a sample might be drawn. In the second place, considerations of efficiency of measurement would often argue against a *random* sample as optimum. For example, in constructing a spelling test, there might be agreement on a certain list of words as constituting the universe; but the most reliable test for a given amount of testing time will almost certainly not be made up of a random selection of the words, but of a sample chosen in part on the basis of their respective difficulties.

The goal of sampling for test-making purposes is usually defined as the production of a sample which is "representative"—a goal which is sometimes at odds with other purposes of the test-maker. In achievement testing, for example, items which measure objectives stated in a course of study, but not reflected in the instructional program, are likely to be poor from the standpoint of discrimination; but if they are eliminated on this count, it is at the expense of "representativeness" of the test as a measure of the objectives.

A "representative" sample is one that *re-presents* the universe—that is, one that duplicates or reproduces the essential characteristics of the universe, in their proper proportion and balance. Presumably these essential characteristics and their interrelationships have been specified in the definition of the universe. How now to insure that the test reproduces them? At a superficial level, it is easy to stipulate that the proportionate emphasis given various content sub-areas be similar in the test to what it is in the universe— that the proportion of test questions devoted to each sub-area be in accordance with the sub-area's importance, however this be judged. If we recall, however, the thought advanced earlier, that content validity is a property of the examinee's responses, as well as of the test content, then it is clear that a more fundamental kind of representativeness must be sought. In essence, it would appear that what we are really after is that the variance in the test scores be attributable to the same sources, and in the same proportion, as the variance in the criterion, or universe, behavior. This implies a far more systematic effort than is usually made to specify the sources of variance in the criterion, and their relative importance.

Assumption 3. **The Sample and the Sampling Process Can Be Defined with Sufficient Precision to Enable the User to Judge how Adequately the Sample Performance Typifies Performance on the Universe.** The function of all validity information is to permit the test user to estimate with what confidence he may make various kinds of interpretations of the test scores. The APA Test Standards prescribe that the test-maker define the universe which he has undertaken to measure, and the nature of his sample and sampling process, assuming that possession of such information will enable the test user prudently to estimate the dependability of various kinds of inferences. In the absence of such information, the test user is indeed at something of a loss in his efforts to appraise the extent to which he may safely generalize from the test data, except perhaps in the case of tests of certain rather simple functions where the intended universe and the nature of sample are virtually self-evident. Even having such information, however, the test user may not have all the information he needs, for the universe with which he is concerned is likely to differ, in some particulars at least, from the test-maker's universe, which difference may or may not limit the confidence to be reposed in the inferences drawn.

Because the sample which constitutes the test is so far removed from being a random sample, all ordinary notions of sampling errors are quite inappropriate as bases for estimating the confidence that may be reposed in the inferences. Because of the impossibility of expressing content validity in quantitative terms, or of expressing the representativeness of a sample in quantitative terms, the test user, regardless of the quality and completeness of information provided by the test-maker, will almost surely have to be satisfied with rather crude answers to his question, "How confidently can I make this, that, or the other inference from these test data?"

One final word about content validity is in order. Content validity, like all other kinds of validity, is specific to the purpose for which, and the group with which, a test is used. Because the content of a test appears to be something fixed and constant, there is more of a temptation to think of content validity as an invariant property of a test than is true of the criterion-oriented predictive and concurrent validity. A moment's reflection makes clear that the universe with which the test user is concerned will ordinarily not be identical with the universe which the test constructor had in mind. Evidences of content validity for a particular group do not necessarily apply to other groups, for the processes by which one group responds to a set of questions may differ from those by which another group responds to the same questions. Thus, we are forced again to the conclusion that there can be no such thing, in the great majority of cases, as *the* content validity of a test but only a content validity for a particular purpose and a particular group of subjects.

17 | Predicting College Success of the Educationally Disadvantaged*

Julian C. Stanley

Because children of the poor tend to score considerably lower on the Scholastic Aptitude Test (SAT) and other standardized ability and achievement tests than do children of the affluent, one can say that in this descriptive sense such tests are "biased against" or "discriminate against" or "penalize" the former. Besides their descriptive denotations, however, these expressions have value connotations. Whether such tests are "unfair" to youth from educationally disadvantaging environments depends on what is meant in this context by the words "unfair" and "disadvantaging."

From the standpoint of an admissions officer, the educationally disadvantaged applicants to his college could be simply those who, on the basis of all available information, including high school grades, test scores, socioeconomic status, race, ethnic origin, and available financial support, are likely to have appreciably more academic difficulty than the typical minimally admissible student. Thus, the son of a distinguished alumnus is educationally disadvantaged for his father's college if it is predicted that he will fail most of his courses and not persist to graduation. The valedictorian of a large high school, who has a sizable national scholarship but whose parents are illiterate and penniless, cannot, by this criterion, be considered greatly disadvantaged educationally.

This definition of educational disadvantage is not in accord with the varied use in the professional literature of expressions such as "culturally deprived," "culturally disadvantaged," and "socially disadvantaged." It is not consonant with tacit assumptions that all persons of a given race, ethnic group, or regional group are educationally disadvantaged. According to this definition, not all blacks or Chicanos or Appalachian whites will have academic difficulties in any particular college. The individual differences in developed academic abilities of high school seniors within each group will be great.

*From *Science*, 1971, **171**, 640-647. Copyright 1971 by the American Association for the Advancement of Science. Reprinted with permission of the author and publisher.

Defining disadvantagement in terms of low predicted grade-point average or low persistence within a specified college, based on all available antecedent information, makes the expression "educationally disadvantaged" or "high-risk applicant" more than a euphemism for "member of a minority group." It involves assessing the educational assets and handicaps of the applicant and estimating his achievement if some of the handicaps can be lessened or removed.

Most published research concerning presumably educationally disadvantaged college students has appeared during the past 8 years. Nearly all of it involved comparisons of black students with a group that might be called "predominantly nonblack students." Many of the black students had good high school grades and test scores; thus according to my definition, they were not educationally disadvantaged (that is, not greatly underqualified academically) for most colleges. That these academically able students tended to do well in college should not be surprising.

In many studies, however, black students of variously developed abilities were lumped together, as though having black skin caused college applicants to be poor academic risks. This practice has made interpretation of the results of such studies difficult, since one often cannot determine from a research report how the black students who had poor high school grades and low test scores performed in relation to those who had good grades and high test scores.

More special programs for educationally disadvantaged Chicanos, American Indians, Puerto Ricans on the mainland, Appalachian whites, and integrated socioeconomic groups are being started. Soon there should be research reports concerning such projects, making it unnecessary to rely as much as before on studies of blacks. Generalized conclusions will increase, and the erroneous identification of nearly all blacks as academically underqualified for most colleges should decrease.

Predicting School Grades

During the first half of the past decade, a number of writers have questioned the validity of standardized tests for ascertaining the developed abilities of children from lower socioeconomic groups. One of these writers, M. D. Jenkins, who was longtime president of predominantly black Morgan State College in Baltimore, stated in 1964: ". . . it is well known that standardized examinations have low validity for individuals and groups of restricted experiential background" (Jenkins, 1964, p. 93). That same year

Fishman and others (1964), presenting the "Guidelines for Testing Minority Group Children" of the Society for the Psychological Study of Social Issues, wrote that the "predictive validity [of standardized tests currently in use] for minority groups may be quite different from that for the standardization and validation groups. . . ."

A year earlier, Clark and Plotkin (1963) had reported results of a study based on "alumni" classes of the National Scholarship Service and Fund for Negro Students in which they concluded that:

> . . . scholastic aptitude test scores are not clearly associated with college grades. It is suggested that college admissions officers weigh test scores less, since they do not predict the college success of Negro students in the same way they do for whites. This study indicates that motivational factors are probably more important than test scores in the demonstrated superiority of Negro students in completing college.

In 1965 Green and Farquhar reported a correlation coefficient of only .01 between School and College Ability Test scores (level not specified) and high school grade-point averages for 104 black males, compared with .62 for the differential aptitude test verbal-reasoning scores of 254 white males.

These four reports do not prove standardized tests to have lower predictive validity for educationally disadvantaged college students. Only the Clark and Plotkin (1963) and the Green and Farquhar (1965) studies, of the four excerpted above, dealt with data. Cleary (Cleary, 1968; Cleary & Hilton, 1968) tried to replicate the findings of Clark and Plotkin with a better controlled design, but failed. The conclusions of Green and Farquhar were questioned in some detail by Stanley and Porter (1967). For black students, especially, the differential-validity hypothesis has been found untenable; indeed, test scores sometimes overpredict the academic achievement of blacks (Thomas & Stanley, 1969).

Hypothetical Example

Let us try to examine the implied logic that leads to assertions such as those made by Jenkins (1964), Fishman *et al.* (1964), and Clark and Plotkin (1963). Suppose that one has two large groups of U.S. high school seniors and that the Scholastic Aptitude Test Verbal (SATV) score of every person in each group is 400. Suppose further that one group is composed of students from inner-city slums: their parents are poorly educated, and most middle-class educational influences are missing from their homes. The students who make up the other group are from affluent suburbs, and most of their parents are college graduates. (To keep the argument uncluttered, assume that each student's 400 is essentially his true score, the average of six SAT scores. Thus, regression toward population means due to errors of measurement will not complicate the discussion. Also, let us assume that both groups had plenty of experience taking tests prior to the SAT.)

One might expect that the SATV scores of the students from the slum group could be increased more easily than the scores of those from the affluent group. This, however, is an empirical issue. Even assuming that the disadvantaged youth had greater SAT potential at the time of conception, it does not follow that this potential persists undiminished to age 17 or 18. Perhaps many of the disadvantaged seniors are so stunted intellectually that massive coaching, tutoring, remediation, and enrichment won't raise their SAT scores much. Such efforts may work, but one has to specify the methods to be used and actually try them out. Not enough has been done yet in a rigorous way and reported adequately.

Alternative Coping Skills

Even when it is recognized that psychologists do not know how to increase the tested SATV ability of disadvantaged high school juniors or seniors appreciably, it is often contended that in order to succeed in college those students need less of this ability than more advantaged ones do. Seldom is it asked why they would need less ability. The contender seems to imply that students who have come up the rough way will study harder and more effectively than advantaged students, or perhaps even that by having survived in the ghetto they have developed coping techniques useful also in schools. Of course, these speculations do not square well with the many other disadvantages besides test-score deficit that most slum-bred students have, nor with the facts of their usual academic difficulties in elementary and high school.

If strong motivation to achieve academically is there, it must in most instances be dormant, ready to awaken in college. One might expect, or at least hope for, satisfactory college work from a person who has either earned fairly good grades in college-preparatory courses at high school or has adequate test scores. However, to expect satisfactory college grades from most students who have neither is asking for a minor academic miracle unless sufficiently massive compensatory education intervenes. Such miracles do happen from time to time, but there does not seem to be any credible evidence that they occur frequently for students who are greatly underqualified, in both respects, relative to other students in the same college.

Persistence to Graduation

A number of academically selective colleges are now more concerned with the disadvantaged student's persistence to graduation than with his grades. For example, preliminary data at Cornell University show that the 56 students who scored below the 5th percentile "of all entering Cornell students for the undergraduate division in question" on two out of three of SATV, SATM, and secondary school class rank "are doing extremely well with regards to academic status, and if the trend continues, about ninety percent (90%) will graduate and less than five percent (5%) will be academically dismissed" (Tetlow, 1969).

In another part of the report, Tetlow shows that the average grades of the group of presumably high-risk students at Cornell were rather low and that "about half of all students in the program have received *at least* a warning for poor performance. Several students have received a 'warning,' a 'final warning,' and a 'post-final warning.' " Of course, more than just persistence to graduation must be demonstrated if such a program is to be considered a success. What have these students learned by the time they graduate, as measured, for example, by achievement, area, and aptitude tests of the Graduate Record Examination? Perhaps they would have learned more if they had attended a less academically demanding college where with the same amount of effort they could have made better grades. However, no objective evidence of this sort seems available for the Cornell graduates or for 19 recent black graduates of Stanford University (Black, 1970).

In an important study, Astin (1970) has used a persistence argument too, though his pooling of grades across 180 colleges of various selectivity levels makes some of his conclusions difficult to interpret. He matched ingeniously, but analyses within each college would have been more convincing. His findings may have little necessary relevance to disadvantaged students recruited into selective colleges, but they do suggest considerable persistence in college by many students with weak academic backgrounds.

A large study of persistence to graduation at Brown University was reported by Nicholson (1970). His data and conclusions are interesting, although his definition of a high-risk student (one whose SATV score is less than 620 and who is therefore in the lower third of the freshman class at Brown) screens out most really educationally disadvantaged persons.

Not many systematic studies of differential persistence between blacks and whites have yet been completed, but the evidence from Tetlow (1969), Black (1970), Nicholson (1970), Clark and Plotkin (1963), Borgen (1970), and Astin (1970) suggests that reasonably able black students from high socioeconomic backgrounds who attend selective colleges persist well to graduation, even though many of them make mediocre or poor grades. Most of these students chose their respective colleges, however, rather than being recruited. Also, they had few black classmates with whom to isolate themselves from the whites or with whom to seek black courses, curricula, departments, and colleges. This situation has changed rapidly within the last few years, so the older data can be suggestive only and apply just to blacks. We know virtually nothing yet concerning the persistence of other disadvantaged minority groups.

The relationship of parental socioeconomic level to academic persistence transcends the race issue. For example, at the University of Illinois Eckland (1964a,b) found that, for persistence to college graduation somewhere within 10 years after initial enrollment, "social class is an important determinant . . . for students from the lower rank of their high-school classes but relatively unimportant for those from the higher rank. . . ." Boys who had poor high school records and who came from families of low socioeconomic status tended to persist to graduation less often than did academically mediocre boys from families of a higher status. Also, giving up pursuit of the degree did not seem closely related to lack of money; those persons who dropped out for what they said were financial reasons tended to return and graduate. Lack of money is a real handicap, but at least in principle a remediable one.

However, persistence to graduation can hardly be the primary criterion. The persister must, in the process, get at least as good an education as he could secure elsewhere for the same effort and cost. Careful objective evaluation of the educational attainments of the students as they progress seems imperative.

Ignoring Test Scores

Recently, many selective institutions have decided to waive test scores (and sometimes high school grades too) in admitting disadvantaged applicants. If the rationale for this is that academic-aptitude and achievement tests lower prediction of criteria such as freshman grade-point average or persistence to graduation, it is a foolish procedure, since in a linear multiple-regression equation a predictor variable cannot lower validity, but only increase it or leave it unchanged. Substituting principals' and teachers' ratings of probable college success for test scores and high school grades appears to me an unfortunate step backward into the subjectivity, invalidity, and social class biases of the 19th century. It would seem more sensible to predict the criterion for each applicant from all available predictors and then, if desired, to set up predictive lists separately for disadvantaged and nondisadvantaged. Those disadvantaged applicants who seem on the basis of all evidence most promising, academically and otherwise, can be accepted, offered financial aid, and, where needed, given massive educational remediation and tutoring.

I would urge a reversal of the current trend. The more disadvantaged a college applicant seems to be socioeconomically, the more objective information one needs about him. For example, one should know such things as how he scores on achievement tests in several specific subjects, such as chemistry and English composition, and what special developed academic ability or other relevant aptitude the student has. It is well to consider noncognitive measures also, but not in lieu of the cognitive ones.

The recent tendency to ignore test scores and rely mainly on the high school academic record may lower predictive validity. As Thomas and Stanley have reported (1969, p. 203), "... high school grades do not consistently make the greatest contribution in predicting college grades of black students, perhaps particularly of men, whereas they do for whites. Unreliability of grade reporting, invalidity of grades in high school, restriction in range due to selection processes, and intergroup differences in personality characteristics [are] advanced to explain this phenomenon."

Predictive Validity

As noted earlier, aptitude test scores and high school grades, when employed together, usually predict college grades at least as accurately for disadvantaged applicants as they do for regular applicants. This is a carefully verified general finding, but if correlation coefficients are used, it depends on the relative range of talent in the two groups. At Cornell, for instance, first-semester correlations for students in a special program tended to be lower than for all freshmen in the College of Arts and Sciences. However, data for the former were from a pooled 4-year period, whereas for the latter they were for a single year. Heterogeneity of grading practices across the years may have lowered the correlation coefficients (Tetlow, 1969, table 5). Also, although there is no way to tell from the report how comparatively homogeneous the two groups are, it seems quite likely that test scores and perhaps high school grades of the special-program students (virtually all of whom were black) were considerably less variable than were those of the regularly admitted students (most of whom were not black). If so, much of the difference in correlation coefficients between the two groups was probably due to restriction of range rather than to invalidity of the tests. A single regression equation might predict college grades with equal accuracy for the two groups there.

Many claims are made that test scores have little or no value for predicting the success of disadvantaged applicants to colleges. Anecdotes are abundant (Somerville, 1967), but upon investigation they are usually found to be atypical or cannot be verified. An admissions officer ignores test scores at his institution's peril. They are certainly useful most of the time in helping to predict college grades, and may also help to identify those students who, persisting through a highly permissive, selective college, will come out with an education rather than a quickly discredited union card.

Biased Items?

The issue of "biased" items was attacked vigorously but largely unsuccessfully in the early 1950's by Eells and others (1951). Investigators worked to devise a "culturally fair" test—one that would still be predictively valid but that would not discriminate as sharply between socioeconomic classes as, for example, the Otis test of mental ability did. The situations and items of the Davis-Eells "Games" were slanted toward urban slum cultures. Nevertheless, the new test differentiated among socioeconomic classes almost as much as its culturally "unfair" predecessors had (e.g., Ludlow, 1956).

A more recent study by Cleary and Hilton (1968) revealed a small but statistically significant interaction of race (black and white) with the items of two forms of the Preliminary Scholastic Aptitude Test (PSAT). As Stanley (1969) showed later, a considerable amount of this interaction was due to a few items that were too difficult for both races and hence did not separate them much. There seemed little likelihood that one could find in either subtest (verbal or mathematical) of the PSAT a subset of item types especially favorable or unfavorable to the blacks, who scored rather uniformly lower than the whites on most of the items.

For a long time it has been well known to specialists that blacks score relatively higher on verbal items than on most nonverbal items (Lesser *et al.*, 1965; Stodolsky & Lesser, 1967). Hence, attempts to create valid, culturally fair tests by reducing their verbal content have slight chance of being successful. Tests such as speed of tapping may not differentiate socioeconomic levels or races much, but they probably will not predict desired academic criteria adequately. Where the criteria are loaded in certain ways, the predictors must be loaded similarly if they are to correlate well with those criteria. If the criteria change (for example, from grades to persistence), the predictors may need to be changed.

Tacitly Different Criteria

If the correlation of certain fixed predictors with a criterion were different for one group as opposed to another, the criterion itself might well be different for each group, even though it is called the same thing by both groups (for example, grade-point average or receiving a diploma). Also, to predict persistence to graduation of high-risk applicants to a college may require considerable knowledge of the special probation policies, financial aid, grading practices, remedial courses, easy regular courses, and fail-safe curricula within the institution. The equation for predicting persistence to graduation from a given college may be quite different from the equation for predicting achievement-test scores of students who entered there quite underqualified academically.

Enrollees Quite Underqualified Academically

A considerable number of minority-group students with weak academic preparation are being recruited into the most selective colleges and universities in the country. There the academic-aptitude and achievement-test scores of many such recruits may be several standard deviations below the average, nonspecial student, and even far below the minimum level for regular admission to the institution. Most colleges do not publish figures for special compared to regularly admitted students, but one can get a few statistics such as the following:

Kendrick (1967-68) infers from the Coleman report (Coleman *et al.,* 1966) that *"not more than 15 percent and perhaps as few as 10 percent of . . . Negro high school seniors would score 400 or more on the verbal section of the SAT. Only 1 or 2 percent would be likely to score 500 or more."* The percentages for all high school seniors in the country are approximately 45 and 20, respectively (*College Board Score Reports,* 1969-70, p. 23). Thus the number of black high school graduates each year who have well-developed verbal ability is quite small. As noted earlier (Tetlow, 1969), the 5th percentile of SATV scores for freshmen in the College of Arts and Sciences at Cornell University is 535. Brown University uses a cutoff of 620 on SATV to define those students who are considered academic risks: "Such a point defines approximately the lower one-third of currently admitted students . . ." (Nicholson, 1970, p. 3), but only about 4 percent of all high school seniors would exceed it (*College Board Score Reports,* 1969-70).

Cornell University may have the ablest large group of black students in the country if SAT scores are used as the criterion. The verbal means of entering freshmen in the special program (composed almost entirely of black students) for 1965-66 through 1968-69 ranged from 530 to 570, whereas the means of the freshmen in the College of Arts and Sciences ranged from 660 to 703. The average difference between the students in the special program and the entire arts and sciences group was 137 points (Comm. on Special Educ. Projects, 1968). No standard deviations are given, but this difference seems likely to be at least two of the standard deviations of the special group. The lowest SATV scores for the 247 students in the special program were reported by year as 430, 340, 400, and 383, respectively.

In the fall of 1967, Michigan State University enrolled "66 not normally-admissible Negro freshmen . . . more than half [of whom] had combined Scholastic Aptitude Test scores [that is, SATV + SATM] of under 789" (Sabine, 1968). No comparative figures for regularly admitted freshmen are given, but the following remarks indicate the discrepancy (Sabine, 1968, p. 13):

> May 28 [1968]: Lunch with four faculty members who want to "do something," meaning tutor Negro freshmen next fall. Their ideas are good, and all went well until they started saying how high the students' grades and test scores should be. They had a hard time believing we haven't even one that high in our special-admission group.

For the University of Illinois during the academic year 1968-69 Humphreys (1969) reported "a difference between the means of the two races that was 2.4 times the standard deviation of the Caucasian distribution." Bowers (1970) provides detailed comparisons of the 111 men and 152 women in the Special Educational Opportunities Program (SEOP) with the regular Illinois freshmen on eight test variables and high school rank. The SEOP students were considerably below the regular students in both respects. Admissions officers have known for many years that a double handicap of this kind (that is, ranking low within the entering class on both aptitude and high school record) makes for pessimistic academic prognosis.

Humphreys (1969, p. 167) forcefully stated the dilemma Illinois faced:

> There will be an intolerable level of dropping of Negro students on academic grounds during the first year unless there is massive intervention. A desirable form of intervention is to establish special sections and special remedial courses. An undesirable form is for the faculty to assign grades in regular racially mixed classes on the basis of skin color rather than performance. In the present emotional climate, if more desirable forms of intervention are not sufficiently massive, this second type becomes inevitable.
>
> There is another effect of bringing in Negro students who are far below their fellow students in readiness to do academic work. A group of young people who are newly imbued with pride in race are placed in a situation in which they are, by and

large, obviously inferior. A scientist qualifies this inferiority by adding "at their present stage of development," but this is slight consolation to the student involved. The causal chain from frustration to aggression is well established. A large ability difference as a source of aggression cannot be ignored. The universities are damned if they don't admit more Negroes, but they are also damned in another sense if they do.

It seems likely that trying to compete far above their comfortable level would confine to the easier courses and curricula most students who are quite underqualified academically, thereby limiting their choice. Also, though such students may pass most of their courses with C's and D's, one wonders what they will be learning, relative to what they might learn in another college where their relative level of ability is average or better. In addition, the negative concept of themselves which they may develop as low men on the academic totem pole must be considered. Perhaps they should be encouraged to attend colleges more geared to their level of academic competence. Not many colleges in the United States are highly selective: at least 2000 others of all sorts can accommodate most levels of developed ability and achievement.

Does Academic Frustration Increase Demands for Relevance?

I am pessimistic about the efficacy of remediation, tutoring, and coaching during the freshman year for overcoming large gaps. Also, I suspect that demands for many "relevant" minority-group courses and instructors are to a considerable extent probably unconscious rationalizations of the pressures of competition with regular students who are much better qualified academically. If the available curricula are too difficult, students must either demand easier curricula, fail, or leave. One's pride is saved, however, by not admitting (even to oneself) how almost impossibly difficult the regular courses and curricula are. Some statements by a black assistant dean of students at Cornell University and her assistant are applicable to the above conjecture (Joseph & Newsom, 1968, p. 10):

> [The black students'] interest in making sure that their course work is relevant—a word they use with even more frequency than white students—has the fervor of a religious cause. It is not, however, a "white" relevance they seek ... [A black student] commented, "Most courses aren't interesting to me. I find it difficult to study them. They are relevant to white students, but not to black students." ... They define relevant courses as those taught by Negroes ... or by professors who understand and take account of the Negro contribution and point of view ... By far the largest number are in the College of Arts and Sciences. And there it is courses in economics, sociology, psychology, and the humanities that arouse their passions most.

It is not easy to assess the contribution of academic unreadiness to demands for segregated curricula, departments, and colleges. However, recent events at a number of colleges seem consonant with the interpretation that academic unreadiness plays more than a minor role in activities which effectively reduce the competition with better-prepared students.

Less Selective Colleges Need Assistance

A major dilemma is that power, resources, and goodwill seem to reside chiefly with the academically difficult institutions, whereas the most suitable institutions for many of the disadvantaged are state colleges, certain private colleges, community colleges, and the less selective state universities. Over the years of this century, the principle that a high school graduate would usually be wise to attend a college neither extremely difficult nor extremely easy for him seems to have been validated rather thoroughly. The educationally disadvantaged should be treated as individuals, not as a species apart from the advantaged. They deserve special consideration and special treatment: adequate financial aid, remediation and tutoring, reduced course loads, extended probation, counseling, and so on. There is, however, no magic in a degree from a usually selective college if it is not in one's preferred field, if it represents little real educational attainment, or if the recipient has falsely convinced himself that he is stupid and convinced others that his entire racial, ethnic, or regional group is vastly inferior to the typical students in the college.

We need massive federal and local aid to put resources such as scholarships, loans, and counselors where they are most likely to yield the greatest educational increments. A number of persons are devising model federal scholarship programs that will include the disadvantaged (Owen, 1970). It should be unnecessary for those educationally disadvantaged students who prefer not to major in racial or ethnic politics or social studies to attend a prestigious, highly selective college simply because a less selective college cannot give them enough financial aid.

Admission and Facilitation

Nothing in this article should be taken to mean that I believe no persons from disadvantaging backgrounds should be in selective colleges. Clearly, some of them will be well served academically, socially, and emotionally there, if, despite their origins, they are not too underqualified academically. I advocate treating each college applicant primarily as an individual, rather than as a member of a group. Logically, that leads to essentially "color blind," "ethnic blind," and "region blind" admission to college, though students from disadvantaging backgrounds who are at the low end of the normally admissible applicant group can be given special consideration for admission and much educational remediation if enrolled. Admitting applicants who are quite academically underqualified for a particular college will necessitate new, easier curricula for that college, not just massive remediation and tutoring for the students.

Rank in high school graduating class, academic-aptitude test scores, and achievement test scores are still the best predictors of grades that an applicant would earn in a particular college and, probably, of his fruitful persistence there. I do not know of any convincing evidence that different predictors or even differently weighted predictors of current criteria of academic success are needed for the disadvantaged.

For the public schools, McPartland (1970) had concluded that the presence of a high percentage of academic and value pacesetters within the individual classroom is essential for stimulating the disadvantaged to greater achievement. If his findings generalize to colleges, many pacesetters seem to be needed in classes, but the disadvantaged students should not be almost hopelessly outclassed.

However, McPartland (1970) does not think that a mixture of whites and blacks is, in principle, crucial to education.

> There is no question but that the desegregated Negro students could have experienced the same kinds of rewards and gains had they switched from the usual segregated school to another all-black school which enrolled students from highly educated and economically advantaged families. In practical terms, though, there simply are not presently enough advantaged black families to accomplish social class desegregation without racial desegregation.

Predicting Occupational Level

It is rather easy to be persuaded that, even if school grades and test scores predict success in school fairly well, they do not predict "life success" and therefore should be ignored. There is a basic flaw in such an argument, as a few examples will illustrate. Suppose one knows the Stanford-Binet IQ scores of a group of children, as Lewis Terman did in his famed "genius" study (Terman & Oden, 1947; Oden, 1968). If their IQ's range from 140 upward, averaging 150, one would predict their adult occupational level to be higher than that of typical adults. Analogously, what is the probability that out of 1000 carefully tested 8-year-boys who have IQ's of 90 there will emerge even one mathematician or Shakespearian scholar on the Ph.D. level?

Suppose that for the 1950 high school graduating classes of 100 students or more one knew the names and present addresses of three males in each class—the top-ranking one, the one who ranked nearest the middle, and the lowest-ranking one. Subsequent education, occupational level, and even income would quite likely be found to differ considerably among the three groups. Of course, since school grades correlate positively with socioeconomic status, intelligence, and other variables, it is hazardous to ascribe causation to academic achievements. Nevertheless, the predictive value of school grades is considerable.

The usual fallacy of an argument against grades as predictors of success in life comes about because it seems to be true that among those persons who, for instance, exactly complete high school—no more and no less—it is difficult to find strong correlations of grades or test scores with measures of life success. Reflect though, that, by eliminating those persons who drop out before high school graduation and those who attend college, one homogenizes the group considerably with respect to motivation, socioeconomic status, intellectual ability, and many other characteristics. That restricts predictive possibilities greatly. Grades and test scores are rather potent predictors of continuation in school which, in turn, leads to increased occupational level and, usually, to increased lifetime earnings (but not invariably, of course, because, for example, a plumber may have a larger annual income than a physicist and may begin drawing it four or more years earlier). For other references and discussion, see Jensen (1969, p. 13), Duncan (1968), Witmer (1970), Stanley (1968), Lindgren (1971), and Claudy (1971).

Increasing Educational Mobility

Viewing the central problem more broadly, one must determine how children of the uneducated poor of any race or ethnic background can be given a better educational chance than they would usually get if not aided. Many such children suffer compound disadvantages: educationally unstimulating homes, poorly developing academic abilities, lack of financial resources, and community influences (especially peers) that are educationally disabling. Our nation is struggling with the problems of helping such youngsters develop their abilities and school motivation more effectively. Much more must be done far earlier than the 11th or 12th grade if efforts then are to be successful. A current dilemma is that present knowledge and funds are so limited that we do not often get to the really disadvantaged. They present so many problems of finance, motivation, and curriculum that nearly everyone tends to work with the more malleable, slightly disadvantaged instead. On the other hand, as Sowell (1970) emphasizes, it is dangerous to ignore the abler members of a minority group while concentrating resources on the least promising ones.

Concluding Remarks

This article covers a complex area, and current practice often seems to me unwise. The many open-admissions programs can be informative, though perhaps often traumatically or even chaotically so. Because of delicate political considerations, objective evidence from most of them will be ruled out for all except a few concerned insiders. If we can devise ways to collect and share information from the many special programs without jeopardizing the positions of the perhaps insecurely placed persons who administer them, it may hasten needed corrective measures (Campbell, 1969). Meanwhile, we must rely mainly on news media, within-college reports, public relations releases, and occasional articles in journals (such as the *College Board Review*) or papers read at professional meetings to discern even vaguely how effective the special programs are.

Summary

Test scores predict the college grades of educationally disadvantaged students at least as well as they do those of the advantaged. High school grades considerably augment the prediction for both groups. Regardless of socio-economic level, students who are predicted to earn quite low grades within a particular college will tend to have academic difficulties if enrolled in it. There are social and educational jutifications for admitting to a particular college some minority-group students who are marginally qualified for it academically, provided that the students are given adequate financial aid and effective remedial courses, tutoring, and coaching. However, if entrants are greatly underqualified academically, new curricula will be required. These may tend to segregate the specially admitted students from the regular student body, thereby diminishing the pacesetter role of the latter. Also, a degree from a special curriculum may not be viewed by employers, graduate schools, and alumni as equivalent to the other degrees awarded by the institution. Thus, admitting students who are seriously underqualified academically for the particular college seems likely to cause frustrations that may be difficult to resolve. Current demands by minority groups for "relevant" courses may reflect the academic difficulties many of their members encounter in present courses more than the educational unsuitability for them of such courses.

18 | The Prediction of Vocational Success*

Robert L. Thorndike

Some four years ago, with Dr. Elizabeth Hagen, I brought out a little volume entitled *10,000 Careers*. This was a report of the follow-up of a group of men who had taken a uniform battery of tests as applicants for aircrew training in the Army Air Force during World War II. As the results of this study got spread around, and received some slight comment in the public prints, my psychometric friends started to hurry by me with averted eyes and without speaking. I seemed on the way to becoming, in my own small way, a psycho-technical pariah. And so naturally I started to brood about the whole thing. Today I plan to share with you some of my soul-searching, for such light as it may throw on the psychological, or more specifically the psychometric bases for vocational guidance.

As I said, *10,000 Careers* was a study of men who were tested with a uniform aptitude battery as applicants for aircrew training during World War II. The group of 17,000 that we undertook to study was an approximately random sample of the 75,000 men tested on one uniform battery that was in operational use during the last half of 1943. Testing for a given individual required a day and a half, one day for paper-and-pencil group tests and half a day for six different psychomotor tests administered to squads of four men at a time. The day and a half of testing yielded 20 separate scores measuring various combinations of verbal-intellectual, numerical, spatial, perceptual, and motor abilities. These test results formed the primary basis for the decision as to the type of Aviation Cadet training a given man should be assigned to—pilot, navigator, or bombardier—subsequently to be commissioned as an officer, or whether he should revert to enlisted status and become a radio operator, tail gunner, or some other enlisted member of the bomber crew.

Fortunately, results from the testing were retained in Air Force files, and in 1955, with funds from the Grant Foundation, it was possible for us to get a roster of names, serial numbers, and test scores and begin our search. To carry out this search, we sought and received the help of many governmental

*From *Vocational Guidance Quarterly*, 1963, **11**, 179-187. Copyright 1963, National Vocational Guidance Association, Inc. Reprinted with permission of the author and publisher.

agencies. The Veterans Administration was our primary resource for locating men, and their comprehensive locator file gave us some sort of a lead on all but eight of our 17,000 cases. Among other things this file immediately identified for us some 1500 of the men who were deceased, and whose careers we could no longer follow with the limited resources available to us. Current military files identified another group of about the same size who were still on active military duty, and who became the subjects of a separate special study. The Air Force Reserve personnel records and the Army Demobilized Personnel Records gave us leads to many others. We salvaged a substantial number of lost souls—or bodies, in any event—through the services of the Retail Credit Company, a resource worth remembering by those interested in longitudinal research.

The hunt was a fascinating one, and we abandoned some of the more interesting trails only reluctantly as it became necessary to get on with the job and analyze our data. In all, we got records on some 10,000 of the men. This represented about a 70% rate of return of those who were alive and in civilian life. We found them everywhere—at home and abroad, wielding the gavel in the board room of a corporation or the broom in the locker room of a country club, in a university teaching psychology, or in a penitentiary serving time for forgery. (Incidentally, the forger became quite a favorite around our shop. We immediately looked up his scores, and found that he had been very low in finger dexterity. We like to think that if he had come to us for vocational guidance we could have told him that forgery was not the career for him.)

In our follow-up of each man, we tried to get as much information as we could, within the limits of a one-page mail questionnaire, on all aspects of his post-war occupational history. We inquired about education, about jobs held, about earned income, about self-perceived work satisfaction and success. Using the information, and drawing upon the experience and wisdom of our colleague, Donald Super, and of Sidney Fine of the U.S. Employment Service, we sorted the men into some 120 occupational groupings, trying to make each grouping as homogeneous as we could in terms of the occupations that we grouped together within it. Then we computed the average score and the spread of scores on each test for each group. Furthermore, we tried to extract from our data any indicators we could find that might serve to represent success in the different occupations. We used such indicators as reported earned income, self-rated success and satisfaction, vertical and horizontal job mobility, as judged by a research worker examining the work record, number supervised, and length on the job. Within each occupational grouping, we correlated each of these indicators with score on each of the 20 tests.

So far as differences within and between occupational groups were concerned, we found a good many. Some were quite substantial, and most of them were sensible and reasonable. Thus, we not only found that those who had become accountants had done better on number tests than those who had become writers; we also found that those who had become accountants had done better on the numerical tests than they had on any of the other tests. We found company presidents highest on intellectual ability, company treasurers highest on numerical fluency, draftsmen highest on visual perception, foremen highest on mechanical ability, and machinists highest on psychomotor coordination. We found that embryo professors were highly verbal, whereas embryo plumbers were not. We found some surprises, due probably to the initial prescreening of our group, for example, a rather surprising level of intellectual ability in our few day laborers, who scored higher in this respect than our high school English and social studies teachers, but most of the patterning was consistent with what you or I would have predicted. Occupational groups did differ in significant and sensible ways on the tests.

However, it is easy to overstate these group differences. Along with differences in mean, it is also true that there was a very wide range of test performance represented within any group. The variability within a single occupation was typically almost as great as the variability in the total group of 10,000. There were accountants whose scores on tests of mathematics, arithmetic reasoning, or computational speed fell almost as far down as the lowest carpenter or truckdriver. There were college teachers—I won't say where or of what—whose verbal comprehension would not have been impressive in our group of auto mechanics. Overlapping was just as real and as impressive as difference.

We turn now to the 12,000 correlations of test scores with indicators of job success. What of these?

I think the simplest and most honest way of summarizing these results would be to say that they clustered around zero—almost as many negative as positive—with the number "significant at the 5 per cent level" making up perhaps 6 per cent of the whole. Of those presumably "significant" correlations, about as many were in the "silly" direction as in the sensible one. Applying these results, taken at face value to the question, "Can tests given at about age 20 predict occupational success 12 years later?" the answer is clearly, "No."

So now you know what has made my friends turn away, and why I have been brooding. Now you can join me as I try to dig behind these results, to see what they really mean, and what message they have for guidance. Why were differences between occupational groups no sharper than they were?

Why did we fail essentially completely to predict our indicators of occupational success? Let me present a series of propositions that might be offered to account for these results and examine each one with you in turn.

Proposition 1

The groups had been pre-screened, and so were too homogeneous to yield significant differences and relationships.

It is true that the groups we studied had been pre-screened by a qualifying examination roughly resembling a scholastic aptitude test, with a cutting score set somewhere near the average of high school seniors. There were few below-average individuals in the group who took the classification test battery. This certainly reduced the sharpness of the differentiation among different occupational groups. That we found a difference of only six-tenths of a standard deviation in reading comprehension between our group of lawyers and our group of truck-drivers stems from the fact that we had a pretty verbal group of truck-drivers. Any others could not have passed the screening test. The effects of pre-screening were certainly most sharply felt in our unskilled and semi-skilled groups, and our samples in these groups are clearly unrepresentative of the total occupational groups to which they belong.

Curtailment is much less likely to have distorted our findings on test validities—especially in the professional and managerial categories that comprised a large proportion of our sample. One feels with some conviction that in these occupations most of the persons excluded by the pre-screening would have fallen by the wayside anyhow in the course of trying to gain entry to or to complete the higher education required for the occupation. At least, it seems to me that any effects of curtailment would have been quite minor, and could not have accounted for the essentially complete lack of significant relationships with the indicators of success.

And I should point out in passing that counselors will often have occasion to deal with groups at least as homogeneous in their abilities as this Air Force group. This would be the case for the counselor in almost any college counseling bureau, and even for one working in a selective high school or with a college preparatory school clientele. So that it would seem reasonable to expect as much difficulty in making long range predictions within many of the groups with which a counselor must work as within ours.

Proposition 2

The tests were inappropriate for civilian jobs.

The tests were, of course, designed for use in a military context. Some concessions to this military context can be found in the content of certain items—for example, an arithmetic rate and distance problem involving an airplane rather than a train or car, a mechanical comprehension item involving the trussed roof of an airplane hangar rather than a bridge truss. But the basic functions covered were in large measure the same ones that appear in current widely-used civilian guidance batteries—verbal ability, numerical ability, mechanical knowledge and understanding, perceptual speed and accuracy, finger dexterity, and eye-hand coordination. A factor analysis of the Air Force battery together with the DAT or the GATB would show that in large part the factors that appear in one also appear in the other. I doubt that we can charge much of the outcome to inadequate tests or testing. If the Air Force battery failed to predict, it seems unlikely that we could expect current commercial aptitude batteries to do so.

Proposition 3

Ability tests picked because they have predicted success in training are of no value for predicting success on the job.

The Air Force battery was initially validated against training school criteria, and those tests were retained in the battery that aided in predicting training school success for some one of the aircrew specialties. Even during the war, there was no convincing evidence that these same tests would predict criteria of combat performance or evaluations by superior officers. Furthermore, predictions of promotions or of proficiency ratings in the military for those of our original 17,000 who stayed in the service were no better than predictions of success in civilian occupations—that is to say, no good at all.

But of course, these findings are consistent with much that we already know concerning the gap between training and job performance. Thus, Ghiselli made an extensive survey of the literature on test predictors of training success and job success, and found that there was essentially no correspondence between the tests that were valid for training criteria and the ones that were valid for job criteria.

It seems likely that much of the distinctiveness in the profiles that we find, especially for the professional occupations, is due to the selection that operated at entry into and during the process of professional education. Thus, the generally high mathematics scores of engineers are probably more a reflection of the hurdle imposed by engineering school than of any further selection that has taken place on engineering jobs. Realistically, it may be that the most helpful counseling that can be given with respect to many occupations will deal with the individuals' prospects of successfully gaining entry to and completing the program of training set as a requirement, either legal or conventional, for entry into the occupation. Perhaps we should be content to estimate Johnny's chances of getting through law school, or medical school, or engineering school, not concerning ourselves with what will happen thereafter.

Proposition 4

The tests were not sufficiently pure and homogeneous measures to bring out occupational differences.

There is a school of thought among test theorists that says that each aptitude test should be a pure measure of some single ability factor, and that each of these pure factor measures should be uncorrelated with all the other tests in a battery. Without question such a test battery has a good deal of appeal to the theoretician. Since each test is measuring a distinct, independent factor, each will give entirely new information; there will be no overlapping or redundance. Each will be able to make a maximum contribution of new validity to whatever validity is possessed by the others and specific ones of the tests will differentiate specific occupations. The prospects for *different* profiles or *different* patterns of validity for different occupations is a maximum.

But in practice, it has more often been the complex tests that have shown high validity as predictors. The Army General Classification Test, for example, was a hodge-podge of verbal, quantitative and spatial material, but this potpourri showed validity quite generally for all sorts of military training programs. It didn't show much *differential* validity but its general validity for many military jobs compared very favorably with that of narrower and more specialized tests.

The Air Force battery, like all others that are known to me, was composed of somewhat impure and somewhat correlated tests. Its ability to differentiate among different occupations may well have suffered somewhat from this fact. However, we can hardly account for its failure to predict *within* occupations on this basis. The battery covered a number of the common ability factors, combined in varying ways and amounts. If these combinations of factors failed to show any signs of validity, it is unlikely that purer measures of the component factors would have done so. Factor purity in the tests of a battery may permit better differentiation between occupations, but it is unlikely to yield validity where none has existed before.

Proposition 5

The tests were too limited in the range of attributes that they covered, and missed the really crucial ones.

The Air Force battery was limited largely to a range of cognitive and motor abilities. The cognitive tests dealt primarily with symbols of one sort or another—words, numbers, maps, diagrams. There was very limited appraisal of the individual's ability to deal with things, and essentially none of his ability to deal with people. Appraisal of aspects of interest or temperament was limited to what may have been revealed in a biographical data blank.

Evidence has been accumulating that, at least in college level groups, differences in interests may be fully as important as differences in abilities in determining curricular and occupational choices. Thus, Berdie found interest test scores to be the most differentiating and aptitude test scores the least differentiating for curricular groups at the University of Minnesota. McCully found large differences by type of job in Kuder interest scores of veterans tested in the VA and followed up several years later—differences that I would estimate were fully as marked as those reported in the Kuder manual. Even in our data, the biographical items seemed to differentiate occupational groups about as well as did the tests. Better interest measures might have sharpened the differentiation still further.

Evidence on temperamental differences between occupational groups is rather less convincing at the present time. Cattell reports some occupational profiles for the 16 Personality Factor Inventory, but these are concurrent rather than predictive data, and most of the groups are distressingly small. Data for occupational groups are reported here and there in the literature, but the material is scrappy, there is rarely any genuine prediction over time, and almost never are there any data on occupational success. My guess at the present time is that most of the useful discrimination between occupations that might be achieved through personality measures is already built into the interest inventories—but I may be wrong.

The evidence concerning interests and temperament relates largely to differences among occupational groups. I am not aware of any convincing evidence that these measures predict success within an occupation, and until we see such evidence we should remain very skeptical that they do so.

How about other sorts of ability measures, beyond those that were included in the Air Force battery? Were there any noteworthy gaps, so far as predicting occupational success is concerned? I would like to call your attention to two areas that seem at least possibilities.

One is the region that Guilford and others have spoken of as divergent thinking, or sometimes more loosely and optimistically as "creativity." These traits are tested with tasks in which the individual is called upon to produce responses, and in which his productions are evaluated with respect to one or more of the attributes of fluency, flexibility, originality, or appropriateness to the demands of the situation. Tests of divergent thinking show only a limited overlap with our conventional ability tests, and in fact they show only a limited overlap with each other. Here is a loosely-knit and as yet poorly-explored area of testing. The plausibility of tests calling for fluency and originality of intellectual production as predictors of occupational success in at least some kinds of jobs is high, so the area is one of promise for future exploration.

A second area that we have long recognized as being important is ability in manipulating people. No tests of such an ability were included in the Air Force battery, nor are any included, so far as I know, in other published aptitude batteries. And perhaps this is because no satisfactory tests of these abilities exist. Certainly, the paper-and-pencil devices that try to use verbal responses to verbal descriptions of interpersonal situations as a way of appraising what the individual will actually do in the real situation have been most unconvincing. Such analyses as we have of them show that they are plausible measures of ability to handle words, but suggest that they are very indifferent indicators of ability to deal with people. After 50 years and more of tests and testing, the development of effective methods of appraising talent for dealing with people is still one of the most obvious and urgent needs.

So in response to Proposition #5, we must cheerfully agree that there were large gaps in our Air Force battery, and that measures which would have filled these gaps *might* have improved our differentiation among occupations, and *might* have even enabled us to predict success within certain of the occupations. And at the same time, we must also admit that measurement procedures for filling some of the most interesting of these gaps are still lacking or at best in an early stage of development.

Proposition 6

Specific abilities of the type included in the Air Force battery show too little stability over time to permit useful prediction.

We know that the individual changes. Particularly in the case of young children, we know that the correlation between ability tests drops as the interval between tests increases, and that in the case of very young children the correlation may drop to substantially zero after a lapse of only a few years. However, we also know that with adults a general measure of intellectual ability is likely to show marked stability over even a long time span. The longest span for which I know of data is the period of about 30 years that was involved in Owens' retest study of men who had taken the Army Alpha as freshmen at Iowa State. For this period, Owens found the rather striking correlation of 0.77 between test and retest. Terman and Oden report a correlation of 0.88 for the original Terman highly gifted group and 0.92 for their somewhat more variable spouses on the Concept Mastery Test over a 12-year span from age 30 to age 42.

But we face a stickier problem when we seek for stability in the *pattern* of *specific* abilities. The reliability of difference scores is typically somewhat low even for immediate retesting. Part of the stability of ability test scores stems from the general factor or factors that they share in common. When we work with score differences, we are typically dealing with a less stable phenomenon—a fact that every guidance worker should keep continually within the fringe of his awareness. So perhaps these differences or patterns don't maintain themselves from one year to the next.

Evidence on the stability of patterns of ability over a period of time is pretty limited, and we sorely need follow-up studies in which a battery such as the GATB is readministered to a group after an interval of 10, 15, or 20 years. Evidence from groups of secondary school age tested after an interval of about 3½ years, in one case with the DAT and in another with the PMA, suggests that the reliabilities of differences between pairs of tests (i.e., numerical ability minus verbal ability) is about as high after several years as it is after a few days or weeks. Correlations of score differences on the one occasion with score differences between the same pair of tests three years later averaged about 0.50, and though this is not impressively high, it is about as high as the reliability of those same difference-scores with no time lapse. So far as evidence is available on the point, it appears that we must reject instability of aptitudes over time as a significant component of our failure to predict—but I would like to see more and better evidence on this point.

Proposition 7

The occupational groups were so heterogeneous that no differentiation or prediction was possible.

It must be admitted that a certain number of our 124 occupational groupings contained a wide range of specific occupations and probably some rather strange bedfellows. It is amazing how meager a sample of even 10,000 becomes when one wishes to identify adequate-sized samples of homogeneous occupational groups. And so we put all our machine operators into two groups—one of fabricating machine operators and one of processing machine operators. We had a single inclusive grouping for laborers, and four groups included all the handicraftsmen. However, at the upper occupational levels, where our yield was better, the groups were generally much narrower, in many cases corresponding to only one or two specific codes in the Dictionary of Occupational Titles. These were such groups as accountant and auditor, architect, airplane pilot, insurance claim adjuster, chemical engineer, civil engineer, electrical engineer, sales manager, and so on. In these cases, the classification is about as homogeneous and restricted as one could hope for in terms of occupations included in a single category. If there is a difficulty, it lies not in our grouping procedure, but in the conception of an occupation as a uniform and homogeneous entity.

Our experience in the conduct of the project gave us a lively sense of the diversity of the specific jobs that are included within even quite a fine occupational code. Thus, the category "lawyer" included trial lawyers and tax lawyers, assistant district attorneys and small town magistrates, individuals whose position was primarily political and individuals who were "organization men" in a large corporation. In activities and setting, they varied widely. Similarly, "college professor" included persons professing speech, physical education, psychology, agriculture, and so on for the full gamut of interests and competence.

The diversity of individuals in a single occupation has been documented more than once. For example, Strong and Tucker's analysis showed the distinctive interest patterns in different medical specialties. Preparing special Vocational Interest Blank keys for pathologists, internists, psychiatrists, and surgeons, they found that these groups could be separated so that there was only a moderate amount of overlapping—though all groups were alike in scoring high on the general "physician" key. And psychiatrists had interest patterns more like those of psychologists than those of surgeons.

Thus, we may suggest that the range of specializations within many occupations that the layman, and perhaps the guidance worker, thinks of in a unitary way is quite wide. People of quite different talents may then be able to find an appropriate niche within the gallery of possibilities. The sharpness of difference *between* occupations may be considerably blurred by this variability *within*. And the task of the counselor may be as much to make a client aware of how he can best achieve fulfillment within a chosen occupation as to identify the occupational category for which he is uniquely best fitted.

Proposition 8

Occupational success was not adequately evaluated, and so could not possibly be predicted.

The evidences of success that we obtained were only those that could be obtained by mail from the respondent. Job satisfaction was rated only crudely. Adequacy of performance was indicated only by increases in pay and in responsibility, and by final level of salary reached. The accuracy of this report could not be checked against independent records, and no performance evaluations could be obtained from associates or supervisors. Our feeling from the flavor of the responses themselves was that when income was reported—and the frequency varied, depending upon the occupation—it was seriously and accurately reported. However, no external verification was possible.

One can argue that the proof of the pudding is in the paying, and that the objective standard of success, at least within a homogeneous occupational category, is the income the person receives from his work. At least to a first approximation, the more successful professors are the better paid professors, the more successful clergymen the better paid clergymen, the more successful accountants the better paid accountants. One can argue that this criterion is more "operational," and consequently more meaningful than any rating or other expression of opinion by an associate or superior. One can argue with somewhat greater force and conviction that ratings obtained from hundreds of different associates and supervisors in hundreds of different companies, regions, and settings would be so lacking in any common point of reference as to be almost completely devoid of meaning.

So though one can quarrel with the self-reported and incomplete measures of success that we were able to obtain, one finds it hard to visualize anything much better as a basis for comparing individuals who have scattered out over the country into hundreds of different work settings. We had wanted to take one or two of our largest groups, our 900 engineers, for example, to work intensively to develop the best possible criterion information on each one, and then to see whether any more meaningful predictions could be obtained from our tests. However, we never found the wherewithal to do this. And frankly, I am not convinced that we would do much better. "Success" is a rather slippery concept, to which it is difficult to give a form and a shape. Perhaps we make a mistake to concern ourselves with it. Let me, offer you instead of Proposition #8, Proposition #8a.

Proposition 8a

Beyond survival in an occupation, "success" is a meaningless concept, which we might as well abandon.

I have pointed out some of the difficulties that we had with appraisals of success. Let me now point to a few others. The one to which I want to give primary attention is what we might call the institutionalization of rewards in certain occupations. Thus, in those occupations in which rates of pay (and sometimes of work) are set by union contract, individual differences in competence beyond the minimum necessary to survive are irrelevant to success in the occupation. In a large other group of occupations, we find pay scales set by civil service schedules, and salary increments coming largely automatically with seniority. It is hard to estimate to what fraction of the total world of work these conditions apply. They are certainly widespread as one drops below the professional and managerial categories, and even those are not entirely exempt. It appears to me that within many occupational categories, it is realistic to say that degree of success has largely ceased to have a meaning, and that success is evidenced only by a shift to another occupation, i.e., from the ranks of worker into the ranks of management, and failure by dropping out of the occupation. If this be so, success must be evidenced primarily by the occupation reached, rather than by indicators within an occupation.

Proposition 9

Long range "success" depends so heavily upon contingency factors that one can never hope to predict it from what can be known about the individual in advance.

As used here, "contingency factors" refer to the whole gamut of things that can happen *to* a person, and that are not known or knowable from any information about him that we could obtain at the time we might be testing or counseling him. On the morbid side, he might be hit by a car or by polio and lose the use of his legs. More happily, his college fraternity brother might be able to get him started in the family business or might introduce him to the boss's daughter. Less dramatically, the jobs that happened to be open the day he started looking for work, the ad he happened to see as he was looking through the paper, the foreman who happened to take over his training as a green hand, the vacancy that happened to become available at the point when he was a candidate for promotion—all of these and many more interact to shape his occupational career.

Nobody knows the extent to which occupational histories are truly dependent upon such external events. Their impact is certainly real. There are certain instances in which they are the swamping influence—as, for example, in the case of our most financially successful farmer, who was making an excellent living leasing out the grazing rights to 20,000 acres of Texas landscape which his wife had inherited from her forebears. The longer the period over which we wish to make our vocational predictions, and the more major choice-points in the vocational career that are included, the more chance there is for these outside factors to come in as determining factors. To the extent that these contingency factors determine success, any attempt to predict it is futile.

Summary

I have tried to share with you some of the thoughts that have come to me as I have pondered over the large regions of negative result in our study of 10,000 civilian careers. Some part of the reason for such negative results may lie in our somewhat curtailed group, and more of it may be found in the incomplete coverage of possibly significant domains of interest, temperament, and ability. But I suspect that most of it resides in the heterogeneity of many occupations, the differences between training and work, the limited meaning of success in occupations in which pay and promotions have become institutionalized, and the impact of contingency factors upon the vocational careers of individuals. These are factors that set a fairly low ceiling on any predictions of occupational success by *any* means. So far as they are determining, they suggest that we may need to focus our attention upon more immediate and more limited objectives—both for our testing and for our counseling.

Anne Anastasi

Within the past decade, psychologists have been especially active in devising novel and imaginative approaches to test validity. In the time allotted, I can do no more than whet your appetite for these exciting developments and hope that you will be stimulated to examine the sources cited for an adequate exposition of each topic. I have selected five developments to bring to your attention. Ranging in scope from broad frameworks to specific techniques and from highly theoretical to immediately practical, these topics pertain to: construct validation, decision theory, moderator variables, synthetic validity, and response styles.

Construct Validation

It is nearly ten years since the American Psychological Association published its *Technical Recommendations* (1954) outlining four types of validity: content, predictive, concurrent, and construct. As the most complex, inclusive, and controversial of the four, construct validity has received the greatest attention during the subsequent decade. When first proposed in the *Technical Recommendations,* construct validation was characterized as a validation of the theory underlying a test. On the basis of such a theory, specific hypotheses are formulated regarding the expected variations in test scores among individuals or among conditions, and data are then gathered to test these hypotheses. The constructs in construct validity refer to postulated attributes or traits that are presumably reflected in test performance. Concerned with a more comprehensive and more abstract kind of behavioral description than those provided by other types of validation, construct validation calls for a continuing accumulation of information from a variety of sources. Any data throwing light on the nature of the trait under consideration and the conditions affecting its development and manifestations contribute to the process of construct validation. Examples of relevant procedures include checking an intelligence test for the anticipated increase in score with age during childhood, investigating the effects of experimental variables such as stress upon test scores, and factor analyzing the test along with other variables.

Subsequently, the concept of construct validity has been attacked, clarified, elaborated, and illustrated in a number of thoughtful and provocative articles by Cronbach and Meehl (1955), Loevinger (1957), Bechtoldt (1959), Jessor and Hammond (1957), Campbell and Fiske (1959), and Campbell (1960). In the most recent of these papers, Campbell (1960) integrates much that had previously been written about construct validity and gives a well-balanced presentation of its contributions, hazards, and common misunderstandings. Referring to the earlier paper prepared jointly with Fiske (1959) Campbell again points out that in order to demonstrate construct validity we need to show not only that a test correlates highly with other variables with which it should correlate, but also that it does not correlate with variables from which it should differ. The former is described as convergent validation, the latter as discriminant validation.

In their multitrait-multimethod matrix, Campbell and Fiske (1959) proposed a systematic experimental design for this twin approach to validation. Essentially what is required is the assessment of two or more traits by two or more methods. Under these conditions, the correlations of the same trait assessed by different methods represent a measure of convergent validity (these correlations should be high). The correlations of different traits assessed by the same or similar methods provide a measure of discriminant validity (these correlations should be low or negligible). In addition, the correlations of the same trait independently assessed by the same method give an index of reliability.

Without attempting an evaluation of construct validity, for which I would urge you to consult the sources cited, I should nevertheless like to make a few comments about it. First, the basic idea of construct validity is not new. Some of the earliest tests were designed to measure such theoretical constructs as attention and memory, not to mention that most notorious of constructs, "intelligence." On the other hand, construct validity has served to focus attention on the desirability of basing test construction on an explicitly recognized theoretical foundation. Both in devising a new test and in setting up procedures for its validation, the investigator is urged to formulate psychological hypotheses. The proponents of construct validity have thus tried to integrate psychological testing more closely with psychological theory and experimental methods.

With regard to specific validation procedures, construct validation also utilizes much that is not new. Age differentiation, factorial validity, and the effect of such experimental variables as practice on test scores have been reported in test manuals long before construct validity was given a name in the *Technical Recommendations*. As a matter of fact, the methodology of construct validity is so comprehensive as to encompass even the procedures characteristically associated with other types of validity (see Anastasi, 1961, Ch. 6). Thus the correlation of a mechanical aptitude test with subsequent performance on engineering jobs would contribute to our understanding of the construct measured by this test. Similarly, comparing the performance of neurotics and normals is one way of checking the construct validity of a test designed to measure anxiety. Nevertheless, construct validation has stimulated the search for novel ways of gathering validation data. Although the principal techniques currently employed to investigate construct validity have long been familiar, the field of operation has been expanded to admit a wider variety of procedures.

The very multiplicity of data-gathering techniques recognized by construct validity presents certain hazards. As Campbell puts it, the wide diversity of acceptable validational evidence "makes possible a highly opportunistic selection of evidence and the editorial device of failing to mention validity probes that were not confirmatory" (Campbell, 1960, p. 551). Another hazard stems from misunderstandings of such a broad and loosely defined concept as construct validity. Some test constructors apparently interpret construct validation to mean content validity expressed in terms of psychological trait names. Hence they present as construct validity purely subjective accounts of what they believe (or hope) their test measures.

It is also unfortunate that the chief exponents of construct validity stated in one of their articles that this type of validation "is involved whenever a test is to be interpreted as a measure of some attribute or quality which is not 'operationally defined.' " (Cronbach & Meehl, 1955, p. 282). Such an assertion opens the door wider for subjective claims and fuzzy thinking about test scores and the traits they measure. Actually the theoretical construct or trait assessed by any test can be defined in terms of the operations performed in establishing the validity of the test. Such a definition should take into account the various external criteria with which the test correlated significantly, as well as the conditions that affect its scores. These procedures are entirely in accord with the positive contributions of construct validity. It would also seem desirable to retain the concept of criterion in construct validation, not as a specific practical achievement to be predicted, but as a general name for independently gathered external data. The need to base all validation on data rather than on armchair speculation would thus be re-emphasized, as would the need for data external to the test scores themselves.

Decision Theory

Even broader than construct validity in its scope and implications is the application of decision theory to test construction and evaluation (see Anastasi, 1961, Ch. 7; Cronbach & Gleser, 1965; Girshick, 1954). Because of many technical complexities, however, the current impact of decision theory on test development and use is limited and progress has been slow.

Statistical decision theory was developed by Wald (1950) with special reference to the decisions required in the inspection and quality control of industrial products. Many of its possible implications for psychological testing have been systematically worked out by Cronbach and Gleser in their 1957 book, *Psychological Tests and Personnel Decisions.* Essentially, decision theory is an attempt to put the decision-making process into mathematical form, so that available information may be used to reach the most effective decisions under specified circumstances. The mathematical procedures required by decision theory are often quite complex, and few are in a form permitting their immediate application to practical testing problems. Some of the basic concepts of decision theory, however, can help in the reformulation and clarification of certain questions about tests.

A few of these concepts were introduced in psychological testing before the formal development of statistical decision theory and were later recognized as fitting into that framework. One example is provided by the well-known Taylor-Russell Tables (Taylor & Russell, 1939), which permit an estimate of the net gain in selection accuracy attributable to the use of a test. The information required for this purpose includes the validity coefficient of the test, the selection ratio, and the proportion of successful applicants selected without the use of the test. The rise in proportion of successful applicants to be expected from the introduction of the test is taken as an index of the test's effectiveness.

In many situations, what is wanted is an estimate of the effect of the test, not on proportion of persons who exceed the minimum performance, but on the over-all output of the selected group. How does the level of criterion achievement of the persons selected on the basis of the test compare with that of the total applicant sample that would have been selected without the test? Following the work of Taylor and Russell, several investigators addressed themselves to this question. It was Brogden (1946) who first demonstrated that the expected increase in output or achievement is directly proportional to the validity of the test. Doubling the validity of the test will double the improvement in output expected from its use. Following a similar approach (see Jarett, 1948), Brown & Ghiselli (1953) prepared a table whereby mean standard criterion score of the selected group can be estimated from a knowledge of test validity and selection ratio.

Decision theory incorporates a number of parameters not traditionally considered in evaluating the predictive effectiveness of tests. The previously mentioned selection ratio is one such parameter. Another is the cost of administering the testing program. Thus a test of low validity would be more likely to be retained if it were short, inexpensive, adapted for group administration, and easy to give. An individual test requiring a trained examiner and expensive equipment would need a higher validity to justify its retention. A further consideration is whether the test measures an area of criterion-relevant behavior not covered by other available techniques.

Another major aspect of decision theory pertains to the evaluation of outcomes. The absence of adequate systems for assigning values to outcomes is one of the principal obstacles in the way of applying decision theory. It should be noted, however, that decision theory did not introduce the problem of values into the decision process, but merely made it explicit. Value systems have always entered into decisions, but they were not heretofore clearly recognized or systematically handled.

Still another feature of decision theory is that it permits a consideration of the interaction of different variables. An example would be the interaction of applicant aptitudes with alternative treatments, such as types of training programs to which individuals could be assigned. Such differential treatment would further improve the outcome of decisions based on test scores. Decision theory also focuses attention on the important fact that the effectiveness of a test for selection, placement, classification, or any other purpose must be compared not with chance or with perfect prediction, but with the effectiveness of other available predictors. The question of the base rate is also relevant here (Meehl & Rosen, 1955). The examples cited provide a few glimpses into ways in which the application of decision theory may eventually affect the interpretation of test validity.

Moderator Variables

A promising recent development in the interpretation of test validity centers on the use of moderator variables (Berdie, 1961; Fulkerson, 1959; Ghiselli, 1956, 1960a, 1960b, 1963; Saunders, 1956). The validity of a given test may vary among subgroups or individuals within a population. Essentially the problem of moderator variables is that of predicting these differences in predictability. In any bivariate distribution, some individuals fall close to the regression line; others miss it by appreciable distances. We may then ask whether there is any characteristic in which those falling farther from the regression line, for whom prediction errors are large, differ systematically and consistently from those falling close to it. Thus a test might be a better predictor of criterion performance for men than for women, or for applicants from a lower than for applicants from a higher socioeconomic level. In such examples, sex and socioeconomic level are the moderator variables since they modify the predictive validity of the test.

Even when a test is equally valid for all subgroups, the same score may have a different predictive meaning when obtained by members of different subgroups. For example, if two students with different educational background obtain the same score on the Scholastic Aptitude Test, will they do equally well in college? Or will the one with the poorer or the one with the better background excel? Moderator variables may thus influence cutoff scores, regression equation weights, or validity coefficients of the same test for different subgroups of a population.

Interests and motivation often function as moderator variables in individual cases. If an applicant has little interest in a job, he will probably do poorly regardless of his scores on relevant aptitude tests. Among such persons, the correlation between aptitude test scores and job performance would be low. For individuals who are interested and highly motivated, on the other hand, the correlation between aptitude test score and job success may be quite high. From another angle, personality inventories like the Minnesota Multiphasic Personality Inventory (MMPI) may have higher validity for some types of neurotics than for others (Fulkerson, 1959). The characteristic behavior of the two types may make one more careful and accurate in reporting symptoms, the other careless or evasive.

A moderator variable may itself be a test score, in terms of which individuals may be sorted into subgroups. There have been some promising attempts to identify such moderator variables in test scores (Berdie, 1961; Fulkerson, 1959; Ghiselli, 1956, 1963). In a study of taxi drivers conducted by Ghiselli (1956), the correlation between an aptitude test and a criterion of job performance was only .22. The group was then sorted into thirds on the basis of scores on an occupational interest inventory. When the validity of the aptitude test was recomputed within the third whose occupational interest level was most appropriate for the job, it rose to .66. Such findings suggest that one test might first be used to screen out individuals for whom the second test is likely to have low validity; then from among the remaining cases, those scoring high on the second test are selected.

Even within a single test, such as a personality inventory, it may prove possible to develop a moderator key in terms of which the validity of the rest of the test for each individual can be assessed (Ghiselli, 1963). There is also evidence suggesting that intra-individual variability from one part of the test to another affects the predictive validity of a test for individuals (Berdie, 1961). Those individuals for whom the test is more reliable (as indicated by low intra-individual variability) are also the individuals for whom it is more valid, as might be anticipated.

Synthetic Validity

A technique devised to meet a specific practical need is synthetic validity (Balma *et al.*, 1959; Lawshe & Steinberg, 1955; Primoff, 1957). It is well known that the same test may have high validity for predicting the performance of office clerks or machinists in one company and low or negligible validity for jobs bearing the same title in another company. Similar variation has been found in the correlations of tests with achievement in courses of the same name given in different colleges. The familiar criterion of "college success" is a notorious example of both complexity and heterogeneity. Although traditionally identified with grade point average, college success can actually mean many different things, from being elected president of the student council or captain of the football team to receiving Phi Beta Kappa in one's junior year. Individual colleges vary in the relative weights they give to these different criteria of success.

It is abundantly clear that: 1) educational and vocational criteria are complex; 2) the various criterion elements, or subcriteria, for any given job, educational institution, course, etc. may have little relation to each other; and 3) different criterion situations bearing the same name often represent a different combination of subcriteria. It is largely for these reasons that test users are generally urged to conduct their own local validation studies. In many situations, however, this practice may not be feasible for lack of time, facilities, or adequate samples. Under these circumstances, synthetic validity may provide a satisfactory approximation of test validity against a particular criterion. First proposed by Lawshe (Lawshe & Steinberg, 1955) for use in industry, synthetic validity has been employed chiefly with job criteria, but it is equally applicable to educational criteria.

In synthetic validity, each predictor is validated, not against a composite criterion, but against job elements identified through job analysis. The validity of any test for a given job is then computed synthetically from the weights of these elements in the job and in the test. Thus if a test has high validity in predicting performance in delicate manipulative tasks, and if such tasks loom large in a particular job, then the test will have high synthetic validity for that job. A statistical technique known as the J-coefficient (for Job-coefficient) has been developed by Primoff (1957) for estimating the synthetic validity of a test. This technique offers a possible tool for generalizing validity data from one job or other criterion situation to another without actually conducting a separate validation study in each situation. The J-coefficient may also prove useful in ordinary battery construction as an intervening step between the job analysis and the assembling of a trial battery of tests. The preliminary selection of appropriate tests is now done largely on a subjective and unsystematic basis and might be improved through the utilization of such a technique as the J-coefficient.

Response Styles

The fifth and last development I should like to bring to your attention pertains to response styles. Although research on response styles has centered chiefly on personality inventories, the concept can be applied to any type of test. Interest in response styles was first stimulated by the identification of certain test-taking attitudes which might obscure or distort the traits that the test was designed to measure. Among the best known is the social desirability variable, extensively investigated by Edwards (1957), Edwards & Diers, (1962), Edwards *et al.* (1962), and Edwards & Heathers, (1962). This is simply the tendency to choose socially desirable responses on personality inventories. To what extent this variable should also reflect the tendency to choose common responses is a matter on which different investigators disagree. Other examples of response styles include acquiescence, or the tendency to answer "yes" rather than "no" regardless of item content (Asch, 1958; Bass, 1955; Couch & Keniston, 1960; Gage *et al.,* 1957); evasiveness, or the tendency to choose question marks or other indifferent responses; and the tendency to utilize extreme response categories, such as "agree strongly" and "disagree strongly."

We can recognize two stages in research on response styles. First there was the recognition that stylistic components of item form exert a significant influence upon test responses. In fact, a growing accumulation of evidence indicated that the principal factors measured by many self-report inventories were stylistic rather than content factors. At this stage, such stylistic variance was regarded as error variance, which would reduce test validity. Efforts were therefore made to rule out these stylistic factors through the reformulation of items, the development of special keys, or the application of correction formulas.

More recently there has been an increasing realization that response styles may be worth measuring in their own right. This point of view is clearly reflected in the reviews by Jackson and Messick (1958) and by Wiggins (1962), published within the past five years. Rather than being regarded as measurement errors to be eliminated, response styles are now being investigated as diagnostic indices of broad personality traits. The response style that an individual exhibits in taking a test may be associated with characteristic behavior he displays in other, nontest situations. Thus the tendency to mark socially desirable answers may be related to conformity and stereotyped conventionally. It has also been proposed that a moderate degree of this variable is associated with a mature, individualized self concept, while higher degrees are associated with intellectual and social immaturity (Loevinger, 1959; Loevinger & Ossorio, 1959). With reference to acquiescence, there is some suggestive evidence that the predominant "yeasayers" tend to have weak ego controls and to accept impulses without reservation, while the predominant "naysayers" tend to inhibit and suppress impulses and to reject emotional stimuli (Couch & Keniston, 1960).

The measurement of response styles may provide a means of capitalizing on what initially appeared to be the chief weaknesses of self-report inventories. Several puzzling and disappointing results obtained with personality inventories seem to make sense when re-examined in the light of recent research with response styles. Much more research is needed, however, before the measurement of response styles can be put to practical use. We need more information on the relationships among different response styles, such as social desirability and acquiescence, which are often confounded in existing scales. We also need to know more about the interrelationships among different scales designed to measure the same response style. And above all, we need to know how these stylistic scales are related to external criterion data.

The five developments cited in this paper represent ongoing activities. It is premature to evaluate the contribution any of them will ultimately make to the measurement or interpretation of test validity. At this stage, they all bear watching and they warrant further exploration.

20 | Incremental Validity: A Recommendation*

Lee Sechrest

The 1954 APA publication *Technical Recommendations for Psychological Tests and Diagnostic Techniques* established minimum standards to be met in the production and promotion of psychometric instruments. Since that time there have appeared a considerable number of articles elaborating or extending the considerations involved in developing tests (e.g., Cronbach & Meehl, 1955; Jessor & Hammond, 1957; Loevinger, 1957; Campbell & Fiske, 1959; Bechtoldt, 1959; Campbell, 1960). In one of the most recent developments, Campbell and Fiske (1959) have suggested that a crucial distinction is to be made between convergent and discriminant validity. It is necessary to demonstrate not only that a measure covaries with certain other connotatively similar variables, but that its covariance with other connotatively dissimilar variables is limited.

Campbell (1960) has suggested several possible additions to recommended validity indicators, all of which focus on the problem of *discriminant* validity, i.e., the demonstration that a test construct is not completely or even largely redundant with other better established or more parsimonious constructs. He has suggested, for example, that correlations with intelligence, social desirability and self-ratings should be reported since these variables are likely to be conceptually and theoretically simpler than most of our constructs. If a new test proves to be reducible to an intelligence or social desirability measure, its *raison d'être* probably vanishes.

It is the purpose of this note to suggest an additional validity construct and evidence which should be presented in the basic publications concerning *any test which is intended for applied, predictive use.*

Incremental Validity

Almost without exception evidence which is presented to support the validity of a psychological test is presented in the form of some improvement

*From *Psychological and Educational Measurement*, 1963, **23**, 153-158. Copyright 1963 by G. Frederic Kuder. Reprinted with permission of the author and publisher.

over results which would be expected by chance. However, in *clinical* situations, at least, tests are rarely, if ever, used in a manner consistent with the chance model. Almost always Rorschachs are interpreted after interviews, reading of case reports, conferences and the like. The meaning of a report that some Rorschach variable will predict better than chance becomes obscure under those circumstances. It seems clear that validity must be claimed for a test in terms of some *increment* in predictive efficiency over the information otherwise easily and cheaply available.

Cronbach and Gleser (1957, pp. 30-32) and, as they point out, Conrad (1950), have both discussed the problem of the base against which the predictive power of a test is to be evaluated. Cronbach and Gleser declare, "Tests should be judged on the basis of their contribution over and above the best strategy available, making use of prior information" (1957, p. 31). They do indicate that tests may be valuable in spite of low correlations if they tap characteristics either unobservable or difficult to observe by other means. Shaffer (1950, p. 76) also suggested, "One can . . . study the degree to which the clinician is valid with and without the aid of a certain technique, and thereby assess the value of the test indirectly." We are not so sure that such an assessment is completely indirect.

In light of the above argument it is proposed that the publications adduced as evidence for the utility of a test in a clinical situation—and probably for most other uses—should include evidence that the test will *add to* or *increase* the validity of predictions made on the basis of data which are usually available. At a minimum it would seem that a test should have demonstrated incremental validity beyond that of brief case histories, simple biographical information and brief interviews. A strong case can also be made to demand that a test contribute beyond the level of simpler, e.g., paper and pencil, tests. As a matter of fact, Campbell's recommendation that new tests be correlated with self-ratings is quite akin to some aspects of incremental validity.

Adequate Statistical Evidence

When a test is added to a battery, the usual way to express its contribution is either by a partial correlation or by an increment to a zero order or multiple correlation. There is, perhaps, one objection to the partial or multiple correlation as a demonstration of incremental validity. That is, the increase, even if significant, is of somewhat undetermined origin and obscures the exact nature of the increment achieved.

Consider the matrix of correlations:

	1	2	0
1		60	40
2			40
0			

in which 1 and 2 are predictors of criterion 0. The multiple $R_{12.0}$ = .45 and the partial $r_{20.1}$ = .22. Both values might be considered to represent improvements over the zero order correlations. And yet, without knowing the reliabilities of 1 and 2 we will be unable to discern whether 2 contributes to the prediction of 0 because it represents a theoretical variable distinct from 1 or whether 2 has only the same, and informationally redundant, effect of increasing the length and, hence, the reliability of Test 1. It will often be important to know whether an increment results from a Spearman-Brown prophecy operation or from some contribution of theoretical importance. Kelley (1927) suggested quite a number of years ago that when correlations between intelligence and achievement measures are properly treated the two measures prove to be almost completely overlapping. Thus, in his view, the two kinds of measures only combine to form a longer and more reliable measure of a single variable.

One solution to the problem might be the correction of inter-test correlations for attenuation. If the reliabilities are so low that the corrected correlation approaches unity, no increment to R nor a significant partial correlation will ensue. In the above example, given reliabilities for 1 and 2 of only .60, the correlation between them would become unity, the multiple would be .40, and the partial r .00. On the other hand, if both variables had reliability coefficients of .90, the correction for attenuation would have little effect on either R or partial correlation.[1]

Exemplary Instances of Incremental Validity Research

Demonstrations of incremental validity are not common in research literature except in prediction of academic performance. Unfortunately, where they occur the data often are discouraging. Winch and More (1956) used a multiple correlation technique in an attempt to determine the increment produced by TAT protocols over a semi-structured interview and case history

---

[1] It is to be noted that correction for attenuation of the validity values is *not* suggested and should not be done.

material. Their results provide no basis for concluding that the TAT contributes anything beyond what is given by interviews or case histories. Sines (1959) discovered that the Rorschach apparently did yield better than chance predictions, but it seemingly not only did not add to other information obtained from interviews and a biographical data sheet, but it actually produced a net *decrement* in predictive accuracy. This in spite of *better than chance* "validity." Kostlan (1954) found that judges made better than chance inferences about patients' behavior from only "minimal data" (age, occupation, education, marital status and source of referral). When test results were used to make the same judgments, only the social history yielded more accurate inferences than those made from simple biographical facts.

In the general area of prediction of academic success, data are widely available indicating the increment over previous grades afforded by predictions based on psychometric data. Even in predicting academic performance, however, it is not always clear that the use of test data accomplishes anything beyond increasing the reliability of the ability measure based on grades. If treated as suggested above, it might be possible to determine whether a test contributes anything beyond maximizing the reliability of the general ability measure afforded by grades. Ford (1950) has presented data concerning the prediction of grades in nursing school making use of among other measures, the Cooperative General Science Test (CGST) and high school point average (HSPA). The correlation matrix between these variables is:

	CGST	HSPA	Grades
1. CGST		.33	.57
2. HSPA			.51
0. Grades			

The multiple correlation $R_{12.0}$ is .66 and the partial $r_{10.2}$ is .50. The split-half reliability of the CGST has been reported to be .88. While no reliability estimate for HSPA is known to the writer, several researchers have reported reliabilities for college grades (Anderson, 1953; Bendig, 1953; Wallace, 1951). If we take the median value of the three reported values of .78, .80, and .90 as a likely estimate for HSPA and then correct the r_{12} for attenuation, the .33 becomes .40. The multiple correlation then drops only to .65 and the partial correlation only to .46. It is obvious that for the prediction of grades in nursing courses the use of the Cooperative General Science Test results in an *increment* in validity over high school grades and that the increment may be regarded as more than a contribution to reliable measurement of a single factor.

Summary

It is proposed that in addition to demonstrating the *convergent* and *discriminant* validity of tests intended for use in clinical situations, evidence should be produced for *incremental* validity. It must be demonstrable that the addition of a test will produce better predictions than are made on the basis of information other than the test ordinarily available. Reference to published research indicates that situations may well occur in which, in spite of better than chance validity, tests may not contribute to, or may even detract from, predictions made on the basis of biographical and interview information. It is further suggested that, when correlations for a given test are entered into a multiple correlation or partial correlation, the inter-predictor correlations be corrected for attenuation to determine whether an increase in the multiple or partial correlations is to be attributed to a mere increase in reliability of measurement of the predictor variable.

Section V

Theories of Mental Abilities

Capsule definitions of intelligence have ranged from Binet's "the ability to judge well, understand well, and reason well" to Wechsler's "global capacity ... to act purposively, to think rationally, and to deal effectively with the environment." Other psychologists, perhaps those with a greater predilection for mathematics and statistics, have been more programmatic in their efforts to define intelligence, or to understand the structure of mental abilities. The first two articles in this section were written by J. P. Guilford and Raymond Cattell, and are representative of the approach via factor analysis. *Factor analysis* is a mathematical procedure for reducing the scores of N individuals on n tests to a more compact description. As discussed in the Guilford and Cattell articles, factor analysis was initiated by Charles Spearman. Spearman's treatment of psychological test data convinced him that intelligence consists of a general factor (g) shared by all tests, plus one or more specific factors (s's) unique to each test. Subsequent refinements of factor analysis and further data collection by both American and British psychologists led to extensions of Spearman's theory to include a number of group factors.

One of the most prominent American factor analysts was Louis Thurstone, whose seven "primary mental abilities" represent an early extension of Spearman's theory. The research of J. P. Guilford, who has postulated over 120 different mental ability factors, resulted in a further breakdown of these seven abilities in addition to many others. In Guilford's *structure of intellect* model, intelligence is viewed as consisting of five mental *operations* (evaluation, convergent production, divergent production, memory, cognition), interacting with four mental *contents* (figural, symbolic, semantic, behavioral), and resulting in six *products* (units, classes, relations, systems, transformations, implications).

More parsimonious than Guilford's model, but also stimulated by Thurstone's work (viz., his discovery of a second-order general factor underlying the seven group factors), is Cattell's conception of two types of intelligence—fluid and crystallized. *Fluid ability* is said to depend less on experience and to reach a peak at about age 15, whereas *crystallized ability* depends

173

more on specific experiences and reaches a peak much later. Crystallized ability consists of complex judgmental skills acquired by applying fluid ability to the environment.

It is noteworthy that both Guilford and Cattell emphasize the importance of experience in the development of intellectual abilities. Heredity is viewed as setting certain limits to intellectual development, but as Guilford points out, few if any people ever reach their limits. The influences of environment in determining intellectual abilities are discussed in greater detail in the last two articles of this section.

Beginning with the postulate that "intelligence is an attribute, not an entity" and "intelligence is the summation of the learning experiences of the individual," Alexander Wesman is critical of much of the theoretical and empirical work on this subject. He considers five issues: 1) the classification of ability tests into aptitude, achievement and intelligence measures; 2) the utility of culture-free and culture-fair tests; 3) is "verbal ability" synonymous with "intelligence"?; 4) the growth and decline of intelligence; 5) the search for purity. Wesman is especially critical of attempts to use factor analysis to search for the "structure of intellect," and he warns against reifying mental abilities "discovered" in this way. He also makes a suggestion that readers of this volume have encountered previously (see articles 11 and 15), namely that in selecting a test one should pay more attention to its validity and less attention to whether it was designed according to certain ideal measurement characteristics. Wesman also points out that the distinction between *bandwidth* and *fidelity* (Cronbach & Gleser, 1965) has proven useful in selecting a test. Thus, traditional omnibus tests of intelligence have broad bandwidths and can predict a wide range of criteria with moderate success. In contrast, tests of more specific abilities, which have narrower bandwidths and greater fidelity, predict fewer criteria efficiently but do a better job with those few.

Wesman's argument that intelligence is the "unstructured . . . sum of learning experiences unique to each individual" serves to underscore the limitations of traditional tests of general ability. But Wesman himself is not entirely free of the tendency toward reification to which he refers. Thus, in several places he states that "intelligence" is a certain thing, when clearly a concept such as "intelligence" can be whatever a consensus of experts desire to call it. In fact, Boring's well-known operational definition of intelligence as "what intelligence tests measure," in spite of its obvious lack of fruitfulness, is probably attractive to certain psychologists because of its apparent objectivity. In this regard, a principle which bears frequent repetition is that concepts, like theories, are not necessarily true or false; they are merely useful or nonuseful. The error in describing "intelligence" as a collection of particular abilities occurs, as Wesman correctly perceives, when theorists begin to believe that their convenient, useful descriptions of mental abilities are actual entities.

The last article in this section, by Anne Anastasi, describes theory and research concerned with two questions: 1) How does behavior become organized into traits? and 2) What do we know about the emergence of behavioral traits? Anastasi recognizes that only categories, not entities, result from factor analysis, and that these categories and their relative importance vary with different samples of examinees and tests. She summarizes data in support of Ferguson's (1954, 1956) hypothesis that the different abilities isolated by factor analysis are the results of overlearning and differential positive transfer in certain areas of learning. Three main approaches to the investigation of intellective traits or abilities are discussed—developmental, comparative and experimental. Although the findings are not entirely consistent, age, sex, socioeconomic and culture differences in the patterning of abilities have been found. In general, the data are viewed as supporting Ferguson's postulate that "As the learning of a particular trait continues, the ability to perform it becomes gradually differentiated from other abilities." (Ferguson, 1954, p. 110)

21 | Intelligence Has Three Facets*

J. P. Guilford

Many a layman who has taken a psychologist's intelligence test, especially if he did not do as well as he thought he should, has the conviction that a score, such as an IQ, does not tell the whole story regarding intelligence. In thinking so, he is absolutely right; traditional intelligence tests fall far short of indicating fully an individual's intellectual status. Just how far short and in what respects have not been well realized until very recent years during which the whole scope of human intelligence has been intensively investigated.

This is not to say that IQ tests are not useful, for they definitely are, as years of experience have demonstrated. Intelligence-quotient tests were originated more than 60 years ago for the purpose of determining which children could not learn at normal rates. This meant that the content of IQ tests weights heavily those intellectual abilities that are pertinent to school learning in the key subjects of reading and arithmetic, and other subjects that depend directly upon them or are of similar nature psychologically. IQ tests (and also academic-aptitude tests, which are essentially similar) predict less well at educational levels higher than the elementary grades, for at higher levels subject matter becomes more varied. Even at the elementary level, predictions of achievement have been poor in connection with the *initial* stages of learning to read, in spelling, and in the arts. The defender of the IQ test might say that intelligence is not involved in such subjects. But he would not only be wrong, he would also be dodging problems.

One Intelligence, or Many Abilities?

The father of IQ tests, Alfred Binet, believed firmly that intelligence is a very complex affair, comprising a number of different abilities, and he manifested this conviction by introducing tests of many kinds into his composite scale. He did not know what the component abilities are, although he suggested that there are several different kinds of memory, for example. He went along with the idea of using a single, overall score, since the immediate practical goal was to make a single administrative decision regarding each child.

Test-makers following Binet were mostly unconcerned about having a basic psychological theory for intelligence tests, another example of technology running far in advance of theory. There was some concern about theory in England, however, where Charles Spearman developed a procedure of factor analysis by which it became possible to discover component abilities (Spearman, 1904). Spearman was obsessed with a very restricting conception that there is a universal g factor that is common to all tests that have any claim to the label of "intelligence tests," where each test has its own unique kind of items or problems. His research, and that of others in his country, found, however, that correlations between tests could not be fully accounted for on the basis of a single common factor. They had to admit the existence of a number of "group" factors in addition to g. For example, sets of tests having verbal, numerical, or spatial material, respectively, correlated higher within sets than with tests in other sets. The extra correlation among tests within sets was attributed to additional abilities each of limited scope.

Factor analyses in the United States have followed almost exclusively the multiple-factor theory of Thurstone (1935), which is more general than Spearman's. In Thurstone's conception, a g factor is not necessary but analysis by his methods would be likely to find it if the intercorrelations warrant such a result. It is not necessary to know the mathematics basic to factor theory in order to follow the remaining content of this article, but for those who wish additional insights the next few paragraphs present the minimum essentials of a mathematical basis. To all readers it may be said that factor analysis is a sensitive procedure, which, when properly used, can answer the taxonomic questions of *what* intellectual abilities or functions exist and what their properties are.

The basic equation in multiple-factor theory, in matrix form, is $Z = FC$, where Z is a matrix of test scores, of order n by N, where N individuals have all taken n different tests. Z indicates that the scores are in standard form, that is, each element $z = (X - \overline{X})/s_x$, where X is a "raw" score on an arbitrary scale, $\overline{X}$ is the mean of the raw scores in the sample of N individuals, and s_x is the standard deviation. In the basic equation, F stands for the "complete factor matrix," which is of order n by $(r + n)$, where r is the number of *common* factors. The addition of n columns indicates that there are n *specific* factors or components, one for each test. In this matrix, f_{ij} is the loading of weight for test I in connection with factor J. C is of the order $(r + n)$ by N and represents the scores of N individuals on $(r + n)$ factors. The basic equation means that for each individual his standard score z_{ij} in a particular test is a weighted sum of his $(r + n)$ factor scores, each factor score also in standard form. An assumption for this form of the equation is that the factors are orthogonal (uncorrelated) variables.

The factor-analysis problem is to derive the matrix of common-factor loadings, A, given the score matrix for N individuals in n tests. The interest is in only the r common factors. The analysis ordinarily starts with intercorrelations among the n tests. The reduced (specifics ignored) intercorrelation matrix R is mathematically related to the factor matrix A by the equation $R = AA'$, where A represents only the common-factor components in F, and A' is the transpose of A. R can be computed from empirical data by the equation $R = ZZ'/N$. Starting with the computed correlation matrix R, the problem is to find the common-factor matrix A. Methods for accomplishing this operation are described by Harman (1967).

Very rarely, indeed, does anyone using the multiple-factor approach find and report a g factor. The reason is that there are too many zero correlations among tests of intellectual qualities, where one genuine zero correlation would be sufficient to disallow a g factor that is supposed to be universal. My examination of more than 7000 intercorrelations, among tests in the intellectual category, showed at least 17 percent of them to be acceptable as zero correlations (Guilford, 1964). The multiple factors usually found are each commonly restricted to only a few tests, where we may ignore factor loadings less than .30 as being insignificant, following common practice.

Discovery of Multiple Abilities

Only a few events in discovering factors by the Thurstone approach will be mentioned. In Thurstone's first major study (Thurstone, 1938) as many as nine common factors were thought to be sufficiently interpretable psychologically to justify calling them "primary mental abilities." A factor is interpreted intuitively in terms of the apparent human resource needed to do well in the set of tests loaded strongly together on the mathematical factor. A distinction between mathematical factors and psychological factors is important. Surface features of the tests in the set may differ, but examinees have to perform well in some unique way in all of them. For example, Thurstone designated some of the abilities as being visual-perceptual, inductive, deductive, numerical, spatial, and verbal. Two others dealt with rote memory and word fluency. Thurstone and his students followed his 1938 analysis with others that revealed a few additional kinds of abilities.

Another major source of identified intellectual abilities was the research of aviation psychologists in the U.S. Army Air Force during World War II (Guilford & Lacey, 1947). More important than the outcome of adding to the number of intellectual abilities that called for recognition was the fact that where Thurstone had found one spatial ability, there proved to be at least three, one of them being recognized as spatial orientation and another as spatial visualization. Where Thurstone had found an inductive ability, there were three reasoning abilities. Where Thurstone had found one memory ability, there were three, including visual memory. In some of these cases a Thurstone factor turned out to be a confounding of two or more separable abilities, separable when more representative tests for each factor were analyzed together and when allowance was made for a sufficient number of factors. In other cases, new varieties of tests were explored—new memory tests, space tests, and reasoning tests.

The third major event was in the form of a program of analyses conducted in the Aptitudes Research Project at the University of Southern California since 1949, in which attention was first concentrated on tests in the provisional categories of reasoning, creative thinking, planning, evaluation, and problem-solving. Nearly 20 years later, the number of separate intellectual abilities has increased to about 80, with at least 50 percent more predicted by a comprehensive, unified theory. The remainder of this article is mainly concerned with that theory.

The Structure-of-Intellect Model

Two previous attempts to put the known intellectual abilities into logical schema had been made by Burt (1949) and Vernon (1950), with similar results. In both cases the models were of hierarchical form, reminiscent of the Linnaeus taxonomic model for the animal kingdom. Following the British tradition of emphasis upon g, which was placed at the apex of the system, there were broad subdivisions under g and under each subdivision some subsubcategories, on down to abilities that are regarded as being very narrow in scope.

My first attempts (Guilford, 1956) found that the hierarchical type of model had to be discarded for several reasons. First, there had to be a rejection of g itself, for reasons mentioned earlier. Furthermore, most factors seemed to be of somewhat comparable level of generality, where generality is operationally defined in terms of the number and variety of tests found to represent each ability. There did appear to be categories of abilities, some concerned with discovery or recognition of information, memory for information, productive thinking, and evaluation, with a number of abilities in each category, but there are other ways of organizing categories of abilities. The most decisive observation was that there were a number of parallels between abilities, in terms of their common features.

Some examples of parallels in abilities will help. Two parallel abilities differ in only one respect. There was known to be an ability to see relations between perceived, visual figures, and a parallel ability to see relations between concepts. An example of a test item in the first case would be seeing that one figure is the lower-left half of another. An item in the second case might require seeing that the words "bird" and "fly" are related as object and its mode of locomotion. The ability to do the one kind of item is relatively independent of the ability to do the other, the only difference being that of kind of information—concrete or perceived in the one case and abstract or conceived in the other.

For a pair of abilities differing in another way, the kind of information is the same for both. One of the abilities pertains to *seeing* class ideas. Given the set of words *footstool, lamp, rocker, television,* can the examinee grasp the essence of the nature of the class, as shown by his naming the class, by putting another word or two into it, or by recognizing its name among four alternatives? The ability pertains to discovery or recognition of a class concept. In another kind of test we ask the examinee to *produce* classes by partitioning a list of words into mutually exclusive sets, each with a different class concept. These two abilities are relatively independent. The one involves a process of understanding and the other a process of production. These processes involve two psychologically different kinds of operation.

A third kind of parallel abilities has pairs that are alike in kind of information involved and in kind of operation. Suppose we give the examinee this kind of test item: "Name as many objects as you can that are both edible and white." Here we have given the specifications for a class, and the examinee is to produce from his memory store some class members. The ability involved was at first called "ideational fluency." The more of appropriate members the examinee can produce in a limited time, the better his score. In a test for a parallel ability, instead of producing single words the examinee is to produce a list of sentences. To standardize his task for testing purposes and to further control his efforts, we can give him the initial letters of four words that he is to give in each of a variety of sentences, for example: W____ c____ s____ d____. Without using any word twice, the examinee might say, "Why can't Susan dance?," "Workers could seldom deviate," or "Weary cats sense destruction." The ability was first called "expressional fluency." The kind of information in both these tests is conceptual, and the kind of operation is production.

But the kind of operation in the last test is different from that for the classifying test mentioned before. In the classifying test, the words given to the examinee are so selected that they form a unique set of classes and he is so told. The operation is called "convergent production." In the last two tests under discussion, there are many possible responses and the examinee produces alternatives. The operation is called "divergent production." It involves a broad searching or scanning process. Both operations depend upon retrieval of information from the examinee's memory store.

The difference between the two abilities illustrated by the last two tests is in the nature of the things produced. In the first case they are single words that stand for single objects or concepts. The thing produced, the "product," is a *unit* of information. In the second case, the product is an organized sequence of words, each word standing for a concept or unit. This kind of product is given the name of "system."

In order to take care of all such parallels (and the number increased as time went on and experience grew), a matrix type of model seemed called for in the manner of Mendeleev's table of chemical elements. The differences in the three ways indicated—operation (kind of processing of information), content (kind of information), and product (formal aspect of information)—called for a three-dimensional model. Such a model has been called "morphological" (Zwicky, 1957). The model as finally completed and presented in 1959 (Guilford, 1959) is illustrated in Fig. 1. It has five categories of operation, four categories of content, and six categories of product.

It is readily seen that the theory calls for $5 \times 4 \times 6$, or 120, cubical cells in the model, each one representing a unique ability, unique by virtue of its peculiar conjunction of operation, content, and product. The reader has already been introduced to three kinds of operation: cognition (discovery, recognition, comprehension), divergent production, and convergent production. The memory operation involves putting information into the memory store and must be distinguished from the memory store itself. The latter underlies all the operations; all the abilities depend upon it. This is the best logical basis for believing that the abilities increase with experience, depending upon the kinds of experience. The evaluation operation deals with assessment of information, cognized or produced, determining its goodness with respect to adopted (logical) criteria, such as identity and consistency.

The distinction between figural and semantic (conceptual) contents was mentioned earlier. The distinguishing of symbolic information from these two came later. Symbolic information is presented in tests in the form of letters or numbers, ordinarily, but other signs that have only "token" value or meaning can be used.

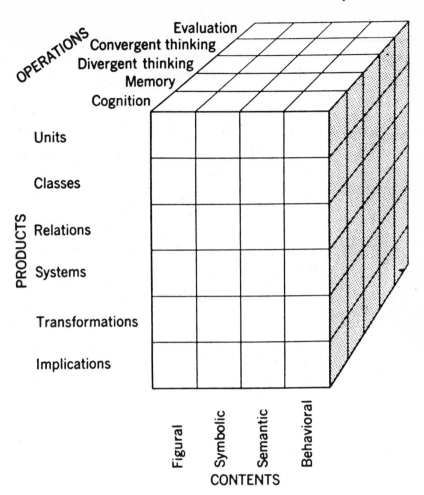

Figure 1. The structure-of-intellect model.

The category of behavioral information was added on the basis of a hunch; no abilities involving it were known to have been demonstrated when it was included. The basis was E. L. Thorndike's suggestion (Thorndike, 1920) many years ago that there is a "social intelligence," distinct from what he called "concrete" and "abstract" intelligences. It was decided to distinguish "social intelligence" on the basis of kind of information, the kind that one person derives from observation of the behavior of another. Subsequent experience has demonstrated a full set of six behavioral-cognition abilities as predicted by the model, and a current analytical investigation is designed to test the part of the model that includes six behavioral-divergent-production abilities. In a test for cognition of behavioral systems, three parts of a four-part cartoon are given in each item, with four alternative parts that are potential completions. The examinee has to size up each situation, and the sequence of events, correctly in order to select the appropriate part. As a test for divergent production of behavioral systems, the examinee is given descriptions of three characters, for example, a jubilant man, an angry woman, and a sullen boy, for which he is to construct a number of alternative story plots involving the characters and their moods, all stories being different.

The reader has already encountered four kinds of products: units, classes, relations, and systems, with illustrations. The other two kinds of products are transformations and implications. Transformations include any kind of change: movement in space, rearrangement or regrouping of letters in words or factoring or simplifying an equation, redefining a concept or adapting an object or part of an object to a new use, revising one's interpretation of another person's action, or rearranging events in a story. In these examples the four kinds of content are involved, from figural to behavioral, illustrating the fact that all six kinds of products apply in every content category.

Implied information is suggested by other information. Foresight or prediction depends upon extrapolating from given information to some naturally following future condition or event. If I make this move in chess, my knight will be vulnerable. If I divide by X, I will have a simpler expression. If it rains tonight, my tent will leak. If I whistle at that girl, she will turn her head. The "If . . . then" expression well describes an instance of implication, the implication actually being the thing implied.

Some Consequences of the Theory

The most immediate consequence of the theory and its model has been its heuristic value in suggesting where to look for still undemonstrated abilities. The modus operandi of the Aptitudes Research Project from the beginning has been to hypothesize certain kinds of abilities, to create new types of tests that should emphasize each hypothesized ability, then factor analyze to determine whether the hypothesis is well supported. With hypotheses generated by the model, the rate of demonstration of new abilities has been much accelerated.

At the time this article was written, of 24 hypothesized abilities in the category of cognition, 23 had been demonstrated. Of 24 expected memory abilities, 14 were recognized. In the other operation categories of divergent production, convergent production, and evaluation, 16, 13, and 13 abilities, respectively, were accounted for, and in all these categories 17 other hypotheses are under investigation. These studies should bring the number of demonstrated abilities close to the century mark. It is expected that the total will go beyond the 120 indicated by the model, for some cells in the figural and symbolic columns already have more than one ability each. These proliferations arise from the differences in kind of sensory input. Most known abilities are represented by tests with visual input. A few have been found in tests with auditory input, and possibly one involving kinesthetic information. Each one can also be placed in the model in terms of its three sources of specification—operation, content, and product.

Having developed a comprehensive and systematic theory of intelligence, we have found that not the least of its benefits is an entirely new point of view in psychology generally, a view that has been called "operational-informational." I have elaborated a great deal upon this view elsewhere (Guilford, 1967). Information is defined for psychology as that which the organism discriminates. Without discrimination there is no information. This far, there is agreement with the conception of information as viewed by communication engineers, but beyond this point we part company. Psychological discriminations are most broadly and decisively along the lines of kinds of content and kinds of products, from which arise hiatuses between intellectual abilities. Further discriminations occur, of course, within the sphere of a single ability. I have proposed that the 4×6 intersections of the informational categories of the SI (structure of intellect) model provide a psychoepistemology, with 24 subcategories of basic information. I have also proposed that the six product categories—units, classes, relations, systems, transformations, and implications—provide the basis for a psycho-logic (Guilford, 1967, Chapt. 10). Although most of these terms are also concepts in modern logic, a more complete representation appears in mathematics.

The operational-informational view regards the organism as a processor of information, for which the modern, high-speed computer is a good analogy. From this point of view, computer-simulation studies make sense. In addition to trying to find out how the human mind works by having computers accomplish the same end results, however, it might be useful, also, to determine how the human mind accomplishes its ends, then to design the computer that performs the same operations. Although a psychology based upon the SI concepts is much more complicated than the stimulus-response model that became traditional, it is still parsimonious. It certainly has the chance of becoming more adequate. The structure of intellect, as such, is a taxonomic model; it provides fruitful concepts. For theory that accounts for behavior, we need operational models, and they can be based on SI concepts. For example, I have produced such a model for problem-solving (Guilford, 1967, Chapt. 14).

There is no one problem-solving ability. Many different SI abilities may be drawn upon in solving a problem, depending upon the nature of the problem. Almost always there are cognitive operations (in understanding the nature of the problem), productive operations (in generating steps toward solution), and evaluative operations (in checking upon both understanding and production). Memory operations enter in, to keep a record of information regarding previous steps, and the memory store underlies all.

There is something novel about producing solutions to problems, hence creative thinking is involved. Creative thinking depends most clearly upon divergent-production operations on the one hand, and on transformations on the other. Thus, these two categories have unique roles in creative problem-solving. There is accordingly no one unique ability to account for creative potential. Creative production depends upon the area in which one works, whether it is in pictorial art, music, drama, mathematics, science, writing, or management. In view of the relative independence of the intellectual abilities, unevenness of status in the various abilities within the same person should be the rule rather than the exception. Some individuals can excel in more than one art form, but few excel in all, as witness the practice of having multiple creative contributors to a single motion picture.

The implications of all this for education are numerous. The doctrine that intelligence is a unitary something that is established for each person by heredity and that stays fixed through life should be summarily banished. There is abundant proof that greater intelligence is associated with increased education. One of education's major objectives should be to increase the stature of its recipients in intelligence, which should now mean stature in the various intellectual abilities. Knowing what those abilities are, we not only have more precise goals but also much better conceptions of how to achieve those goals.

For much too long, many educators have assumed, at least implicitly, that if we provide individuals with information they will also be able to use that information productively. Building up the memory store is a necessary condition for productive thinking, but it is not a sufficient condition, for productive abilities are relatively independent of cognitive abilities. There are some revealing findings on this point (Guilford & Hoepfner, 1966). In a sample of about 200 ninth-grade students, IQ measurements were available and also the scores on a large number of tests of various divergent-production (DP) abilities. Table 1 shows a scatter diagram with plots of DP scores as a function of IQ. The striking feature of this diagram pertains to the large proportion of high-IQ students who had low, even some very low, DP scores. In general, IQ appears to set a kind of upper limit upon DP performance but not a lower limit. The same kind of result was true for most other DP tests.

TABLE 1   *Scatterplot of Expressional Fluency (one aspect of divergent production) scores in relation to CTMM (California Test of Mental Maturity) IQ.*

DP score	Intelligence quotient								
	60-69	70-79	80-89	90-99	100-109	110-119	120-129	130-139	140-149
50-59						1	3		1
40-49						2	4	1	
30-39			2	3	4	11	17	6	2
20-29			1	3	10	23	13	7	
10-19	1	5	3	9	11	19	7	3	1
0- 9	1	3	1	4	10	11	2		

On the basis of present information, it would be best to regard each intellectual ability of a person as a somewhat generalized skill that has developed through the circumstances of experience, within a certain culture, and that can be further developed by means of the right kind of exercise. There may be limits to abilities set by heredity, but it is probably safe to say that very rarely does an individual really test such limits. There is much experimental evidence, rough though it may be, that exercise devoted to certain skills involved in creative thinking is followed by increased capability (Guilford, 1967, p. 336). Although special exercises have their demonstrated value, it is probably better to have such exercises worked into teaching, whatever the subject, where there are opportunities. Informing individuals regarding the nature of their own intellectual resources, and how they enter into mental work, has also been found beneficial.

There is not space to mention many other problems related to intelligence—its growth and its decline, its relation to brain anatomy and brain functions, and its role in learning. All these problems take on new aspects, when viewed in terms of the proposed frame of reference. For too long, many investigators have been handicapped by using a single, highly ambiguous score to represent what is very complex but very comprehensible.

Without the multivariate approach of factor analysis, it is doubtful whether any comprehensive and detailed theory of the human intellect, such as the model in Fig. 1, could have been achieved. Application of the method uncovers the building blocks, which are well obscured in the ongoing activities of daily life. Although much has already been done by other methods to show the relevance and fruitfulness of the concepts generated by the theory (Guilford, 1967), there is still a great amount of developmental work to be done to implement their full exploitation, particularly in education.

Summary

In this limited space I have attempted to convey information regarding progress in discovering the nature of human intelligence. By intensive factor-analytic investigation, mostly within the past 20 years, the multifactor picture of intelligence has grown far beyond the expectations of those who have been most concerned. A comprehensive, systematic theoretical model known as the "structure of intellect" has been developed to put rationality into the picture.

The model is a cubical affair, its three dimensions representing ways in which the abilities differ from one another. Represented are: five basic kinds of operation, four substantive kinds of information or "contents," and six formal kinds of information or "products," respectively. Each intellectual ability involves a unique conjunction of one kind of operation, one kind of content, and one kind of product, all abilities being relatively independent in a population, but with common joint involvement in intellectual activity.

This taxonomic model has led to the discovery of many abilities not suspected before. Although the number of abilities is large, the 15 category constructs provide much parsimony. They also provide a systematic basis for viewing mental operations in general, thus suggesting new general psychological theory.

The implications for future intelligence testing and for education are numerous. Assessment of intellectual qualities should go much beyond present standard intelligence tests, which seriously neglect important abilities that contribute to problem-solving and creative performance in general. Educational philosophy, curriculum-building, teaching procedures, and examination methods should all be improved by giving attention to the structure of intellect as the basic frame of reference. There is much basis for expecting that various intellectual abilities can be improved in individuals, and the procedures needed for doing this should be clear.

22 | Are I.Q. Tests Intelligent?*

Raymond B. Cattell

The dilemma of the Mensa Society dramatizes the current upheaval in intelligence testing. Roughly three out of four of the prospective members selected on one kind of intelligence test failed to be selected by a second test, and three out of four of those chosen by the second type could not meet the standards of the first test. This international society, which limits entry to those at the 98th percentile or above in intelligence, was forced to make a policy decision on *which* kind of intelligence the society would consider.

Present controversy on the meaning of intelligence and of intelligence testing has erupted only in the past decade. It centers on whether there is a single factor of general intelligence and on the adequacy of present tests to measure it. My research indicates that there are two kinds of intelligence, fluid and crystallized, and that the former, which is independent of culture, can be measured as accurately as the latter.

To grasp what we now know of intelligence and the devices which attempt to measure it, one first must understand the background of the current dispute. In the first decade of this century, Charles Spearman brought to a field crowded with untutored, arbitrary, and generally naive definitions of intelligence, the theory of the "g" factor, a unitary, objectively defined, general-intelligence factor. For 50 years, Spearman's g factor has remained the only firm basis for the objective determination and measurement of intelligence.

This factor was defined by weights applied to different kinds of intellectual performances, and its existence was proved by the peculiar form of correlation coefficients that appeared in correlations of ability measurement. If correlation coefficients show that four abilities, a, c, e, and g, are mutually positively related when measured over a group of 300 people, whereas the correlations are essentially zero on the abilities b, d, and f, we can assume some underlying unity behind a, c, e, and g.

*Reprinted from *Psychology Today* Magazine, March, 1968. Copyright © Communications/Research/Machines, Inc.

There is no reason that there could not be two, three, or more such correlation clusters in a large group of abilities. But Spearman argued that the squared table of all possible correlations among a widely sampled set of abilities had a uniform slope which pointed to the existence of only one factor. To support this argument, he went beyond correlation clusters and developed factor analysis—a means of discovering the influences behind clusters.

Factor analysis is a method of calculating—from the various correlation coefficients of measured individual performances—the number and the general natures of the influences that account for observed relations. Through such an analysis, Spearman found the tests that bore most heavily on his general intelligence factor were those that had to do with reasoning and judgment. He therefore defined this factor as the capacity to educe relations and correlates.

Factor analysis also tells us how much of the individual variation in some particular performance is accounted for by each of the several factors that combine to produce that kind of behavior. Spearman concluded that g had about a 9:1 ratio to special abilities in determining mathematical learning rate; about 7:1 in accounting for the size of one's properly used vocabulary; about 2:1 in determining musical ability; and about 1:4 in judging drawing ability.

Decades later, Louis Thurstone developed a multiple-factor analysis. This improvement over Spearman's methods led to Thurstone's discovery and definition of a dozen primary abilities, among them verbal comprehension, word fluency, number space, and reasoning. Neither g nor the I.Q. were invalidated by Thurstone's work. On the contrary, advances in factor analysis rectified the only known statistical and structural flaw in Spearman's work. General intelligence now emerged from multiple-factor analysis as a single *second-order factor,* based on the intercorrelation among primary factors. The general intelligence concept was strengthened, for the pyramids of primary factors provided a far more reliable base then did the grains of innumerable small variables.

The question of how Thurstone's primary abilities grew out of Spearman's general ability remained unanswered, but researchers tended to neglect its importance. Instead of investigating the natural structure of abilities, the experts devised tests to fill the holes in a subjective framework. And so, for 30 years, there has been only trivial consolidation in this field, with a consequent hardening of attitudes and custom among professional intelligence testers.

As one who investigated with both Spearman and Thurstone, I at first was as much disturbed as intrigued when I thought I saw flaws in their monolithic structure. The first signs appeared in data on the second-order analysis of primary abilities. There was evidence that *two* general factors rather than one were involved. On rather slender evidence, I put forward in 1940 the theory of two *g*'s. Those original disquieting conceptions since have been strengthened by the accumulation of evidence.

The breadth of a factor and the number of factors depend upon what tests an experimenter uses to gather his data. From the 20 primary abilities surveyed by John French, John Horn obtained some four or five broad abilities, such as fluid intelligence, crystallized intelligence, speed, and visualization. But the broadest of all such abilities, and the ones with a semantic claim to the label "intelligence," are fluid and crystallized.

Crystallized general ability, "g_c," shows itself in judgmental skills that have been acquired by cultural experience: vocabulary, good use of synonyms, numerical skills, mechanical knowledge, a well-stocked memory, and even habits of logical reasoning. G_c is high on the subtests that traditionally have been built into intelligence tests: vocabulary size, analogies, and classifications involving cultural knowledge of objects in the problem. Crystallized ability stretches across the whole range of cultural acquisitions. Mechanical knowledge—which is negligible or even negative on fluid ability—has a measurable effect on crystallized ability.

Tests of fluid ability "g_f," have little relation to a well-stocked memory. They are culture-fair perceptual and performance tests and those specially developed tests of judgment and reasoning which have been considered relatively culture free. They involve solutions to tests of classifications, analogies, matrices, topology, and problems that do not involve much educational acquisition. Fluid ability does have a role in numerical reasoning and even in verbal skills. It is fairly powerful in spatial reasoning and very powerful in inductive reasoning. (See Table 1)

The difference between fluid and crystallized general abilities becomes apparent when the intellectual responses of two persons who contrast in them are described. To find a person high in fluid ability but low in crystallized, we should have to take someone who accidentally has missed schooling. I have measured deck-hands and farmers who scored much higher than average professors in fluid ability but who acquired no comparable level of crystallized ability because they had not systematically applied their fluid intelligence to what is usually called culture. Such men will astonish you in a game of chess, or by solving a wire puzzle with which you have struggled in vain, or in swift insights into men and motives. But their vocabularies may be arrested at a colloquial level, their knowledge of history negligible, and they never may have encountered algebra or geometry. These men often excel at the strategy of games, and one suspects they are naturally good soldiers. Lord Fisher, who

TABLE 1   *Fluid and Crystallized General Ability Factors at Various Ages. Crystallized general ability shows itself in those judgmental skills dependent upon cultural experience, while fluid ability affects tests unrelated to well-stocked memory. Flexibility is distinct from either g_c or g_f. Note the consistent level of g_f scores throughout all the age groups.*

Primary Abilities of Specific Batteries	Research I: Boys (57) and Girls (5) of 6½ Years Old		Research II: Boys (151) and Girls (154) of 9, 10, & 11 Years Old		Research III: Boys and Girls (277) of 12 & 13 Years Old		Research IV: Men and Women (297) Adult Range	
	g_f	g_c	g_f	g_c	g_f	g_c	g_f	g_c
Verbal	-17	74	22	63	15	46	10	69
Spatial			73	03	32	14	30	-07
Reasoning	10	72			08	50	23	30
Number	43	49	47	35	05	59	24	29
Fluency					07	10	-03	25
Series: Culture Fair					35	23		
Classification: Culture Fair	58*	-11*	78*	09*	63	-02	48*	-08*
Matrices: Culture Fair					50	10		
Topology: Culture Fair					51	09		
Perceptual Speed							20	06
Flexibility							-03	03
Induction							55	12
Intellectual Speed							51	10
Mechanical Information							-15	48
Ego Strength	-07	-09					01	43
Self Sentiment							01	43
Super Ego								
Surgency								
Anxiety	10	-33	04	-04			-05	-26

192

designed the Dreadnought battleship, said, "In war you need surprise." Surprise bursts from situations in which crystallized intelligence is useless. Napoleon claimed that he would make his despairing opponents "burn their books on tactics." The characteristic of fluid intelligence is that it leads to perception of complex relationships in new environments.

The individual with a high level of crystallized intelligence has different capacities. He will have learned many intelligent responses to problem situations. He will recognize an engineering problem as requiring solution by differential calculus, and he will diagnose a defective sentence by pointing to a dangling participle. He could not have acquired these skills, however, unless he had the fluid ability to see them.

To illustrate a case where crystallized ability is clearly higher than fluid ability, we must take either a person in whom there has been some recession of fluid ability, as through aging or brain damage, or a person who has been overeducated for his ability—say, someone like Sheridan's Mrs. Malaprop, taught a bigger vocabulary than natural judgment permits handling.

Crystallized and fluid intelligence abilities could not be isolated until technical progress in factor analytic experiments made their recognition possible. These two structures have been confirmed repeatedly by researchers over the whole age range, from five to 50.

Fluid and crystallized ability factors are positively correlated. According to the theory of two broad intelligences, fluid intelligence is a general relation-perceiving capacity, independent of sensory area, and it is determined by the individual's endowment in cortical, neurological-connection count development. It is a broad factor because such integrating power can be brought to bear in almost any perceptual or reasoning area. Crystallized ability, on the other hand, appears as a related circle of abilities—verbal, numerical, reasoning—that normally are taught at school. The extent to which an individual takes or leaves what he is taught depends on his fluid ability, on his years of formal education, and on his motivation to learn. Thus, crystallized general ability reflects both the neurological integrative potential of the individual and his fortune in cultural experience.

Crystallized ability is not identical with scholastic achievement. Many scholastic skills depend largely on rote memory, whereas what factor analysis shows is crystallized ability in that section of school learning involving complex judgmental skills that have been acquired by the application of fluid ability. (See Figure 1)

Once these two general abilities are located and independently measured, further distinguishing characteristics appear. The age curve of growth for the two abilities turns out to be quite different. Fluid ability follows a biological

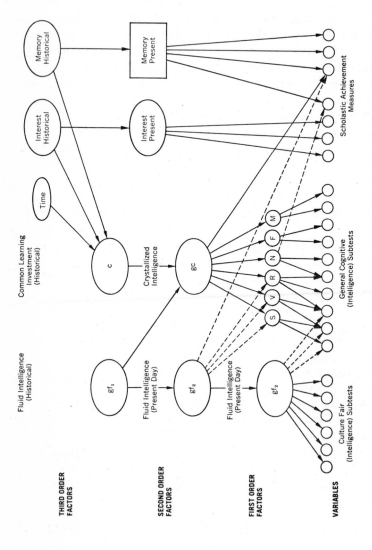

Figure 1. Causal Relations Between Fluid and Crystallized Ability Factors. Scores on the general intelligence subtests and on scholastic achievement measures are the result of time, interest, memory and both fluid and crystallized intelligence. Arrows indicate the direction of influence and solid arrows show major lines of influence. Note the lack of other influence on culture fair subtests.

growth curve and approaches a plateau at about 14 years, whereas crystallized ability shows an increase to 16, 18, and beyond. The evidence points to some steady decline in fluid intelligence after about 22 years of age, but crystallized intelligence keeps its level as far into later years as adequate samples have been taken. (See Figure 2)

The standard deviation of the calculated I.Q.—mental age divided by actual age—is almost exactly 50 per cent greater for fluid than for crystallized ability, 24 points instead of 16 points. Socio-educational research might determine whether arranging brighter and duller streams of classroom instruction would permit more divergence of crystallized I.Q.

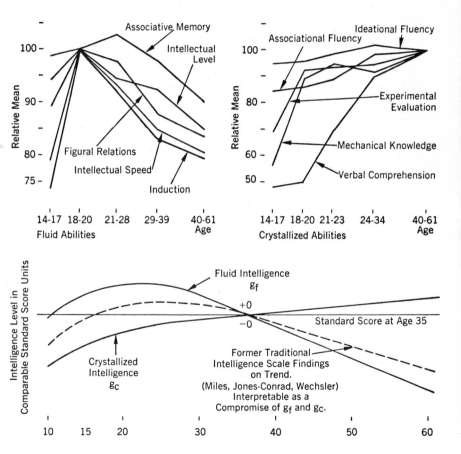

Figure 2. Age Curves Compared for Fluid and Crystallized General Ability and Traditional Tests.

There are substantial indications that fluid and crystallized intelligence respond differently to brain damage. Localized injury may produce localized loss of skills, while leaving other abilities untouched. By the nature of fluid ability, an impairment in any cortical locality should produce some loss of general fluid-ability performance.

A pilot study on nature-nurture ratios suggests that heredity bears a greater relation to fluid than to crystallized intelligence. Tentative estimates of relative variance are 90 per cent for g_f and 70 per cent for g_c. An independent demonstration of the higher hereditary influence of fluid-ability levels has been given by John Loehlin, who compared the primary factor within pairs of both fraternal and identical twins. Verbal ability, fluency, and reasoning primaries naturally showed environmental influence, but a general genetic factor corresponding to fluid ability was apparent.

My own research and that of others indicates that day-to-day changes do occur in intelligence. Our subjective conviction that we are brighter on some days than we are on others is borne out by measures of g_f variability over time, as might be expected from the closer dependence of fluid intelligence upon total physiological efficiency.

Many of the puzzling phenomena in intelligence testing are explained if we consider that the traditional intelligence test actually is a mixture of fluid and crystallized factors. Discoveries of different ages for the end of intelligence growth, significant differences in the standard deviation of I.Q.'s, and different ratios of the weight of heredity and environment on the I.Q. all result from a confusion of the two factors in the usual intelligence test.

When I first called attention to the flaws in the general intelligence theory, I at once proceeded to investigate the correlations with the general fluid ability factor of a variety of "perceptual" tests. From my research came the culture fair intelligence test associated with present uses in cross-cultural studies and Head-start programs. But whatever its present practical importance, the origin of these culture fair tests was in the first place the theoretical goal of defining the new form of intelligence.

In our first attempt at developing a fluid-ability test appropriate to all cultures, I took such common elements as parts of the human body, sun, moon, rain and stars, as well as random blotches. But only the perceptual forms have been retained in later tests, for experiment has shown that these give accurate results. (See Figure 3)

In choosing test elements, the effect on the score of cultural experience can be reduced by taking either what is overlearned in all cultures or what is absolutely strange to all. Anything in between these extremes is bound to show the influence of the culture in the test scores. To take overlearned items

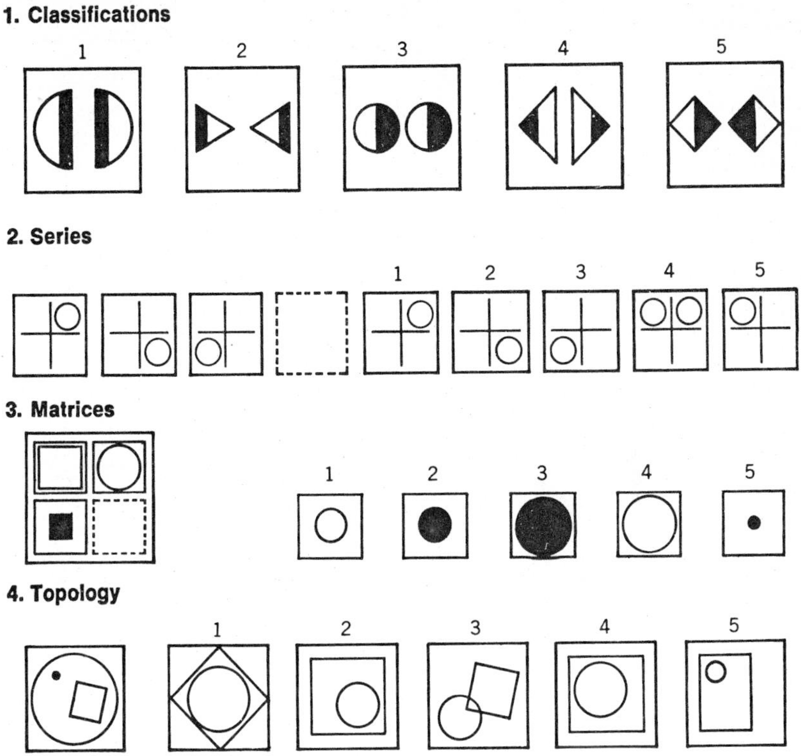

1. Classifications

2. Series

3. Matrices

4. Topology

Figure 3. Sample items from a Culture Fair Test.

1 Which one of these is different from the remaining four? (No. 3)
2 Which of 5 figures on right would properly continue 3 on left, i.e., fill blank? (No. 5)
3 Which of figures on right should go into square on left to make it look right? (No. 2)
4 At left, dot is outside the square and inside the circle. In which of the figures on the right could you put a dot outside the square and inside the circle? (No. 3)

is more practical, because valuable test time is wasted in getting responses on completely strange items.

To avoid pointless sociological arguments, we called fluid-ability measures culture *fair* rather than culture *free*. Objection from teachers to a culture-free concept arises from confusion between the cultural familiarity and test sophistication effects on test scores. *All* tests, culture fair tests included, are susceptible to test sophistication, and scores may continue to improve for some four to six retests. Scores increase due to familiarity with instructions, with layout, with timing, and with the tricks any good person being tested can learn. Studies by Sarason, Feingold, and me have shown that practice in the culture-fair type of spatial and analogies perception produced no real gain, unlike training in the verbal and numerical fields that dominate the traditional intelligence test. But with subjects unused to paper-and-pencil tests, and with subjects from other cultures, it would be ideal always to repeat testing several times and to throw away the results of the first three or four encounters.

The culture-fair concept does not imply that no significant differences ever should be found between different populations living in different cultures or subcultures or social classes. The bright people in most societies tend to migrate to higher socio-economic levels. The correlation of .20 to .25 between fluid ability measures and social status presumably is a measure of the relation of real ability to status, but the correlation of .38 found with

TABLE 2   *Cultural Differences and Culture-Fair Scores. That culture is no barrier when a culture-fair test is used shows in American and Chinese scores on the same test. The correlation between g_f and social status measures the relation of real ability to the status.*

1. *Comparison of American and Chinese Children, 10 Years of Age, by IPAT Culture Fair Scale 2 (Rodd, 1959).*

	American (1007)		Chinese (Hong Kong) (1007)	
	Mean	Stand. Dev.	Mean	Stand. Dev.
Culture-Fair Form 2A	24.10	6.66	24.04	5.70

2. *Comparison of American and Chinese College Students (Mean Age 18 yrs.) by IPAT Culture-Fair Scale 3(Rodd, 1959).*

	American (1100)		Chinese			
			Taiwanese(765)		Mainland Chinese(525)	
	Mean	Stand. Dev.	Mean	Stand. Dev.	Mean	Stand. Dev.
Culture-Fair Form 3A	21.99	4.50	21.99	4.50	22.88	4.47
Culture-Fair Form 3B	26.90	4.50	26.95	4.47	27.23	4.53

3. *Correlation of Culture-Fair and Traditional Tests with Social Status (McArthur and Elley, 1963).*

Traditional Test (California Test of Mental Maturity)	+0.38
Traditional Test (Modified) (Lorge-Thorndike)	+0.27
Fluid Ability (IPAT Culture Fair) (On 271 12-and 13-Year-Olds)	+0.24

traditional intelligence tests represents also the scholastic gain of those with the luck to be born into more-educated families.

Where ulterior evidence suggests that peoples *are* equally gifted, a culture-fair test must show absolutely no difference of score despite profound differences of culture. No differences have been demonstrated on the culture-fair scales among American, British, German, French, and Italian samples. A more severe test was made by William Rodd, who compared Chinese (Taiwanese) and American school children and university students on identically printed culture-fair tests. The raw scores are identical to three significant figures for Midwestern American and Taiwanese school children. American college students do not differ from the Taiwanese, but there is a significant difference between Taiwanese and mainland Chinese, which could be the result of differences in methods of student selection. (See Table 2)

But testing does suggest that significant mean population differences *can* exist. Samples have shown higher means in the south than in the north of Japan, in the north than in the south of Italy, and in New Zealand migrants as compared with unselected British Isles stock. Further research might develop a world map of intelligence resources.

For school-age children, when intelligence tests are most used, the correlation between g_f and g_c scores is positive and substantial. It will probably become even higher if regular school attendance becomes universal and methods used in more efficient school systems become uniform. From this high correlation, casual administrators may argue that one kind of test—the old kind, of course—is enough. Indeed, hard-headed realism may assert that the traditional I.Q. test is preferable, because the g_c test predicts this or next year's scholastic performance slightly but systematically better than does the g_f test. (See Table 3)

But if a maximum prediction of next year's academic achievement were all that one desired, one would not use an intelligence test at all! For a higher correlation can be obtained from *this* year's grades, or from a proper combination of intelligence, personality, and motivation measures, as our research has shown.

The purpose of an intelligence test is different. It should help us to understand the causes of a given person's good or poor grades or to predict what he will do in the future in radically changed circumstances. Over an interval of a year or so we can expect habits and situations and the momentum of interest to make scholastic performance *now* the best predictor of grades in the future. But when a person's life turns a corner, as when he goes from liberal education in the school to technical education in a career, the crystallized-ability measure may be quite misleading. A fluid-ability I.Q. from a culture-fair test is likely to be a better predictor of performance.

TABLE 3   Correlations of Fluid and Crystallized Intelligence Tests with other Measures. The validity in terms of general ability saturation is highest for the culture-fair scales, but correlation with school grades is higher when the traditional intelligence test is used.

	Validity General Factor	Correlation with School Total Achievement					Other Intelligence Tests		
		Marks by Teacher Amer. Chin.	Stand. Ach. Test	English Amer. Chin.	Reading	Math Amer. Chin.	Calif. Mental Verb.	Test of Maturity Numer.	Wisc. I.Q.
Fluid Abil. (IPAT Cult.-Fair Scale 2)	.79*	.34*	.35*		.52++				.72++
Fluid Abil. (IPAT Cult.-Fair Scale 3)	.78[0]	.35** .35**	.59 .49	.40 .30+		.64 47+	.42	.56	
Crystal. Abil. (Cal. Test Ment. Mat.)	.58*	.66* 0?	.65*	0?		0?			
Crystal. Abil. (Lorge-Thorndike)	.52*	.43* 0?	.35*	0?		0?			
Army Beta				.25		.34	.27	.58	
Henmon Nelson			.81						
Pintner					.85++				.80++

*McArthur & Elley, 271, 12 and 13 year olds
**Domino, 94 college students

+Rodd & Goodman (Atten. corrected on school test)
++79 children in Bridge Project School

[0]Bajard

The same principle holds if we compare children of fundamentally different backgrounds. The Binet in French, administered to a mixed group of 100 French, 100 American, and 100 Chinese children, would show a correlation of I.Q. with French language skills, but the Binet score would be no general predictor of language ability among the Americans and Chinese. In the same situation, a culture-fair test would correlate with the native-language performance about equally in each of the three language groups.

During the school years, culture-fair tests are both theoretically and practically useful, especially in localities with language or cultural differences. But the dual I.Q. becomes indispensable almost anywhere when testing adults. The two I.Q. values for a given person may be very different, and the kinds of prediction made from each will differ. Crystallized ability may remain steady or even climb, for it increases with age and experience, but fluid ability falls after age 22. A middle-aged man handles most situations in our culture more intelligently than he would have when he was 20, but if a younger and an older man were transferred to an absolutely new society, the probably higher fluid-intelligence level of the younger man would be likely to show itself. Where performance in radically different situations is involved, the man of 50 will perform very differently from what would be predicted for him on the basis of his g_c mental age. The g_f mental age would have predicted this difference.

Despite the tremendous accumulation of experience concerning intelligence testing between 10 and 20 years of age, there has been comparatively little over the 20- to 70-year range, and we know little about what happens to age trends, distribution, or sex differences of intelligence in that period.

Our society, which values high intelligence, must make some kind of policy decision on *which* kind of intelligence should be given emphasis in this period. A decision on culture-fair and traditional test usage becomes even more imperative for the psychologist whose testing helps determine jobs and clinical outcomes. As men leave school and go into their special occupational fields, the statistical general factor begins to disintegrate, or to persist only as an historical relic. Vocabulary tests for the average man reveal a distinct falling off in ability after school. And if women in middle age are tested by intelligence tests (at least as mostly designed by men), they undergo an apparent drop in crystallized ability not shown by men.

To continue to regard the traditional intelligence tests as a general intelligence measure when applied after the age of 20 is pure illusion. If a g_c score predicts relation-perceiving capacity in new fields, it does so indirectly by harking back to the fact that scholastic ability at 18 was a measure of g_f intelligence. If that happens not to be true for a person, or if such things as brain damage have occurred since, the g_c prediction can be badly in error.

The need for a dual I.Q. score is rooted not only in what happens to the man but in what happens to the culture. A comparison that I made of all 11-year-olds in a city of 300,000 before World War II with 11-year-olds in the same city after the war and 13 years later showed no trace of any significant difference on a culture-fair test. Yet Godfrey Thomson's comparisons on the British Binet at about the same period showed a very significant upward shift. Results in America by Frank Finch with various traditional crystallized-ability tests showed an even greater upward shift. The standardization of a traditional test becomes unanchored from the moment it is made, and it drifts in whatever direction the tide of educational investment happens to take. In this more prosperous age, the direction is upward. Since no such drift is demonstrable with culture-fair, fluid-ability measures, error of prediction is less flagrant.

New answers to educational, political, and social questions may be reached through culture-fair intelligence testing. Culture-fair tests are not toys for anthropologists to take to remote cultures. They need to be used here and now to open equal educational opportunity to all our subcultures of class and race.

23 | Intelligent Testing*[1]

Alexander G. Wesman

The nature of intelligence has been a favorite subject for contemplation and disputation for centuries—perhaps from the dawn of man as Homo sapiens. The topic is being studied and debated today by educators, sociologists, geneticists, neurophysiologists, and biochemists, and by psychologists specializing in various branches of the discipline. Despite this attention and effort, however—or perhaps *because* of it—there appears to be no more general agreement as to the nature of intelligence or the most valid means of measuring intelligence than was the case 50 years ago. Concepts of intelligence and the definitions constructed to enunciate these concepts abound by the dozens, if not indeed by the hundreds.

With so many diverse definitions of intelligence, it is perhaps not surprising that we cannot agree on how to measure intelligence. It is my conviction that much of the confusion which plagued us in the past, and continues to plague us today, is attributable to our ignoring two propositions which should be obvious:

1. Intelligence is an attribute, not an entity.
2. Intelligence is the summation of the learning experiences of the individual.

We have all too often behaved as though intelligence is a physical substance, like a house or an egg crate composed of rooms or cells; we might better remember that it is no more to be reified than attributes like beauty, or speed, or honesty. There are objects which are classifiable as beautiful; there are performances which may be characterized as speedy; there are behaviors which display honesty. Each of these is measurable, with greater or lesser objectivity. Because they can be measured, however, does not mean they are substances. We may agree with E. L. Thorndike that if something

---

*From Wesman, A. G. Intelligent testing. *American Psychologist,* 1968, **23**, 267-274, Copyright 1968 by the American Psychological Association, and reproduced by permission.
[1]Presidential Address presented to Division 5 at the meeting of the American Psychological Association, Washington, D.C., September 1967.

exists it can be measured; we need not accept the converse notion that if we can measure something it has existence as a substance.

Intelligence as here defined is a summation of learning experiences. The instances in which intelligent behavior is observed may be classified in various ways that appear to be logical or homogeneous, but they are individual instances all the same. Each instance represents a response the organism has learned; each learned response in turn predisposes the organism for learning additional responses which permit the organism to display new acts of intelligent behavior.

For our present purposes, it matters little whether we are more comfortable with stimulus-response bonds, with experience-producing drives, with imprinting, or with neuropsychological explanations of *how* or *why* learning occurs; whatever the learning theory, the fundamental principle is universal. We start with an organism which is subject to modification by interaction with the environment; as a product of that interaction, the organism has been modified. Further interaction involves a changed organism—one which is ready to interact with its environment in a new way.

Organisms may differ from one another in their susceptibility to modification. One organism may need a more potent stimulus to trigger reaction to the environment than does another. A particular organism may respond to a given class of stimuli more readily than it does to other kinds of stimuli. Organisms may differ from one another in their readiness to respond to different classes of stimuli. There may be important differences in the ability of organisms to modify their behavior in effective ways as a result of experience.

We may develop and investigate hypotheses as to whether such differences in response as are displayed arise from variations in neurological endowment or in conducive environment. All that we can be sure of, at least as of now, is that what we are dealing with is a response-capable organism which has been exposed to environmental stimuli, has interacted in some way with those stimuli, and has been modified thereby.

The bits or modules which constitute intelligence may be information or may be skill; i.e., they may be content or process. Furthermore, they are multidimensional, and some modules may have more dimensions than do others. Each module is subject to essential change as the individual is exposed to further learning experiences. Each act of learning serves to create new modules, change the existing ones, or both. Modules are not independent; rather, they may overlap with several or many other modules; thus, they are complex both in their number of dimensions and in their interrelationships. Even early percepts are rarely if ever simple. A toy ball when first seen has at least size, shape, and color; if it is touched, it has texture and hardness as well. Accordingly, few if any modules of learning are truly simple.

The whole of a person's intelligence at any given moment may well be thought of as an amorphous mass—not a regular geometric figure. Within this mass, modules may cluster with greater or lesser permanence, and may be organized along principles of relatedness. Thus, word knowledge may form a cluster—but the words of which one has knowledge will be components of other clusters as well. A pencil is an object one writes with; it has shape in common with other objects, it has function in common with pens and crayons, it produces color of varying intensity, it has a number property, it is usually associated with paper. The learned module "pencil" may thus be part of many clusters.

One need not posit that a learning module is permanent. It could, presumably, disappear entirely, although far more often we would expect it to undergo essential change by taking on a more complex character. This model does assume that higher learning depends so intimately and essentially on certain previous learnings that the more complex modules cannot exist without the antecedent modules from which they grew. For example, if the ability to subtract numbers should disappear, the ability to do long division could not remain unaffected. Thus, retention of learning is integral to the concept here proposed.

The simple-minded conceptualization outlined above may have horrified those of my colleagues who are even moderately sophisticated with respect to modern learning theories. To those colleagues I apologize, but I also beg their indulgence. Oversimplified as the conceptualization undoubtedly is, I believe it does no *essential* violence to any current theory; it has, I hope, the virtue of permitting a view of the organization of intelligence, and of the nature of the testing of intelligence, which may prove illuminating for several issues which confront us.

Issue I: The Classification of Ability Tests into Aptitude, Achievement and Intelligence Measures

As soon as we have agreed that what we know and what we can do intellectually is learned, the artificiality of the above classification becomes self-evident. Historically, we have recognized that what achievement tests measure is what the examinee has learned. We have been less ready to accord similar recognition to intelligence tests. In their case, we have too often behaved as though what these tests measure is somehow independent of the learning phenomenon. We have played the role of Aladdin seeking a magical lamp, complete with a genie ready to spring forth with full power to accomplish all sorts of wondrous things. We have pondered wistfully on the number of critical issues that would be resolved if we could only somehow measure "intelligence" separately from "achievement."

We have been similarly unrealistic in treating the concept of "aptitude." Our textbooks enunciate the distinction that aptitude tests measure what the individual *can* learn, while achievement tests measure what he *has* learned. Some of our leading theorists aggravate the confusion by ignoring the implications of their special use of the term. "Aptitude" is typically used in laboratory learning experiments as a matching or otherwise controlling variable; it is employed to assure that groups to be compared start the experiment as equal in initial ability. One gets a strong impression that the aptitude instrument is perceived as measuring the innate potential of the individual as distinguished from what is to be achieved (i.e., learned) in the experimental process. If learning theorists recognize that what they are calling "aptitude" (or, for that matter, "intelligence") is "previously learned" (as, clearly, at least some of them do), the artificiality of the distinction between "aptitude" or "intelligence" and "achievement" should be eminently apparent.

I wish that at least a few of my psychometric colleagues would leave off searching for *the* structure of intelligence, and devote their wisdom and energy to learning more about the learning process, and to teaching learning theorists about testing. I am convinced that both specialties would profit immeasurably from the cooperative enterprise. It is my strong impression that the inattention of the psychometrician to the facts of learning is matched fully by the unsophisticated treatment accorded to testing by many learning theorists.

All ability tests—intelligence, aptitude, and achievement—measure what the individual *has* learned—and they often measure with similar content and similar process. Let us take, for example, an item[2] such as this: A square and a rectangle have the same perimeter. The square has an area of 10,000 square feet. The rectangle has an area of 9,324 square feet. What are the dimensions of the rectangle?

This item would clearly be deemed appropriate whether it appeared in an achievement test in high school mathematics, a test of aptitude for mathematics, or the numerical portion of an "intelligence" test. I submit that a great many items can equally readily fit any of the three categories.

---

[2] This item was proposed by G. K. Bennett in another context as an example of an arithmetic problem which might be correctly answered by any of several methods.

Such justification as we have for our labeling system resides entirely in the *purpose* for which the test is used, not in the test document itself. If our intent is to discover how much the examinee has learned in a particular area, such as a school course, we may select items which probe for the distinctive learnings the schooling was intended to stimulate. We label the test an "achievement" test. If our intent is to predict what success an individual is likely to attain in learning a new language, or a new job, we seek those specific previous learnings the possession of which bodes favorably for that future learning, and we label the test an "aptitude" test or a "special aptitude test." If our intent is to predict future acquisition of learning over broad areas of environmental exposure, we seek those previous learnings the possession of which will be relevant to as many, and as important, future learning situations as we can anticipate. This test we label an "intelligence" test. The selection of test items or sample tasks for the three purposes may or may not differ; but in each instance what is measured is what was previously learned. We are not measuring different abilities; we are merely attending to different criteria. It is the *relevance* of the learnings we select for investigation that largely determines how we name our test, and whether we will succeed in our purpose.

Issue II: The Utility of Culture-Free and Culture-Fair Tests

The notion of relevance of previous learnings leads naturally to a consideration of some follies we have committed in the search for culture-free or culture-fair instruments. I do not wish to impugn the high social motives which stimulate the search for such devices; I do wish to question that such a search, in its usual setting, is sensible. A culture-free test would presumably probe learnings which had not been affected by environment; this is sheer nonsense. A culture-fair test attempts to select those learnings which are common to many cultures. In the search for experiences which are common to several different cultures or subcultures, the vital matter of relevance of the learning for our purpose is subordinated or ignored.

The implicit intent in the attempt to create culture-free or culture-fair tests is somehow to measure intelligence without permitting the effects of differential exposure to learning to influence scores. This contains the tacit assumption that "native intelligence" lies buried in pure form deep in the individual, and needs only to be uncovered by ingenious mining methods. If we recognize that intelligence comprises learning experiences, it becomes clear that our attempts are not ingenious, but ingenuous.

It is true that we can probe learnings that have occurred in nonverbal, nonnumerical domains. This means only that we can test selected aspects of intelligence. The question immediately arises of the relevance of these special domains to the kinds of learnings we will want to predict. The measurement purpose for which culture-fair tests are ordinarily developed is that of predicting academic or industrial performance. Most academic courses and most industrial jobs involve some use of verbal abilities. Since further learning is conditioned by relevant past learning, the individual who has developed more of the prerequisite ability inevitably has an advantage over the individual with less of the prerequisite ability. If we wish to predict whether an individual will profit appreciably from additional exposure to learning, our best predictor must be a measure which appraises what prerequisite learning he has acquired heretofore. Appropriate verbal abilities are more relevant to the largely verbal learning we usually wish to predict than other abilities are.

It has on occasion been suggested that tests be developed which sample the verbal skills or factual information which are peculiar to a given subculture. Such tests are proposed as a "fairer" measure of the "intelligence," or readiness to learn, of the members of that subculture. The response to this proposal is "readiness to learn *what?*" If our purpose is to distinguish members of that subculture from their peers with respect to how much of that special culture they have assimilated, such a test might well be useful. If, as is more likely the case, we wish to predict future learnings of the content of the more general culture (e.g., the so-called white, middle-class culture such as typifies what the majority of our schools are organized to transmit), tests designed for the subculture will be less relevant than those which sample from the general culture. This is not intended to imply that the members of the subculture *could* not learn what the schools as constituted are offering. It does emphasize that, at the moment at which we make our appraisal, what the individual has already learned from the general culture domain is the most significant information as to what he is then ready to learn. The less relevant the previous learnings we appraise, the more hazardous must be our predictions of future learnings.

As long as our educational system and our general culture are dependent on conventional verbal abilities, those who aspire to progress in that system and that culture will need to command those abilities. In a verbal society, verbal competence cannot sensibly be ignored.

Issue III: Is "Verbal Ability" Synonymous with "Intelligence"?

To say that we cannot afford to ignore learnings in relevant verbal areas when we are appraising "intelligence" does not imply that *only* the verbal domain is important. The development of tests of "general mental ability" which sample only the verbal domain implies that since verbal tests predict school criteria best, it is unnecessary to attend to other cognitive abilities the student has developed; in other words, that, in effect, "verbal ability" is synonymous with "intelligence." It would be most unfortunate if, consciously or unconsciously, we adopted this too narrow perspective.

That verbal tests are typically good predictors of grades in many academic courses is undeniable. *Why* this is the case warrants some thought. Is it because all, or even most, of what constitutes "intelligence" is represented by verbal ability? Certainly the chief symbol system of our society is verbal. Even when we deal with numerical, spatial, or figural problems we often transform them to verbal expressions. It is one thing, however, to recognize the involvement of verbal abilities in all kinds of learning experiences and quite another to grant them exclusive sovereignty over learning domains. Many domains require the possession of other abilities as well, but our appraisal methods are often inadequate to reveal that need. Because it is easier to employ verbal criteria, or more convenient—or because we have given insufficient thought to criterion validity—we predetermine the finding that verbal abilities dominate the scene.

A particularly revealing demonstration of this phenomenon came to the attention of the authors of the Differential Aptitude Tests some years ago. Grades in an auto mechanics course were found to be better predicted by the Verbal Reasoning test of the DAT than by the Mechanical Reasoning test. We had the unusual good fortune of having access to further information about the course. We discovered that early in the course the teacher had been called from the room for almost a half hour. In his absence, the students had disobeyed his instructions not to fool around with the automobile motors. To let the punishment fit the crime, he conducted the rest of the course almost entirely by lecturing, giving the students minimum opportunity for actually working with the engines. That grades in a course taught by lecture and evaluated by a written test should be best predicted by a verbal test is not too surprising!

An illustration such as the above should force us to stop and think. As we study tables replete with validity coefficients, how many of those coefficients represent similar instances? As we develop hypotheses as to the importance of particular aspects of intelligence, how well do we understand the *criteria* which gave rise to the coefficients on which our hypotheses are based? Would the use of more valid criteria in courses for which curricular goals transcend verbal skills, have produced similar data, or different? Would the admittedly broad pervasiveness of verbal skills seem quite so broad if more appropriate measures of learning were employed? If we remain complacent about criteria composed largely of behaviors from the verbal domain, we are unlikely to see the relevance of other abilities.

In his APA presidential address in 1964, McNemar paid flattering attention to the Differential Aptitude Tests; he quite accurately reported that the verbal tests were most frequently the best predictors of course grades. The data he cited certainly supported the point he was making: Verbal tests predict grades in many academic courses. What might well have been added was recognition that the nature of our educational criteria exaggerates the real importance of verbal skills. If (and it is hoped *when*) grades or other criterion statements become more content valid, the relevance of a number of other skills will be more demonstrable.

Industry has perforce learned this lesson. Few mechanical apprentices are selected solely, or even primarily, because they can describe a process, rather than perform it. The military has learned that the ability to diagnose a malfunctioning torpedo is poorly demonstrated by verbal exposition, but well demonstrated by a work sample requiring actual mechanical repairs. It is to be hoped that education will increasingly become more realistic with respect to what *its* criteria *should* be.

Issue IV: The Growth and Decline of "Intelligence"

So preoccupied have we been with reifying intelligence as some mystical substance that we have too often neglected to take a common-sense look at what intelligence tests measure. We find ourselves distressed at our failure to predict with satisfactory accuracy the intelligence test scores of a teen-ager from his intelligence test scores as an infant. Why should this occasion surprise, let alone distress? If we look inside the tests, it should be obvious that the kinds of learnings we typically appraise at the earlier ages bear little resemblance, and may have little relevance, to the kinds of learnings we appraise later.

At the earlier age levels, we have typically tested for such characteristics as motor dexterity, perception, and similar features of physical development. When intellectual concepts become available for testing as baby grows to infant, to child, to teen-ager, we change the focus of our testing from the physical domains to the cognitive—we appraise knowledge, concept formation, and reasoning.

It is possible that future research will disclose that possession of certain physical abilities or tendencies is prerequisite to the development of concept formation, and that earlier possession of these characteristics will foretell the future intellectual development of the individual. Interesting and promising research now being conducted is directed toward this goal. It is my opinion that, because learning experiences vary so from one child to another, there is some practical limit beyond which we will be unable to predict, however penetrating our research. In any event, we would do well at this moment to recognize that since we are measuring in different ability domains at infant and school-age levels, we should not expect good prediction from one level to the other—and we should certainly not behave as though the data permitted confident prediction.

At the other end of the age spectrum we have, with similar lack of insight, proceeded to corollary errors. We have accepted the gloomy dictum that once we have passed the age of 18, or 25, or 35, we have passed our peak; from that age, our ability to learn declines. Our texts are peppered with charts showing that depressing downhill slide. What is the basis for this widely accepted conclusion? The principal basis is that when we apply our conventional measures of intelligence to older people, we find that average scores decrease. We have implicitly accepted the idea that intelligence is defined by what is measured by these particular intelligence tests. If, however, we return to our previous formulation of intelligence as what we know in a wide variety of domains, and hence as a base for what we can learn at a given moment, our perspective changes. We then proceed to compare what the intelligence tests measure with the kinds of learning individuals have engaged in from age 30 or 40 on. The relevance of the tests, except perhaps as measures of retention, is seen as increasingly remote with each passing year. Most individuals have not failed to learn more with added years of life. Their learnings have occurred in areas (science, business, politics, psychology, psychometrics), often relatively specialized, which are not measured by conventional intelligence tests.

It is true that new learnings of adults occur in such a variety of endeavors that it would be virtually impossible to find a common core on which all could be examined. We should not, however, pretend we do not suffer this psychometric disability; we should not continue to use less relevant measures to support deceptive graphs and curves of the decline of "intelligence." We might better recognize the limitations of our measure, until such time as we can devise relevant measures of the significant learnings which do occur. For the present, we can conclude only that with each passing decade older people do less well on tests designed for younger adults.

Issue V: The Search for Purity

A discussion of the nature of intelligence, and of intelligent testing, should not ignore the topic of factor analysis. It is a method which has influenced test construction and test selection. It is a technique which has stimulated the promulgation of theories of the structure of intellect.

The history of psychometrics gives evidence that each new major technique has attained a heyday of popularity, during which unrealistic hopes led to unbridled use. In the 1920s and 1930s, Pearson product-moment coefficients held the stage; everybody seemed to be correlating everything with everything else with wild abandon. We appear, in more recent times, to have been engaging in factor analyses with almost equal frenzy. With so much activity going on, it is perhaps to be expected that some studies, and some conclusions, would be characterized more by enthusiasm than by wisdom.

To criticize factor analysis as a procedure because individuals have misled themselves through its use would be very silly indeed. Among the benefits it has provided are the ability to summarize vast masses of data, and to facilitate the organization of information in a way that inspires, and then leads to investigation of interesting and often fruitful research hypotheses. At the same time, we need not believe that the power of the tool assures the validity of the product. Some of the conclusions which have been drawn, some attitudes which have been adopted, and some theories which have occasionally been treated as though they were established fact might well be exposed to scrutiny.

There have been instances in which a test battery was chosen for practical use *because* it had its origins in a program of factorial research. Presumably, the rationale was that such a battery consists of relatively "pure" tests, and would show near-zero intercorrelation among the tests; it would therefore be more efficient than a battery of similar measures not derived from factorial studies. If this rationale survived empirical study, it would still not of itself be adequate justification for selecting one set of tests rather than another. Efficiency is certainly desirable—but *validity* is *crucial.* How tests were constructed is interesting and even germane; how they *work* is the critical issue.

Let us return, however, to the rationale. Is the leap from "factorial origin" to "purity" defensible? The "pure" tests developed in psychometric laboratories often do correlate very little with one another. To some degree, at least, this low correlation is frequently ascribable to the unreliability of short, experimental tests, or to restriction in range of the various abilities of the subject, or both. For exploratory and research purposes, these conditions represent a reasonable situation. Practical test use situations are something else again.

When batteries of reliable tests with factorial ancestry, and batteries testing in similar domains but not factor oriented, are given to the same students, the within-battery intercorrelation of scores is ordinarily of about the same order. For example, with one ninth-grade group of boys, the average inter-*r* among the Differential Aptitude Tests was .37; for the same group, the average inter-*r* of the Primary Mental Abilities Tests was .36. Similar results were obtained in a comparison of the DAT and the General Aptitude Test Battery scores for a twelfth-grade group. Thus, there was little evidence of greater "purity" in the factorially derived batteries than in the DAT, which were not so derived. (In the everyday world, it appears, "purity" is all too likely to be an illusion.) Accordingly, we would be well advised when choosing tests for practical use to concentrate on how they work, not on how they were built.

Let us now turn briefly to the role of factor analysis as a stimulator of hypotheses concerning the structure of intellect. Its influence has often seemed to be not so much mathematicodeductive as mathematico*se*ductive! The power of the method as a way of manipulating great masses of data appears all too often to have led us astray. Even our more eminent protagonists of the technique have not always appeared immune. When expounding on the theory of factor analysis, experts almost invariably agree that factors are merely descriptive categories; they are not functional entities. But when engaged in interpreting the factors which have emerged from their studies, some analysts apparently succumb to the mystic charm of rotating axes and perceive entities which, they have told us, do not exist. The lure of the temptation to discover a psychological structure analogous to the periodic table of the elements is too powerful to resist. We then hear of "primary mental abilities" or are shown "the three faces of intellect." Though the authors of such creations have sometimes demonstrated in other writings that they well understand the difference between the reality of descriptive categories and the illusion of underlying entities, some of their disciples and many of their readers seem less clear in their perception.

If we accept the thesis that the modules or bits which constitute intelligence are themselves complex, a combination of such modules can hardly be expected to be simple or "pure." A 6-year-old who assembles three alphabet blocks to spell out "cat" has employed, at a minimum, verbal and spatial skills; if he is aware that there are three blocks or letters, he has engaged in numerical perception as well. The ability to perform the task has required cognition, memory, convergent thinking, and evaluation. The product is figural, symbolic, and semantic. All this, and we have not yet taken into account such considerations as the motor-manipulative activity, the perception of color, the earlier learning experiences which enabled him to perform the task successfully, or the imagery which the concept "cat" induces in him. We, as analysts, may choose to attend to only a single aspect of the behavior—but the behavior itself remains multifaceted and complex. To assume that we can abstract from a host of such activities a pure and simple entity is to ignore the psychological meaning of intelligent behavior.

Let us continue to explore, by all means available to us (including factor analysis) the nature of man's abilities. Let us *not* assume that the results of research obtained under closely managed conditions in the laboratory will hold true as realities in day-to-day situations. Let us not unwittingly forget that the descriptive categories we adopt for convenience in communication do not have real existence as ultimate psychological entities.

Conclusion

To what view of a structure of intellect am I led by the ideas I have enunciated here? Essentially, I believe intelligence is *un*structured. I believe that it is differently comprised in every individual—the sum total of all the learning experiences he has uniquely had up to any moment in time. Such structure as we perceive is structure which we have imposed. We can so select samples of previous learnings to examine as to reveal a general factor, or group factors, or specifics. We can sample from domains that are relatively homogeneous and apply labels such as verbal, numerical, spatial; we can sample from a wider variety of learnings, and apply labels such as "general mental ability" or, simply, "intelligence."

There are many bases on which we may choose which kinds of learnings we will sample. The most reasonable basis, I believe, is that of predictive purpose. Those previous learnings should be probed which are most relevant to the particular future learnings we wish to predict. In addition to criterion—or, more likely, *criteria*—relevance, the principles of band width and fidelity (as enunciated by Cronbach and Gleser) might well serve as guides. If we are interested in forecasting narrow-band criteria, selection of highly homogeneous, directly relevant behaviors is indicated. If we are interested in a wide range of criteria, we have at least two options: we may choose to select small samples from widely scattered domains—as in a Binet, a Wechsler, or a broader gauge instrument still to be devised—or examine more intensively with several narrower gauge tests, as in the Differential Aptitude Tests. The broader gauge instruments will offer economy, but lesser fidelity for selected criteria. The narrower gauge instruments will be longer and more time consuming—but the possibility of more direct relevance to one or more particular criteria should permit higher fidelity.

The critical issue, then, is not which approach measures intelligence—each of them does, in its own fashion. No approach save sampling from every domain in which learnings have occurred—an impossible task—fully measures intelligence. The question is rather which approach provides the most useful information for the various purposes we wish the test to serve. Recognition that what we are measuring is what the individual has learned, and composing our tests to appraise *relevant* previous learnings, will yield the most useful information. We, and those who utilize the results of our work—educators, personnel men, social planners—face problems for which intelligence test data are relevant, and sometimes crucial. We must remember, and we must teach, what our test scores really reflect. The measurement of intelligence is not, and has not been, a matter of concern only to psychology. It has always been, and continues to be, an influence on educational and social programs. If we are to avert uninformed pressures from government agencies, from school administrators, from the courts, and indeed from psychologist colleagues, we must understand and we must broadly communicate what these scores truly represent. Only then can we who build tests and they who use them properly claim that we are indeed engaged in intelligent testing.

24 | On the Formation of Psychological Traits*

Anne Anastasi[1]

It is a special privilege to give this first lecture of the Robert Choate Tryon Memorial Lectureship. I welcome the opportunity to honor an outstanding psychologist and a valued friend. In choosing a topic related to one of Dr. Tryon's own contributions, I had a wide field available to me. There was, of course, his pioneer research on behavior genetics (Tryon, 1940) and the subsequent methodological and theoretical developments that continued to engage his efforts over the years (Hirsch & Tryon, 1956; Tryon, 1963). There were his many contributions to statistical method, especially within the area of factor analysis (Tryon, 1939, 1967). That the work of a single psychologist should span the genetics of animal behavior and the techniques of factor analysis is itself a striking indication of the unusual breadth of Dr. Tryon's activities. His applications of factor-analytic methodology to substantive problems gave further evidence of the varied and innovative nature of his research. To cite only one example, his cluster analysis of census data for different neighborhoods (Tryon, 1955, 1968) represents one of the early uses of factor-analytic techniques with variables other than test scores—and it highlighted the need for analyzing the variables of man's cultural environment with the same thoroughness traditionally followed with organismic variables.

What I finally chose as the point of departure for my talk was a 1935 article in the *Psychological Review* that illustrates still another facet of Dr. Tryon's contributions, namely, his theoretical insight into the nature and origins of psychological traits (Tryon, 1935).

Let me first clarify some terms. When psychologists speak of the development of traits, they usually refer to the level or amount of a given trait that the individual manifests at different times, as when plotting growth curves or learning curves. The term "trait pattern" is employed in more than one sense

---

*From Anastasi, A. On the formation of psychological traits. *American Psychologist*, 1970, **25**, 899-910. Copyright 1970 by the American Psychological Association, and reproduced by permission.
[1] First Annual Robert Choate Tryon Memorial Lecture presented at the University of California at Berkeley, February 26, 1970.

but usually signifies the relative amounts of different traits displayed by an individual or group. Thus, cultural differences in trait patterns characteristically pertain to the relative performance of different cultural groups in, for example, verbal, numerical, and spatial tests (e.g., Lesser, Fifer, & Clock, 1965). If Group A scores highest in verbal and lowest in spatial tests, while Group B scores lowest in verbal and highest in spatial tests, these findings are reported as a group difference in trait patterns.

In the factor-analytic literature, on the other hand, trait pattern traditionally connotes the very dimensions or traits identified by factor analysis and in terms of which the performance of individuals or groups may then be described. It is with trait patterns in this sense that the present discussion is concerned. How does behavior become organized into traits? What do we know about the origin or emergence of behavior traits? It is apparent that these questions do concern the development of traits or trait patterns, but because of the alternative connotations of these terms I have chosen the less familiar expression, "formation of psychological traits."

Insofar as the traits under consideration are those identified by factor-analytic techniques, the question of trait formation becomes essentially an inquiry into the causes of correlation among different behavioral samples, as represented, for example, by test scores. It should be added that for simplicity the discussion will be limited to abilities. The same mechanisms, however, would undoubtedly apply to the formation of personality traits, albeit the specific substantive details might differ.

Theoretical Analyses of Trait Formation

From the earliest discussions of trait organization, one can find explicit recognition of the fact that factor-analytic techniques yield only descriptive categories and that different schemas of classification are applicable to the same data. This approach to factors has been more fully presented in the writings of British investigators, such as Burt (1941, 1954), Thomson (1916, 1948), and Vernon (1961, 1969). These writers, moreover, have gone on to explain the empirically identified group or general factors in terms of the overlap or association of innumerable intrinsically unrelated determiners. To be sure, other factor analysts have occasionally expressed agreement with these interpretations of factors. Thus, even Thurstone (1940) observed in one of his articles that factors should not be regarded as ultimate psychological entities but rather as "functional unities" or aggregates of more elementary components. His treatment of factors in other publications and especially his continued use of the term "primary mental abilities," however, strongly suggest the concept of factors as relatively permanent, underlying, causal entities.

In his 1935 article, Tryon explored the process of trait formation fully and systematically, proposing a psychological interpretation of factors and outlining three mechanisms whereby correlations among specific behavioral determinants may develop. First, he suggested that the elementary psychological components of behavior are concepts and conceptual relations, which themselves evolve when the appropriate environmental stimuli occur in conjunction with an adequate conceptual background in the behaving organism. This process thus recognizes the need for a suitable set of stimuli or external environmental field, as might be provided by an educational program, as well as the prerequisite antecedent conceptual development of the organism.

To account for correlation among different psychological measures, such as test scores, Tryon proposed three mechanisms: overlap of psychological components, correlation between independent environmental fields, and correlation between independent gene blocks. The major source of correlation he attributed to overlap among the many conceptual components brought into play by different tasks. The magnitude of correlation between two tests, he argued, depends on the extent to which they "sample similar universes of conceptual components." The correlations among different intelligence tests, for example, are generally high, "not because some mystic general factor saturates them all heavily, but because all these tests sample to a marked extent the same complex welter of concepts determining vocabulary, reading, and arithmetic abilities." [Tryon, 1935, p. 450] Intercorrelations among tests or test items also depend in part on the breadth of application or generality of the individual concepts themselves. For instance, the concept expressed by the verb "to sing" has much more limited applicability than does the concept corresponding to the verb "to be."

A second source of correlation among test scores is to be found in the correlation between the environmental fields in which the different psychological components originated. This can be illustrated by the fact that a child reared in a cultural milieu that provides environmental fields eliciting superior verbal concepts tends also to be exposed to environmental fields eliciting superior numerical concepts. The third source of test correlation, arising from the correlation of independent gene blocks, is attributed to assortative mating. Since individuals tend to marry within their own general socioeconomic and educational level, persons superior in quite different respects are likely to interbreed. Their offspring would thus tend to receive genes for superior development in a number of initially unrelated characteristics; and the same type of selection would occur in the interbreeding of persons of diverse inferiority.

It should be noted that cultural factors may operate in all three of the mechanisms described by Tryon. The nature and breadth of concepts available to an individual in solving a problem or performing an intellectual task obviously vary not only with the language he has been taught but also with many other aspects of his cultural background. Culture also determines which environmental fields covary in quality in the individual's experiences. From another angle, it determines which environmental fields are encountered in the same temporal or spatial context, as when different academic subjects are included in an organized educational curriculum, or when different topics are covered within a single course. Similarly, cultural factors provide the opportunities and social pressures that encourage inbreeding within subcultures or social classes having certain common characteristics. From these considerations it follows that different traits may be formed in different cultures.

Approaching the question from a somewhat different angle, Ferguson (1954, 1956) proposed an explanation of the formation of factors in terms of transfer of training. Regarding abilities as prior overlearned acquisitions, he attributed correlation among abilities to the result of positive transfer. According to Ferguson, abilities emerge through a process of differential transfer. Because cultural factors influence what the child shall learn at each age, moreover, different cultural environments lead to the development of different ability patterns. The breadth of the transfer effect determines whether the resulting factor is a broad one, like verbal comprehension, or a narrow one, like a specialized perceptual skill. Traditional intelligence tests measure intellectual skills that transfer widely to tasks in our culture. Similarly, many of the skills acquired through formal schooling, as in reading or arithmetic computation, are applicable to a wide variety of subsequent learning situations. Individual differences in the extent to which these skills have been developed will thus be reflected in the performance of many different tasks. In a factor analysis of such tasks, these widely applicable skills would emerge as broad group factors.

From still another angle, Whiteman (1964) pointed to a relation between the formation of learning sets, as illustrated in Harlow's classic experiments with monkeys (Harlow, 1949, 1960), and the development of factors. Establishing a learning set to differentiate between certain shapes, such as triangle and circle, enabled the animal to learn more rapidly when presented with a new problem requiring the differentiation of *other* shapes. The animal had established a learning set for differentiating shapes; he knew what to look for when faced with a new problem. Differences in the amount of such prior shape-discrimination experience or in the degree to which the individual had profited from this experience would be reflected in individual differences in the strength of the learning set. These individual differences would in turn increase the correlation among all tasks to which such a learning set was applicable. Whiteman (1964) also relates trait formation to Piaget's concept of operations, as does Hunt (1961). For the present purpose, the most relevant features of Piaget's operations are their intersituational or intertask consistency, their development through the organism's interaction with his environment, and their progressive organization into a hierarchy of increasing complexity.

The similarities among these explanations of the origin of factors in terms of generality of concepts, extent of transfer effects, and the intersituational applicability of learning sets and operations should now be evident. Still other writers have focused on other mechanisms of factor formation. While recognizing the importance of transfer and learning sets, Vernon (1961, 1969) repeatedly cites examples of the emergence of factors through contiguous educational experiences. Thus, what he designates as the broad verbal-educational factor (v:ed) is commonly found across intellectual functions taught in school, and its nature and breadth may vary in different cultures as a function of varying content coverage in formal schooling. Narrower group factors are likewise seen to be associated with the organization of course content in different types of schools or training programs.

In a discussion of the factors of verbal achievement, Carroll (1966) refers to several possible mechanisms for the emergence of factors, among which he lists prerequisite learning, transfer, and contiguous occurrence in experience. Commenting on these mechanisms, he writes: "Note, now, that this last possibility makes no appeal to any psychological considerations about the two responses; it merely refers to the actuarial fact of their co-occurrence, beyond chance, in the particular sample under study." [p. 408] Much of Carroll's further discussion centers around the operation of this mechanism of co-occurrence through the clustering of experiences in the school, the home, and the community.

Age Changes

Now we may turn from these theoretical analyses of trait formation to some illustrative empirical investigations. Such studies may be grouped under three principal approaches: developmental, comparative, and experimental.

Since the mid-1930s, a fairly large number of factor-analytic studies followed a developmental approach, at least in the sense that trait patterns were investigated in different age groups. Few utilized longitudinal procedures. After surveying the results of research conducted prior to 1946 on groups ranging from preschool children to college students, Garrett (1946) concluded that "intelligence" is relatively undifferentiated in early childhood and becomes increasingly specialized with age. Later investigations raised doubts regarding this simple differentiation hypothesis. As a group, they yielded highly inconsistent results regarding age trends in factor patterns (see Anastasi, 1958, p. 358, for references). A careful analysis of these studies, however, led Burt (1954) to the conclusion that their contradictory findings resulted from methodological deficiencies. Having himself proposed an age differentiation hypothesis as early as 1919, Burt reaffirmed his position after this survey of intervening research.

When one considers the remarkable potpourri of tests, subject characteristics, and factor-analytic techniques represented by studies purporting to test the differentiation hypothesis, it is not surprising that every possible trend (or lack of trend) can be found in their results. Many of the studies failed to provide an adequate test of the hypothesis because unsuitable instruments or statistical techniques were employed; some failed to maintain comparability in test content, reliability or variability at different age levels; in still others, the subjects employed at different age levels were not comparable in other important respects, or the age range covered was too narrow to permit the detection of age trends.

Another notable limitation of many of these studies stems from their failure to consider what experiences the subjects were undergoing during the time spans covered. To be sure, both Burt and Garrett explained age differentiation chiefly in terms of maturation rather than experiential factors. But the data become more intelligible when examined in the light of the previously considered hypotheses of trait formation. What are the implications of such hypotheses? On the one hand, exposure to a more or less standardized educational curriculum in our culture should lead to the emergence of a very broad factor, variously designated as Spearman's *g*, intelligence, or Vernon's verbal-educational factor. Those children who receive better schooling, or who for motivational or any other reasons profit more from their schooling, will tend to excel in all the abilities fostered by the school curriculum; those exposed to poorer schooling or who respond less favorably to the school experience will tend to fall behind in the same combination of academic abilities. The resulting broad factor can be more clearly identified in educationally heterogeneous groups and may appear of negligible magnitude when factor analyses are carried out in fairly homogeneous samples.

On the other hand, as the child advances through school, the academic curriculum becomes increasingly structured and differentiated into traditional subject matter areas. Thus, his instruction in verbal and numerical areas comes gradually to be separated into different class periods and eventually is even given by different teachers and possibly in different classrooms. Similar separations occur with regard to instructional areas involving predominantly perceptual or spatial abilities, as in art, mechanical drawing, shop work, and other "practical" subjects. This differentiation of academic experiences is accompanied by the increasing prominence of somewhat narrower group factors, such as those represented by Thurstone's primary mental abilities or Guilford's Structure of Intellect model. It is with this type of change over time that the proponents of the differentiation hypothesis have been concerned.

When we examine relevant research conducted since 1960 with appropriate procedures and more carefully controlled conditions, the results do in fact indicate an increasing differentiation of group factors from early childhood to late adolescence (Dye & Very, 1968; Lienert & Crott, 1964; Mukherjee, 1962; Osborne & Lindsey, 1967; Quereshi, 1967). By way of illustration, we may consider a study by Quereshi (1967), in which 14 test scores were separately factor analyzed in seven groups of 100 children each, ranging in age from 3 to 9 years. The factor-analytic techniques employed ensured that the same general and group factors would be identified in each age group. Increasing differentiation of performance with age was demonstrated in three ways. First, the percentage of variance attributable to the general factor decreased consistently with age from 41.3% to 22.8%. Second, with only minor exceptions, the percentage of variance attributable to each group factor increased with age. Third, the mean intercorrelation among the factors decreased with age from .68 at age 3 to .38 at age 9.

A word should be added about age changes in factor patterns among adults. Although several investigators have reported such adult data as evidence for or against the differentiation hypothesis, it should be noted that this hypothesis as originally formulated was restricted to developmental changes in childhood and adolescence. Moreover, the interpretation of such differentiation in terms of school experience cannot be extrapolated to adults who have completed their education. Beyond maturity, subsequent individual experiences vary too widely to suggest any clear hypothesis applicable throughout a culture. Different factor patterns might be expected to develop, for example, in persons pursuing different occupations.

It is nevertheless interesting to observe that when the older subgroups in an adult sample have had less education than the younger, or when their level of performance is significantly lower than that of the younger, the older groups usually show *less* differentiation of abilities than do the younger (Balinsky, 1941; Green & Berkowitz, 1964; Lienert & Crott, 1964; Weiner, 1964). Greater educational heterogeneity in the older groups would also have the effect of increasing the relative weight of the general factor and decreasing the contribution of the narrower group factors (Balinsky, 1941; Weiner, 1964).

Group Differences

A second major type of investigation is characterized by a comparative approach to the understanding of trait formation. Trait patterns have been compared among groups differing in type of educational program, socioeconomic level, sex, and national or other broad cultural categories. In order to test hypotheses arising from the previously cited theoretical analyses of the origin of factors, several conditions need to be met. The investigator must administer a fairly large number of suitable tests to sufficiently large groups; he must employ appropriate factor-analytic techniques; and he must have access to at least some data regarding relevant cultural and other experiential variables. These conditions are admittedly difficult to meet in any one study. Consequently, few if any available studies provide definitive or clearly interpretable data on trait formation. What we find instead is a number of interesting leads and provocative results, frequently gathered incidentally in connection with the investigation of other problems.

Both *educational* and *socioeconomic* differences in factor patterns were found by Filella (1960) in a study of high school students in Colombia, South America. In all groups, two factors were identified in a battery of six tests, representing an adaptation of the Differential Aptitude Tests for use in Colombia. The nature of these factors, however, varied among the groups, as indicated by the tests yielding high loadings in each factor. Among boys enrolled in technical high schools, the two factors could best be described as quantitative reasoning and spatial-mechanical reasoning. In this group, the two verbal tests in the battery had marginally low loadings in one or the other of these factors. Among academic high school boys, on the other hand, the same tests revealed a verbal and a nonverbal factor.

Socioeconomic differences were explored by comparing factor patterns in public and private high schools, in which an identical curriculum was followed but the students differed in socioeconomic level. A major difference between these two groups was to be found in the sharper differentiation between verbal and nonverbal factors in the private school group. One indication of this difference was the lower correlation between the oblique axes in the private than in the public high school group (.42 versus .77). In addition, a number of differences were observed in the relative weights of the two factors in specific tests, suggesting certain differences in the nature of these factors. Thus, in the public high school group, the verbal factor appears to be a broad academic factor (akin to Vernon's v:ed), while the nonverbal factor is more nearly a spatial factor. In the private high school group, on the other hand, the nonverbal factor appears to be primarily an abstract reasoning factor; and the verbal factor emerges in the strictly verbal tests, with some additional loading in mechanical reasoning problems, which these students may solve largely in verbal terms.

A similar study was conducted in England by Dockrell (1965). Taking as his point of departure the theoretical orientation provided by Ferguson (1954) and Vernon (1961), Dockrell hypothesized certain differences in the degree of differentiation as well as in the nature of group factors as a function of both social class and secondary school curriculum. A battery of 10 tests covering verbal and nonverbal aptitudes, linguistic and numerical skills, and practical or spatial ability was administered to 10-, 12-, and 14-year-old school children classified according to father's occupation into middle and lower social groups. The 12- and 14-year groups, who were attending secondary schools, were also subdivided with reference to type of school attended, including academic, technical, and general. With regard to social class, the results confirmed the hypothesis that the middle class would show more differentiation of ability than the lower class. This finding agrees with those reported by Filella (1960) for Colombian students and by Mitchell (1956) in a study of American school children. In Dockrell's study, differentiation also occurred at an earlier age in the middle than in the lower class.

Comparisons among types of secondary schools in Dockrell's study revealed more differentiation of abilities in the academic and technical schools than in the general schools. The general factor accounted for the largest proportion of battery variance in the general school group, less in the academic school group, and least in the technical school group. Moreover, the differences among schools increased from the 12-year-old to the 14-year-old group. As in Filella's study, verbal skills tended to be more clearly differentiated in the academic schools, while spatial and numerical skills tended to be more highly differentiated in the technical schools. In this connection, mention may also be made of similar variations in the organization of abilities reported by Vernon (1961, pp. 116-120) from factor-analytic studies of several groups of technicians in the British military services.

Relevant data are also reported by Sutherland (1960) who compared the performance of students exposed to departmentalized and nondepartmentalized school instruction. The SRA Primary Mental Abilities Tests were administered to students enrolled in Grades 6-10 in four school systems in

Kentucky. Departmentalized instruction, whereby each subject is taught by a different teacher, was introduced at different grade levels in the different school systems. Separate analyses by age and type of instruction suggested a possible effect of departmentalization on trait organization. The correlations between verbal and numerical subtests revealed a significant decrease approximately two to three years following the introduction of departmentalization. The spatial subtests, which are less closely related to school instruction, showed no consistent changes in their correlations with other subtests.

There is a considerable body of scattered data regarding *sex differences* in factor patterns. A number of early studies conducted in the United States and Great Britain at the elementary, high school, and college levels indicated greater differentiation of those abilities in which each sex excels (see Anastasi, 1948, pp. 133-134). For example, girls excelled in verbal tests and also yielded higher intercorrelations among verbal tests and lower correlations between verbal and other types of tests than did boys. Thus, among girls, verbal aptitude showed more evidence of having become differentiated into an identifiable trait. The same was true of memory tests, in which girls likewise excelled. In numerical and spatial tests, the reverse was true, boys excelling in mean scores and also providing more evidence of trait differentiation.

Several more recent studies report sex differences in the number, nature, or distinctness of factors identified in male and female groups (Avakian, 1961; Dye & Very, 1968; Filella, 1960; Irvine, 1969; Lindsey, 1966; Tyler, 1951; Very, 1967). In a few instances, interesting parallelisms are noted between sex differences in educational curricula or other cultural experiences and the particular differences in factor patterns found between the sexes (Filella, 1960; Irvine, 1969). Some investigations provide further evidence for the association of ability level with degree of differentiation in particular areas. Thus, in a study on primary school children, two verbal factors were required to account for the test performance of girls, while a single verbal factor was sufficient for the boys (Lindsey, 1966). An investigation on high school students identified two spatial-visualization factors among boys in addition to a spatial factor found for both sexes (Very, 1967).

Some investigators have approached the relation between *ability level* and trait differentiation more directly. In an early study, Segel (1948) compared the intercorrelations among some of the primary mental abilities tests and other linguistic and mathematical tests in two contrasted groups of ninth-grade boys selected on the basis of total scores on the battery. There was a clear tendency for the correlations to be lower in the high-scoring group, suggesting greater differentiation in the more able individuals. Similarly, in a factor-analytic investigation of normal six-year-old children and institutional-ized retardates of the same mental age, Myers and his associates (Myers et al., 1962) found more clearly differentiated abilities in the normal children. Lienert and Crott (1964) report a number of German studies which corrobo-rate these findings with subjects at several intellectual and age levels. Differences were found with regard to magnitude of mean intercorrelations among tests, number of factors isolated, and weights of the first centroid in individual variables. The same authors even cite supporting data from psycho-pharmacology. In a study by Lienert (1964), the experimental lowering of performance by pharmacological stress (LSD or alcohol) was accompanied by a dedifferentiation of the factor structure. From still another angle, Manley (1965) found different factor loadings in concept attainment tasks when comparing "solvers" with "nonsolvers."

The correspondence between all these findings and the previously reported results on age and educational differences in both children and adults is clearly evident. It is also interesting to note that Ferguson (1954) deduced the relationship between ability level and trait differentiation from his transfer theory, concluding that "as the learning of a particular task continues, the ability to perform it becomes gradually differentiated from . . . other abilities." [p. 110]

The decade of the 1960s has seen an increasing number of *cross-cultural studies* of trait organization (Das, 1963; Guthrie, 1963; Guttman & Guttman, 1963; Irvine, 1969; Vandenberg, 1959, 1966; Vernon, 1965, 1969). Factor analysis has been applied to the results of test batteries administered in Israel, India, the Scottish Hebrides, the Philippines, the West Indies, and several African nations; to Indian and Eskimo boys in Canada; and to Chinese and Latin American students in the United States.

In one of the most far-flung of these projects, Vernon (1965, 1969) administered an extensive and highly diversified battery of individual and group tests to school boys in southeastern England, the Hebrides, Jamaica, and Uganda, and to Indian and Eskimo boys in Canada. The number tested in each group varied from 40 to 50, except that the English sample used for normative purposes numbered 100. Testing was followed by individual inter-views to elicit background information.

Although Vernon's factor patterns exhibited many cross-cultural similar-ities, some noteworthy differences were found which appeared to have a basis in cultural characteristics. For example, in the Hebrides and in Jamaica, the verbal-educational factor was actually a general factor, having substantial loadings not only in educational tests but also in many tests of a noneduca-tional nature. In other words, verbal reasoning, perceptual, and spatial abil-ities were less clearly differentiated in these groups. In the light of its correlation with certain background factors, this broad verbal-educational factor was interpreted as reflecting the extent of assimilation of the culture represented by the schools. In Uganda, on the other hand, no general factor was found, but only a verbal-educational factor that was quite distinct from other aspects of cognitive functioning. It had negligible loadings, for example, in the Progressive Matrices and Draw-a-Man tests. These tests would thus have little or no predictive value for school work in this culture, where educational achievement depends so heavily on the specific ability to acquire the English language. Vernon (1969) identified another broad factor in the Uganda data, with loadings in many of the performance and nonverbal tests, which he described as "an ability to cope with perceptual analysis, concrete operations, and the world of objects, quite distinct from educational attainments." [p. 187]

Another extensive investigation was that conducted by Irvine (1969) on several thousand elementary and high school students in Kenya, Zambia, and Rhodesia. The batteries consisted of group tests covering verbal, numerical, spatial, mechanical, and perceptual content. Cross-cultural uniformities in the loadings of certain broad factors were attributed by Irvine to uniformity of education in the British-style schools attended by his samples. The greatest uniformities of factorial composition were found in overlearned drill skills, such as language usage and the mechanics of arithmetic. On the other hand, perceptual and reasoning skills requiring manipulation of nonverbal stimuli showed much less factorial consistency, being more dependent on culturally diverse learning outside of school.

It should be added that cross-cultural studies usually employ selected samples, because the individuals who attend school are generally more highly assimilated to the Western culture than are those not in school. Moreover, the test batteries administered in such studies are frequently overloaded with tests requiring the intellectual skills taught in these Western-style schools. Such a choice of tests is understandable in cultures that are in the process of adopting at least to a limited degree the skills and values of the Western culture. Most of the tests employed in these studies were undergoing development or evaluation as instruments for use in this assimilation process. Had the investigations been designed primarily to study cultural differences in trait development, a quite different selection of subjects and tests would have been appropriate.

Experimental Studies

The third major approach to the investigation of trait formation represents the experimental alteration of trait relationships. Such studies provide a condensed and relatively controlled version of what probably occurs more gradually, over a longer time period, in the individual's daily experience. The investigator thus tries to reproduce the process of trait formation that can be inferred from the observation of age changes, educational differences, and variations among other experientially dissimilar groups.

One type of study following this approach is concerned with the effects of *practice* upon factor patterns. Early studies by Woodrow (1938, 1939) and by Greene (1943) found many changes in the factorial composition of tests in the course of practice. Some of these changes showed interesting correspondences to changes in observed performance or in subjects' reports. More recently, Fleishman and his co-workers have investigated the factorial composition of several complex perceptual-motor tasks at different stages of learning (see Fleishman & Bartlett, 1969; Fleishman & Hempel, 1954; Fleishman & Rich, 1963). Their results revealed progressive and systematic changes in factor loadings with practice. In the course of learning, there was a decrease in the contribution of such "nonmotor" factors as verbal and spatial aptitudes relative to motor factors, as well as an increase in the contribution of a factor specific to each task. These general findings were confirmed in a subsequent independent investigation (Kohfeld, 1966) and were extended in still other studies to conceptual (Bunderson, 1964; Dunham, Guilford, & Hoepfner, 1966), memory (Frederiksen, 1969; Games, 1962), and perceptual (Fleishman & Fruchter, 1960) tasks. The nature of the observed changes in factor patterns with practice suggests an increasing differentiation of functions as learning proceeds. This finding is consistent with the previously cited results of studies on age, educational differences, and ability level.

A somewhat related procedure follows directly from Ferguson's hypothesis regarding the role of *transfer* in the emergence of factors. Subjects are given practice in one test, which may be supplemented by verbal explanations and other instructional procedures. The effect of such learning on the factorial structure of a battery of related tests is then investigated. This approach is illustrated by two Swedish studies, one using motor tests (Heinonen, 1962), the other using a variety of verbal, numerical, and spatial tests (Melametsa, 1965). Both found evidence of increasing differentiation of factor patterns following training.

Still another procedural variant is represented by an early exploratory study by Anastasi (1936). Five tests, including vocabulary, memory span for digits, verbal reasoning, code multiplication, and pattern analysis, were administered to 200 sixth-grade school children. All subjects were then given one session of *instruction* in the use of special techniques that would facilitate performance on the last three tests only. In its general nature, this instruction resembled that received in the course of schooling, as, for example, in the teaching of arithmetic operations, shortcuts, and the like. After a lapse of 13 days, parallel forms of all five tests were administered under the same conditions as in the initial testing.

The rationale of this study was derived from the mechanism of contiguous experience, or Tryon's correlation of independent environmental fields. Essentially, it was hypothesized that the more an individual profited from the interpolated experience, the greater gain he would show on the three "instructed" tests. Consequently, the interrelations of the three "instructed" tests should alter, while the relations of the "noninstructed" tests to each other and to the "instructed" tests should remain virtually unchanged. A comparison of the correlations among initial and final tests supported this hypothesis. The factor patterns showed a number of changes, several of which could be understood in terms of the interpolated experience. For example, the factor accounting for the largest proportion of battery variance in the initial tests had the highest loading in tests most closely related to school work; in the final tests, on the other hand, this factor had the highest loadings in the three "instructed" tests.

An ongoing *longitudinal study of job performance* by MacKinney (1967), although not strictly experimental in approach, bears some resemblance to these learning studies. Beginning with the premise that the job performance of individual workers changes over time, not only in level but also in nature, MacKinney has been investigating the factorial composition of criterion job performance at annual intervals. The specific job chosen was that of second-echelon managers, although its choice was fortuitous. Department heads in several plants of a large manufacturing company were given the Minnesota Scholastic Aptitude Test, the California Psychological Inventory, and the Strong Vocational Interest Blank, together with an extensive series of questionnaires covering biographical data, leadership style, job satisfaction, and the subject's perception of his working environment and his job activities. In addition, ratings of the subject's job performance and personal traits were obtained from his supervisors and subordinates. The hypothesized time changes are expected to occur not only as a function of worker variables—as illustrated by the effects of practice in job skills—but also as a function of changing situational variables to which the same individuals may be exposed over time. In terms of both duration and experimental design, MacKinney's research appears to fall about midway between the age studies and the learning experiments.

From a different angle, French (1965) investigated the relationship of individual differences in *problem-solving styles* to the factorial composition of tests. Fifteen cognitive tests were administered to 177 male high school and college students. Individual problem-solving styles were explored through questionnaires, interviews, and oral solution of typical test items. Factor analysis of the stylistic variables thus identified, together with the 15 test scores, yielded 17 psychologically meaningful stylistic factors. Many of these factors fell loosely into a category that could be described as a tendency toward "systematizing" or toward "analyzing versus scanning." The entire sample was divided successively into two subsamples differentiated on the basis of these stylistic factors, and the test scores were separately factor analyzed in the two subsamples. The resulting factor patterns exhibited a number of differences that were related to the problem-solving styles. Not only did the factorial composition of individual tests differ as a function of response style, but the factor patterns also differed in number and nature of factors that emerged and in the magnitude of correlation between oblique factors.

The problem-solving styles studied by French bear some resemblance to the "cognitive strategies" posited by Frederiksen (1969). In the course of learning, an individual may change his choice of strategy and thereby alter the factorial composition of the task as performed by him. Moreover, the applicability of a given cognitive strategy to several tasks may account for transfer of improvement from practice as well as for the clustering of these tasks into an identifiable trait.

For our final example of the experimental approach to trait formation, we may ask what research on infrahuman organisms has to offer. The answer is: very little thus far, although potentially it should be a rich field for testing the hypotheses that have been proposed. Most factor-analytic studies on animals are purely descriptive and cross-sectional (see Anastasi, 1958, pp. 326-364). The large majority have used the familiar laboratory white rat, although a few other species have occasionally been investigated. As in the human studies, there is evidence that the factor structure of the same task may change in the course of training (see, e.g., Anastasi, Fuller, Scott, & Schmitt, 1955). On the whole, however, the animal studies have yielded factors that proved more difficult to interpret than the factors obtained with humans. Rarely do we find broad aptitude factors such as have been identified in human studies. What factors are found are usually quite limited in scope. Some have been defined in terms of specific techniques applicable to the solution of more than one problem, such as the principle of turning alternately right and left, or the utilization of visual cues. To be sure, this type of finding now appears to be of considerable interest in connection with the role of transfer, learning sets, problem-solving styles, and cognitive strategies in the development of factors.

It is also characteristic of the animal data that cognitive and emotional aspects of behavior are not sharply differentiated. Thus, even when the variables analyzed are derived from performance on typical learning tasks, such as mazes, discrimination apparatus, and problem-solving situations, one finds such factors as docility, wildness-timidity, and impulsiveness or activity. This intertwining of aptitude and emotional factors may have an experiential origin. Unlike the school children or college students of the typical human factor-analytic studies, animals have not been exposed to that classic dichotomy between curricular and extracurricular experiences, between standardized intellectual development and unstandardized emotional development.

Probably the most significant contribution that animal research can make to our understanding of traits is to be found in experimental studies of the development of factors under controlled conditions. This approach is exemplified in a well-designed study by Whimbey and Denenberg (1966), in which the investigators quite literally created group factors through the experimental control of early experiences in a homogeneous group of rats. Within a total sample of 96 rats, three males and three females were randomly assigned to each of 16 experimental treatment groups. Each of these 16 groups was exposed to a different combination of the following four treatment variables: (a) whether or not the mother had herself been handled in infancy; (b) whether or not the subject was handled in infancy; (c) whether the mother and litter were housed in a maternity cage or in a free environment between birth and weaning; (d) whether the subject was housed in a laboratory cage or in a free environment between weaning and the age of 42 days.

Between the ages of 42 days and 220 days, all animals lived under identical conditions. Beginning at 220 days, they were put through a test battery that yielded 23 score variables. The mean scores of each of the 16 groups on each of these 23 variables were intercorrelated and factor analyzed. Because of the random assignment of animals to each group, these intergroup score differences, which proved to be significant, could be attributed to the experimental treatments. Hence, the obtained correlations were a function of known experimental inputs. Six factors were found, of which four could be clearly idenitified as emotional reactivity, avoidance learning, consumption-elimination, and field exploration. Whimbey and Denenberg's own concluding remarks are noteworthy. They write:

> The factor structure obtained in this experiment is surprisingly similar to ones obtained when heterogeneous groups of rats or mice were employed in factor analytical studies. . . . This could mean that one can generate as great and complex a range of individual differences by means of experimental manipulation as one can by capitalizing on random genetic variations; or it may mean that the uncontrolled ("random") life experiences of the animals played a much more important role in shaping and establishing the behavioral patterns (individual differences) of the animals than has been realized heretofore [p. 285].

Section VI

Individual and Group Differences in Mental Abilities

Several of the articles in Section V refer to variables which are correlated with individual differences in mental abilities. Thus, Guilford's (no. 21) concluding reference to the effects of experience on factor structure and Cattell's (no. 22) discussion of the relative influence of environment on fluid and crystallized intelligence are pertinent to the heredity/environment controversy over the origins of mental abilities. Although both of these theorists admit that environment is important in determining intelligence, Wesman's (no. 23) view of intelligence as the "sum total of an individual's learning experiences" appears to give even more weight to environment. Finally, Anastasi (no. 24) discusses a number of variables which affect the patterning of intellectual abilities: age, sex, culture, socioeconomic status, education and training.

The articles in Section VI represent a continuation of the focus on individual and group differences in mental abilities and other psychological characteristics. The issues described in these articles are currently topics of lively controversy, both in psychology itself and in the wider social context. Since heredity and environment interact in a complex way to determine all human characteristics, it is pointless to argue that a certain portion of an *individual's* intellectual ability is caused by heredity and the remainder by environment. However, a proportion figure (b^2) is often legitimately used in discussions of how much of the total variability of a characteristic in a given *population* can be accounted for by hereditary determinants.[1] For example, Jensen (1969) has argued on the basis of a review of population studies of intelligence test scores that, in an unselected population, $b^2 = .80$. Thus,

---

[1] The *heritability index* (b^2), defined as the portion of variance in a characteristic attributable to heredity, applies to populations but not to specific individuals within those populations. Thus, we cannot say that if $b^2 = .80$ for intelligence, 80% of a given person's intelligence is produced by hereditary factors. All that can be said is that 80% of the variance of scores on an intelligence test administered to a given population is attributable to genetic differences among the individuals comprising that population.

233

Jensen estimates that 80% of the variability in intelligence test scores obtained by the population is due to hereditary factors and 20% to environmental factors. This conclusion in itself has not aroused as much controversy as his related conclusion that the reason why blacks, on the average, score lower than whites on intelligence tests is because the number of intelligence genes in the black population is less than those in the white.

Although Jensen's (1969) review was published more recently than the article by Otto Klineberg reprinted in this section, Klineberg's summary of the issues and related literature is fairly complete. Since Klineberg is admittedly somewhat biased in favor of an environmental explanation of the data on black-white intelligence differences, for purposes of comparison the student is encouraged to consult Jensen's discussion as well as the remarks of several critics of his position in volume 39 (1969) of the *Harvard Educational Review* (also see Herrnstein, 1971).

The second article in this section, by Anne Anastasi, is indirectly concerned with the heredity/environment controversy. Anastasi, noting that the Stanford-Binet and similar intelligence tests are biased toward Western culture, describes early attempts to construct "culture-free" tests of intelligence. Subsequent recognition of the fact that a score on any test reflects the examinee's culture led to replacement of the older term "culture-free" with "culture-fair." *Culture-fair tests* represent attempts to devise test items that deal with experiences common to different cultural groups. But as Anastasi points out, the culture-fairness of a test is not universal; also, a test's factorial composition may vary across cultures. Finally, since the performance criterion against which a test is validated is typically culturally-loaded, a culture-fair test may be less valid as a predictor in a given culture than a more culturally-biased test.[2]

Another current controversy in the area of intelligence testing, also related to the heredity/environment issue, was provoked by the book *Pygmalion in the Classroom* (Rosenthal & Jacobson, 1968). The book is a report of an investigation concerned with the effects of teachers' expectations on the intelligence test scores and other behaviors of their pupils. A major conclusion of the study, that simply telling teachers that certain pupils are "potential intellectual bloomers" can raise the IQs of the pupils, has been the topic of much discussion and further empirical research. In a review of *Pygmalion in the Classroom*, Robert Thorndike (1968) pointed out a number of methodological flaws of the investigation. Furthermore, in a second look

---

[2] The article by Julian Stanley (no. 17) in Section IV also includes some discussion of the question of the cultural biasness of test items and its effects on the validity of tests as predictors of grades and persistence in college.

at the Rosenthal and Jacobson data, two Stanford University researchers concluded that, "Our reanalysis reveals no treatment effect or 'expectancy advantage' in Grades 3 through 6. The first and second graders may or may not exhibit some expectancy effect. . .," but "a conclusive analysis of these data is not possible." (Elashaff & Snow, 1970) The author of the third article in this section, in a similar investigation, failed to find an "expectancy effect." However, there are admittedly many variables on which an "expectancy effect" might depend, and the topic is certainly worth pursuing through more carefully designed experiments.[3] Unfortunately, random assignment of people to experimental treatments, as required by analysis of variance designs, is difficult in educational settings. Even Claiborn's rather carefully planned investigation (no. 27) can be questioned on its use of analysis of covariance, since neither pupils nor groups were randomly assigned to treatment conditions.

The final article in this section on individual and group differences deals with a broad range of psychological variables—achievement, intelligence, personality—correlated with birth order or ordinal position in the family. William Altus cites the results of numerous investigations conducted during the past century as support for his hypothesis of the "eminence of primogeniture." These findings reveal a tendency for firstborn children to be higher achievers, higher scorers on tests of intelligence or scholastic ability (especially verbal ability), and to differ in other respects from later-borns. Several studies referred to have also shown that, in relation to accomplishment, birth order interacts with sex of siblings and age differences. Altus explains the preeminence of the firstborn as being due to differences in the ways that parents treat these children, as compared to later-borns. Thus, parents appear to stress "conscience" development, independence training and achievement more in the case of firstborns who become higher achievers. Of course, Altus's summary refers to tendencies; the firstborn child is not invariably the brightest nor the most successful child in the family. But the "environmentalist" explanation that parental encouragement of independence and achievement at a certain age level (6-8 years) is associated with superiority of the firstborn is provocative. In any event, it would appear difficult to argue for a hereditary explanation of the data cited by Altus.

---

[3] Barber's (1969) description of five failures to demonstrate the experimenter bias effect casts considerable doubt on the potency of the "pygmalion phenomenon."

25 | Negro-White Differences in Intelligence Test Performance: A New Look at an Old Problem*

Otto Klineberg

I have written this article at the suggestion of the Society for the Psychological Study of Social Issues (SPSSI), Division 9 of the American Psychological Association. It is based in part on some of my own earlier publications and in part on a chapter which I have prepared for a forthcoming book; it represents an attempt to bring up to date a psychological analysis of an old problem. The substantial number of recent publications in this field, some of which have attracted considerable popular attention; the many "letters to the editor"; the unfortunate tendency, all too frequent, to stray from an interpretation of the data to an attack on the ethnic origins or the alleged political positions of the persons involved; the accusation of a "conspiracy"; and finally, the practical implications which have been drawn for public policy—all of these developments have made a factual reappraisal desirable. I had hoped that this might be done by another psychologist, one less closely identified with a definite stand on one side of this issue. As the next best thing, I have tried to look, as honestly as my own biases would permit, at the evidence which has accumulated on both sides. It goes without saying that I am writing as an individual, and that neither the Council nor the membership of SPSSI should be held responsible for what follows.

The Issue

I shall restrict my discussion of Negro-white differences to that aspect of the issue on which we, as psychologists, may claim to speak with professional competence, namely, the interpretation of the results obtained from the application of mental tests. There are other aspects of at least equal impor-

*From Klineberg, O. Negro-white differences in intelligence test performance. *American Psychologist*, 1963, **18**, 198-203. Copyright 1963 by the American Psychological Association, and reproduced by permission.

tance; whether, for example, there is any acceptable indication of biological superiority or inferiority; whether one can argue from the nature of a culture to the genetic factors responsible, etc. On these and related questions the anthropologists are better qualified than we are to express a judgment. I leave these matters, therefore, with the single reminder that the American Anthropological Association has taken the position that there is no scientifically acceptable basis for a genetic hierarchy among ethnic groups.

As far as mental tests are concerned, the issue is *not* one of whether *on the average* Negro children obtain lower test scores than whites. Of that there can be no doubt. My own earlier survey (Klineberg, 1944), in which I was greatly aided by Kenneth B. Clark, was based on 27 studies, and led me to the conclusion that an IQ of 86 represented the approximate Negro median. Shuey (1958), after a much more thorough and complete survey, obtained substantially similar results; on verbal group tests alone, she located no fewer than 72 studies, based upon tests of 36,000 colored children, and her estimate of the average IQ is 85. (I might add parenthetically that in my own earlier survey I found median IQs for children of Italian, Portuguese, and Mexican parentage at or below those of American Negroes, and those of American Indians definitely below.) Shuey's estimate is therefore very close to mine.

The addition of so many further studies has, however, supplied very little new insight. One is reminded of the *Literary Digest* poll in connection with the Roosevelt-Landon electoral contest in 1936; on the basis of more than 2,000,000 ballots, it was predicted that Landon would win an overwhelming victory. As is well known, there was a systematic bias in the sample. The addition of another 100 studies of Negro children would not strengthen Shuey's (1958) conclusion that there are "some native differences between Negroes and whites as determined by intelligence tests" (p. 318), if some systematic error entered into the test results.

As far back as 1933, Garrett and Schneck in their book on *Psychological Tests* reminded us that "the examiner must always remember that comparisons are permissible only when environmental differences are absent, or at least negligible" (p. 24). This appears to be the crucial issue. What comparisons of Negroes and whites have been made under such conditions?

The Argument for "Some Native Differences"

There are three major studies cited by Shuey and others as demonstrating that differences persist even when environmental factors have been "equated." (I have put this word in quotation marks for reasons which will appear later.) One of these is by Myrtle Bruce (1940), who matched Negroes and whites in a rural community in southern Virginia on the Sims Socioeconomic scale, and still found a difference, with a resulting mean IQ on the Binet of 86 for the whites and 77 for the Negroes. Those who have used Bruce's results have not always gone on to note her careful qualifications.

> Although the white and Negro samples equated for social status still show statistical differences in IQ on each of the three intelligence tests, this fact cannot be considered proof of the superiority of the white group, since the equation of the two groups *is not entirely valid* (p. 20, italics supplied).

Even a quick look at her graph on page 20 shows more whites at the upper levels and more Negroes at the lower. Bruce herself "is inclined to believe that there is an innate difference between the particular white and Negro groups studied" (p. 97). She does not, however, extend this conclusion to the ethnic groups in general; she speaks, for example, of the skewness of the Negro IQ distribution as something which "prevents this study from being used as evidence for the superiority of the white race to the Negro race" (p. 97).

Suppose, however, that the two groups had really been "equated" for their scores on a satisfactory socioeconomic scale. Can this possibly be regarded as taking care of all the relevant environmental variables? This appears to be the assumption underlying the study by McGurk (1951) in New Jersey and Pennsylvania. Negro and white high school seniors were matched for socioeconomic level, and still there was a difference, the Negroes overlapping the white means by 29%. This would be an important finding (as would also the demonstration that there was about as much difference between the two groups on test items identified as "cultural" and "noncultural," respectively) if socioeconomic level were all that mattered. Can anyone really believe that? Do motivation, self-confidence, opportunity for wider experience, and other related factors count for nothing?

In a recent critical review, Dreger and Miller (1960) insist that it is not enough to equate ethnic groups in terms of social class and economic variables; that there is a caste as well as a class difference; that even those Negroes whose economic status is higher than that of most white persons will still in most cases be prevented from living the same kind of life in all respects; these writers insist that many other factors may also be important. Incidentally, they emphasize that they "are not taking sides at this point in the hereditary-environment controversy . . ." (p. 367). They show their impartiality in a striking and (to me) slightly painful manner by stating that "Shuey does the same rationalizing from an hereditarian standpoint that Klineberg did in his earlier 'review' from an environmental standpoint" (p. 364). To return to McGurk, it is impossible to accept the contention that all relevant environmental factors have been considered, just because socioeconomic status has been controlled.

The third study which has figured prominently on this side of the argument is by Tanser (1939). This was conducted in Kent County, Ontario, Canada, where the Negroes have lived since before the Civil War; Tanser writes that they are on a level with the whites in regard to "every political and social advantage." On the Pintner-Paterson tests, the mean white IQ was 109.6, the Negro, 91; on the Pintner nonlanguage test, the means were 111 and 95; on the National Intelligence Test the respective figures were 104 and 89. On this last test, 20% of the Negroes reached or exceeded the white median; 29% of the Negroes and 56% of the whites reached or surpassed the *National* test norms. (Tanser's study is unfortunately not available to me in Paris; I have quoted these figures from Shuey.)

If Tanser is right with regard to "every political and social advantage," these results must be taken seriously. A comment by Anastasi (1958) is, however, pertinent.

> Nevertheless significant differences were found in the socioeconomic level of the two groups. Moreover, it is reported that the white children attended school more regularly than the Negro, a difference often associated with social class differences. Thus within the entire sample of white children tested, school attendance averaged 93.38%; within the Negro sample, it averaged 84.77% (pp. 556-557).

I have only one comment to add. I was born in Canada, and lived there the first 25 years of my life. I would have said that Negroes were reasonably well off there, but emphatically not that they lived under conditions of complete equality, or that the social environment was free of prejudice. I would have thought that Canada was in this respect similar to the northeastern United States, with Negroes occupying about the same relative position. As a matter of fact Chant and Freedman (1934) report a correlation of .98 between scale values assigned to the same list of ethnic groups, including Negroes, by Canadian as by American students. I do not know Kent County, Ontario, and I cannot take it for granted that the same attitudes would be found there. I cannot help wondering, however, whether this particular Canadian community can be so exceptional. I would like to see a replication of this study, with full attention to social and sociological variables, and to patterns of personal development and interpersonal relations. In the meantime, Tanser's results cannot be dismissed, but they appear to me to be outweighed by the evidence on the other side.

The Argument Against Native Differences

The evidence against the assumption of native differences in intelligence test performance between Negroes and whites still seems to me to be very convincing. The relevant studies, most of which are already well known and will therefore be presented in brief outline, include the following.

Among infants during the first year of life the earlier finding by McGraw (1931) was that southern Negro babies showed inferiority on the Hetzer-Wolf tests. McGraw concludes:

> It is significant that with even the very young subjects, *when environmental factors are minimized* [italics supplied], the same type and approximately the same degree of superiority is evidenced on the part of the white subjects as that found among older groups.

In New Haven, however, where Negro mothers obtained more adequate nourishment and where the general economic level of the families had improved, Pasamanick (1946) found no Negro inferiority or retardation. A follow-up of 40 cases at a mean age of about two years still showed no retardation (Knobloch & Pasamanick, 1953; Pasamanick & Knobloch, 1955). Using different tests, Gilliland (1951) also reports no significant differences between Negro and white infants in Chicago.

For preschool children, Anastasi and d'Angelo (1952), found no significant differences on Goodenough Draw-a-Man IQ between samples of Negroes and whites attending Day Care Centers in New York City. Dreger and Miller (1960) comment:

> With due recognition of the limitations of the Goodenough as a test of intelligence, we may yet regard Anastasi and d'Angelo's results as a challenge to nativist theories of intellectual differences between the races (p. 366).

It is as the children get older that differences in test performance appear. Surely this is to be expected on the basis of the cumulative effect of an inferior environment. Such an effect has been demonstrated in the case of white children as well. To mention only one example out of many, Sherman and Key (1932) found a striking decrement with age among white children living in the "hollows" of the Blue Ridge Mountains; there was a Pintner-Cunningham IQ of 84 at ages 6-8; 70 at 8-10; and 53 at 10-12. This is a much more dramatic drop than any with which I am familiar in the case of Negro children; it shows what *can* happen when a poor environment persists over a long period.

Conversely, when the environment improves, test scores go up. In the case of Negro children they do not usually go up all the way to meet the white norms, but this is to be expected if the discriminatory treatment persists, and even *for a time* if discrimination were to be completely eliminated. The atmosphere in the home, the conversation around the dinner table, the use of leisure time, the books read and discussed—these and other factors contributing to "intelligence" cannot be expected to change over night or even possibly in one generation. With this in mind, the changes that have been reported in Negro IQs become all the more impressive.

When my students and I indicated (Klineberg, 1935) that test scores of southern Negro children improved in proportion to their length of residence in New York City, we were perfectly aware that they still did not reach the white norms, and we pointed that out. Could anyone have expected them to do so under Harlem living conditions, and in the Harlem schools as they were at that time? Could anyone possibly suggest that in New York or in Philadelphia, where Lee (1951) obtained similar results, there is *no* discrimination against Negroes? There was improvement, however, because there was *less* discrimination than where they came from.

In some cases, the improvement has even been dramatic. Shuey (1958, p. 87) points out that in my review of Negro intelligence testing (Klineberg, 1944) I gave special prominence to a study by W. W. Clark in Los Angeles (1923). This I did because of the striking finding that the Negro children attending 5 elementary schools obtained an average National Intelligence Test IQ of 104.7 as compared with an IQ of 106 for all the children in 15 schools. Shuey indicates that she wrote to Clark asking for further details, and was informed by him that "the *National* norms available in 1922 were probably *about 5 per cent too high*" (p. 87, italics supplied). Surely 5% does not change the results greatly. Besides, in that case the results for the comparison group of 15 schools would also have to be reduced by a similar proportion.

I also wrote to Clark for further information, and he indicated that the obtained IQs were too high, but that he could not determine by how much. The fact remains that if they were too high for the Negroes, they were also too high for the rest of the Los Angeles school population. Clark's original article indicates that there was *no significant difference* shown in the intelligence level of the Negro children and the 15 schools in general, nor were there significant differences in reading comprehension, arithmetic ability, spelling, as well as educational accomplishment in general. He writes: "The average accomplishment and range of accomplishment for Negro children is practically the same as for the total population of the fifteen schools."

Shuey reports further that research conducted in Los Angeles Public Schools in 1928 (unpublished) revealed a median IQ for Negro children of 95. If that is the case, it is difficult to understand Clark's finding of "no significant difference." Even if we accept this estimate, however, the fact remains that in the relatively friendly climate of Los Angeles, Negro IQs have shown a tremendous leap upwards. Compare even this lower estimate of 95 with the 76 reported by Bruce for rural Virginia. Could "selective migration" account for this large difference? Shuey writes:

> If we were correct in assuming an IQ difference of about 9 points between northern and southern Negro children, then about half to two-thirds of this difference may reasonably be attributed to environmental factors and the remainder to selective migration (p. 314).

Here the difference is 19 points, and "half to two-thirds" would suggest that Shuey would accept an improvement of 10 to 12 points in IQ as attributable to the superior environment. I am putting this figure *at its most conservative*, since I have found no acceptable evidence for this kind of selective migration, but even then the environmental rise is clear, and it is considerable.

The desegregation of elementary schools, particularly in the border states and cities where the process has more than a "token" character, gives us another opportunity to see what an improved educational environment may accomplish. This situation has been studied in Washington, D. C., although the measures used were tests of achievement rather than of intelligence. Stallings (1960) writes:

> The Washington study showed that during the five years following integration, marked progress has been made in academic achievement . . . a gain was made in the median score for every [school] subject tested at every grade level where the tests were given.

With regard to Louisville, Kentucky, Omer Carmichael, Superintendent of Public Schools, reported (1959) as follows:

> When we tested, we looked at the results the year before desegregation and then looked at them after the second year of desegregation and found that the Negro in all grades had improved—and by an amount that was statistically significant.

This does not mean that average differences between Negroes and whites have disappeared; it does mean that they have been reduced. Nor has this occurred as the result of "pulling down" the white level. Carmichael reports that there "was a slight improvement for the whites; a substantial improvement for the Negroes." For the difference to disappear completely, much more has to happen. (Even among whites, the difference in the IQ of occupational classes is substantial.) Until that "more" has happened, we have no right to assume that Negroes are, on the average, innately inferior.

Averages and Individuals

In many of the recent analyses of ethnic differences, including the extensive one by Shuey, a great deal of emphasis has been placed on the extent of overlapping. Her own estimate is that the median overlap among school children was between 10 and 20%. (In McGurk's study it was 29%, and presumably in Clark's it was close to 50%.) As every psychology student (but unfortunately not every layman) knows, this refers to the percentage of the "inferior" group who reach or exceed the mean of the "superior." As Anastasi (1958) points out:

> If 30 per cent of the Negroes reach or exceed the white median, the percentage who reach or exceed the lowest score of the white group will be approximately 99. Under these conditions, therefore, the ranges will overlap almost completely (p. 549).

Clearly, then, statements to the effect that there was "only 20% overlap" obscure the degree of similarity in the total distributions.

This fact comes out strikingly when one looks more closely at Bruce's findings on the Kuhlmann-Anderson scale. For the total population examined (521 whites and 432 Negroes), the range in IQ was 52 to 129 for the former and 39 to 130 for the latter. When equated on the Sims scale, the range was 51 to 115 for the whites, and 41 to 130 for the Negroes. On the Binet, the two ranges were 51 to 125, and 51 to 130; on the Grace Arthur scale, 46 to 140, and 51 to 120, respectively. On three out of these four comparisons, one or more Negroes obtained higher scores than *any* of the whites; on two out of the four, one or more whites obtained scores as low as, or lower than, those of *any* Negro.

Let us suppose for the purpose of this argument (a supposition for which I perceive no acceptable evidence) that there is a difference in averages due to genetic factors. What about the individuals who "overlap"? I learned my statistics from a good teacher, a former psychologist at Columbia University, who kept reminding us not to forget the *range* when we compared two distributions. We were both students of that wise man, R. S. Woodworth, for whom the essence of psychology, as I understood him, was the behavior and characteristics of the *individual*. In one of his texts (1929) he defined psychology as the scientific study of the activities of the individual.

It is perhaps beyond the scope of this paper to consider the practical implications of psychological research on Negro-white differences and similarities, but I hope I may be permitted one observation. Lines of demarcation between groups of people, in employment, in education, in opportunities for development, based on alleged differences in averages which are essentially abstractions, do violence to the facts of individual capacities and potentialities. At the most, group differences are obscure and uncertain; we are faced with the living reality of individual human beings who have a right to the opportunity to show what they can do when they are given an equal chance. Perhaps I am allowing my own value system to influence me to look at the whole range of individual variations and not just at averages. I should have thought, however, that concern with the individual represented one value on which all psychologists might find themselves in agreement.

Conclusion

I can only conclude that there is no scientifically acceptable evidence for the view that ethnic groups differ in innate abilities. *This is not the same as saying that there are no ethnic differences in such abilities.* In the first place, I do not feel that mental tests can by themselves alone be used to prove this negative proposition. Perhaps in the future new techniques will be developed, better than our present tests, less subject to possible variations in interpretation, more conclusive in their results. I doubt that this would really change the picture, but the possibility must be kept open. Secondly, it is exceedingly difficult ever to prove the absence of something, because one can never be certain that all the relevant factors have been taken into account. We can, however, say to those who have claimed to find evidence for ethnic differences in innate mentality: You have not proved your case. You have not been able to demonstrate that such differences exist.

We can go a little farther than that. We can point to the improvement in achievement when conditions of life improve. We can emphasize the tremendous variations within each ethnic group, much greater than the differences between groups even under discrepant environmental stimulation. We can insist that since innate psychological differences between ethnic groups have never been satisfactorily demonstrated, we have no right to act as if they had been. The science of psychology can offer no support to those who see in the accident of inherited skin color or other physical characteristics any excuse for denying to individuals the right to full participation in American democracy.

26 | Culture-Fair Testing*

Anne Anastasi

The title of my talk illustrates one of the "Innovations in Testing" with which this panel is concerned. Had the organizer of this program been less sophisticated and up-to-date than she is, I might have been asked to talk about culture-free tests. This more traditional title would have provided me with a convenient opening sentence, in which I could have disclaimed the existence of any such tests. At that point either I could have sat down or I could have proceeded to talk about something else. But no such easy solution is open to me now.

I shall approach my topic from several angles, including rationale, varieties, universality, factorial composition, and validity. First we may ask, "What is the current *rationale* of culture-fair tests and how does it differ from that of the older 'culture-free' approach?" When psychologists began to develop instruments for cross-cultural testing some fifty years ago, they hoped it would be at least theoretically possible to measure hereditary intellectual potential independently of the impact of cultural experiences. The individual's behavior was thought to be overlaid with a sort of cultural veneer, whose penetration became the objective of culture-free testing.

Subsequent developments in genetics and psychology have demonstrated the basic fallacy in this concept. We now recognize that hereditary and environmental factors interact at all stages in the organism's development, from conception to death, and that their effects are inextricably intertwined in the resultant behavior. For man, culture permeates nearly all environmental contacts. Since all behavior is thus affected by the cultural milieu in which the individual is reared and since psychological tests are but samples of behavior, cultural influences will and should be reflected in test performance. It is therefore futile to try to devise a test that is *free* from cultural influences. The present objective in cross-cultural testing is rather to construct tests that presuppose only experiences that are *common* to different cultures. For this reason, such terms as "culture-fair," "culture-common," and "cross-cultural" are gradually replacing the older "culture-free" label.

It follows that there can be many *varieties* of culture-fair tests—as many varieties as there are parameters along which cultural groups differ from each

*From *Educational Horizons*, 1964, 43, 26-30. Copyright 1964 by Pi Lambda Theta. Reprinted with permission of the author and publisher.

other. A well-known example of such a parameter is language. If the cultural groups to be tested speak different languages, we need a test that requires no use of language on the part of either examiner or subjects. This type of test is illustrated by the *Army Group Examination Beta* and the *Pintner Non-Language General Ability Test*. It is also illustrated by some of the earliest individual performance tests, such as those developed by Knox during the early part of this century to test immigrants at Ellis Island. The *Knox Cube Test*, later incorporated into the *Pintner-Paterson Performance Scale, the Arthur Point Scale of Performance Tests*, and the Wechsler scales, originated in that project.

Another type of culture-fair test is the non-reading test, which calls for extensive use of spoken language by the examiner, but no reading by the subject. Illiterates, persons with inadequate schooling, and those with special reading disabilities are among the groups for which this type of test is culture-fair. A relatively recent example of such tests is provided by Flanagan's *Tests of General Ability*, or TOGA. Extending from the preschool to the adult level, this test demands good understanding of spoken English and considerable information specific to the modern American culture; but it requires no reading. Another example is the nonverbal part of the *Lorge-Thorndike Intelligence Tests*. Many individual performance tests also fit into this category.

Cultures and subcultures frequently differ in the emphasis they place upon speed. Not only the tempo of daily life, but also the motivation to hurry and the value attached to rapid performance vary widely among national cultures, among ethnic minority groups within a single nation, and between urban and rural sub-cultures. Accordingly, cross-cultural tests have often—though certainly not always—tried to rule out the influence of speed by allowing long time-limits and giving no premium for faster performance.

Still other parameters along which cultures differ pertain to test content. Most non-language and non-reading tests, for example, call for items of information that are specific to certain cultures. Among the culturally linked objects in such instruments as the Army Beta and other non-language tests may be found violin, postage stamp, gun, pocketknife, telephone, piano, and basketball player. A reservation Indian in the United States or an Australian aborigine would lack the experiential background to respond correctly to such items. It was chiefly to control this type of cultural parameter that the classic "culture-free" tests were first developed. Currently available examples include the *Leiter International Performance Scale, the IPAT Culture Free Intelligence Test*, and Raven's *Progressive Matrices*. In all these tests, the attempt was made to include only content common to a wide variety of cultures. The *Davis-Eells Games* represent an attempt to control content parameters with regard to socioeconomic classes within the urban American culture. Thus in this test, the authors tried to employ only items that would be as familiar to lower-class as to middle-class children in American cities.

The examples cited suffice to show that culture-fair tests have been devised with reference to several specific purposes and for use with specific groups. To be sure, the classical "culture-free" tests, such as the Leiter, IPAT, and *Progressive Matrices,* were developed with very broad objectives in mind. Moreover, the original concept of a "culture-free" test carried strong implications of *universality.* No available test, however, can be accepted as universally applicable or equally "fair" to all cultures. Although less restricted than other tests, cross-cultural tests are never completely unrestricted in their cultural reference. Any test tends to favor individuals from the culture in which it was developed. The mere use of paper-and-pencil or the presentation of abstract tasks having no immediate practical significance will favor some cultures accustomed to representative drawing. A two-dimensional reproduction of an object is not a perfect replica of the original; it simply presents certain cues that, as a result of past experience, lead to the perception of the object. If the cues are highly reduced, as in a simplified or schematic drawing, and if the necessary past experience is lacking, the correct perception may not result. Cultural differences in emotional and motivational factors may also influence test performance. Examples include intrinsic interest of test content, rapport with the examiner (who may be a member of another culture), drive to do well on a test, desire to excel others, and past habits of solving problems individually or cooperatively.

Obviously no single test can control all these cultural parameters. Even if it were possible to construct a test that included only content and functions common to all cultures and to so manage its administration as to admit only emotional and motivational variables shared by all mankind, the usefulness of the resulting test might be questionable. Its universally culture-fair residue of behavior would probably prove to be so minute and trivial as not to be worth measuring.

Paradoxical as it may seem, the culture-fairness of a test is itself culturally limited. In other words, a given test may be culture-fair when applied to groups A and B, but heavily culture-bound when used in comparing groups B and C. An entirely different test may be culture-fair in the comparison of groups B and C. This limitation in the applicability of culture-fair tests may be illustrated with the verbal-nonverbal dichotomy into which intelligence test content is often classified. It is commonly assumed that nonverbal tests are more nearly culture-fair than are verbal tests. This assumption is obviously correct for persons who speak different languages. But for groups speaking a common language, whose cultures differ in other important respects, verbal tests may be less culturally loaded than tests of a predominantly spatial or perceptual nature.

Cultural factors may influence relative performance on verbal and non-verbal tests in a number of ways. Interests, value systems, work habits, problem-solving attitudes, or emotional insecurity arising from cultural conditions may foster or retard the development of specific aptitudes. When the *California Test of Mental Maturity* was given to university students in Ceylon, the Ceylonese greatly surpassed the American norms on the language part while falling far below the norms on the non-language part. This difference is the reverse of what might have been expected in a bilingual population such as the Ceylonese. The investigator attributed these results to the value systems of the upper-class Ceylonese culture, which included rejection of manual tasks and attachment of high prestige to verbal scholarship. The nature of the Ceylonese educational system, with its emphasis upon feats of memory and upon learning by precept and rote, was also cited as a possible contributing factor.

As a result of a somewhat different combination of cultural pressures, Jewish groups tested in America usually perform much better on verbal tests than on tests involving concrete objects, spatial relations, and numerical problems. These results have been corroborated in several studies, employing a variety of tests and extending from the preschool to the college level. This intra-individual difference between verbal and non-verbal performance has also been found to increase with age. The traditional emphasis in most Jewish families on formal education and abstract intelligence has often been mentioned in explanation of such findings.

Still another example is provided by studies of American Negroes, who generally perform more poorly on perceptual and spatial tests than on most types of verbal tests. One explanation proposed for these differences centers around problem-solving attitudes. Insofar as the social environment of the American Negro has traditionally encouraged attitudes of passive compliance rather than active exploration, it would be more conducive to rote verbal learning than to perceptual manipulation of stimuli and problem solving.

Here then are three groups—two of them bilingual and one with a relatively poor educational background—which for very different reasons perform better on verbal than on nonverbal tests. These findings challenge the common belief in the greater culture-fairness of nonverbal tests and suggest that the problems of cross-cultural testing are too complex to be solved by a single, all-purpose type of test.

At this point we may well ask: "When is a culture-fair test not culture-fair?" The answer is: "When it fails to control relevant cultural parameters." It follows that in choosing a culture-fair test, we must take into account the cultural similarities and differences between the particular groups to be tested, as well as the specific cultural parameters controlled by each test.

There is still another important way in which culture-fair tests differ from each other, namely in their *factorial composition.* In their individual efforts to rule out language, reading, or other culturally biased content, test constructors have followed a variety of paths and have produced tests measuring widely different intellectual functions. When psychometricians regarded all intelligence tests as measures of Spearman's *g*, specific test content was a matter of indifference. But later research with the techniques of factor analysis has demonstrated that the aptitudes measured by different item types or different content may be quite distinct.

Non-language and other cross-cultural tests differ from one another in the extent to which they draw upon spatial and perceptual functions, as contrasted with symbolic manipulation of concepts and abstract relations. The latter functions resemble more closely those required in traditional verbal tests of intelligence. To be sure, the substitution of pictorial for verbal content may itself alter the nature of the test. At the same time, we cannot indiscriminately group together all pictorial or non-language tests. Some, like the *Pintner Non-Language Test,* concentrate on spatial and perceptual factors to the almost complete exclusion of other factors. Other non-language tests utilize item types calling primarily for ideational or symbolic responses as illustrated by Raven's *Progressive Matrices.*

Although all these tests may yield similar-sounding "intelligence quotients," their similarity is deceptive. The difference in the intellectual functions sampled by different culture-fair tests of intelligence, as well as in their proportional coverage of these functions, provide one more reason for evaluating each test individually, in the light of specific testing purposes and needs.

A final question concerns the *validity* of culture-fair tests. Whether we are interested in predictive validity in the narrow sense or in concurrent, construct, or even content validity, we always want to be able to generalize beyond the test itself. We give a test so that we may draw some conclusion about what this individual will do in *other* situations. Therefore, whether the elimination of cultural differentials from a test will raise or lower its validity depends upon the *breadth* of the cultural differential.

For example, if a test item requires the interpretation of a proverb familiar to children in one cultural group but not in another, its inclusion would probably lower the validity of this test against most criteria. On the other hand, if one group performs more poorly on certain items because of inadequate facility in the use of English, the inclusion of these items would probably not reduce the validity of the test for certain purposes. In this case, the same factor that lowered the test score would also handicap the individual in his educational and vocational progress and in many other activities of daily life. Similarly, slow work habits, emotional insecurity, low achievement drive, lack of interest in abstract problems, and many other culturally linked conditions affecting test scores are also likely to influence the relatively broad area of criterion behavior.

To be sure, these cultural handicaps are remediable—many within the individual's own lifetime. Other cultural handicaps such as the brain damage resulting from improper maternal nutrition or other inadequacies of prenatal environment, may require more than one generation for their elimination. But cultural handicaps cannot be remedied by removing cultural differentials from test scores while leaving them in the criterion behavior that the tests are designed to predict. This ostrich-like approach only evades the problem.

The purpose of tests is to show what the individual is able to do at the time of testing. Tests are not designed to show the causes of behavior or the origins of individual differences in performance. To identify causal factors, we need to investigate the experimental backgrounds of the individuals or groups tested. Nor can tests be used as instruments of social reform. To compensate for a cultural handicap, we need remedial programs directed toward the individual as well as toward society. Masking the handicap by the use of a culture-fair test is no solution.

To summarize: culture-fair tests endeavor to utilize what is common in the experiential backgrounds of different cultural groups. They include many varieties of tests, each eliminating one or more parameters along which cultures differ, such as language, reading, speed, or culturally loaded content. The culture-fairness of any test is not universal but must be evaluated in terms of the cultural differentials of particular groups. Culture-fairness depends upon the control of relevant cultural parameters. Culture-fair tests also differ among themselves in factorial composition, or in relative coverage of different intellectual functions. While an IQ on one such test may be largely a measure of abstract reasoning, on another it may depend chiefly on spatial and perceptual aptitudes. Finally, whether or not cultural differentials should be eliminated from a test depends ultimately upon the effect their elimination will have upon the test's validity for specific purposes.

27 | Expectancy Effects in the Classroom: A Failure to Replicate*

William L. Claiborn

Summary. Twelve first-grade classrooms were divided equally among four groups representing the combinations of presence or absence of the expectancy bias and classroom observers. In the bias classes, each teacher received a list of approximately 20% of her pupils who could be expected to show "intellectual blooming" when these pupils were in fact picked without regard to intellectual potential. Retesting 2 months later showed no relative gains for pupils who were the object of the expectancy bias; there were no clear changes in observed teacher-pupil interaction. Differences between the present study and previous studies were discussed in light of this "failure to replicate." It was concluded that the evidence for bias effects in the school remains equivocal.

Rosenthal and Jacobson (1968) and others have reported that changing a teacher's expectation of a particular pupil's intellectual potential results in changes in that pupil's performance on a standardized group IQ test. This research has grown out of a long line of E bias studies (Rosenthal, 1964, 1966, 1967) which have demonstrated that the expectations of E are a significant factor in determining the outcome of the experiment. This appears to occur with the greatest regularity where the demands of the task are relatively vague (Shames & Adair, 1967). However, Barber and Silver (1968) presented an analysis of 31 studies which have attempted to demonstrate the E bias phenomenon. According to their reanalysis and reinterpretation of the design and statistics presented in these studies, the majority did not clearly or unequivocally demonstrate the unintentional E bias effect. Barber and Silver are particularly critical of post hoc analyses following failure to reject the null hypothesis and of post hoc probability pyramiding. They conclude that the bias effect is more difficult to demonstrate and less pervasive than has been previously assumed.

*From Claiborn, W. L. Expectancy effects in the classroom: A failure to replicate. *Journal of Educational Psychology*, 1969, **60**, 377-383. Copyright 1969 by the American Psychological Association, and reproduced by permission.

A thorough reading and analysis of the recent book, *Pygmalion in the Classroom* (Rosenthal & Jacobson, 1968), shows that the same difficulties discussed by Barber and Silver (1968) are inherent in their presentation. Rosenthal and Jacobson randomly chose approximately 20% of the children in each of three classes in Grades 1-6. Teachers were told that these "special" children could be expected to show intellectual blooming in the coming months. What follows is an example of the kind of difficulty present in the authors' interpretation of their data. At the end of the first year, the special children had gained more IQ points relative to the control children ($p < .02$, one-tailed). This effect is largely attributable to substantial changes in one first-grade classroom in which the special children showed a relative advantage of 15.4 IQ points. There was no significant IQ gain reported for Grades 3-6. Thus, there was no teacher expectancy effect in two-thirds of the grades examined. More importantly, only 2 of the 18 classes (one first and one second grade) yielded any reliable IQ increase; one third grade showed a significant decrease. Examination of the pretest IQs for the special and nonspecial pupils in the three first grades shows differences in initial IQ. Significance tests indicated that one first grade differed on the verbal subtest; the special children had the lower pretest scores. When this −28 point initial discrepancy is compared with the posttest discrepancy of +8 (*ns*) points, it is apparent that regression effects could account for the observed changes. It is this class which produces the significant IQ change score. Randomization failed to protect the selection of special children and resulted in uninterpretable effects. The authors' pre- to posttest difference-score analysis clearly does not permit unambiguous statements attributing changes to treatment. In a real sense, no expectancy effects can be claimed for the first grade.

Analyses of other results reported by Rosenthal and Jacobson (1968) make it reasonable to fail to reject the null hypothesis that no reliable teacher expectancy effects were observed. In any case, the findings upon which Rosenthal and Jacobson (1968) based their conclusions were difference scores, not corrected for known pretest differences, and partially attributable to regression effects. Further difficulties relating to post hoc hypothesis support, partial data analysis, and probability pyramiding are presented in Claiborn (1968).

Despite these weaknesses, Rosenthal and Jacobson (1968) conclude that telling a teacher that some of her children are likely to show intellectual blooming is sufficient to result in changes in the pupil's obtained IQ. It is implied that the measured changes are not artifacts of the experimental procedure.

> Teachers may have treated their children in a more pleasant, friendly, and encouraging fashion when they expected greater intellectual gains of them. Teachers probably

watched their special children more closely, and this greater attention may have led to more rapid reinforcement of correct responses with a consequent increase in the pupil's learning. . . .Such communication together with possible changes in teaching technique may have helped the child learn by changing his self-concept, his expectations of his own behavior, and his motivation, as well as his cognitive style and skills [Rosenthal & Jacobson, 1968, p. 180].

The primary purpose of this present research was to observe and quantify some in-class teacher-pupil behavior in an attempt to "capture" changes in teacher behavior which would follow the introduction of a fictitious statement about the intellectual potential of some of her pupils. The second purpose of the study was to "replicate" the earlier purported finding that providing a teacher with a bias for the intellectual growth of some of her pupils results in the improvement in intellectual performance for those special pupils. Most generally it was hypothesized that altering the teacher's expectancy for the intellectual potential of some of her pupils would result in (a) an increase in the child's IQ as measured by difference between pre- and posttest on a standardized group IQ test; (b) a differential change in teaching behavior toward the children who were the objects of the expectancy bias. The biased teacher would have more frequent contact, express more positive affect, and would tend to expand upon the contributions of the special children.

Method

Design

The study can be described as a 2 X 2 factorial experiment. The two levels of the first factor consisted of the presence or absence of raters in the classroom; the two levels of the second factor consisted of the presence or absence of induced expectancies for intellectual blooming. As Table 1 illustrates, the research plan provided for four experimental groups. Each group consisted of three classrooms chosen from the available sample of 12 first grades.

In brief, in the beginning of the spring term a 2-week observation period in Rated classrooms was followed by a testing session in all classes. The results of the testing for "potential intellectual bloomers" was made known to the Bias classroom teachers following the first testing period; observation was continued for an additional period. Two months later, near the end of the school year, the IQ test was readministered to all children.

TABLE 1   *Treatment Conditions for Each of the Four Experimental Groups*

Group	Class-room be-havior ratings	Pretest	Expect-ancy bias	Class-room be-havior ratings	Posttest
Rated—Bias	X	X	X	X	X
Rated—No Bias	X	X	0	X	X
Unrated—Bias	0	X	X	0	X
Unrated—No Bias	0	X	0	0	X

NOTE.–"X" indicates the presence of a treatment, "0" indicates its absence.

Sample

The schools from two predominately middle-class suburbs of a major upstate New York community each provided four first-grade classes. Each cell of the 2 X 2 (Rated—Bias; Rated—No Bias; Unrated—Bias; Unrated—No Bias) contained three classrooms, one from each of the three different schools. Within the school, classes were assigned to the Bias and No Bias conditions (with one exception) at random. Assignment of classes to Rated and Unrated conditions was made by the school principal. The mean pretest IQ for classes ranged from 92.4 to 118.4.

Within each classroom, approximately 20% (from four to five) pupils were designated as "special" and subject to special analysis. The special pupils in the Bias classrooms were presented to the teachers as "potential bloomers." The 20% were chosen proportionately from the males and females in the class, and within sex randomly, from the upper and lower half of the pretest IQ distributions.

Measures

The primary dependent measure was pre- to posttest IQ differences obtained from the group administration of Tests of General Ability (TOGA) developed by Flanagan (1960). The limits at the high end of the tabled norms for this test necessitated extrapolations for IQ scores for a few pupils. A similar problem, though at the opposite end of IQ range, developed in the Rosenthal and Jacobson (1968) experiment.

The second major set of dependent variables was obtained from systematic ratings of classroom behavior. Each classroom in the Rated condition was scheduled for regular observation sessions. The 20-minute sessions were divided into a pretest unit of 2 weeks and a posttest unit of 7 classroom days. The system of rating was designed to evaluate teacher interactions regarding particular pupils rather than to assess the teacher's general teaching behavior. Each interaction was scored for the particular pupil involved. The rating attempted to assess the nature and frequency of teacher-pupil interactions, including affective aspects.

Procedure

The period from the beginning of the classroom rating to the final post-testing was just under 3 months in the spring of a regular school year. In the beginning of the spring term, following some preliminary observation, the first formal rating period lasted 2 weeks and was introduced to the teachers as part of a requirement for a graduate education course. Following this observation period, children in each of the 12 classes were tested with the TOGA. Teachers were told that the test was designed to predict "intellectual blooming." At the end of the same week, "test results" were distributed to the teachers in the Bias classes only. These results in fact reported the names of the 20% who had been independently chosen from each class. Immediately following the testing and the introduction of the expectancy bias, classroom observation continued for an additional period of about 1½ weeks. In the first week of the last month of school, all classes were retested with the same IQ test. Teachers also completed a questionnaire which assessed their awareness of the nature of the experiment, and their ability to remember the names of the students who had been designated as "bloomers."

The classroom observers and the author were aware of the major experimental hypotheses. The teachers, however, were not told the nature of the experiment and the raters did not know which were the Bias and which were the No Bias classrooms. In addition, only the Biased teachers and the author were aware of which children were designated as "potential bloomers."

Results

From the questionnaires it was evident that the teachers were able to accurately remember the names of the "potential bloomers," providing evidence that the teachers attended to the bias presentation.

The major hypothesis, similar to the hypothesis tested in the Rosenthal and Jacobson (1968) experiment, that pupils who were the object of the expectancy bias would show greater pre- to posttest IQ improvement when compared to the remaining pupils, was tested with a three-factor analysis of covariance, using the pretest IQ as the covariate to control for initial IQ differences. Lord (1963) points out that the use of simple difference scores such as pre- to posttest IQ differences, may result in distortion due to uncontrolled regression effects. It also requires more rigid assumptions about the linear and ratio nature of the variable scale. Covariance used in randomly assigned groups may minimize some of these problems (see Evans & Anastasio, 1968). However, where groups are not randomly assigned, or where other assumptions are not met, it may not be possible to determine the appropriate adjustment for initial differences. Finally Lord points out that the use of a poor measure to adjust for initial differences is of negligible value. The reliability co-efficients reported for the TOGA are sufficiently high (Flanagan, 1960) to reduce concern regarding the use of the IQ pretest score as a covariance adjustment.

IQ changes in the special and nonspecial pupils within the bias classes were compared, blocking on Rated and Unrated classrooms and on schools. The test for the hypothesis yielded an F of 2.12 ($df = 1/101$), which was not significant, indicating no effect as measured by the IQ change for the pupils who were designated as "bloomers" when compared to the remaining pupils in the class. Similarly, there were no significant differences when IQ subtest scores were compared. These findings are in contrast with those reported in Rosenthal and Jacobson (1968). The mean pre- and posttest IQ scores for the various groups are presented in Tables 2 and 3.

As can be seen from the tables, there was considerable variability between classes in initial and follow-up IQ. Comparison of pretest IQs for critical groups (e.g., the between comparison of the special Bias pupils with pupils in No Bias classes and the within comparison of the special Bias pupils with the nonspecial Bias pupils) shows that randomization yielded special and nonspecial groups within schools of sufficiently similar pretest IQs.

Examination of Table 4 shows a substantial practice effect or gain from pre- to posttesting. The mean full scale gain for all pupils was 11 points, ($t = 14.86$, $df = 245$, $p < .0001$). The gains reported across schools and classes were not consistent and no simple explanation for these differences is apparent.

Further analyses nominally evaluated hypotheses relating to cross-class comparisons, such as the prediction that special children in the Bias classes would show more gains than the children in the No Bias classes; that children designated as nonspecial in the Bias classrooms would show less IQ gain than the children in the No Bias classrooms; and that children in the Rated classrooms would show greater pre- to posttest IQ gains than would the children

TABLE 2   Mean Pretest Full Scale IQ for All Groups

Group	School 1			School 2			School 3			All schools	
	IQ	n	SD	IQ	n	SD	IQ	n	SD	IQ	n
Bias—Rated	108.9	19		117.2	19		109.9	23		111.9	61
Special	110.2	4	22.0	117.8	4	19.5	109.8	5	11.7	112.4	13
Nonspecial	108.6	15	10.9	117.0	15	13.6	109.9	18	15.1	111.7	48
Bias—Unrated	111.0	20		96.8	23		109.8	21		105.5	64
Special	114.0	4	15.5	93.4	5	9.3	113.5	4	15.8	105.9	13
Nonspecial	110.3	16	10.8	97.8	18	10.4	108.9	17	15.4	105.4	51
No Bias—Rated	118.4	20	15.6	99.5	21	12.7	114.8	23	15.1	110.9	64
No Bias—Unrated	101.1	19	12.4	92.4	16	5.2	113.8	22	20.0	103.6	57
Bias	110.0	39	12.2	106.0	42	15.8	109.8	44	14.5	108.3	125
No Bias	110.0	39	16.5	96.5	37	10.7	114.3	45	17.5	107.5	121
Rated	113.8	39	15.1	108.0	40	16.1	112.4	46	14.7	111.4	125
Unrated	106.1	39	12.8	95.0	39	8.7	111.8	43	17.8	104.5	121
Bias Special	112.1	8	17.7	104.2	9	18.7	111.4	9	12.9	109.1	26
Bias Nonspecial	109.4	31	10.7	106.5	33	15.3	109.4	35	15.0	108.4	99
All pupils	109.9	78		101.7	79		112.1	89		108.2	246

TABLE 3   Mean Posttest Full Scale IQ for All Groups

Group	School 1			School 2			School 3			All schools	
	IQ	n	SD	IQ	n	SD	IQ	n	SD	IQ	n
Bias—Rated	114.4	19		133.9	19		123.7	23		124.0	61
Special	109.5	4	16.1	142.0	4	14.6	121.4	5	19.8	124.1	13
Nonspecial	115.7	15	15.1	131.7	15	13.2	124.3	18	18.3	123.9	48
Bias-Unrated	120.8	20		103.3	23		125.1	21		115.9	64
Special	117.0	4	22.4	97.6	5	8.6	128.5	4	5.7	113.1	13
Nonspecial	121.8	16	10.6	104.9	18	12.3	124.3	17	21.7	116.7	51
No Bias—Rated	131.9	20	14.4	107.6	21	13.7	132.7	23	20.1	124.2	64
No Bias—Unrated	106.3	19	18.2	102.7	16	14.0	124.4	22	23.5	112.3	57
Bias	117.7	39	14.3	117.1	42	20.0	124.3	44	18.7	119.8	125
No Bias	119.4	39	20.7	105.5	37	13.8	128.7	45	22.0	118.6	121
Rated	123.4	39	17.0	120.0	40	19.0	128.2	46	19.5	124.1	125
Unrated	113.7	39	17.3	103.1	39	12.6	124.7	43	21.4	114.2	121
Bias Special	113.2	8	18.5	117.3	9	25.8	124.6	9	14.9	118.6	26
Bias Nonspecial	118.9	31		117.1	33		124.3	35		120.2	99
All pupils	118.6	78	13.1	111.7	79	18.4	126.5	89	19.7	119.2	246

TABLE 4   *Adjusted Mean Full Scale IQ Gains*

Group	School 1	School 2	School 3	All schools
Bias Special pupils	1.63	13.74	10.70	8.69
Rated	-.60	25.83	5.62	10.26
Unrated	3.86	1.64	15.77	7.09
Bias Nonspecial pupils	9.39	10.50	16.97	12.29
Rated	7.02	16.10	16.13	13.08
Unrated	11.76	4.89	17.81	11.49
Bias Rated classes	3.21	20.97	10.88	11.69
Bias Unrated classes	7.81	3.27	16.79	9.29
No Bias Rated classes	12.00	8.19	13.31	11.17
No Bias Unrated classes	4.68	12.21	7.79	8.23
All Bias classes	5.51	12.12	13.83	10.49
All No Bias classes	8.34	10.20	10.55	9.66
All classes	6.93	11.16	12.19	10.09

in the Unrated classrooms. Only the last of these three hypotheses was supported ($F = 8.39$, $df = 1/197$, $p < .005$). Since the classes comprising this test were not randomly assigned, factors relating to assignment, observation or their interaction may be the source of the results.

The other major set of hypotheses dealt with predictions related to teacher-pupil interactions. The hypotheses were tested with multivariate analyses of variance (Cooley & Lohnes, 1962). The hypotheses that within the Bias Rated classes, teacher-pupil interaction ratings would change more with the special children than with the nonspecial children, and that across classrooms, teacher-pupil interactions with special pupils in the Bias classrooms would show a differential change when compared to teacher-pupil interactions with special pupils in the No Bias classrooms were not supported. There was, however, weak evidence of a differential change in the teacher-pupil interactions with the nonspecial pupils in the Bias classrooms when compared with the nonspecial pupils in the No Bias classrooms ($F = 3.60$, $df = 8/95$, $p < .01$). The contributions of the various teacher-pupil interaction variables were not predicted a priori, and are not easily or clearly related to teaching practice.

Discussion

The major hypotheses were not supported. There were, however, certain crucial differences in procedure which distinguish this finding from those presented by other authors. First, however, a noting of similarities is in order. The IQ test and the bias statements which accompanied the "test results" were exactly the same as those used by Rosenthal and Jacobson (1968). Approximately the same percentage of designated "bloomers" was chosen from each class. Two major differences between the present procedure and the Rosenthal and Jacobson study do exist: (*a*) the bias in the present study was introduced about 1 month into the second semester of the school year, presumably well after the teacher had formed impressions of her pupils; (*b*) retesting followed 2 months after the introduction of the bias. In the Rosenthal and Jacobson study, the bias was introduced at the beginning of the school year, and retesting for IQ change was performed at the end of each semester. Their teachers, presumably, had not had time to form stable impressions before the introduction of the bias; similarly, the duration of the experiment was several months longer than in the present study. In the study by Conn, Edwards, Rosenthal, and Crowne (1968) the bias was introduced at the beginning of the second semester and pupils were retested at the end of that semester. Anderson and Rosenthal (cited in Rosenthal & Jacobson, 1968, p. 145 f) observed expectancy bias effects within the summer camp season. Likewise, Beez (1968) found bias effects within an 8-week period. Considering these studies together, it appears that neither the duration of the experiment nor the nature of the teacher's prior impressions have been shown to be critical variables.

Rosenthal (1969) combines 11 studies dealing with expectancy effects in educational settings. He computes a directional standard normal deviate for the "comparable" findings. By considering all the findings as essentially similar, he computes a joint one-tailed probability of .00033 supporting the position that expectancy effects have been reliably demonstrated. However, examination of the studies which he has combined shows that the findings were not at all similar and certainly not directly comparable. For example, while the Claiborn (1968) study, reported here, was based on approximately 2 months of "bias effects" for first graders, the comparison presented from Rosenthal and Jacobson (1968) apparently refers to the results of all classes after 1 year. The most similar comparison would seem to be the one-semester results of Rosenthal and Jacobson for first graders. Had that been used, substantially different standard normal deviates would be in the table. Similar arguments can be made for and against the inclusion of the nine other studies, and it does little to the strength of the expectancy-effect position to juxtapose substantially incongruent and dissimilar findings and represent them as parallel.

A major difference between the Rosenthal and Jacobson (1968) and the present study is the level of pretest IQ. Generally, in the present study, the pretest IQ was substantially higher than that reported in Rosenthal and Jacobson. In both cases, the TOGA norms proved to be inadequate resulting in added error variance.

There are two major conclusions to be drawn from the present study: (a) Further research needs to be conducted before the conclusions of the Rosenthal and Jacobson experiments become accepted as psychological fact. It should be clear from this short paper that at least one study which was sufficiently similar to the original paradigm has produced results which do not support, nor suggest that there is, an expectancy effect. (b) It would appear that the assessment of teacher-pupil interaction variables in terms of a relatively easily rated set of behavioral interactions has yet to prove its usefulness. Since the hypotheses relating to IQ change were not supported, little can be said about the ability of the rating procedures to capture teacher changes which were a result of the bias. There was some evidence that the presence or absence of the expectancy bias was related to the teaching behavior toward those children who were *not* included in the bias statement. However, the nature of the relationship and the configuration of the variable weights were not predicted and have little face validity. A more tenable general hypothesis is that as a result of biased expectations, some teachers changed their behavior but that these behavior changes cannot accurately or adequately be assessed by analysis in terms of identical changes for all variables for all Ss.

From this study, it appears that teacher behavior is moderately resistant to the kinds of bias or expectancy statements which make up much of our standardized testing programs. The evidence concerning the effects of giving teachers information about the abilities of their pupils on the pupils' academic performance remains equivocal. Considering the discussion presented in this paper and by others (Barber & Silver, 1968), caution should be used in accepting significance levels and verbal conclusions at face value. Data can be combined in ways designed to maximize desired outcome and to capitalize on chance or other factors (as exemplified by the use of uncontrolled difference scores).

Unlike much research in education and psychology, the Rosenthal and Jacobson (1968) report has already begun to have an effect on educational practice. Of course, even if the teacher expectancy effects are accepted without qualification, the issue as to the magnitude of these effects (or amount of variance accounted for) has not been discussed. It is essential that psychologists be particularly careful in drawing conclusions from ambiguous data.

28 | Birth Order and Its Sequelae*

William D. Altus

The relation of order of birth to achievement has been investigated for nearly a hundred years. The first known data appear in Sir Francis Galton's *English Men of Science,* published in 1874. Galton selected his scientists according to objective criteria, such as being a Fellow of the Royal Society, and then asked them for biographical data, including their order of birth. He found more only sons and first-born sons among them than his calculations showed chance should have allowed. This finding he thought easy to interpret: Through the law of primogeniture, the eldest son was likely to become possessed of independent means and to be able to follow his own tastes and inclinations. Further, Galton argued, parents treated an only child and a first-born child (who is also an only child for a period of time) as a companion and accorded him more responsibility than other children were given. Thus first arrivals on the family scene were favored from the start.

A generation later Havelock Ellis (1904, 1926) published *A Study of British Genius,* based on 975 eminent men and 55 eminent women selected from the 66 volumes of the *Dictionary of National Biography.* In the main, he chose those to whom three or more pages were devoted in this dictionary, but excluded those who were of the nobility and also those whom he judged to be notorious rather than famous. Among those eminent people, Ellis found some striking linkages to order of birth: The probability of appearance was much greater for a first-born than for an intermediate child, and the youngest likewise was favored over the intermediate child, though not to the same degree. Ellis does not interpret his finding; he merely reports that it is congruent with an American study (Yoder, 1894) published a decade earlier:

This predominance of eldest and youngest children among persons of genius accords with the results reached by Yoder in studying an international group of 50 eminent men; he found that youngest sons occurred oftener than intermediate sons and eldest sons than youngest.

*From *Science,* 1966, **151,** 44-49. Copyright 1966 by the American Association for the Advancement of Science. Reprinted with permission of the author and publisher.

About the time Ellis published his survey of eminent Britishers, the American psychologist Cattell (1917) published data based on 855 American scientists, which showed the same relation between birth order and eminence, the eldest and then the youngest being favored.

In 1915, Corrado Gini showed a linkage between order of birth and being a university professor. From 445 replies to a questionnaire he sent to his fellow professors in Italian universities, he found that twice as many were first-born as would have been expected from chance, and that all the other birth orders were below expectancy or no higher than expectancy. Gini's published data do not allow comparisons between the youngest and the in-between. I report these data with considerable diffidence, since most of us have had personal experience with university professors who would not qualify as eminent people, no matter how lax a criterion one employed. Still, it is of some interest to know that the first-born also takes precedence in the academic milieu, if data gathered a half century ago in Italy have generality beyond that time and place.

In his dissertation, on the nature and nurture of American men of letters, E. L. Clarke (1916) reported that eldest and youngest sons appeared in greater than chance numbers. He rationalized his findings in a somewhat different way from his predecessors:

> First-born and last-born children frequently enjoy greater educational opportunity than do their intermediate brothers and sisters. First-borns often succeed in getting a start before adversity befalls the family, or before the expense of caring for an increasing family of young children becomes so great that it is necessary to curtail the education of some of the older children.

He also notes that the youngest comes along when older brothers may be grown up and in a position to help the youngest through school.

In 1938, the American geographer Ellsworth Huntington published a book primarily concerned with what he felt were sequelae of one's season of birth. He collected data on 1210 Americans whom he thought to be the most distinguished of those whose vitae he found in genealogical works. Of those who came from two-child families, 59 were first-born and 33 were second-born. While his finding is typical of all those reported thus far, his explanation of the linkage is not typical: He argued that the first-born probably tend to be physically stronger and healthier. The more vigorous eminent, he claimed, tended to be born early in the year (perhaps, though he doesn't say so, as the first fruits of the traditional June wedding). One may safely accept his data on the birth order of the eminent without accepting his explanation.

In a study of the birth order of Rhodes Scholars, mainly those from the United States, Apperly (1939) found the first-born to be overrepresented. Among two-child family representatives, 144 were first-born, 91 second born. He also found the youngest child to take precedence over the in-between one.

Jones (1954) gives some statistics on birth order of persons listed in *Who's Who*. Some 64 percent of the representatives of two-child families were first-born; if inclusion in *Who's Who* were a strictly chance affair, one would expect, of course, a 50-50 distribution of the older and the younger from two-child families. Of the three-child family representatives 52 percent were first-born, instead of the 33 percent to be expected.

The last of the studies relating to eminence to be reviewed here, though it is by no means the latest, is that by Anne Roe (1953), who published in 1953 her researches on 64 eminent scientists, selected for their distinguished contributions by the elder statesmen in their respective specialties. Thirty-nine, or 61 percent, were first-born. But the evidence for primogeniture of talent is even more overwhelming, according to Roe:

> Of the 25 scientists in my groups who were not first-born, five are oldest sons, and two of the second-born were effectively the oldest during their childhood because of the death of older sibs, one at birth, one at age two.

Therefore, Roe concludes, some 46 of the 64—72 percent—were actually or effectively the oldest sons in their respective families. Roe's data corroborate in an accentuated way all the evidence which has been marshalled on the topic of birth order and eminence, beginning with Galton's study in 1874. I have found no study that shows trends divergent from those here reported.

Birth Order and Intelligence

Forty years ago Lewis Madison Terman published the first volume (1925) of his studies of 1000 "gifted" school children—that is, children with IQ's of 140 or higher, which is the IQ of the top 1 percent of the general population. Most of these children came from small families; only a few came from families of five or more children. Among those from families of two, three, and four children, Terman found the eldest the most numerous, followed by the youngest, and then by the in-between children. Terman noted that the breakdown was quite similar to the one Cattell had found for eminent American scientists some 20 years before, but he did not attempt to bind these separate studies together by theory.

Terman's findings, which indicate that—at least among the very bright—birth order may be of some significance, have to my knowledge never been checked on a large sample until quite recently. In June 1964, Robert C.

Nichols, of the National Merit Scholarship Corporation, sent me some data on 1618 high school students who were finalists in the National Merit competition and who earned exceptionally high scores among this restricted group. Nichols reports the average score of this selected group of finalists to be "almost three standard deviations above the mean of the general population," which would imply an aptitude at least in the top 0.5 percent of the general population. This level of aptitude is superior to that of Terman's gifted group. Nichols reported that of the 568 representatives of the two-child family, 66 percent were first-born. Of the 414 from three-child families, 52 percent were first-born; the other two ranks obviously contributed 48 percent. Of the 244 students from four-child families, 59 percent were first born, the other three ranks contributing 41 percent. Of the 85 representatives of the five-child family, 52 percent were first-born, the other *four* birth ranks contributing 48 percent. In summary, nearly 60 percent of the Merit Finalists who came from families of two, three, four, and five children were first-born. Here is intellectual primogeniture with a vengeance! But Nichols shows that birth order is effectively linked to aptitude *only at the top level.* In the very large number of high school students who took the first round of tests before any were eliminated, birth order does not appear to be related to the scores earned. In one respect Nichols' data do not corroborate the findings on eminence: Youngest children are less numerous among his restricted Merit Finalists than the in-betweens. In fact, Nichols' data show a stairstep progression downward, from the first-born to the last in each family group, whether of two children, three children, four children, or five children.

I have found birth-order linkages to aptitude-test data among students in the University of California (Altus, 1962, 1963, 1964, 1965b), about whom I have been collecting statistics since 1959. Students at this university are a select group, since in general only those applicants who rank in the top 10 to 15 percent with respect to high school grades are eligible for admission. In two samples, one consisting of 1800 undergraduates and another of 2500, the first-born scored higher to a small though statistically significant degree than did the later-born on tests of verbal intelligence, which measure such things as the size of general vocabulary and the ability to infer correctly the right words to make sense of statements from which key words have been omitted. On the other hand, measures of quantitative ability were not found to be associated with birth order per se. However, when birth order is linked to another parameter, the sex of the sibling, certain correlations are noted. First-born students, either male or female, from two-child families earned a significantly (.05 level of confidence) higher mean score on a test of quantitative ability if their siblings were male. This finding corroborates in part an earlier study by Helen Koch (1954), who found that 5- and 6-year-old boys and girls in two-child families earned higher scores on the Primary Mental Abilities Test if the other child in the family was a boy rather than a girl. Koch's finding is independent of birth order: Having a brother for a sibling helped both the younger and the older in the two-child family. My data on college students show a facilitating effect only for the first-born with a brother and only in a measure of quantitative ability.

Nichols' data on the National Merit Scholarship contestants suggest that there may be hierarchies of aptitude related to birth order and family size. For instance, the first-born with three siblings had the highest mean aptitude scores of all birth ranks among those who came from families of two, three, four, and five children. The mean score of contestants with two older siblings was the lowest of all these ranks, significantly lower (.01 level of confidence) than that of the first-born from four-child families. My data from the University of California confirm these findings: The first-born in the four-child family is significantly brighter (.01 level of confidence) in verbal aptitude than the youngest from the three-child family; he has the highest verbal aptitude among all students who come from families of two, three, and four children—a group which accounts for four-fifths of the student population. The only child scores even higher, but he is eliminated from these comparisons because Nichols did not include the only child in his reported data. Schachter (1963) shows the only child to be markedly overrepresented among graduate students at the University of Minnesota. These two items of data may be related: The only child may be the ablest and thus persist longer as a student.

It seems reasonable to infer from the foregoing that order of birth may well be associated with aptitude if the population is quite bright. Terman's findings, Nichols', and mine all point in this direction. The data are obviously neither conclusive nor definitive, but they are consistent and compelling. There is, additionally, some evidence that the sex of the sibling, where there is only one, may affect one's aptitude score. Finally there is a suggestion that there may be hierarchies of aptitude levels among the intellectually able related to birth order and family size.

Birth Order and College Attendance

Given the data on birth order and eminence and birth order and aptitude, one would expect to find some degree of correspondence between birth order and college attendance. I first became aware of the correspondence in tabulating the birth ranks of certain of the students on the Santa Barbara campus in

1959. During the next 4 years, 1960 through 1963, I gathered annual data for all—or nearly all—students who matriculated there for the first time. Of the 1817 representatives of the two-child family, 63 percent were first-born. The figures for men and women are almost exactly alike. During the same period, 1299 representatives of the three-child family matriculated; 50.5 percent of these were first-born, 30.8 percent were second-born, 18.7 percent were third-born. Matriculants from four-child families numbered 538, of whom 50.5 percent were first-born, 25.8 percent second-born, 14 percent third-born, 9.7 percent fourth-born. We noted this downward progression by birth order also in Nichols' data for Merit Finalists. Here the data on college attendance and Merit Finalists part company with the data on eminence: The youngest is not favored over the intermediate sibling; he is at the bottom step in the progression.

Are the data on college attendance and birth order thus far reported merely a parochial accident? Sufficient data are not at hand for a definitive answer, but there is some evidence that it would be no. At Yale, 61 percent of an undergraduate sample proved to be first-born (Capra & Dittes, 1962); at Reed College, 66 percent; at the University of Minnesota, slightly over 50 percent (Schachter, 1963). The differences in percentages may be a function of the degree of selectivity exercised by the various institutions—the more stringent the standards for admission, the higher the percentage of first-borns. This inference is based, of course, upon what has been found in the realm of aptitude testing. If the inference proves to be correct, then public junior colleges should have the lowest percentage of first-borns, since in most states, if not all, their entrance requirements are least stringent. Cal Tech, Rice University, and Harvard should, according to this hypothesis, enroll a very high percentage of first-borns. It does not seem likely, however, that in any college the percentage should much exceed the 66 percent of the Reed College sample.

Mary Stewart, in 1962, reported (Stewart, 1962) a study of 7000 boys and girls in grammar and modern secondary schools in a London borough. The grammar school is mainly college preparatory and is entered by virtue of passing a state examination, the "11 plus." Those who do not pass may attend the modern school. Stewart found the first-born to be overrepresented in the grammar school, and the later-born in the modern school. However, of those who remain in school after the legal attendance requirements have been met at age 15, roughly the same proportion of first-borns is found in both schools, when the ratio of the first-to the later-borns becomes slightly greater than two to one. It seems clear that birth-order influences on schooling are present in England and are just as sharp as they are here.

Schachter (1963) reported data from colleges and certain professional schools in the United States which show that at the graduate level, also, the first-born is overrepresented. This overrepresentation holds not only for the ratio of all first-born to all later-born, but also for families of any given size.

Several studies (Altus, 1965a, 1965b) in the psychological journals show that birth-order linkage to college attendance goes back at least to the '20's. Bender (1928) reported some data in 1928 which show that the first-born were clearly in excess at Dartmouth at that time. His focus was on something other than the relation of birth order to college attendance; consequently, he missed the significance of this aspect of his data. In this he was like all others who reported birth-order data for college students, until Schachter, in 1963, finally noted the connection between order of birth and going to college.

The evidence is of course not all in. The reports are fairly numerous by now, and they are consistent in their findings. Since the evidence is congruent with what has been consistently found for various degrees of eminence for nearly 100 years, and also with what has recently been found concerning the linkage of verbal aptitude and birth order among the very bright, it seems a fairly safe assumption that there is a kind of academic primogeniture operating at the college level.

Birth Order and Personality

Alfred Adler believed that order of birth was influential in the channeling of the socially very significant power drives. The first-born, he said (Adler, 1928), is a "power-hungry conservative." The foregoing data suggest that the later-born may come out poorly in competition for position in our technological society, but it does not necessarily follow that industrial or professional achievement derives from a hunger for power. As to the allegation that the first-born is a conservative, I have been unable to find convincing evidence on the college campus. I have found at Santa Barbara that the first-born is somewhat more likely to say he attends church services than is the later-born, but this bit of evidence is about all I have found linking the first-born with conservatism. None of the measures of liberalism-conservatism I have tried out thus far show consistent trends related to birth order.

Sears, Maccoby, and Levin (1957) came to the conclusion that the first-born shows greater "conscience" development than does the later-born. They thought that the differences they found in children were probably due to differences in handling of the first-born by parents, that the first-born had more metes and bounds set to his behavior and was more likely to be punished for transgressions. The father, it was noted, often participated in the disciplining of the first-born, a practice he did not usually continue with the later children. Dean (1947) found the first-born to be more cooperative and more given to curiosity, the later-born to be more pugnacious and also more affectionate. This latter finding—that the later-born are more affectionate—may have a sequel in a recent report by Schachter (1964) that first-born were not so well liked as later-born by their fraternity brothers in the University of Minnesota.

Koch (1956) found in her study of 5- and 6-year-old boys and girls from two-child families that the sex of their siblings together with birth order could influence their social behavior. For instance, a boy who is junior to a sister close to him in age (within 30 months, say) will often be rather "sissy" in comparison with a boy who has an older brother. The boy with the not-much-older sister will more commonly admit to liking to play with girls and with dolls than will boys reared in other sibling relationships. Recently I have found some similar evidence among college students. Male students with older sisters close to their own age were significantly less masculine on two measures of masculinity-femininity than were other males from two-child families.

Schachter (1959) in 1959 concluded from a series of studies conducted over several years that the first-born is more driven by "affiliative needs" than is the later-born, especially when danger threatens. If the first-born feels that danger or pain lurks in the offing, he wants to share his anxiety by being with others; the later-born shows considerably less need to be with other people under similar circumstances. In this sense, the first born is more dependent on others. These generalizations of Schachter's derive largely from studies of undergraduates at the University of Minnesota.

Capra and Dittes (1962) have reported that among Yale undergraduates first-borns were more likely to volunteer for a psychological experiment than were later-borns. I have also found, in a study recently concluded (May, 1965), that first-born males showed up for voluntary experimental testing in somewhat greater proportion than did later-borns. The differences among the female undergraduates were in the same direction but were not statistically significant. It may be that there is a sex factor here; it is also plausible that the nature of the experiment influences the ratio of volunteers. More research is certainly necessary to determine the significant parameters, if any, relating to birth order and volunteering for experimentation. If first-born do tend, even though only under certain circumstances, to offer themselves as subjects with greater alacrity, this would have great significance for those who base research on samples drawn from college students, especially where the first-born is already considerably overrepresented. Social scientists, in particular, who often use college populations in their studies, would have to control another parameter in their experimental designs.

It seems a reasonable hypothesis that birth-order effects are seldom unitary, but are mixtures involving other family aspects, such as the sex of the siblings and their difference in age. It has already been mentioned that a boy whose only sibling is an older sister, especially a close-up older sister, tends to be somewhat more effeminate than a boy with an older brother. I have found at Santa Barbara that on self-rating tests a girl from a two-child family tends to check more disparaging adjectives about herself if she has an older brother than if she has an older sister. The same girl with an older brother tends to check more unfavorable adjectives about her sibling and about their father than does the second-born of two sisters. What lends interest to this datum is that there are more girls here who have older brothers than who have older sisters. One may conjecture that such a girl's academic motivation might be at the expense of self-esteem and esteem for her brother and father. In any event, there is some tentative evidence that the junior member of either sex in the two-child family has some unfortunate attitudinal residuals if the older sibling is of the opposite sex.

There have been many studies of the relation of mental disorder to birth order. Since the data reported tend to be confusing and generally rather contradictory, they will not be introduced here, except for those of Schooler (Schooler, 1961, 1964), who has done two studies on birth order and schizophrenia. He found that females who were among the younger in large families, that is, of five or more children, were overrepresented in his two samples of schizophrenics. Schooler believes that the difference in incidence is probably social in origin rather than biological, but he does not attempt to explain the presumed social genesis. In students at the University of California I have been unable to find any relation between birth order or family size and maladjustment, as measured by such a standard device as the Minnesota Multiphasic Personality Inventory. There are differences, to be sure, in the way certain items in this test are answered by first-borns as compared with later-borns, but generally these differentiating items bear no relation to symptoms of a neurotic or psychotic nature. This is not to say that personality differences do not obtain, as both family size and birth order are varied, for they do; but the differences in this admittedly parochial population seem not to be related to deviant adjustment to any significant degree.

An Attempt at a Synthesis

In England and in the United States, there appears to be an indubitable relation of birth order to the achievement of eminence, however it has been defined. The dice are loaded in favor of the first-born. There is also some evidence that in the *quite bright* segment of our population the first-born are not only present in greater numbers, but are also somewhat more verbally able. The first-born is overrepresented among college populations, and there is some indication that the more selective the college, the greater the over-representation. It seems reasonable to believe that the aptitude data and the college attendance figures must be interrelated, and it seems equally reasonable that both sets of data are linked, quite possibly in a causal way, to the numerous data on eminence that have been presented.

Cattell (1917) observed that the preeminence of the first-born was "probably due to social rather than to physiological causes." In my opinion the most prominent of the presumed social "causes" is likely to be the differential parental treatment accorded children of different ordinal positions, to greater "conscience" development, greater dependence on adult norms, and higher expectations of achievement falling to the lot of the first-born. I have already mentioned the report of Sears *et al.* (1957) that parents tend to be stricter with the first-born child. Lasko (1954) noted that later-born children tend to be treated in a more relaxed, permissive way. This difference in rearing practices may explain why Dean (1947) found the first-born to be more dependent upon adults and the later-born more physically aggressive—that is, less hampered by social restraint. She also reported that the first-born showed more curiosity—that is, he asked more questions—and that he sought adult attention more frequently. Finally, one further difference which sets the first-born apart is that he is the only child who has access for an indeterminate period of time to parental interaction which he does not have to share with a sibling.

The foregoing data suggest fairly strongly, I think, why the first-born may do better in school. His curiosity, dependence upon adults, and greater conscience development doubtless make him respond more affirmatively to the teacher and to the school. He should thus more frequently win the teacher's approval, which should serve to augment further his tendencies to do that which is expected of him as a student. If this inference is correct, it is easy to understand why the colleges attract such a high proportion of the first-born.

Schachter (1963) argues that the greater predilection of the first-born for college explains his greater eminence: His superior educational attainments make the achievement of eminence easier for him when he competes for place and position with the less well-trained later-born. This would appear to be unquestionable today, at least as regards eminence in science and technology. I would suspect, however, that in creative writing, sculpture, painting, music—the arts generally—the dependence on college training is not nearly so marked. I would also suspect that a century ago it was easier to achieve eminence, however defined, without having gone to college. Still, the greater incidence of the first-born among the eminent must have somewhere its origin: Educational attainment cannot be discounted as an important source of the observed differences in eminence among the birth orders.

The intellectual superiority of the first-born noted by Terman, by Altus, and by Nichols among the very bright segment of the population deserves further comment. Hunt (1961), who has summarized the literature on the development of intelligence, leaves room to believe that the child can increase his intelligence by hard intellectual work. If the first-born, by virtue of his different treatment in the home, takes to school more readily, works harder, persists longer (as the college attendance figures attest), then it might be expected that he may well increase his intellectual stature in the process. The first-born who arrives at college has given himself a boost, as it were, by hard tugging at his intellectual bootstraps.

Finally, one must grapple with this problem: If differential treatment of the first-born by his parents makes him a better prospect for higher aptitude, for college training, and for eminence, why does it affect relatively few of the total available first-borns? McClelland (1961), who has given two decades to research on motivation and achievement, has generalized his findings on optimal home influences thus: " . . . what is desirable . . . is a stress on meeting certain achievement standards between the ages of six and eight." The child is given, he continues, training in independence and mastery, and he is held in warm regard by both parents, who are ambitious for him but not too dominating, and who have a strong, positive attitude toward education.

Not many parents would fill this bill of particulars in all details. Even when they do, their offspring must have an initial aptitude for learning that places them in the upper half of the total pool of children, if the parental impetus toward achievement is to have the desired result. It seems to me that the preceding considerations impose sufficient restrictions to ensure that only a minor portion even of the relatively fortunate first-born will attain a college degree. And to the extent that aptitude and eminence are a product, even partially, of the educational process, they would tend to vary with education.

In conclusion, the viewpoint embodied in this paper may be fairly summarized by a single sentence: Ordinal position at birth has been shown to be related to significant social parameters, though the reasons behind the relations are as yet unknown or at best dimly apprehended.

Assessment of Interests and Personality

Although for many psychologists the term *personality* comprises all mental and behavioral characteristics of the individual, traditionally it has referred to the somewhat more limited nonintellective or affective aspects of a person. Attempts to measure these nonintellective variables—interests, values, dispositions, motives, temperaments, traits, etc.—have resulted in a number of psychometric devices. Rating scales, inventories and projective techniques are among the many instruments for assessing personality, or the *typical performance* of an individual. Such measuring instruments are generally less reliable and valid than intellective tests, or measures of *maximum performance.* However, when combined in a battery with intellective tests, personality and interest inventories have frequently contributed something to the prediction of behavioral criteria. In addition, although their use in educational and vocational settings has sometimes aroused controversy, these instruments have proven valuable in clinical studies and research investigations.

Interest inventories in particular have been viewed as important additions to interview and aptitude test data in academic and vocational counseling situations. Clearly, there are factors which operate to invalidate scores on interest inventories—faking, response sets, failure to understand the directions, among others. For example, in the first article of this section, Charles Bridgman and George Hollenbeck report the results of an empirical study which show that, when directed to do so, college students can fill out an interest inventory (Kuder Form D) in such a way that their responses do not differ significantly from those of the corresponding occupational groups. Furthermore, the verification or validity keys on interest inventories do not always detect dissimulation of this sort. But simply because an individual *can* fake does not imply that he *will* fake his answers in a counseling situation where he is seeking help and the need for responding accurately is explained to him. Also, general response sets, e.g., the tendency to answer in the perceived socially desirable direction, can be controlled to some extent by the forced-choice item format.

In any event, scores on interest inventories, which predict occupational persistence and satisfaction, if not occupational success, appear to have fairly impressive long-term reliabilities (see Strong, 1955). In addition, many of the occupational scales on inventories such as the Strong Vocational Interest Blanks (SVIB) tend to hold up over several decades, the occupational interest patterns of yesteryear's population having their counterparts in today's. David Campbell, who has assumed major responsibility for further development of the SVIB since E. K. Strong's death, reviews the evidence for the above statement in the second article of this section.

The third article, by Wayne Holtzman, is a rather brief discussion of each of six unanswered questions or issues concerning personality assessment: 1) What is meant by personality assessment? 2) How much must be known about an individual in order to really understand his personality? 3) How can personality variance be separated from method variance? 4) Is the theory and technique of assessment that is now being constructed culture-bound within Western industrialized society? 5) Is it possible to develop a personality theory that is systematic and comprehensive, but still closely linked with empirical data? 6) How can the moral dilemmas created by personality assessment be dealt with? In this article Holtzman gives particular attention to the second and fourth questions. His conclusion, that most of these issues will continue to be debated and unsolved for some time to come, seems reasonable if the past is any indicator of the future in personality assessment. Incidentally, in reading this article, the student may find it helpful to refer to the following definitions:

Acquiescence. The tendency of an examinee to answer in the affirmative (e.g., "Yes" or "True") on personality tests and in other situations in which he is uncertain of the "correct" answer.

Idiographic. This pertains to the detailed analysis of an individual's behavior by means of observations, interviews, tests and other clinical assessment techniques, for the purpose of determining his unique pattern of personality characteristics. Each personality is considered as a lawful, integrated system to be studied in itself.

Multitrait-multimethod matrix. A table displaying the correlations among measures of: 1) the same trait measured by the same method; 2) different traits measured by the same method; 3) the same trait measured by different methods; 4) different traits measured by different methods. This type of information is important in determining the *convergent validity* (relationship to other measures of the same construct) and *discriminant validity* (lack of relationship to measures of different constructs) of a test.

Nomothetic. In contrast to *idiographic*, this refers to the search for laws or principles which will serve as explanations of the behavior and personalities of people in general.

Social desirability. A response set (response style) affecting scores on personality inventories. It refers to an examinee's tendency to give answers that appear to him as more socially desirable, rather than necessarily accurately describing himself.

The last two articles in this section, by Gardner Lindzey and Paul Meehl, respectively, represent a description and critique/discussion of two investigations concerned with the relative effectiveness of the clinical ("seer") and statistical ("sign") approaches to diagnosis and prediction. Lindzey's investigation, like many others conducted during the 1950s and 1960s, was a response to Paul Meehl's (1954) challenge to clinical psychologists for demonstrations that the clinical/impressionistic approach to personality assessment is equal to or more accurate than the statistical/psychometric approach of regression equations and expectancy tables. In the article reprinted here, Lindzey reports that two clinicians were able to detect homosexuality by using blind analysis of TAT protocols better than by using a statistical "signs" procedure. Although Lindzey did not specify the particular techniques employed by the clinicians, Meehl argues that they were responding to "highly subtle, stylistic-expressive aspects" of the TAT responses.

Meehl recognizes Lindzey's investigation as the first and only empirical demonstration that the clinical approach can, under certain circumstances, be clearly superior to the statistical approach. On the other hand, he cites data from over 50 other studies which point to the superiority of the statistical approach in two-thirds of the cases and equal effectiveness of the two approaches in the remaining one-third. Meehl's advice, that one should "... predict by actuarial methods, except when empirical information is available as to the predictive efficiency of the clinician's functioning..." appears sound when all of the evidence is considered. However, human behavior often seems to be inconsistent, intransitive and nonlinear, so a multidimensional computer of the sort which resides in the heads of certain people (SDAC, or "simply divine automatic computer") will continue to prove more effective than an equation under certain circumstances. As both Lindzey and Meehl recognize, what is needed is further exploration of the perspicuity of some clinicians and other insightful observers of human behavior. Certainly, the ability to make accurate impressionistic judgments from psychological test responses or behavioral observations, if it is consistent, can be understood and need not remain forever in the realm of extrasensory perception.

29 | Effect of Simulated Applicant Status on Kuder Form D Occupational Interest Scores*

Charles S. Bridgman and George P. Hollenbeck

Kuder (1950, 1957) has developed an interest inventory (Occupational, Form D) which provides scales for various occupations. He suggests in the manual (1956a, p. 5) that these scales and others which could be developed for additional occupations might be of assistance in selection of industrial personnel.

Each Kuder scale is developed by selecting items which differentiate maximally between a group already employed in the given occupation and a base group representing employed people in general (Kuder, 1956b). Applicants presumably would be influenced by a desire to make a good impression to a greater extent than would individuals who are already established in the occupation. Therefore, use of such an inventory for selection purposes raises the problem of response bias. Kuder provides a verification scale to help identify respondents who either have answered incorrectly or carelessly, or who may have answered insincerely. His data indicate relatively little overlap between verification scores obtained when subjects responded sincerely and when they were instructed to make a good impression. For example, only 10% of a group of 50 college students obtained verification scores in the "acceptable" range, when instructed to conceal their faking while giving "best impression" responses (Kuder, 1956a).

The question still remains whether scores can be biased in the desired direction on such occupational scales, and if so, whether the bias will be revealed by a shift in verification scores, when respondents answer under conditions more closely approximating the application situation, i.e., where the set for faking is less firmly and explicitly established than is presumably the case with the "best impression" set which Kuder used to demonstrate the effectiveness of the verification scale.

*From Bridgman, C. S., & Hollenbeck, G. P. Effect of simulated applicant status on Kuder Form D occupational interest scores. *Journal of Applied Psychology,* 1961, **45**, 237-239. Copyright 1961 by the American Psychological Association, and reproduced by permission.

279

Method

To explore these and related questions, Kuder's Form D was administered to four groups of students in elementary psychology classes under instructions outlined below. Groups were asked to fill out the interest inventory as they would if applying for a specific sales job (sanitary supply salesman), the job of industrial psychologist, and an unspecified "job in industry." The salesman job was described briefly for the first group, and the psychologist job was described briefly for the second group. In each case the subjects were told to assume that they had the necessary background and were interested in obtaining the position. However, no explicit instructions were given to make a good impression or to falsify their responses.[1] For comparison purposes a fourth group was given vocational guidance instructions, i.e., they were asked to complete the inventory accurately in order to obtain help in making a vocational choice.

The answer choices of these four groups were scored on a sanitary supply salesman scale (developed at the University of Wisconsin) and on the Kuder industrial psychologist scale. Verification scores were also obtained.

By comparisons among scores of the experimental groups and available reference groups, we have been able to consider the following questions:

1. Can students approximate the responses of individuals actually employed in the occupations under consideration, after instructions to respond as though they were interested applicants?

2. Are the effects of assuming the role of job applicant specific to the particular occupation, or are these effects the result of a generalized effort to "look good"?

3. Do the unbiased scores of student groups differ from those of Kuder's base group on these occupational scales?

4. Can Kuder's verfication scale differentiate between biased and unbiased groups when the bias set is established through instructions to assume the role of job applicant?

Results and Discussion

The mean scores for groups instructed to act as applicants for sales and for psychologist jobs did not differ significantly from the mean scores for the

[1] Copies of the detailed instructions can be obtained from the Bureau of Industrial Psychology.

TABLE 1 *Mean Occupational Interest Scores and Standard Deviations for Groups Given Specific Job Instructions and for the Corresponding Occupational Groups*

Scale	Group	N	Mean	SD
Salesman	Sales instructions	70	71.5[a]	10.5
	Actual salesmen	50	73.1	9.6
Industrial Psychologist	Psychologist instructions	50	53.2[a]	7.9
	Actual psychologists	200	54.5	9.7

[a]Mean not significantly different from mean of corresponding occupational group.

corresponding occupational groups (Table 1).[2] The students, simply by assuming an applicant set based on a brief job description, obtained distributions of scores comparable to those of individuals actually employed in the two occupations.

Among the experimental groups, the highest occupational interest scores on each key were obtained by the group given specific instructions appropriate to the key (Table 2). Nonspecific instructions to apply for a job in industry were significantly less effective than the specific instructions appropriate to the key, but did produce mean scores significantly higher than vocational guidance (sincere) instructions.

It might be argued that presentation of the salesman and psychologist job descriptions merely established more firmly a generalized set to look good, in comparison to the job-in-industry instructions, and that this could account for the higher scores. However, evidence for the specificity of the effects of the specific job instructions was found when the groups given these instructions were scored on the noncorresponding scale (i.e., salesman instructions group scored on psychologist key, and psychologist instructions group scored on salesman key), as shown in the appropriate cells of Table 2. Salesman instructions were only as effective as nonspecific job instructions in increasing scores on the psychologist scale. On the other hand, psychologist instructions did not produce an increase in scores on the salesman scale above the mean obtained by the vocational guidance group.

[2]Analyses of variance indicated significant ($p < .01$) differences between means for the groups in Table 1 on both occupational scales and the verification scale. Subsequent t tests were employed for differences between specific means. A probability level of less than .05 was accepted as significant. Significant differences between specific means are indicated in the text and tables.

TABLE 2   *Mean Occupational Interest Scores and Standard Deviations for Experimental Groups*

			Scoring Key			
			Salesman		Psychologist	
Type of Set	*Instructions*	*N*	*Mean*	*SD*	*Mean*	*SD*
Specific Applicant	Salesman	70	71.5[a]	10.5	48.7	9.2
	Psychologist	50	61.4	8.2	53.2[a]	7.9
Nonspecific Applicant	Job in industry	55	64.8[a]	6.9	48.9	9.1
Sincere	Vocational guidance	100	61.8	9.1	44.6[a]	8.9

[a]Mean significantly different from the means of the three remaining groups.

It may be concluded that the specific job instructions produce answer choices appropriate to the given occupation. The resulting scores cannot be attributed simply to a more effectively established general set to make a good impression.

The vocational guidance group did not differ significantly from a sample of Kuder's representative employed group when both were scored on the sales interest scale.[3] (Data for Kuder's group: N = 97, mean = 60.7, standard deviation = 9.9. Data for our group is in Table 2.) However, the industrial psychologist scores of these two groups differed markedly. The mean of the students (44.6) fell approximately halfway between that of the representative employed group (33.2) and that of the actual industrial psychologists (54.5). (Data for Kuder's group: N = 97, mean = 33.2, standard deviation = 9.8. Data for the other two groups can be found in Tables 1 and 2.)

It is not particularly surprising that, in their unbiased responses to this inventory, our students are more like industrial psychologists than is Kuder's representative employed group. However, this finding raises an important question as to the appropriate base group which should be used in developing these specialized occupational interest scales. If the scale is to be used to discriminate among applicants or potential applicants, then samples of applicants can be suggested as appropriate for use as a base in developing the occupational scale. At least this procedure should be considered when there is any reason for suspecting that the responses of the applicants will differ systematically from Kuder's representative employed group.

[3] The employed group is a sample of 97 whose answer sheets were obtained from Science Research Associates.

TABLE 3   *Verification Mean Scores and Standard Deviations of Experimental and Comparison Groups*

		N	Mean	SD
Instruction Group	Salesman	70	46.8[ab]	5.5
	Psychologist	50	45.5[ab]	4.6
	Job in industry	55	48.9[b]	4.9
	Vocational guidance	100	51.1[b]	4.5
Comparison Group	Kuder's representative employed	97	54.0	3.8

[a]Significantly different from vocational guidance mean.
[b]Significantly different from representative employed mean.

The verification mean scores of the bias groups were significantly lower than that obtained by the vocational guidance group, except in the case of job in industry set, as shown in Table 3. (The scale is designed to give lower scores for individuals who are trying to make a good impression.) However, the observed means for our applicant set groups are not nearly as low as those found by Kuder for best impression responses, since he has reported mean scores in the vicinity of 35 for a number of groups responding under this set. Another Kuder group, instructed to conceal its bias, obtained a mean of 41 on the verification scale (Kuder, 1956a). The overlap of the distributions of the sample of Kuder's representative employed group and his group instructed to conceal its bias was 16%. However, the overlaps between the vocational guidance instructions group and the salesman, psychologist, and "job in industry" instructions groups were, respectively, 67%, 54%, and 82%. Thus it must be concluded that effective bias of occupational scores can be achieved without a sufficiently large shift in verification scores to ensure identification of the presence of bias in individual cases. The possibility remains that more discriminative modified verfication scales could be developed for use with each occupational scale.

Summary

Separate groups of college students were instructed to assume they were applying for specific jobs (sanitary supply salesman and industrial psychologist). When scored on the appropriate scale of Kuder's interest inventory (Form D), both groups obtained scores comparable to the groups employed in these occupations.

College students instructed to apply for an unspecified "job in industry" showed significantly higher means on both scales than a group given vocational guidance instructions, indicating that some part of the bias noted above can be introduced by such a general nonspecific set. However, evidence was presented that the instructions to apply for specific jobs produced responses appropriate to the specified occupation, rather than simply inducing a more effective nonspecific set.

College students given vocational guidance instructions obtained scores comparable to the base group (representing employed people in general) on the sales interest scale, but scored significantly above the base group on the industrial psychologist scale. This result was interpreted as implying the need to use a base group comparable to the applicant group when it is the purpose of the investigator to develop Kuder-type interest scales to be used for selection purposes.

Kuder's verfication scale differentiated significantly between the groups responding with an applicant set and the vocational guidance group. However, the differentiation was not nearly as effective as reported by Kuder between sincere and best impression groups. The differentiation was not sufficient to warrant use of the verification scale in the manner recommended by Kuder.

30 | The Stability of Vocational Interests Within Occupations Over Long Time Spans*

David P. Campbell

Summary. Counselors and those responsible for the construction and maintenance of vocational interest inventories need to be aware of change in interest patterns over time within occupational groups. That issue is explored here for the SVIB by asking three questions: first, do the SVIB scales developed in the 1930's hold up in cross-validations today? Answer: yes, they appear to. Second, when various SVIB scales have been revised, have the revised scales differed drastically from the originals? Answer: not much; in a few instances, there has been no change whatsoever. Third, do the people who today hold exactly the same jobs as those held by Strong's criterion groups of the 1930's have the same interest patterns as the original group? Answer: yes, at least in one occupation, i.e., bankers. Further speculation suggests that men with similar interest patterns have sifted into similar occupations throughout recorded history.

Do the characteristic interests of occupational groups change over time?

This is an important question for the counseling psychologist who needs to know something of the nature of these groups, and it is an absolutely crucial point for psychometricians involved in the development of vocational interest inventories. If occupational interest patterns do change, then interest inventories should be continually revised. As such revisions wipe out accumulated data on existing forms, disrupt on-going research programs, and require substantial amounts of time and money, some effort should be expended to determine just how necessary these revisions i.e., to find out just how much occupational groups do change.

To study change over time is not easy as it requires the collection of data over long periods, and even when such longitudinal data are available, they are usually not organized as one would wish. However, even with these restrictions, some pertinent information is available. As the Strong Vocational Interest Blank (SVIB) has been in existence almost 40 years, it has been

*From *Personnel and Guidance Journal,* 1966, **44**, 1012-1019. Copyright 1966 by the American Personnel and Guidance Association, Inc. Reprinted with permission of the author and publisher.

possible to locate data, already "aged," that permit some exploration of change over time.

Studies of Change Over Time

Relevant information can be grouped into three categories: the first includes those validity studies that are continually being published on the SVIB scales. If occupational groups are changing rapidly, then scales developed years ago should no longer be valid, but that is clearly not the case. Several recent studies of groups such as medical students (Thrush & King, 1964), life insurance salesmen (Ferguson, 1958, 1960), psychologists (Campbell, 1965), and policemen (Matarazzo, Allen, Saslow, & Wiens, 1964) make it clear that the SVIB scales still discriminate between occupations. A brief review of just two such studies will provide the flavor of the results.

In 1948, Berdie and Hagenah tested 70 lawyers in Minnesota who had been classified by the Minnesota law school as good practitioners. The comparison between these Minnesota lawyers, tested in 1948, and Strong's sample, drawn from the California Bar Association and tested about 20 years earlier, is shown in Figure 1. Obviously, there is a great deal of similarity between the groups, even though they came from different geographical areas, were sampled by different techniques, and were tested 20 years apart. Note that both groups scored highest on the Lawyer scale.

Another recent validity study, concerned with the Policeman scale, was reported by Matarazzo and his associates from the University of Oregon Medical School. They found considerable similarity between successful police applicants in Portland in 1959-62 and earlier applicants for the same positions. Their conclusion was: "The comparisons make clear that the 1959-62 police recruit is a remarkable facsimile . . . of the police officer appointed to the same force in 1946-47" (Matarazzo, et al., 1964, p. 132).

While these validity generalization studies certainly imply that there must be some stability in the characteristics of occupations, they are not sufficient to establish that fact conclusively. For one thing, the time spans are not very long—12 years in the case of the policemen and 20 years for the lawyers. However, the main reason for indecision is that it seems naive and contrary to common sense to believe that occupations are static and unchanging. Before that conclusion is acceptable, the evidence must be absolutely unassailable.

There is a second kind of study that provides further relevant data. For various reasons, several occupations have been studied a second time to review the appropriateness of the original scale. The occupations are as follows: psychologists (Kriedt, 1949), accountants (Strong, 1949), physicians (Strong

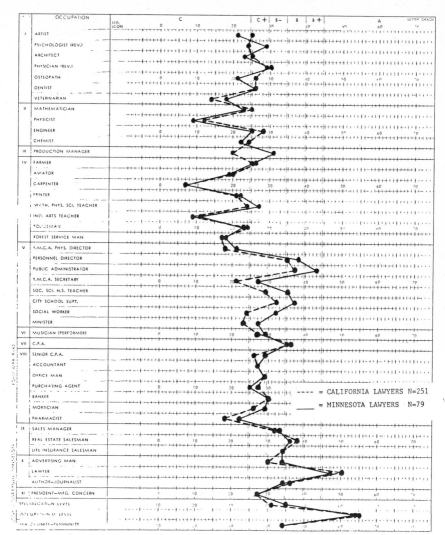

Figure 1. SVIB profiles for California (1930) and Minnesota (1948) lawyers.

& Tucker, 1952), personnel directors (Kriedt, Stone, & Paterson, 1952), and women social workers. (McCornack, 1956). In each case a new scale was developed and compared with the original scale developed in the 1930's.

Two of these new scales, Accountant and Personnel Director, were so similar to the original scales that no attempt was made to publish any changes. In the other three studies, those dealing with psychologists, social workers, and physicians, there were some changes and revised scales were published. However, even in these instances, the changes were mild; for example, the revised Physician scale correlated .85 with the original scale.

Furthermore, it is not at all clear that the revisions were necessary because of changes in the occupation. Usually the second study was methodologically better than the first, that is, the sampling was better or the sample was larger, and these sampling changes may have been sufficient to explain the changes. For example, the original 1930 Physician scale was based almost solely on the graduates of Stanford Medical School, while the 1950 Physician scale was based on a random sample of the American Medical Association. This difference in sampling method may have been sufficient to explain the difference between the original and revised scale. The same comments apply to both the psychologist and social worker studies. Clearly, these studies cannot be considered definitive answers to the question of occupational change.

The type of information that would be most useful in deciding whether occupational groups change would be comparisons, across time, of two samples from the same occupation where the sampling technique had been held constant. Some studies of this type, the third relevant category, are reported below; essentially, what has been done is to study pairs of men where each pair held exactly the same job, separated by about 30 years in time.

The first group studied was bankers (Campbell, 1966). In the old Strong files, about 190 booklets were found that had been filled in by Minnesota bankers in 1934, just after the banks reopened after the National Bank Holiday. Because the banking profession keeps very good records, it was possible to identify the exact job held by almost all of these men. In 1964, the men who held those same jobs were approached and asked to fill in the SVIB. For example, if we had a 1934 SVIB from the cashier in the First National Bank in Duluth, Minnesota, we asked the current cashier in that same bank to fill it in for us. One hundred and three pairs of bankers, matched in this way, were collected.

There are several reasons why one might expect the two groups to differ in their interest patterns as the banking business has changed considerably in the last 30 years. The public image of the banks has evolved from that of a sober, conservative old patriarch to that of an aggressive, hard-driving community servant, an image most visibly expressed in the architecture of the bank building. Not infrequently the bank is the newest and boldest appearing building in the small Minnesota town. Other changes include the improvement in accounting and data processing methods with the advent of computers, and the growth of external control exercised over these institutions by federal agencies since the 1930's.

Considering these possible sources of disruption, the similarity between the profiles of these two groups, shown in Figure 2, is remarkable.

This similarity is possibly an underestimate as the seven percent of the sample in which the same man was holding the same job 30 years later was not included.

Figure 3 reports some further findings from the banker study, i.e., test and retest profiles for a group of 48 bankers who were part of the original 1934 criterion group and who were retested in 1964. They were about 40 years old when originally tested, and about 70 years old when retested. Strong has earlier reported that interests are stable after about age 25 through age 55; from the results reported here, it appears that these characteristics remain constant well into old age. These figures also lend little support to the notion that long-term membership in an occupation changes an individual's interests toward the mode.

While such comparisons showing great stability between matched groups over time in one occupation are reassuring, the demonstration of similar results among other occupations would be very welcome.

A slightly different design has been used to replicate this study, using psychologists as subjects. Instead of working with pairs of psychologists holding the same job, one position, that of president of the American Psychological Association, has been studied by examining the characteristic interests of the men holding that position over a long time span.

In Figure 4, the average profile of 25 men who were presidents of the American Psychological Association before 1939 is compared with the profile of 25 APA presidents since that time.

While the similarity is dramatic, there are some relevant differences. The more recent presidents tend to score higher on the biological science scales and slightly lower on the physical sciences scales. The more recent ones also score higher on the social service scales. Profiles for all of these presidents have been published in an earlier article (see Campbell, 1965), and one of the more intriguing findings was that the latest available SVIB profile from an APA president (from the president in 1965) was a close duplication of the earliest available SVIB profile from an APA president (from the president in 1900).

Three further replications of occupations over time are now being conducted. In one, those ministers who today are serving in the same churches as the ministers studied by Strong 30 years ago are being tested. Thus, the church is being held constant over 30 years. The second replication concerns corporation presidents, where the presidents of the same corporations over 30 years are being tested; the third includes city school superintendents where

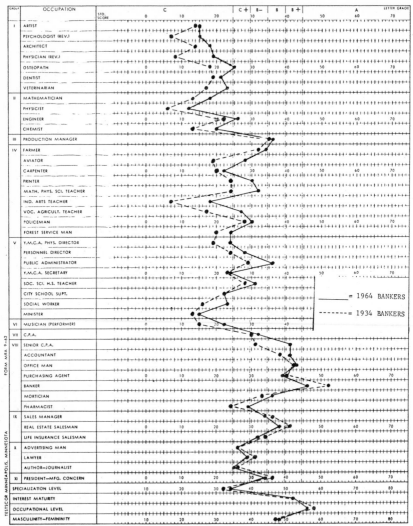

Figure 2. Comparison of 1934 bankers vs. 1964 bankers holding identical jobs (103 in each group).

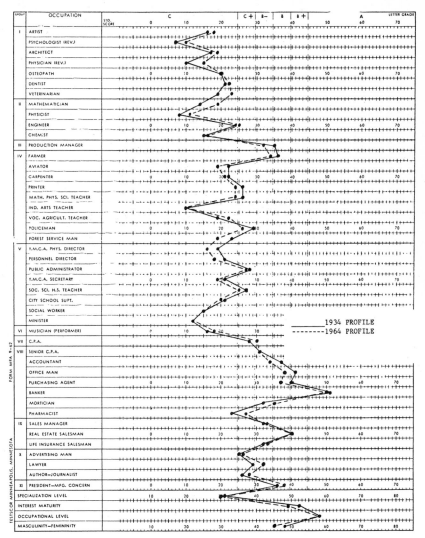

Figure 3. Test-retest results over 30 years for 48 bankers.

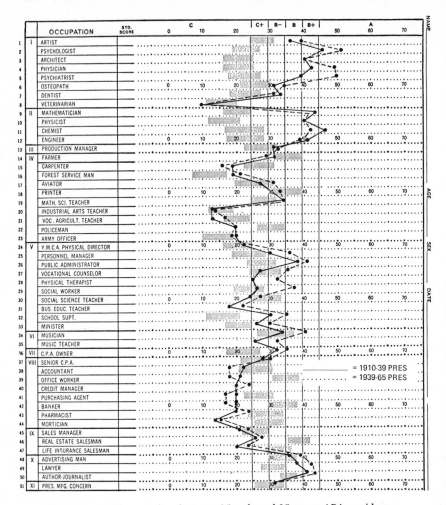

Figure 4. SVIB comparison between 25 early and 25 recent APA presidents.

the school system is being held constant over 30 years. When these three projects are finished, the nature of occupational change over time will be more clearly understood.

Discussion

However, it already is safe to conclude that there is considerable stability across time within occupations on interest measures, much more than one might expect intuitively. Further, these studies collectively imply that individuals in the 1930 culture were similar in their interest patterns to those in the 1964 culture, and that the mechanisms of occupational choice—whatever they may be—are fairly constant over long time periods. Somehow men with banking interests gravitated into the banking business 30 years ago, and men with those same interest patterns are found in the same jobs today.

But cultures change, occupations come and go, and one wonders what happens to those individuals who today have the interest patterns of yesterday's occupations. For example, what happens to the men who today have interests similar to the blacksmiths of earlier generations?

To suggest a way to study such questions, a brief digression is necessary to bring in some further methodology. Kenneth Clark, in his work on the vocational interests of nonprofessional workers, has developed two kinds of scales for the Minnesota Vocational Interest Inventory (Clark, 1961). The first are empirical occupational scales, developed just as the Strong scales were; the second are scales that contain items highly correlated with each other. These latter scales are called Homogeneous scales. Clark developed nine of these Homogeneous scales and found, quite surprisingly, that all but one of these scales correlated very highly with some occupational scales, that is, one of his homogeneous scales correlated highly with his Truck Mechanics scale, another with the Electrician scale, another with the Stock Clerk scale, and so forth. Thus, using two different psychometric approaches, Clark found scales with the same item content. His interpretation of this was that men have cut up the world of work in the same fashion as their interests are structured. For example, for the cluster of interests called mechanical, jobs have been shaped that contain primarily these activities.

These clusters of interests, closely tied to occupations, may offer one method of understanding the evolution of occupations, and of answering the question of what happens today to people with interest patterns characteristic of yesterday's occupations. Take the cluster of mechanical interests. This would seem to be a recently emerging area. Even 30 years ago, the number of machines around was very much less than today—what occupations did people with mechanical interests enter? The answer to that question appeared almost accidently recently when about 60 blacksmiths were tested at the University of Minnesota. It was clear from the results that the blacksmiths of yesterday are the mechanics of today. This cluster of interests has emerged intact though there have been dramatic changes in the demands of society.

Work is now under way to establish the same kind of clusters for the SVIB, with the hope that they will provide the necessary techniques to better understand changes over time.

The conclusions that I have drawn up to this point have been cautious and based on fairly substantial data; let me now do some far out speculating. It seems likely that if we but had the data, we could show similarities in interest patterns within occupations extending back to the edge of civilization, or at least back to the time that occupational groups began to appear. Take, for example, the people in charge of throwing Christians to the lions— would you agree with my hunch that they might have some common interests with the Nazi storm troopers of a much later era, and perhaps even with the knock-out squads of the Ku Klux Klan of today?

Or take another group. What common interests might we find among men such as Sir Francis Drake, Magellan, Columbus, and their current day counterparts, men such as John Glenn, Gus Grissom, and the Soviet astronauts? Anyone who would step out of a spaceship with nothing but a rope between him and the stars must surely have something in common with a fellow who thinks at any moment he might sail over the edge of the world.

That men choose different ways to interact with their environment is already known; that there is some consistency across generations in these modes of interaction seems now to be a reasonable assumption. Our search now should be for ways to describe these modes and to understand how they are reflected in the occupational world.

31 | Recurring Dilemmas in Personality Assessment*[1]

Wayne H. Holtzman

Summary: Six unresolved issues related to recurring dilemmas in personality assessment are 1) the meaning of personality assessment, 2) how many things must be known about an individual to understand his personality, 3) how personality variance can be separated from method variance, 4) whether we are building a culture-bound theory and technique of assessment, 5) whether we can ever develop a systematic, comprehensive personality theory closely linked with empirical data, and 6) the moral dilemmas created by personality assessment.

It is highly fitting that this symposium has been organized to commemorate the 25th anniversary of the classical publication, "Explorations in Personality," by Henry Murray and his associates at the Harvard Psychological Clinic. Murray's emphasis upon the intensive study of normal individuals, his use of a diagnostic council for weaving together into a coherent whole the rich and often contradictory bits of information about an individual, and his ingenious, tailor-made techniques of assessment still stand today as methods to be emulated by others. Much of what I see as recurring dilemmas in personality assessment was recognized by Murray although their manifestations take a different form today than 25 years ago.

To attempt to cover in any systematic manner all the dilemmas still current in the field of personality assessment would indeed be presumptuous of any one person, particularly within the few minutes available to a symposium speaker. It's bad enough to look squarely at one or two dilemmas. Being confronted by all of them at once is sufficiently overwhelming to drive out of the field all but the stouthearted or foolhardy. Being both foolhardy and stouthearted, I shall present what I see as six major, unresolved issues that continue to plague us in our attempts to develop the theory and technique of assessment.

*From *Journal of Projective Techniques,* 1964, **28**, 144-150. Copyright 1964 by the Society for Projective Techniques, Inc. Reprinted with permission of the author and publisher.
[1] Presented at the annual meeting of the American Psychological Association in Philadelphia, August 31, 1963.

1. *What do we mean by personality assessment?*

Whether one prefers to emphasize the social stimulus value of the individual, the way in which he adjusts to his environment, the manner in which his behavior is organized, or the subjective aspects of the phenomenal self depends largely upon the theory of personality employed. In a similar manner, what a given psychologist means by personality assessment is determined mainly by the particular techniques he chooses to employ and the assumptions implicit in them. We all tend to use the same words though rarely the same music. The resulting cacophony is confusing indeed, even to the untrained ear. Thus one person will insist on *his* set of personality traits as defined by *his* techniques, while another uses the same trait names with entirely different operations. Most of us are guilty of such egocentrism in the name of operationism. Certainly it's a free world where everyone can choose his terms and techniques as long as he states at least some of his conditions, but it frequently leads to rather silly statements, misunderstanding, and even public rejection.

Until recently within the field of individual differences, the domain of personality assessment was largely reserved for what was left over after covering human ability, interests, and attitudes. In the usual textbook survey of techniques, the various tests were neatly classified according to the domain covered, leaving personality as the residual and lulling the student into a false sense of security that he had a firm grip on things. Today, however, the world of individual differences is again in ferment. Some claim the whole of the field as the rightful domain for personality assessment; others prefer to abandon any classification system for different domains, concerning themselves with assessment in general. The fad among personality psychologists is to look closely at cognition, perception, and learning, while the expert on abilities worries about motivation, response sets, and other non-cognitive aspects of test behavior. In all probability such a diffusion of ideas will lead to a more satisfactory theory of assessment than previous piecemeal efforts. In the meantime, however, it is likely to become even more difficult to specify clearly what we mean by personality, a dilemma of definition and conception to which I see no good answer in the immediate future.

2. *How many things about an individual must we really know to understand his personality?*

The strong criticism of atomistic approaches in personality assessment that was so characteristic of much debate during the past thirty years has had its effect. The battleground has shifted but the basic issue is the same. To understand an individual's personality, must one take into account all aspects of the individual and his situation as they interact to produce manifestations of the personality? Or, is it possible that sufficient understanding for effective differential prediction of behavior can be achieved by increasingly complex, multivariate approaches to assessment? The current issue concerns how holistic must one be, not atomism versus holism.

If indeed it is true that a huge amount of past and present information about an individual must be properly digested, together with detailed knowledge of the future circumstances likely to prevail, then it is highly unlikely we will ever reach a very satisfactory level of understanding in the sense of prediction from personality assessment. While I'm inclined to think we can still achieve efficient differential prediction of important things about a person by improving our techniques of assessment, I must admit that this belief is based largely on faith rather than hard evidence.

Nevertheless, we have moved a long way in our conception of how to deal with complex information about an individual obtained simultaneously from different levels of his functioning and at different points in time. Even the old arguments about idiographic versus nomothetic assessment of personality are rapidly breaking down in the face of multivariate models which can account for both kinds of information at the same time. The general model suggested years ago by Cattell (1946) is a useful one from which to proceed since it allows for any amount or kind of assessment on one axis, any number and type of persons on a second axis, and any number of repeated measures on different occasions or situations on a third axis. These three broad, orthogonal dimensions—traits, persons, and occasions—yield the general case for almost any conceivable way in which the individual is approached, requiring only the assumption that individual differences exist and are measurable, an assumption that underlies all empirical approaches to personality assessment. What one stresses within this general model and how he goes about measuring and analyzing it can vary greatly, of course, and accounts for the wide variety of theory and technique prevalent today.

The general case itself, when taken seriously, is exceedingly difficult to achieve since it requires repeated measures on the same individuals using the same techniques of assessment. Most of our methods of personality assessment have questionable validity when applied on more than one occasion, let alone many, unless a rather long time period intervenes. One good example of the possibilities for Cattell's general model is the ambitious investigation undertaken by Mefferd, Moran, and Kimble where a small number of schizophrenic patients is assessed daily for a large number of days under different courses of treatment. In one preliminary report (Mefferd *et al.*, 1960), they describe the first results obtained in the analysis of about 100 measures repeated for 245 successive days on a single patient. Among the techniques employed are included ward behavior ratings, brief mental tests, indices of physiological arousal, constituents of blood and urine, and such exogenous variables as air temperature, drug treatment, and ward environment. The overwhelming rate at which information accumulates in such a study would make analysis impossible if it weren't for some automatic coding, high speed computers, and multivariate statistical processing. The appropriate statistical model is multiple time series analysis. Elsewhere (Holtzman, 1963a), I have outlined some of the problems in such analysis, with illustrations drawn from the data collected by Mefferd and his colleagues.

Whatever method of analysis is employed, Cattell's P-technique model for the single case is thoroughly idiographic in nature. It is in the choice of a particular method of analysis that one encounters serious controversy similar to the nomothetic one of actuarial versus clinical prediction. The important point is that one no longer needs to think simply in terms of idiographic versus nomothetic or of statistical versus clinical. The general model for personality assessment allows for any combination of these approaches. It is largely a matter of purpose, personal preference, or feasibility with existing techniques rather than theoretical considerations as such, although one's theory is relevant to this choice.

But the fundamental issues still remain as to choice of which persons to study under what conditions and with what techniques of assessment. And even if one develops a complex, multivariate model for prediction purposes, there is little empirical evidence as yet that it will work that much better than the relatively simple, isolated methods of the past, as far as prediction is concerned. The concept of hostility provides as good an example as any of the problems that will be encountered. One can speak of hostility as a generalized state, a predisposition to become hostile, or as a specific state which is linked to particular situational and internal conditions. The generalized trait of hostility requires trait stability over different occasions, while the specific state of hostility only demands valid measurement of hostility under specific conditions. The former requires a nomothetic approach across different individuals while the latter is best studied by repeated testing of single individuals. Only rarely are the two approaches combined. And yet, without some such combination, important, unevaluated interactions between the steady and fluctuating trait systems may completely obscure the meaning of the results.

Quite aside from the problem of coping with both generalized and specific manifestations of the same process is the difficulty encountered in choosing assessment techniques and scores or signs for the techniques which are appropriate to the personality construct in question. At least four systems or levels of functioning have been studied with regard to hostility though rarely at one time: (a) hostility in *fantasy* and imaginal processes as revealed by such devices as the Thematic Apperception Test, the Holtzman Inkblot Technique, or story completion tests; (b) the *inferred conscious self* as revealed by various self-report inventories; (c) the *objective observed self* as indicated by peer ratings; and (d) the intervening *psychophysiological processes* as reflected by Lacey-type indices of autonomic reactivity or hormonal balance from analysis of biochemical constituents. It is easy to see why serious attempts to take into account various levels of functioning while also dealing with the problems of interaction between steady and fluctuating traits are almost non-existent, even when attention is focussed on a single general concept such as hostility or anxiety.

A major dilemma is that in any practical situation one must continually make rather arbitrary choices and exclude all but a small portion of the general model for personality assessment. One is repeatedly haunted by the question, Can we ever really understand a personality?

3. *How can one separate personality variance from method variance?*

A third fundamental dilemma of great concern to many psychologists is the inevitable confounding of personality traits with the particular method for assessing them. In recent years, special attention has been given to the difficulties arising from such response sets as Tendency to Acquiesce or Social Desirability which often overshadow the substantive meaning of items in personality inventories. The interaction between examiner and subject in such projective techniques as the Rorschach or TAT poses a similar dilemma that has led many clinicians to insist that the examiner himself is part of the instrument, that he must listen with his "third ear" and sharpen his intuitive acumen to a high degree or he will surely fail.

Campbell and Fiske (1959) have suggested that for most personality constructs it should be possible to design experiments employing a multi-trait multi-method matrix for teasing out the relative contributions of content and method. Given two or more traits and two or more methods for assessing the traits, the resulting scores can be intercorrelated and the results arranged in a rectangular matrix for close inspection and possible further analysis. Placing one's data in such a matrix is a sobering experience that usually serves to dramatize how much the measurement of a given personality trait is really a function of the method used rather than the theoretical construct.

4. *Are we building a theory and technique of assessment which is culture-bound within western, industrialized society?*

As the psychologist in the United States and Western Europe reaches out to other societies he is becoming acutely aware of the restricted bounds within which his work applies. Many react by quickly closing the curtain and renewing their efforts to develop a theory based on college sophomores or hospitalized schizophrenics who are at least somewhat malleable and readily available. Others are struggling to establish cross-cultural comparative studies or replication in foreign cultures to test the limits of their systems. The most difficult problems of translation to maintain equivalence arise with respect to questionnaires, inventories, and other verbally loaded instruments. Even with the best of literal translations across different western societies one can hardly be sure of the semantic properties of the words used. The recent study by Peck and Diaz-Guerrero (1963) of the meaning of the term, "respect", in Mexico and the United States revealed marked differences in the connotations of the word, both cross-culturally and among subcultures of both countries.

As Lindzey (1961) has pointed out in his survey of projective techniques and cross-cultural research, the relationships between the subject and examiner, problems of communication, and the confounding of culture and personality create serious dilemmas in any attempt to extend personality assessment to other cultures, especially primitive ones. Even in the case of nonverbal, "meaningless" stimuli such as inkblots, serious difficulties of interpretation arise.

An anthropologist, Edwin Cook, recently returned from a two-year visit to a most inaccessible part of New Guinea where he and his wife have been conducting studies of culture change with increasing western contact. He reduced the problems of communication and his relationship to the tribesmen to a negligible minimum by living within the community and meeting the inhabitants strictly on their own terms many months before beginning any personality assessment. The fact that culture and personality are confounded in his study is irrelevant to his particular problem of culture change. The stimuli and methods of administration for the Holtzman Inkblot Technique are about as culture-free as it is possible to get (Holtzman *et al.*, 1961). While most of the variables with which he is working appear to be satisfactory for his purposes, the problems of interpretation from a personality rather than cultural point of view still loom large. Let me illustrate more specifically by citing a particular response that he obtained and the rich local meaning associated with it.[2]

---

[2] Personal communication from Edwin A. Cook to the writer.

The response, "kotsamba", was given to Card 7A, an inkblot which is mostly black and white with little red spots often suggestive of blood. Kotsamba is a small, greenleafed, purple flowering plant which seems devoid of particular significance until viewed in the light of additional ethnographic information. According to Cook, the flowered plant is important in at least two contexts. After a person is buried, a few of these plants are uprooted and thrown on top of his grave. Ancestor worship and the local animistic beliefs suggest more than mere decorative value for the plant. A second association of considerably deeper meaning to kotsamba is indicated by the following context. At the conclusion of a ceremonial pig festival which may last for 15 months, the majority of pigs are killed as sacrifices to the ancestors. Kotsamba is dipped in the pig blood by men, brushed over a woman, and stuck under the thong of her rear net covering to insure that her pigs will grow big and fat. Since Card 7A has only red color suggestive of blood, rather than purple or green color like the flowering plant, the response of "kotsamba" must refer to the ceremonial plant covered with pig's blood, an association charged with emotion and superstition. Given the difficulty of grasping the nuances of a strange vocabulary and the problem of understanding a sharply divergent world view, even a skilled anthropologist intimately acquainted with the culture has difficulty of interpretation while a psychologist would be completely lost.

5. *Can we ever develop a personality theory that is systematic, comprehensive, and closely linked with empirical data?*

Closely related to the first four dilemmas posed is our recurrent failure to develop a satisfactory theory of personality. In their comprehensive review of personality theories, Hall and Lindzey (1957) were notably impressed by the diversities, disagreements, lack of formal clarity, and lack of demonstrated empirical utility characteristic of personality theories. About the best that can be said of most theories is that they stir the imagination, strike a respondent chord here and there, and have a heuristic value in stimulating research. Certainly there is no single widely accepted theoretical position today, nor does it seem likely that one will emerge in the near future. Man is simply too complex an animal to capture so easily.

Implicitly or explicitly, we all have some kind of theoretical position that we employ as a point of departure in personality assessment. As often as not, however, we are hard-pressed to rationalize our personality theory with our assessment techniques. Perhaps it is expecting too much to ask that our practice be in accord with our theory. Perhaps we should be content with theory that is sufficiently vague and general to allow maximum freedom for what we want to do.

A rather interesting and fresh approach to this dilemma has been opened up by high speed computers and the possibility of constructing models that can be tested by computer simulation of personality. If one does not require that a theory account for all personality phenomena but only for a limited segment of human behavior, then it is possible to conceive of a small system of formal constructs and properties which can be spelled out in a logic diagram and incorporated in a computer program. Loehlin (1963) has recently achieved some success in the simulation of a rather primitive personality he calls Aldous. Three subsystems provide Aldous with a means of mediating his response to his environment—recognition, emotional reaction, and action preparation. Aldous has both immediate and permanent memory, with a learning subsystem that modifies the latter. Aldous can introspect in a superficial way by responding to questions in a verbal report that is printed out by the computer. The press of his environment can be manipulated along several dimensions to study its impact upon his personality development and, with additional programming, several Aldouses can be constructed to form a small social system.

As I have indicated elsewhere (Holtzman, 1963b), Loehlin's simulated personality model is actually static and fairly simple in design. It should not be difficult, however, to build into Aldous additional properties, including the attribute of self-modification which is essential to any realistic personality model. The use of a higher capacity computer would make it possible to introduce more dynamic features that would lift Aldous above his present primitive level to a degree that would make computer simulation of personality a highly useful approach to model construction and the testing of theory. It should be kept constantly in mind, however, that the psychology of machines is only a pseudopsychology unless a reasonable goodness of fit is assured between the machine model and real organisms, at least with respect to the limited system of traits and relationships being simulated.

6. Moral dilemmas created by personality assessment.

Most of us are so concerned with the substantive and theoretical problems of personality assessment that we often overlook the ethical and social implications of our work. It comes as a rather rude shock to find the general public crying out in righteous indignation about our techniques and the way in which we use them. While there has always been a small group of extremists who want to censor the work of psychologists and who demand an end to personality assessment, the reactionary movement has developed sufficient force recently to push numerous legislative bills aimed at banning personality testing in schools and other public agencies. Although the fears of some people that we have powerful, secret techniques for uncovering private information about an individual or controlling his personality are obviously unjustified at present, there is strong evidence to suggest that such methods will indeed be developed in the near future.

Several principles in the current version of the APA Code of Ethics are of particular interest since they embody unresolved moral dilemmas which face us. Corollaries of Principles 6, 7, and 16 deal with confidentiality of information and invasion of privacy, the welfare of individuals who submit to personality assessment, and the problem of harmful after-effects where stressful situations are involved in assessment. The basic moral dilemma in each instance arises from a conflict of two values: (a) the individual human being has a right to maintain his privacy and personality without threat of intrusion; and (b) a better understanding of human behavior, which can only be achieved in its fullest sense by experimentation and probing investigation of the human personality, is of benefit to mankind. The current ethical code reduces the dilemma to specific issues that confront us every day in personality assessment, issues that in the last analysis can only be settled by repeated juridical review rather than by simple pronouncement.

These six dilemmas, five substantive and one moral, hardly cover all that can be said about recurring dilemmas in personality assessment. Much can also be said about the really significant progress that has been made in the past 25 years. Perhaps some of these issues will simply fade away with time. But if past experience is any indication of the future, we can expect most of them to be with us for a long time to come.

32 | Seer Versus Sign*

Gardner Lindzey

Thematic Apperception Test (TAT) protocols from homosexual and normal college Ss and homosexual and normal prisoners were employed in two consecutive studies concerned with clinical and actuarial prediction. In the first study a clinician blindly predicted the criterion from TAT protocols with 95% accuracy. Twenty objective TAT indices, when combined after-the-fact using actuarial methods, functioned nearly as well as the clinician. When applied to the prison population, the actuarial methods were totally ineffective, while two clinicians were more successful in predicting the criterion. The findings are discussed in terms of their implications for the clinical-actuarial prediction controversy as well as the probable utility of objective "signs" derived from projective technique protocols.

The task of the investigator is inextricably linked to the individual observer, and nowhere is this more frustratingly evident than in the study of personality. Although the efforts of psychologists to dehumanize—more positively, to "objectify"—the process of data collection have been many and ingenious, it remains true that behind every validity coefficient or network of justifying concepts and operations there lurks, at some point, an observer, hopefully a sensitive and unbiased observer. Few psychologists have accepted this fact more gracefully than Henry A. Murray and none has labored more diligently and imaginatively to maximize the contribution of the observer and to provide him with a respected position within the field of psychology.

The present investigations may be viewed as minor attempts to assess the relative merits of the trained human observer in a particular setting. More specifically, they compare the judgment of one or more unaided clinicians with objective and actuarial methods of prediction under conditions where the special strengths of the clinician are given a reasonable opportunity to manifest themselves. As such they belong to a growing body of investigations concerned with the relative merits of mechanical, objective, and (typically) quantitative methods of prediction as opposed to the relatively subjective and qualitative predictions of the clinician. Such studies have been summarized

*From *Journal of Experimental Research in Personality*, 1965, 1, 17-26. © 1965 by Academic Press, Inc. Reprinted with permission of the author and publisher.

ably by Meehl (1954), Cronbach (1956), and Gough (1962) among others, and the area of investigation owes much to the earlier writing of Allport (1937, 1942), Sarbin (1941, 1942), and Murray (1938, 1948).

It is worth noting that this issue possesses certain significant links to the idiographic-nomothetic question, and like the latter controversy it has proved sturdily resistant to the frequent suggestion (for example, Holt, 1958; Zubin, 1956) that sophisticated examination of the problem reveals little or no real basis for maintaining such a distinction or issue. Just as species survival may be considered the ultimate test of "fitness," so too the persistence of a conceptual distinction or empirical issue over many years in the face of repeated efforts to obliterate or dissolve it may be considered evidence of theoretical-empirical fitness or significance.

Study I

In this study, which already has been reported in part (Lindzey, Tejessy, and Zamansky, 1958), it was possible to compare the predictive (literally, postdictive) effectiveness of a number of objective TAT indices of homosexuality (individually and in combination) with the comparable effectiveness of clinical predictions by an experienced interpreter of the TAT.

Method

Subjects. The *S*s consisted of 20 undergraduate male students who had acknowledged overt homosexual acts and a group of 20 undergraduates comparable in sex, age, and educational level but with no known history of homsexuality. They were volunteers and received no pay for their participation.

Procedure. Five TAT cards (4, 6BM, 7BM, 10, 18BM) were administered individually by an experienced male administrator. The resultant protocols with all identification of individual *S*s removed were then scored for 20 different variables or indices that were believed on the basis of prior research or formulation to be indicative of homosexual tendencies (Lindzey, Bradford, Tejessy, and Davids, 1959). The variables, scoring procedures, and reliabilities are described in greater detail in an earlier publication (Lindzey *et al.,* 1958), and they are briefly identified in Table 1.

The TAT protocols were also sorted blindly by an experienced interpreter of the TAT who was generally familiar with all the objective indices used in the study but was permitted to make his classification without justification or specification of the basis for his decision. He also divided the predictions into those of which he was confident and those of which he was uncertain.

Results

The results summarized in Table 1 indicate clearly that the objective indices functioned very well in comparison with similar indices derived from TAT protocols that have been examined in previous studies (Lindzey and Newburg, 1954; Lindzey and Tejessy, 1956). However, it is equally clear that none of the indices serves by itself as a powerful basis for discrimination between the homosexual and normal groups. Indeed, when compared with the judgments of an experienced clinician they fare very poorly. The judge was able to sort the protocols with 95% accuracy—classifying incorrectly one S from each group. Moreover, of the 29 judgments which he considered "confident," there were no incorrect classifications.

TABLE 1   *Dimensional TAT Comparison of College Students*

Variable	Normal (N = 20) M	Normal (N = 20) Freq.	Homosexual (N = 20) M	Homosexual (N = 20) Freq.	p^a
1 Misrecognition of sex		3		3	—
2 18BM: Attack from the rear		4		9	<.10
3 Feminine identification	1.05		1.55		<.005
4 Attitude toward marriage	−.32		.48		<.005
5 Man killing woman		0		5	<.02
6 Sexual references	.55		1.25		NS
7 Unstable identification	1.65		2.25		<.005
8 Feminine feelings, emotions	2.10		2.05		NS
9 Shallow heterosexual relations	.90		1.75		<.005
10 Male embrace		0		1	—
11 Attitude toward opposite sex	−.32		.18		NS
12 Tragic heterosexual relations		2		7	.06
13 Attachment to mother		2		4	NS
14 18BM: Symbolism or allegory		0		6	.01
15 Attachment to father		5		1	.18
16 Derogatory sexual terms applied to women		0		7	.004
17 Homosexual content		0		6	.01
18 Incest		0		1	—
19 10BM: No elderly couple		16		11	NS
20 18BM: Positive introduction of female		5		0	.02

[a]Values of p for differences between means are based on t tests. Those for variables 2 and 19 are based on x^2, and the remainder, on Fisher's Exact Test. Only the variables on which the difference was not in the predicted direction (8, 15, 19) were assigned to a two-tailed test of significance.

The question remains whether it is possible to combine after the fact the information contained in the 20 objective indices and produce findings that parallel, or closely resemble, those produced by qualitative, clinical judgments. The first step in answering this question was simply to arrange all indices (no matter what the prediction or expectation had been) so that a high score was typical of the homosexual group and a low score of the normal group. This involved reversing two variables (15 and 19). We then cumulated raw scores across all variables for each *S*, ignoring the different ranges of scores permitted by the various scoring procedures. The resultant distribution of scores for the two groups are reported in Fig. 1. Next we divided the scores for each variable as close to the median as possible so that we had a high and low group. Then for each *S* we simply counted the number of variables in which his score placed him in the high group, and the results for the two groups are summarized in Fig. 2. Both of these procedures functioned effectively; indeed, if we permit ourselves the luxury of maximizing diagnostic accuracy by identifying a cutting point after-the-fact, we are able to identify such a score for each distribution that will correctly classify 34 of the 40 *S*s.

A third objective approach used in the attempt to extract the diagnostic information potentially available in these indices emphasized pattern or configural analysis. We employed an ingenious technique devised by Lykken (1956; Lykken and Rose, 1963) that utilizes dichotomous predictor variables to make up actuarial tables for the various patterns of scores. Each table represents the observed frequency from each criterion group for one particular pattern; for example, for the pattern low, high, high for variables 14, 16, and 17 there were 5 homosexual *S*s and 0 normal *S*s, thus leading to the prediction of homosexuality from this pattern, while for the pattern low,

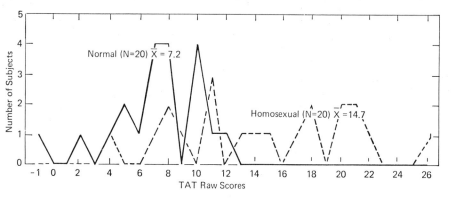

Figure 1. Comparison of normal and homosexual college students on total TAT scores.

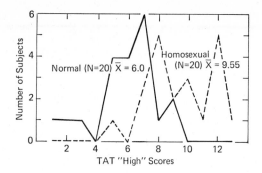

Figure 2. Comparison of normal and homosexual college subjects on total TAT "high" scores.

low, low for variables 14, 16, and 17 there were 7 homosexual Ss and 20 normal Ss, leading to the prediction of normality. It is also possible to provide a "validity coefficient" for each pattern which is based upon the number of cases in the original group displaying the pattern and the amount of difference between criterion groups in frequency for this pattern.

In the present study we used five actuarial tables, consisting of three variables each, which included most of the individual indices that seemed to function effectively. The variable groups employed were 14-16-17, 12-19-20, 2-12-16, 6-2-11, and 3-4-15. With this method it proved possible to predict correctly (after the fact) 34 out of the 40 cases when the prediction for each case was that indicated by three or more of the five tables. This performance could be increased slightly (36 correct identifications) if the prediction was based upon the difference for each S between the summed validity coefficients for the homosexual predictions as opposed to the normal predictions.

In summary, we find that the informed but unfettered and nonquantified clinician functioned slightly better than any of the actuarial combinations of objective scores. The relative similarity in performance of the two approaches must be evaluated against the background of a deliberate maximizing after-the-fact of the information contained in the objective indices, even when this meant reversing the intended direction of scoring. Thus, the clinician made his predictions before the fact while the objective procedure was adjusted to maximize its sensitivity after the fact. Under these circumstances one may naturally expect a great deal of shrinkage when the actuarial procedure is applied to an independent sample of observations. Study II was intended to permit an estimate of just how effectively the two systems would function when applied to a new source of data.

Study II

In this study we compared clinical judgment with our actuarial procedures when applied to two groups of Ss that were distinguished from each other in terms of overt homosexual acts but otherwise were quite different from the Ss of the previous study. We were interested in further evaluating the two different methods of prediction and also in examining the situational generality of findings concerned with the relation between a particular TAT sign or index and an underlying disposition or personal attribute.

Method

Subjects. The Ss consisted of 30 male prisoners in a state maximum security prison. The group was divided into 14 who were known to have been overtly homosexual prior to imprisonment (11 were convicted of sodomy charges) and 16 who provided no evidence of homosexuality prior to imprisonment or during incarceration. The groups were matched in terms of age, education, intelligence, period of imprisonment, and place of residence. The normal group was selected in such a manner as to exclude persons convicted of crimes of violence, and consequently it included predominately persons convicted of charges related to crimes against property. The Ss were paid for their participation in the study and all knew that they were participating in a study that involved, among other things, an interest in homosexuality.

Procedure. The TAT was administered individually (Cards 2, 3BM, 6BM, 9BM, 10, 12, 13MF, 18BM) by two male administrators who were unaware of the group to which any S belonged. Each examiner tested an equal number of normal and homosexual Ss.

The stories were scored for 20 variables according to the procedures developed in the earlier studies by two raters who were unaware of the group to which any S belonged. Discrepancies between the two sets of scores were eliminated by discussion between the two raters so that the final score represented a composite rating. The scoring was the same as in the previous study except that the larger number of cards increased the range of scores for a number of variables, and for two variables (4, 11) the numerical score assigned for the five categories was changed from $(-2$ to $+2)$ to $(0$ to $+4)$.

The Ss were classified by two judges independently as being homosexual or nonhomosexual on the basis of the TAT stories and knowledge of the true distribution of cases in the two categories. One judge (A) was unfamiliar with

TABLE 2   *Dimensional TAT Comparison of Prisoners*

Variable	Normal (N = 16) M	Normal (N = 16) Freq.	Homosexual (N = 14) M	Homosexual (N = 14) Freq.
1	2.31		1.86	
2		2		4
3	3.50		3.79	
4	15.75		15.00	
5		4		4
6	1.75		1.93	
7	1.44		1.43	
8	1.94		1.79	
9	.56		.64	
10		0		0
11	15.94		15.86	
12		5		5
13		3		8
14		1		1
15		0		0
16		4		4
17		0		0
18		0		2
19		6		6
20		14		12

the objective indices and the findings of the previous studies, but the other judge (B) was intimately familiar with these findings although he did not make any systematic effort to use this information. Judge B was the same judge who had made the comparable ratings in the first study. Each judge divided his predictions into those of which he was confident and those of which he was uncertain.

Results

Examination of the findings summarized in Table 2 indicates a consistent failure of the objective indices to differentiate between normal and homosexual Ss in a manner comparable to that revealed in the first study. Of 20 comparisons only one achieved conventional significance in the predicted direction; there were four reversals in the expected direction of the difference, and most of the 10 group differences in the predicted direction were minute. It seems clear that these indices, even though "validated" in several previous studies (Davids, Joelson, and McArthur, 1956; Lindzey *et al.*, 1958), have little merit when applied under the conditions of the present study.

Not surprisingly, in view of the results for the individual variables, the application of the actuarial procedures used in the previous study to combine these indices were highly ineffective. Whether we use raw scores cumulated (Fig. 3), number of high scores (Fig. 4), or the configural scoring method, we arrive at the same "hit rate" of 17 out of 30, or 57%. Even an additional, and more complicated application of Lykken's technique failed to improve upon the 57% figure. In this method each S was compared with all 40 of the Ss in the previous study, and for each pair-comparison a deviation score was computed that represented the number of times the two Ss were discrepant on a variable (one high and the other low). Then those Ss in the comparison group who had deviation scores of six or less were identified, and a prediction was made based upon whether the majority of these similar patterns had been drawn from homosexual or normal Ss.

In contrast, the judges' performance (Table 3), although variable, appears distinctly better. The most efficient of the judges were able to identify group membership with 80% success. While the less successful judge was able to identify correctly only 60% of the cases, of those 14 judgments in which he

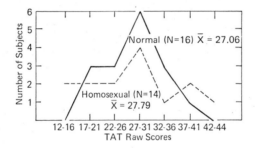

Figure 3. Comparison of normal and homosexual prisoners on total TAT scores.

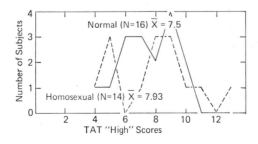

Figure 4. Comparison of normal and homosexual prisoners on total TAT "high" scores.

TABLE 3   *Accuracy of Judges' Predictions for Normal and Homosexual Prisoners*

| Predictions | N | Per cent correct | |
		Judge A	Judge B
Over-all	30	80	60
Confident	14	71	86
Uncertain	16	88	38

indicated confidence he was correct in 86% or 12 of the cases. Thus Judge A was able to predict significantly better than chance for all Ss, and Judge B functioned well above chance for those predictions of which he was confident; none of the actuarial methods proved able to function above the level of chance.

Discussion

Clinical versus Actuarial Prediction

The studies we have just discussed may be viewed as a direct, although modest, response to a challenge issued by Paul Meehl following a comprehensive review of the clinical-statistical research literature. His survey failed to reveal any clear evidence for the superiority of the clinical method, and he concluded, "I have reservations about some of these studies; I do not believe they are optimally designed to exhibit the clinician at his best; but I submit that it is high time that those who are so sure that the 'right kind of study' will exhibit the clinician's prowess, should *do* this right kind of study and back up their claim with evidence" (Meehl, 1957, p. 272). Our findings, although far from definitive, do provide evidence that, at least under some circumstances, clinical judgment may function somewhat more efficiently than objective and actuarial prediction.

For such findings to be of more than glancing importance, however, it must be possible to state something about the conditions that may have played a role in producing these discrepant results. In the present study it seems to us the events predisposing in favor of the sensitive and informed clinician relate to the psychometric intractability of the TAT. In brief, we have here an instrument that elicits a large amount of complex response data and which is accompanied by very little in the way of rules for effectively transforming or encapsulating these responses within a finite number of scores, variables, or indicants. Thus, although there have been many attempts to establish dimensions or categories for analyzing TAT responses (cf. Lindzey *et al.,* 1959), none of them has met with spectacular success. It appears that the massive and unwieldy qualitative data of the TAT continue to provide predictive cues for the skilled clinician that are not represented adequately in the objective indices upon which actuarial prediction must rest. To generalize, it seems reasonable to expect that, under circumstances where there is little available in the way of sensitive and objective guidelines, the experienced clinician is likely to function relatively better than in a psychometrically highly developed terrain.

It may appear that I am suggesting that clinical predictions function better only in very primitive areas of psychological measurement. Indeed, overlooking the role of the clinician as a source of ideas or hypotheses that may lead to further objectivity and specification, this is precisely what is implied. Insofar as the objective basis for clinical prediction's operating better than chance can be made explicit and verbalized, it will usually prove possible to devise substitutive methods that are freer of error than the human mind. On the other hand, there is little doubt that much of psychological measurement, defined broadly, is still in a very primitive state, consequently, it may be no trivial accomplishment to function relatively well under conditions such as those that prevailed in this study.

It is clear, in addition, that conditions in the present study come closer than most studies in this area to meeting the demands that the criterion to be predicted is at least as familiar to the clinician as to the psychometrician. Comparison of the two methods of prediction in connection with academic achievement, or some comparable outcome variable, favors the actuarial method both because this area of behavior is more often studied by psychometrist than clinician and also because the objective indices for predicting such behavior are relatively efficient and readily susceptible to quantitative analysis. McArthur (1956), Meehl (1956), and Cronbach (1960) have pointed to the importance of studying clinical predictions on their home terrain, and all have suggested that here the performance of the clinician may be relatively more encouraging, as indeed it appears to be.

It is worth emphasis that, contrary to a frequent misunderstanding, Meehl has always believed in the probable superiority of the clinician over the actuary under certain circumstances. Indeed, in a recent paper (Meehl, 1959) he has identified six factors that should favor the clinician. The first is *open-endedness,* where the event to be predicted cannot be represented by means of a single dimension or a small number of categories but where the predictor himself is determining the terms or content of the prediction. Second is *unanalyzed stimulus-equivalences,* where the rules for analyzing or classifying the relevant data are not objectively specifiable. Third is the existence of *empty cells,* where particular events or combinations of events have not been observed in the past and consequently have not yet gained a place in the actuarial tables. Fourth is the possible role of *theory-mediation,* where there is an active process of theoretical reasoning and hypothesis formation intervening between the observational data and the particular prediction to be made. Fifth is the situation which offers *insufficient time* for the application of actuarial methods simply because an immediate decision must be made. Sixth is the case where there is a *nonlinear* and particularly a *configural* or pattern association between the predictor variables and the criterion. The performance of the clinicians in the present studies is presumably consistent with the implications of Meehl's statements in regard to "unanalyzed stimulus equivalences" and "empty cells" as factors favoring the effectiveness of clinical prediction. That is, the clinicians responded to stimuli that had not yet been objectively identified and classified, and among these cues there may even have been some that had not been encountered in previous studies and consequently could not have been used by the actuarial methods. It is impossible to completely rule out the role of theory-mediated hypotheses, but the subjective report of the judges and the state of theory in this area make such a contingency most unlikely.

Our findings are only obliquely related to Holt's (1958) distinctions between pure actuarial, naive clinical, and sophisticated clinical prediction. However, insofar as the distinction between naive clinical and sophisticated clinical can be mapped into this study, we would have to place Judge A in the naive category and Judge B in the sophisticated class, on the basis of the fact that Judge B had made comparable predictions from a similar data base before and was intimately familiar with objective findings in this area. Our evidence suggests that the naive clinical judge did at least as well as the sophisticated clinical judge, contrary to Holt's expectation, although one would not like to generalize far from only two judges.

If we recklessly accept the difference between Judge A and Judge B as a real and stable difference, we are faced with the mild embarrassment of increased experience and sophistication appearing to diminish accuracy or sensitivity. Obviously this is not necessarily the case. Judge A may simply have been a better diagnostician, and with increased experience his advantage might have been even greater than it was. However, it is at least possible that experience with predicting this variable under conditions of the first study, and a thorough knowledge of the TAT literature on homosexuality, might make a negative contribution to prediction in the second study. Remembering how poorly the objective indices functioned in the second study, it seems altogether conceivable that if Judge B was deriving many of his diagnostic cues from these indices, he might have operated at a disadvantage.

Utility of Projective Technique "Signs" or Objective Indices

In view of the fact that the indices and related variables studied in the present investigations comprise one of the most successful sets of "signs" in the history of TAT research, their almost total collapse upon further cross-validation might be considered a serious indictment of this entire approach to measurement. On the other hand, such a finding should scarcely come as a surprise in view of the many investigations (for example, Kenny, 1954, 1961; Lindzey and Silverman, 1959; Masling, 1960) and formulations (Lindzey, 1952, 1961; Gleser, 1963) that have made clear the extent to which these instruments are responsive to a wide array of diverse determinants. Given this multiplicity of conditions that determine projective technique response, only a small proportion of which are related to personality variables or dispositions, it is inevitable that strictly empirical findings secured in one situation will not be likely to generalize effectively if we change a great many of the situational factors as well as nonpersonality attributes of the Ss.

Let us consider some of the respects in which the Ss and conditions of test administration differed between our first and second studies. The Ss of the second study were much more heterogeneous than Ss of the first study in age, socioeconomic status, education, intelligence, employment history, indeed on almost any other variable one might care to mention other than criminality. Not only was the second group more variable on these attributes but also there were sizeable differences in the group average for most variables, including verbal facility, intelligence, and socioeconomic status. The differences in situational determinants of test performance were at least as striking as the differences in demographic and personal attributes. To mention only the most salient of these differences, one group of tests was given in a maximum security prison and another in an institution of higher learning; one group of Ss was paid for participation and the other was not; one group of homosexual Ss knew the examiner was aware of their homosexual behavior while the other group did not; one group of homosexual Ss included a large number who had been harshly punished by society for homosexual acts while the comparable group in the other study included no such Ss. A large number of studies have been conducted that demonstrate projective technique responses to vary with conditions such as those just described. Many of these investigations are described or referred to in recent publications by Masling (1960) and Lindzey (1961).

Generalizations of the sort dealt with in this study must be accompanied by a statement of the parametric limits within which they operate, and among the group differences mentioned above there are undoubtedly many such parameters that must be attended to in order to permit effective generalization of findings. To cite only a single illustration, a great deal of the research and clinical literature on projective techniques has tended to ignore the difference between the situation in which the S sees the examiner as sympathetically involved in a cooperative and supportive enterprise and the situation in which the S, accurately or not, perceives the examiner as hostile, as a barrier to some desired goal, or as the potential revealer of some deeply defended aspect of the S's inner world. There seems little doubt that one of the reasons for the failure of the second study to even approach a replication of the findings of the first study concerns just this difference. Indeed, when reporting the initial results of the first study we indicated that " . . . most of the indices of homosexuality that functioned successfully tended to be relatively directly related to homosexuality and thus might be expected to be readily subject to censoring or inhibition" (Lindzey *et al.,* 1958, p. 74). Given this observation it is altogether predictable that, with less cooperative Ss, the TAT indices would fare more poorly.

What has just been said concerning the parametric limits within which one may expect a given relation between projective technique sign and personality disposition to be maintained might be considered banal if it were not for the fact that the majority of studies concerned with such diagnostic relationships fail even to mention the importance of such parameters. Thus, much of the existing interpretive lore, both that based upon controlled research and that derived from clinical observation, is certain to be misleading because there has been no attempt to state the reasonable bounds within which the interpretation or relationship is likely to be sustained.

The sensitivity of the TAT to situational variation is obviously a serious problem for the person interested in enduring and personological traits, albeit the problem is equally perplexing with structured tests and other techniques for assessing personality. Until and unless we are able to identify objective cues that prove to be linked with personality traits in an invariant manner over many different situations, the clinician or investigator must be exceedingly cautious in attempting to make personality inferences concerning respondents who are examined in a novel setting.

33 | Seer Over Sign: The First Good Example*

Paul E. Meehl

Professor Lindzey's study is the first (in some fifty published) which demonstrates a clear superiority of the clinical judge over formalized (actuarial) methods of data combination. These clinicians' superiority lay in validity generalization, the semi-objectified "signs" derived from research on college students having negligible validity singly and collectively when applied to a population of maximum-security prison inmates. The data indicate that the clinical experts were not employing the "signs" reported in the research literature. It is suggested that TAT-skilled judges rely on subtle stylistic features of the protocol, which are refractory to scoring categories. Because of their atypicality and the crucial role played by moving to a very different population, the findings should not be generalized to other prediction tasks, kinds of data, or an unselected population of clinicians.

Ten years ago I made a rather unsuccessful attempt to arouse clinical practitioners from their dogmatic slumbers (Meehl, 1954). I call the attempt unsuccessful because, while it mobilized emergency emotions and made some sparks fly, I have not as yet been able to detect any significant impact upon clinical practice. In his daily decision-making the clinician continues to function, usually quite unabashedly, as if no such book had ever been written. However, I can perhaps lay claim to having focused attention on a research problem of both theoretical interest and practical importance, thereby generating numerous research studies. Monitoring of the literature in the decade since the book appeared yields a current bibliography of some fifty empirical investigations in which the efficiency of a human judge in combining information is compared with that of a formalized ("mechanical," "statistical") procedure. The design and the range of these investigations permits much more confident generalization than was true on the basis of the eighteen studies available to me in 1954. They range over such diverse substantive domains as success in training or schooling, criminal recidivism and parole violation, psychotherapy (stayability and outcome), recovery from psychosis, response to shock treatment, formal psychiatric nosology, job

*From *Journal of Experimental Research in Personality*, 1965, 1, 27-32. © 1965 by Academic Press, Inc. Reprinted with permission of the author and publisher.

317

success or satisfaction, medical (nonpsychiatric) diagnosis, and general trait ascription or personality description. The current "box score" shows a significantly superior predictive efficiency for the statistical method in about two-thirds of the investigations, and substantially equal efficiency in the rest. (In 1954 I mistakenly classified one paper as favoring nonformalized judgment, because I failed to detect its use of a spuriously inflated chi-square.)

It would be difficult to mention any other domain of psychological controversy in which such uniformity of research outcome as this would be evident in the literature. Since Professor Lindzey's paper is the first and *only* empirical comparison of the relative efficiency of the two methods showing clear superiority for the clinical judge, it is deserving of special attention.

Since, as Lindzey points out, commentators have tended to polarize and oversimplify my own views, in reacting to his paper I should like first to say clearly that I incline strongly to accept his results and interpretation. It would be my judgment that we have here the first clear instance of somebody's accepting the statistical challenge and exhibiting a significantly superior predictive performance by the human judge. What I have to say by way of further comment or questions should not, therefore, be construed as meaning that I disagree with the author's essential conclusions.

I take it as not in controversy that the clinical judge (proceeding informally or impressionistically) and the "sign" list (employed mechanically) do not differ significantly in the hit-rate achieved on a college population. While the statistical method is given an advantage through the lack of cross-validation, I would be inclined not to assign this factor as much weight as the author does. Cross-validation shrinkage (in the narrow sense) is a very important influence for prediction systems such as regression equations where the actual magnitude of a rather unstable statistic like a beta-weight is used with the idea of maximizing predictive power. But this effect is very considerably reduced when a simple count of signs, based on a median cut or similar dichotomous procedure such as the author employed, is involved. I have seen some striking examples where such an unweighted sign-counting procedure results in negligible cross-validating shrinkage. Presumably the reason for this is that the discriminating *power* of a dichotomous sign is not being weighted, so as long as the signs are at least scored "in the right direction," an unweighted sign-count is not a statistic greatly biased by capitalizing on random error in the criterion sample. (This is especially true, of course, when the selected signs do not represent a small minority of a large potential set such as the MMPI item pool).

On the clinician's side, we have no accurate means within the data of estimating how much of the fluctuation in hit-rate between the two samples (a drop from 95% hits in Sample I to 80% hits in Sample II) is attributable to random sampling error and how much to the (presumably much more important) factor of validity generalization to a different population. That is, we have no good means, either from theoretical considerations or estimators calculable from the data, of deciding whether there is a difference between the efficiency of the statistical method and the judges in the first study. If we were dealing with the first study taken by itself, we would have to record it in the box score as "no substantial difference." I shall therefore confine my discussion to the striking superiority of the clinical judges in Study II.

In explaining the clinical judges' marked superiority over the statistical sign-combination in Study II, the fascinating question is, of course, "What were the clinical judges *doing?*" I put it this way because the data make it quite clear that the difference in results between Studies I and II lies in the failure of the sign-statistical method to hold up, while the clinical judges did almost as well as in Study I. It is important to realize that we deal here not with shrinkage on *cross-validation* in the strict sense, i.e., that attributable to random sampling fluctuation within the same population, but the very different situation of *validity generalization,* i.e., the extent to which predictor variables function in the same way in a different population. Granted that in theory it will never be the case that any two clinical populations are mathematically identical in their parameters, in practice one can usually assume that shrinkage in passing from one VA Mental Hygiene Clinic sample, say, in Minnesota in 1956 to one in Michigan in 1958 will be largely attributable to sampling fluctuations; whereas moving from a population of college students to a population of prisoners involves a rather marked change in a number of presumably critical variables (demographic, intellectual, psychiatric, test-attitudinal, stylistic). A hard-line protagonist of the statistical method might be tempted to view this fact as a defect of the experimental design, saying that it is "not fair to the statistician" to expect him to make estimates of parameters in a prediction function for a population which he has not yet sampled. I am sure that Lindzey would accept the substance of that observation as a statistical truism. However, as regards the "fairness" aspect, I think that this line of rebuttal would be improper, for the same reason that I think it improper when clinicians dismiss the adverse studies by saying it is "unfair" to expect the clinician to know in advance whether a certain predictor variable is relevant to a certain criterion. If the clinician makes judgments under the erroneous impression that the current state of psychological theory or the generalizability of his accumulated clinical experience is such as to permit him to make powerful predictions of a given criterion, this error is part of the clinician's weakness as a predictive instrument. Similarly, I would insist that given the pragmatic context in which the whole issue makes sense—and it is only, I believe, in the pragmatic context that it can be properly formulated as a competition between techniques—then it seems obvious that the ability of a clinician to move successfully into a new population, when the statistical method collapses upon attempting such movement, must be viewed as a manifestation of the clinician's pragmatic superiority under the particular circumstances.

The data indicate that, whereas the clinical judges suffered some loss of predictive power in moving to the prisoner population, their attrition was not nearly as great as the attrition suffered by the sign-statistics, which collapsed to a clinically useless magnitude. That the latters' collapse is mainly a matter of validity generalization rather than pure sampling-error shrinkage is shown by the data in Table 2,[1] where we see that the component signs in the sign-statistic had individually no discrimination power, with a couple of exceptions. Thus we deal here not with a situation in which purportedly "optimal weights" fail because they capitalize excessively upon random error in the initial sample; rather we deal with a situation in which the very *dimensions* being utilized for prediction are for the most part predictively irrelevant within the new population.

On first reading the paper I was impelled to criticize the emphasis in its first two paragraphs upon the clinical judge as "observer," but I think I understand on further thought why the author emphasizes the "observer" aspect as he does. It seems the most parsimonious interpretation of the data to say that the clinical judges were able to do almost as good a job on the prisoner sample as on the college sample, in spite of the fact that the samples differ so greatly in respect to the variables used as statistical signs, because the clinical judges were relying largely, perhaps almost wholly, upon other aspects of the protocol than those aspects represented in the signs. Hence I would myself look upon the author's comments on the "psychometric refractoriness" of the TAT protocol as getting closest to the heart of the matter. Of the (practically) unlimited number of facets or aspects of the verbal behavior recorded in a TAT protocol, it seems that those which the research, and even the articulated clinical tradition, have fixed upon as TAT "signs" of homosexuality are just not the best ones, i.e., "best" in the sense of possessing high validity generalizability.

If we inquire into what these superior aspects might be, we leave the realm of the data for speculation. But if it is permissible to record a hunch, I would hazard a guess that we deal here with some subtle aspects—subtle because highly configural—of a stylistic-expressive nature. I do not, of course,

---

[1] See page 310. [Editor's note]

mean something crude like sentence length or verb-adjective quotient or what not, but I do mean some features of the patient's discourse which are relatively closer to the *formal* than to the *contentual* aspects of the stream of speech. It is a pity that the article does not report any introspective account by the judges of what they at least *thought* they were attending to in making the discrimination. But this general line is what has made me more comfortable with the author's "observer" emphasis, because pending further investigation of the inferential process in this situation, I would opt for the working hypothesis that the judges were scanning the material with responsiveness to features of it that have as yet eluded anything like an adequate reduction to scoring categories.

This latter point perhaps renders the investigation somewhat less central in regard to the clinical-statistical issue than it would otherwise be. As I formulated the distinction (Meehl, 1954, pp. 15-18) the question of relative efficiency is most appropriately asked having first settled upon a defined class of data, whether these data are rockbottom epistemologically or are themselves, strictly speaking, inferences, constructions, or behavior summaries. Thus, for example, in predicting academic success one would normally treat the student's Stanford-Binet IQ as part of the "data." But a little reflection upon the process of administering an individual intelligence test makes it obvious that "clinical judgments" already occur close to the behavior level, as when the examiner must decide how a patient's definition of a word is to be scored when precisely that definition cannot be found among the scored samples in the manual. There is, admittedly, an arbitrary element here because of the ambiguity of the verb "observed" in ordinary language and even in conventional scientific usage. In moving from the patient's stream of behavior to the scored signs, two reductions of data occur: First, only the words are recorded and such behavioral features as rate, tone, expressive movements, and the like are ignored, a factor not relevant in the present study. Second, only certain features of the word sequence as found in the protocol are selected for attention and classified with respect to specified properties, i.e., "scored." Here again, I can understand a temptation on the part of the actuarial protagonist to say that the study does not quite fulfill the criteria for a meaningful test because the two predictive methods do not "start with the same body of data." While this is true in one sense, a sense of which Lindzey is fully cognizant, it is not true in that sense which is pragmatically important. The fact is that the skilled judge reading the protocol impressionistically and the statistical system putting together scores obtained by attending selectively to prespecified features of the record, *do* have access to the "same data," namely a transcript of verbal behavior. At the risk of overstressing a methodological abstraction, one could say as a matter of strict logic or epistemology that, when the statistical method does not begin by scoring the aspects of verbal behavior which the judge responds to impressionistically, from the mathematical point of view this amounts in effect to the actuarial method's assigning a zero weight to those aspects and meanwhile assigning nonzero weights to other aspects which are less predictive, or at least less generalizably so.

I think it is less important to argue the semantic merits of a broad versus narrow use of the verb "observe" than it is to get as conceptually clear as we can about what is actually going on in the situation. There is an interesting symmetry here between the special disadvantages of the two predictive methods, in that Holt's distinction (1958) between the "naive" and the "sophisticated" clinical judge finds its counterpart in the "naive" versus "sophisticated" actuary. Holt wants to make sure, before he will be happy with a comparison of the two methods' efficiencies, that the clinical judge has had an adequate opportunity to consult actuarial experience (including actuarial experience with his own previous judging behavior) so that he can adjust and hopefully improve his subjective weights by whatever psychological means clinical judges do this. Similarly, it will not do much good for the statistician to employ formally powerful mathematical methods of combining scored dimensions if those dimensions are not the right ones to start with. Noting this symmetry, we must nevertheless give due recognition within the pragmatic context of predictive efficiency to a finding that the efforts of clinically knowledgeable investigators to identify the predictively relevant and *population-generalizable* aspects of the stream of TAT speech, and to subject them to a semiobjective response classification procedure ("scoring"), has thus far apparently failed. I should think that the observational and classificatory problem involved here would partake to a considerable degree of the same elements that enter into skillful functioning as a psychotherapist and, therefore, that many of the theoretical considerations I raised in that respect would be relevant in understanding the findings of the present study (Meehl, 1954, Chapters 6 and 7). I am also inclined to agree with the author's identification of two of my proposed six "pro-clinical" factors (Meehl, 1957) as being most likely operative in this predictive situation.

As must be evident from the character of my comments, I find very little in the paper with which to disagree. I am not entirely happy about the terminology adopted to describe the two clinical judges, especially since the judge characterized as "naive" paradoxically did the better job in both samples and, I take it, significantly better in the prisoner sample. This judge, the late Ephraim Rosen of the Minnesota Psychology Department, was trained by Nevitt Sanford and was an unusually gifted clinician. As the author points out, the other judge's "sophistication," consisting in his own research experience and familiarity with the statistical sign list, may actually have worked to his disadvantage. There is the further consideration that whereas the explicit identification of predictive signs can never systematically reduce the power of an actuarial method, it may sometimes reduce power when the signs are not treated actuarially but are filtered through the thinking process of a clinical judge. This possibility arises because one of the changes that is likely to occur when a judge succeeds in making explicit a proper subset of the cues to which he is potentially responsive is that his subjective beta-weights on these cues will increase, to the disadvantage of the residual subset of cues which he has not yet brought to the reporting level. Thus Sarbin, in his classical study (1942), found that the well-recognized scholastic predictors HSR and CAT were being subjectively assigned a *larger* proportion of criterion variance by counselors than these two variables actually accounted for. A beautiful instance of this effect can be found in the fascinating article by Berne (1949) in which an intuitively gifted psychoanalyst who had been doing remarkably well diagnosing certain occupations of inductees "at sight" suffered a marked decline in his efficiency as a result of identifying only a *portion* of the cue-family to which he had been originally responding unconsciously.

The only other partial disagreement I would have with the author is based upon literature not extensively known to him, in that he lays some stress upon the relative lack of studies in which the clinician is operating on his own terrain and attempting to predict a criterion with which he has some meaningful clinical familiarity. This criticism has been considerably reduced by the studies appearing since 1954, and I am not convinced that on the basis of the total body of presently available evidence one can plausible attribute the highly consistent and sometimes marked superiority of the statistical method to the use of an inappropriate setting and criterion for assessing the clinician's predictive skills.

Finally, I believe it is needful to enter a *caveat* with regard to the general application of these findings in the pragmatic context of daily clinical decision-making. I have little doubt, on the basis of my long personal acquaintance with them, that both of these clinical judges would be superior to the modal practitioner in a number of dimensions that I can hardly think irrelevant in this task, particularly abstract intelligence, good common-sense judgment, flexibility, and responsiveness to subtle nuances. [While revising the draft of this paper, I received a research report on counselor predictions in which 12 accurately predicting counselors differed from 12 inaccurately predicting ones by 27 raw score points on the Miller Analogies Test, a mean difference of approximately two sigma. No other counselor variable showed any such large differentiation as this measure of "Ph.D.-type brains"; see Watley and Vance (1964).] Investigations involving several clinicians characteristically show significant differences in predictive skill. The average judge does no better than the statistical method and usually somewhat worse; a minority of judges will sometimes succeed in bettering the actuarial procedure. While the functioning of a consistently superior judge is of great theoretical interest, and also could presumably provide one basis for refurbishing the less adequate average judge who performs below the actuarial method, unless individual judges are empirically calibrated with respect to their predictive efficiency over the range of recurring clinical tasks, the present empirical demonstration that these two judges were doing something validly that the scoreable signs were not doing does not help us much in adopting an over-all administrative policy with regard to the optimal method of clinical decision-making. As I have earlier pointed out, a pretty strong case can be made for an overarching decision-policy *to predict by actuarial methods, except when empirical information is available as to the predictive efficiency of the clinicians functioning in an installation;* and the specificity of abilities surely makes it dangerous to assume that these can be assessed by an indirect general method (except perhaps general intelligence) instead of carrying out a major predictive study on each clinic's personnel (Meehl, 1954, pp. 114-116).

With these minor reservations and qualifications, let me conclude by saying that, so far as I am concerned, Professor Lindzey has successfully responded to my "challenge" to do the right kind of study enabling the clinical judge to emerge victorious.

Ethical Issues
and the Social Impact of Testing

During the decade of the 1960s, criticism and concern over the ethics of psychological and educational testing showed a rapid upsurge. A number of background factors were associated with the increased questioning of the purposes and effects of testing: the extension of testing to greater numbers of students, applicants, employees and counselees; repercussions of communist witch hunts of the 1950s; the civil rights movement and the resulting focus on individual rights; increased use of testing in publicly-supported research. The National Defense Education Act of 1958, which was designed to support the identification of high-ability students in public shcools, and similar programs provided funds for more testing. The results were reflected in the growth of the College Entrance Examination Board, the National Merit Scholarship Corporation, the American College Testing Program and related organizations. Industry and government, responding to the successful use of tests for selection and placement in the armed services during and after World War II, have added to the number of tests administered. Finally, large-scale, publicly-financed programs in mental health, mental retardation and other areas related to psychology and education resulted in the further development and application of tests.

Of course, psychological and educational testing has had critics almost from the time of its inception during the first quarter of this century. But the criticism became more vociferous during the 1960s, as attested to by the writings of Banesh Hoffmann (1962), Martin Gross (1962), Hillel Black (1963) and others. In addition to these more professional critics, testing has occasionally become a kind of "political football," condemned on the one hand by extreme right-wingers as a "communist plot" and on the other hand by extreme left-wingers as an "establishment system." In the first article of this section, Gwynn Nettler describes the circumstances leading to the burning of several thousand test answer sheets by order of the Houston School Board. Although this incident took place several years ago, the following conclusions drawn by Nettler are valid even in the decade of the 1970s:

1) the public relations of testers are in need of repair; 2) the public should be informed beforehand of the purposes and methods of research involving large-scale testing programs; 3) the "scientific ethic" of psychologists is not necessarily shared by those whom they serve.

In the second article, Marvin Dunnette considers several criticisms of testing presented by Banesh Hoffmann in his book *The Tyranny of Testing.* Perhaps Dunnette is a bit one-sided and occasionally defensive in his counter-arguments, but this article is a readable introduction to some of the most salient criticisms of multiple-choice items and standardized ability tests. Lest the editor of this volume be accused of biasness, the student is encouraged to consult the books by Hoffmann (1962) and Black (1963), as well as the more extensive reply to critics of testing prepared by Chauncey and Dobbin (1963).

Dunnette also refers to a few useful points made by Hoffmann, in particular the inadequacy of terms such as "underachiever" and "overachiever," and the fact that rational analysis of item content should take precedence over statistical analysis. A third matter, the possibility of nonlinear and hetero-schedastic relationships between item responses and criterion scores, and the need to inspect item characteristic curves, involves some new terminology for many readers. As a brief explanation, two of the assumptions involved in interpreting a predictive validity coefficient are that: 1) the underlying relationship between predictor (item or test) and criterion scores is a straight line (linear); 2) the frequency distributions of criterion scores obtained by examinees having each test (or item) score all have the same variance. Failure of assumption 1 is referred to as *nonlinearity,* and failure of assumption 2 as *heteroschedasticity.* Both assumptions can be roughly checked by examination of the *item characteristic curve,* a graph showing the proportion of examinees attaining each criterion score who answered the particular item correctly. The steeper the item characteristic curve, the greater the discriminating power (validity) of the item.

The third article, by David Goslin, is a more comprehensive treatment of criticisms of testing. Five types of criticism related to test validity are considered, the facts that tests: 1) may be unfair to the gifted, the disadvantaged and other groups; 2) are far from perfect predictors of performance; 3) are sometimes used too rigidly; 4) do not measure innate characteristics; 5) may result in a self-fulfilling prophecy. Five other criticisms which are more or less independent of test validity and reliability are also discussed. These pertain to the effects of testing on 1) thinking patterns, 2) school curricula and 3) self-image, motivation and aspiration, as well as problems regarding testing for 4) ability grouping and other categorizing schemes, and 5) invasion of the individual's right to privacy. Goslin, who has directed extensive surveys for the Russell Sage Foundation on the use of tests in public schools, concludes that the social effects of tests as well as their statistical characteristics need to be taken into account. In particular, more rational policies for using tests with the disadvantaged, more careful attention to how test results are employed, and greater concern for the problem of testing as a possible invasion of privacy are urgently needed.

A similar list of criticisms and suggestions, although more optimistically worded from a tester's standpoint, is provided in the article by Sidney Marland. Nine criticisms are considered: excessive testing; misinterpretation or improper use of tests; limited characteristics measured by current tests; formalizing or overemphasizing numerical scores; the charge that test scores result in a self-fulfilling prophecy; possible dehumanizing effects of tests; use of tests to test schools and teachers; personality tests as invasions of privacy; curriculum control by means of tests. Of particular interest is the contrast between Marland's viewpoint and that of Goslin with regard to the argument that showing pupils' IQ scores to their teachers results in a self-fulfilling prophecy (see the introduction to Section VI and also article 27). Goslin considers this to be a serious problem, whereas Marland does not feel that it occurs as frequently as Rosenthal and Jacobson (1968) imply. In Marland's opinion, many of the problems related to testing in the schools can be handled administratively and by properly trained teachers.

Furthermore, Marland, who was appointed U.S. Commissioner of Education in 1971, argues for a Job Entry Examination Program (JEEP) with the prestige of the College Entrance Examination Board (CEEB) for evaluation and placement of the 50 percent of young people who do not go to college. It should be noted that John Gardner (1961) and other officials have considered related proposals to increase the prestige and effectiveness of nonprofessional occupations, but the conception held by so many American parents and young people of a "college education" as *the* pathway to social and material success has proven difficult to modify.

The last article of this section, by Theodore Sizer, is somewhat more critical of the social and political impact of testing than the preceding ones. Sizer argues that, because of preoccupation with the "engineering" aspects of testing, the compatibility of testing with the ideals and social practices in this country and the narrow viewpoint of many early mental testers, these scholars were unable to prevent their ideas from being misapplied. Quoting at length from S. B. Cutten's 1922 presidential address at Colgate University, Sizer maintains that Americans at the time needed mental testing, which, together with the principle of local control of schools, led to a perpetuation of school segregation along social and ethnic lines and an espousal of the notion of rule by an intellectual aristocracy. One of the few critical voices concerned with the applications of testing during the first quarter of this century was that of Walter Lippmann (1922), who pointed to the inconsistency between the formulas originating from Lewis Terman's work on the Stanford-Binet and those obtained by Robert Yerkes with the Army Alpha.

An examination of the history of mental testing reveals that in spite of the class bias of these early tests and the "undemocratic" conclusions of certain psychometricians, testing actually had a minimal effect (if any) on social legislation. Nevertheless, mental testing has helped maintain social stratification according to scholastic ability, not only in public schools but in a wide range of employment situations as well. Furthermore, Sizer and other critics maintain that overemphasis on the measurement of cognitive abilities has resulted in the neglect of measures of attitudes, moral development and other affective variables. Sizer concludes that we still need to predict individual achievement in a variety of intellectual, vocational and affective skills, but the tests should be designed to carry as little class bias as possible. In addition, efforts to determine the effects of social, cultural and ethnic variables on the development of skills and attitudes must be continued.

34 | Test Burning in Texas*

Gwynn Nettler

By a 5-1 vote the governing board of the Houston Independent School District, one of the largest in the nation, in June 1959 ordered burned the answer sheets to six sociopsychometrics administered to some 5,000 ninth graders. Four of these instruments were taken from a pilot study of the National Talent Project to be administered by the University of Pittsburgh and the American Institute for Research in 1960; the remaining instruments were added by local psychologists interested in forecasting the realization of talent and in the assessment of psychological health.

The board also instructed the assistant superintendent in charge of special services, whose office had served as repository for tests administered in other school systems within the county, to return several thousand additional answer sheets to a dozen participating districts that they might reconsider submission of these results.

The action of the Houston trustees destroyed the labors of responsible school personnel and social scientists. It countermanded the administrative decision of its own school executives to participate in such a study and challenged the thoughtfulness of all the other school officials who, at a March meeting of the County Superintendent's Association, had agreed to take part in this project guided by its own members and subsidized by the Hogg Foundation for Mental Health of the University of Texas. The board's public action, and the response of the metropolitan press, exposed a prevailing misunderstanding of the nature of a psychometric and suspicion of the good sense of psychologists.

The instruments that had been used included a Vocabulary-Information Profile Test, an Interest Blank, a High School Personality Test, a Student Information Blank that included self-evaluating items on health, a sociometric rating device, and the Youth Attitude Scales. These last measures, which contained most of the troublesome items, concern students' perceptions of

*From Nettler, G. Test burning in Texas. *American Psychologist,* 1959, **14**, 682-683. Copyright 1959 by the American Psychological Association, and reproduced by permission.

themselves and their relations with their families, teachers, and peers. These scales are not part of the National Talent Project but were adapted from questionnaires used in the 1956 Texas Cooperative Youth Study that had been administered to more than 13,000 children in 169 schools throughout the state without parental objection.

The Houston test burning came as a result of a few telephone calls (no one knows how many) from parents complaining, at the outset, to two of the seven trustees concerning the content and purpose of the tests. The metropolitan press was alerted and published stories in advance of the school board meeting promising a ruckus (board meetings are televised) under such headlines as PARENTS PROTEST TEST QUESTIONS, PARENTS STILL BOILING OVER THOSE "TALENT HUNT" QUESTIONS, and DR. McFARLAND [the superintendent] FACES TOUGH MONDAY NIGHT.

According to newspaper accounts parents were objecting to having their children respond to such items as:

> I enjoy soaking in the bathtub.
> A girl who gets into trouble on a date has no one to blame but herself.
> If you don't drink in our gang, they make you feel like a sissy.
> Sometimes I tell dirty jokes when I would rather not.
> Dad always seems too busy to pal around with me.

Houston school board members, with one exception, seconded the allegation of some parents that these and similar questions a) could serve no useful function in a talent search or in the guidance of children ("If you can show me one iota of value to these tests," one trustee is quoted as saying, "I'll quit the board.") and that b) such questions might undermine a child's moral character. One board member saw the tests as an additional symptom of the encroachment of "outside agencies" upon local school systems.

News items and exchanges in the letters-to-the-editor columns continued for at least two weeks after the Houston board's decision. Within 24 hours of the televised meeting one citizen prepared an application for a court order restraining officials from burning test results only to learn that the answer sheets had been destroyed earlier in the day.

The clamor spread to the suburban Spring Branch school district where the superintendent was called upon for an explanation in a meeting at which it was announced, incidentally, that the DAR was interested in the possible subversive uses of psychological instruments and that it had prepared a list of proscribed tests. A spokesman for the antitest group also suggested that answers to some of the questions—as, for example, those on family income, family size, and home ownership—would be of value to communists. The Spring Branch board decided that, rather than destroy the answer sheets of all students for all tests, parents who objected to the inclusion of their child's responses would be given the opportunity to request deletion. As of this writing, some six weeks after this decision, 11 parents of a possible 750 have made this request.

Social scientists and interested citizens, concerned that the Houston board action not go unprotested, conferred informally to discuss measures that might effectively indicate to the community the questionable wisdom of the board's decision (Once the tests had been administered, why destroy the *results?* And why without a hearing? And why the results of *all* tests of *all* students?). As a result of these telephonic and luncheon conclaves, it was apparent that no organized civic or professional body felt justified in making further remonstrance and that, pragmatically, any continued debate with the school board and its supporters aired in the press would probably result in victory for the board with possible harmful consequences for other phases of school testing programs.

Each man will read his own lessons from the events outlined above; I should like to suggest these:

1. In general, the public relations of psychometricians is in a sad state and in need of repairs.

a. There are national bodies interested in attacking psychology and psychologists as potential instruments of state control, *ergo,* of communism.

b. We have not been able to explain the role of tests in personnel selection procedures to a wide audience.

c. The press, with few exceptions, is a dubious factor in the fair reporting of our case if only because the rationale of testing is difficult to explain to editors and reporters.

2. It seems advisable that future large-scale testing programs be preceded by a public "warm up" explaining to as broad a segment of the public as possible the purposes and methods of such research. For example, effort spent in the education of PTAs and boards of education in advance of such surveys may prevent such loss as Houston has suffered.

3. Psychologists are behaving "ethnocentrically" in assuming that their ethic is shared by the people they study. The statement of "Ethical Standards of Psychologists" carried in the June (1959) issue of the *American Psychologist* holds:

> As a scientist, the psychologist believes that society will be best served when he investigates where his judgment indicates investigation is needed . . . (page 279).
>
> The psychologist in the practice of his profession shows sensible regard for the social codes and moral expectations of the community in which he works . . . (page 279).

When the student of behavior works in a xenophobic and individualistic community, he cannot assume that his scientifically honorable intentions will be considered morally justifiable by those whom he seeks to help. Even though the scientist says, in effect, "I am studying you, and asking you these questions, for your own good," his subject may respond, "It is part of my 'good' that you desist from your intrusion of my privacy."

As with all such conflicts in ethics (in ultimate values), facts are irrelevant—and consequences too.

35 | Critics of Psychological Tests: Basic Assumptions: How Good?*

Marvin D. Dunnette

First, let us consider some of the major assumptions made by Hoffmann (1962) in his book, *The Tyranny of Testing,* and consider the relative validity of each. Later, we will comment on some of the broader charges made by other critics and the relative validity of these.

Conveniently, Hoffmann spells out his assumptions on page 150 of his book. The first is as follows:

> The tests deny the creative person a significant opportunity to demonstrate his creativity and favor the shrewd and facile candidate over the one who has something to say.

I personally know of no evidence to suggest that tests stifle the creative person. The major problem with making such a charge or assumption is that little satisfactory research has been done to define the so-called trait of creativeness. The usual procedure has been simply to call people "creative" who happen to score high on so-called "creativity" tests. Recently, Robert Thorndike (1963) has analyzed the relative factorial purity of the content of the standard IQ tests and of the so-called creativity or divergent thinking tests. He finds that tests of creativity actually correlate more highly with convergent thinking tests than they do with themselves. Evidence such as this is hardly sufficient to sustain an argument that the so-called trait or behavior which we label "creative" has been successfully measured by tests now available. Unfortunately, the usual approach is to label persons as creative who score high on these factorially poorly defined "creativity" tests rather than on the basis of any behaviorally defined reference outside the tests themselves.

Hoffmann cites the study by Getzels and Jackson (1962) described in their book, *Creativity and Intelligence.* Unfortunately the Getzels and Jackson study is a particularly poor example of what I have just discussed. In their study Getzels and Jackson define creativity on the basis of scores on a variety

*From *Psychology in the Schools,* 1963, **1**, 63-69. Copyright 1963, Clinical Psychology Publishing Company, Inc. Reprinted with permission of the author and publisher.

of measures of fluency and divergent thinking. In one part of their study they contrast two groups selected on the basis of high scores on IQ tests and creativity tests, respectively. The average IQ of the students selected on the basis of IQ tests was 150 whereas the average IQ of students selected on the basis of the "creativity" tests was only 127. Getzels and Jackson report that these two groups who differ by 23 points in IQ *did not differ on standard multiple choice achievement examinations.* Yet Hoffmann says on page 146 of his book,

> In view of the above how much faith can we have in the IQ as an unbiased predictor of scholastic achievement even when the scholastic achievement is measured by multiple choice methods? Think of the number of gifted students who were penalized in our schools because they lack the IQ knack.

It is difficult for me to understand how Hoffmann can use the data of the Getzels and Jackson study to make such a comment. Just the opposite is, in fact, true: the "low ability" (IQ = 127) students were *not* penalized on achievement examinations; they scored the same as the "high ability" (IQ = 150) students.

Even so, there seems to be a widely held misconception that teachers somehow like the highly "creative" children less well than the highly intelligent children. As a matter of fact Getzels and Jackson are often cited as evidence and they do state that "the high IQ students are preferred over the average student by their teachers, the creativity students are not." The actual facts as shown by the Getzels and Jackson data are that teachers' preferences were in the same direction for *both* groups and of very nearly the same magnitude. The difference, however, was not statistically significant for the "creative" children. Thus the reader and the public is left by this cavalier treatment of data with the unjustified impression that the teachers prefer the "high IQ's" to the "high creatives." In my opinion, this is irresponsible reporting of research data—reporting that is nicely designed to lead people with an axe to grind (such as Mr. Hoffmann) astray.

Let us consider a second assumption made by Hoffmann. He says:

> They penalize the candidate who perceives subtle points unnoticed by less able people including the test makers. They are apt to be superficial and intellectually dishonest with questions made artificially difficult by means of ambiguity because genuinely searching questions did not readily fit into the multiple choice format.

A comment such as this of course ignores the massive amount of careful research which actually goes into the construction and final validation of a test item. For example, it is well known that distractors are purposely written to "fool" the less able person. We know that information about responses made by persons of different levels of knowledge shows without question that the degree of ambiguity perceived by the examinee is inversely related to his knowledge of the subject matter. In other words in a good test item the less one knows the more ambiguous does the question appear. In spite of this, Hoffmann states on page 67 "and the more one knows about the subject the more glaring the ambiguities become." Hoffmann, of course, has no evidence to support this assumption.

A further assumption made by Hoffmann may be stated as follows:

> they take account of only the choice of answer and not of quality of thought that lead to the choice, and They neglect skill and disciplined expression.

Hoffmann apparently feels very strongly that objective examinations fail to assess a mysterious entity which he calls "quality of thought" or that they give little opportunity for "disciplined expression." Naturally, he offers no definitions for these mysterious attributes and he certainly suggests no reliable nor valid way of measuring them. In fact Hoffmann seems diligently to resist all references to the concepts of reliability and validity.

In addition to the fact that Hoffmann fails to define quality of thought or disciplined expression, it is noteworthy that he gives in Chapter 3 a series of very convincing arguments for *not* using essay examinations to measure so-called quality of thought or disciplined expression. For example, Hoffmann states that it is difficult in writing an essay question to choose a topic which will be fair to all examinees. He further states that even if a topic finally is chosen it is extremely difficult to determine whether the essay is actually relevant to the question, further that it is difficult to overcome the problem of negative halo due to poor handwriting, poor spelling, or poor punctuation. He brings up the problem of different graders of essay examinations using different standards and he even cites the difficulty of the grader changing his standards as he moves through the examinations which he must grade. Hoffmann concludes that essay exams may be unfair, indeed that they are unfair for the testing of the students.

Thus Hoffmann works himself into a corner by criticizing objective exams because they fail to assess quality of thought on disciplined expression; yet he leaves no alternative for assessing these non-defined entities by any other means (such as by essay exams).

In his discussion of this problem he cites a study by the Educational Testing Service showing that a 90-minute essay test was less good than an objective exam, the English Composition Test, for predicting faculty ratings in English Composition. Faced with this evidence that an essay exam is less worthy, Hoffmann simply argues that these results are silly and that they could not possibly have been obtained. He appears to be using logical analysis in order to overcome or to reject empirical results. Essentially, of course, Hoffmann is simply confusing content with predictive or concurrent validity.

Finally, perhaps the potentially most damaging assumption and the one which would be the most difficult for Hoffmann to sustain has to do with the effect of tests in the identification of individual merit. He states,

> They have a pernicious effect on education and the recognition of merit.

Furthermore he seems to be concerned about the idea that multiple choice testing might somehow be "efficient" and he feels that efficiency is bad in and of itself. For example, on page 90 he states,

> Let us not sacrifice too much for the sake of efficiency. In some respects the dictatorship is more efficient than a democracy and the lie detector more efficient and scientific than the jury. The efficient Nazis made medical experiments directly on men and women.

After reading this I find myself very curious about Mr. Hoffmann's stand on fluoridation of water which certainly must be regarded as one very efficient way of decreasing the incidence of dental caries. However, lest I be charged with arguing in the same manner as I am accusing Mr. Hoffmann of doing, let me hasten to offer something in a more positive vein.

Actually, standardized testing is one of the great success stories of our time. Perhaps this has been no better pointed out than in the book, *Excellence*, by John Gardner (1961). Psychological testing for the first time enables us to look at the many facets of an individual instead of making judgments based on the so-called "lump of dough" doctrine. Now we can truly measure and assess the individuality of each person in society and through careful guidance help individuals realize the potentialities indicated by psychological testing instruments. Gardner illustrates the lump of dough doctrine and the lack of any recognition of individuality by citing the experience of a friend who visited a small provincial school in France. Gardner states,

> The teacher seemed to find it impossible to separate his judgment of a pupil's intelligence from his judgment of the pupil's cleanliness, good manners, neatness of dress and precision of speech. Needless to say his students from the upper and upper-middle social class excelled in these qualities.

Today, through objective tests we can identify the many abilities of children and for the first time do a good job of mapping the true individuality of each and every child. In other words, tests provide us with the best means available for assessing individuality and discovering and rewarding individual merit. In my opinion this function is undoubtedly the greatest strength of testing and it is an entirely fallacious and unfounded assumption on the part of Hoffmann that tests are instead working against the recognition of individual merit and the wise and humane utilization of human resources. The creative genius of men such as Terman, Thurstone, Guilford and Strong cannot be nullified by a few Hoffmanns, Packards, Grosses, or Whytes.

Now I would like to turn briefly to points made by Hoffmann which I believe are essentially worthwhile and with which I am in essential agreement.

First, Hoffmann is unhappy with the terms "underachiever" and "overachiever." So am I. As a matter of fact, tests have never shown predictive or concurrent validities which exceed .60 or .70. It would seem under these conditions to be wiser to use the terms "over-scorer" and "under-scorer" rather than to assume and to label persons in terms of their achievement as is done by the widely used terms, under and overachiever.

Secondly, Hoffmann argues that statistics should not take precedence over rational analysis of an item's content. I would tend to agree with this statement. Even if empirical validity did show that an item was valid, if a wrong answer were keyed, I would not then proceed to use this wrongly keyed answer. Thus, I would say that empirical validity should not necessarily carry the day over content validity and in so saying I am in essential agreement with Hoffmann. Unfortunately, Hoffmann completely ignores the fact that statistical validation of test items is most often an effective means of discovering poor and ambiguous items. Nowhere in his book does Hoffmann mention that item analysis is primarily a means of identifying poorly keyed and ambiguous items.

Finally, Hoffmann may not be aware of it but he does call attention to the possibility of heteroschedastic and non-linear relationships. It would certainly be well for more psychologists to recognize the possibility of such relationships more generally. One of the approaches to item analysis which is suggested then by this complaint of Hoffmann's is a more thorough analysis of the item characteristic curve for each of the items in the pool being submitted to analysis. This is a wise and a needed procedure as has already been pointed out by Dr. Astin.

Now, I should like to consider more generally some of the assumptions made by other writers who have complained about psychological testing, including such persons as Vance Packard, Jacques Barzun, Martin Gross, William Whyte, Allan Harrington and others.

One of the major assumptions running throughout these writings is that "mind" can't be measured. It would appear that most of these gentlemen feel that "mind" somehow is such a warm and mysterious human quality that they resist the idea of being able to learn or to predict anything about it. It is as if they seek to retain this particular "mystery system" as being outside the realm of scientific study. We know, of course, that if "mind" is defined as behavior, it can indeed be measured. As a matter of fact, as has already been stated, perhaps the greatest accomplishment of psychology thus far has been the measurement of the individuality of man. We know that we can, through various psychological techniques assess the individuality of persons and make rather good predictions about their future behavior. Perhaps the greatest recent success attesting to this is the selection of the Peace Corps candidates who are now serving overseas. I do not know what the current "hit rate" is for the Peace Corps selection project but I do know that of the first 600 persons who went overseas only 6 had to be returned and that 2 of these returned because of a death in the family. I would say that the assumptions that "mind" or behavior cannot be measured is entirely negated by the evidence we have at hand.

Secondly, the writers against psychological testing seem to make an assumption which is the exact opposite from that just discussed. They assume that testing will lead to conformity by picking persons who are all of the same mold or all of the same type. This, of course, assumes that "mind" can be measured only too well and is a sharp contradiction from the assumption that mind can't be measured. Of course we know that our psychological measures aren't *that* good, but even if they were we have widespread evidence showing that the compensatory model seems to be of major significance for predicting behavior. Thus, even though we have a series of tests which combine into a multiple prediction which is highly valid, we know that any given person would show a great deal of intra-individual trait variability. This was pointed up nicely by a recent study involving the early identification of management potential conducted by the Standard Oil Company of New Jersey. In their study it was possible to develop a battery with a cross-validated multiple correlation of .70 for identifying more effective and less effective managers. However, the managers did not fit a common mold when the various individual tests of the battery were examined. Some managers were high on one kind of test (such as verbal fluency); other managers, though low on this test, seemed to "make-up for it" by having a pattern of education and work experience in their backgrounds which compensated in a sense for their lower measured ability. Thus, again, one of the great principles of psychological testing which is ignored by these critics is the fact of intra-individual trait variability. The fact that people do differ within themselves has long been recognized and submitted to careful study by psychologists.

A third common complaint about psychological testing is that it is an invasion of privacy. It is possible that this criticism may have some merit.

This is the point, of course, at which it is incumbent upon the users of psychological tests to demonstrate the validity of any items which might otherwise be regarded as an invasion of privacy. A major point usually ignored by critics of psychological testing when they discuss the invasion of privacy is the distinction between institutional and individual decisions. If a firm is using a test to assess candidates and an individual desires employment with that firm, the use of the test is for the purpose of helping the institution to make a hiring decision; the purpose is not to give guidance or to protect the privacy of the individuals being tested. It is true, but perhaps beside the point, that an increase in the accuracy of institutional decisions will, over the long run, be accompanied by an increasing proportion of accurate or "correct" individual decisions.

Finally, it should be noted that the critics very rarely suggest any alternatives to psychological testing. Gardner in his book, *Excellence,* says the following:

> Anyone attacking the usefulness of the tests must suggest workable alternatives. It has been proven over and over again that the alternative methods of evaluating ability are subject to gross errors and capable of producing grave injustices.

Thus it would appear that the alternatives are to return to the Industrial Dark Ages when personnel decisions were made on the basis of hair color or shape of head or perhaps more realistically on the basis of family background or family status. Although most critics carefully avoid suggesting alternatives, Allen Harrington in his book, *Life in the Crystal Palace,* does suggest some interesting ones; on p. 60 he says,

> Once long ago it seems hiring was done in a rough and ready way. It still is by the firms that are too small to maintain an employee relations staff or by companies that expect a certain amount of turnover.

And on p. 61 he states further:

> Employer and applicant made an intuitive connection. By intuition, I mean perception through unconscious logic. We tried to see into each other beyond the things we said, behind the polite formalities. We sought to discover what the other was really like. Sometimes one was the victim of whimsical judgment. A businessman I know always scrutinized a visitor's shoes in order to determine his character. He could, he said, "Read" an applicant by studying his footwear, the shine, the repair of the heels, and so on. Another employer after World War II despised anyone who had been in the Air Force. He was a former infantryman and had once been bombed and wounded by our own planes.

Thus it is apparent that the alternatives, when they are suggested, are clearly ridiculous. Let us consider, for example, how Harrington would have reacted to a personality test inventory which had the following three items in it:

1. My heels are often run down   True or False.
2. I love to have my shoes shined   True or False.
3. I worry a good deal about the appearance of my feet.   True or False.

Certainly items such as this would be received by great anguish and gnashing of teeth. However, they are simply objective statements of the examination of the visitor's shoes which seems in Harrington's rather inconsistent manner of thinking to be a preferred selection technique.

Conclusion

I believe that our careful examination of the assumptions made by the various critics of psychological testing can lead to only one conclusion: The basic assumptions are erroneous and fallacious; they are based for the most part on lack of information, as apparently is the case for Hoffmann, or more seriously on a refusal to accept the strong evidence showing that individuality *can* be assessed with *accuracy* and in such a way as to give better recognition to real merit than has ever before been the case in either our educational or industrial institutions.

36 | Standardized Ability Tests and Testing*

D. A. Goslin

Standardized ability tests have been a source of considerable controversy in recent years. Growing competition for jobs and for all educational opportunities has intensified the search for better ways to evaluate individual abilities and aptitudes and to identify intellectual potential at progressively earlier ages. Standardized tests of various types increasingly are used to identify applicants throughout the educational system, as well as by the military, the civil service, and business and industry (Brim *et al.,* 1964; Goslin, 1967; Goslin *et al.,* 1965).[1]

This reliance on results of standardized tests has caused questions to be raised about the validity of the tests used, as well as their effects on those who take them and on the society that uses them to differentiate among its members. Thus far, there have been very few, if any, attempts to bring together all of the criticisms that have been leveled against tests, and to place them in an analytical framework that would permit a systematic evaluation of their validity. In this paper the validity of standardized tests is discussed, and major criticisms of tests are summarized within such a framework.

Three Variables of Criticism

Criticisms of testing relate to three variables: the type of test, how it is used, and assumptions regarding its validity. First, the type of test being used must be considered. Ability tests may be divided into tests that attempt to measure inherent capabilities, potentials, or abilities acquired over a long time, and tests designed to measure specific achievements.

Intelligence and aptitude tests are implicitly assumed to measure a relatively deep and enduring quality. This quality may be viewed as changeable;

*From *Science,* 1968, **159,** 851-855. Copyright 1968 by the American Association for the Advancement of Science. Reprinted with permission of the author and publisher.
[1] A number of surveys of the extent of testing and test use have appeared in recent years. See, for example, Goslin, D. A. *The search for ability.* New York: Russell Sage Foundation, 1963.

however, startling changes are assumed to be rare except under specific conditions, as when extreme cultural deprivation is ameliorated. Intelligence and aptitude tests therefore generate anxiety in people tested. The high cultural value placed on intellectual abilities in our society also makes any instrument which purports to measure general intellectual abilities a source of fascination. For these reasons, such tests have been a major source of controversy and debate.

Although less often perceived as unfair, since they measure skills acquired in a particular area over a short time, achievement tests potentially exert a considerable influence on subject matter and teaching methods, as well as on what skills appear desirable. Among all tests, they are distinctive in that it is easier in the case of an achievement test to see what one is measuring, since the universe of abilities being sampled by the test is theoretically finite and far more easily specified.

The second variable is the use to which the test is put. Test results may be used for selection and placement, or counseling, and sometimes both. A test used to select among a group of candidates for a job, or among applicants for admission to a school, or a test used to assign individuals to specific groups (like tracks in a school) has an essentially predictive function. It is used to predict individual performance with respect to that of the other members of the group.

Tests may also be used as a basis for providing an individual with information about his abilities and aptitudes. This use of tests is theoretically different from that previously mentioned because the information provided to the "counselee" is intended to enable him to decide about his future. In the former case, although the individual sometimes decides for himself (as whether or not to apply), others ultimately decide for him. However, counseling frequently directs the individual to one of several alternatives. In this case, depending on the information and how it is transmitted, the counselor may actually be the decision-maker.

Finally, criticisms may either question the validity of tests or they may have little or nothing to do with whether the test measures what it is supposed to measure. Here we must ask: Is the force of the criticism affected by whether we assume the test to be a valid measure of what it is supposed to measure, or not?

Criticisms of the Validity of Ability Tests

Several critics have claimed that certain characteristics of tests make them unfair and invalid predictors for certain individuals or groups. These critics have singled out three types of individuals.

First, Hoffmann (1962) and others have claimed that these tests are unfair to deep thinkers. Critics who take this position claim that certain items
on standardized tests penalize bright students because they are ambiguously
worded or because the alternatives presented included one or more options
(scored as incorrect) that the mediocre student passes by, but which the
extremely bright student correctly perceives as being possibly correct
answers. One cannot dispute the fact that Hoffmann and others have demonstrated clearly the existence of such items on tests that are currently in use.

Although it is not known whether any extremely bright students have
actually suffered because of poorly written tests, Hoffmann's point is valid, at
least in the abstract. It seems unlikely, however, in our achievement-oriented
society, that very many geniuses remain undiscovered, regardless of their
performance on standardized tests (or more important, that more geniuses are
missed because of standardized tests than would be missed with alternative
selection techniques).

Second, any test designed to be given to individuals in our heterogeneous
society will discriminate against people with a cultural background different
from that of the majority. To take an extreme case, if a pupil cannot read
English because Spanish is spoken at home, he is not likely to do well on tests
of reading comprehension in English, or, in fact, on any test written
in English. Members of any group whose life experiences differ significantly from those on which the test was standardized will also be at a disadvantage.

Partly, this is a problem of standardization. Conceivably, special norms
could be developed on any test for every distinctive group likely to take the
test, so that both inter- and intragroup comparisons could be made. But
another principle is involved. Most standardized tests are designed to predict
success of individuals in the broader society, or in the setting in which the
individual wishes to gain admission. Thus, tests are doing their job when they
discriminate. If facility in English is assumed necessary for success, then a test
of that facility is not unfair. In such cases, it can be pointed out that it is not
the test which is unfair, but rather the circumstances which have permitted
the deprivation to persist. However, any inferences about the general intellectual abilities of members of disadvantaged or other special groups based on
test scores should be avoided at early ages.

Finally, tests may be unfair to individuals who lack special skills required
for taking standardized tests. For almost everyone, these skills may be
assumed to develop as a result of repeated contact with tests. Some individuals, however, take more tests than others. The amount of experience required to make this factor an unimportant influence in test performance is
unknown. It may be assumed, however, that tests are unfair to individuals

without the requisite experience with tests.[2] Hence, extensive testing in elementary and junior high school is beneficial, but inequalities may be created when some schools test more frequently than others. The problem is acute for foreigners from countries where tests are not widely used (for example, foreign applicants to American graduate and professional schools).

Factors Affecting Validity of Tests

Standardized ability tests are not perfect predictors of subsequent performance, even in situations that require abilities similar to those required on the test. Highest coefficients of correlation between test scores and measures of subsequent performance are obtained for short-range academic performance.[3] For example, scores of standardized tests given in the 12th grade predict first-year college grades fairly well. As the length of time between the test and criterion situation increases, the magnitude of the correlation is reduced. Similarly, as the criterion situation becomes more dissimilar from the test situation, the correlation is reduced. Thus, most existing studies show no correlation between test scores and subsequent occupational success (nor is any correlation shown between academic performance as measured by grades and subsequent occupational success). Because test scores correlate only moderately with long-range academic performance and not at all with postacademic performance, one can raise serious questions about their usefulness and reliability.

Three factors contribute to this lack of correlation. First, it is often difficult to establish clear criteria for successful postacademic performance. Many studies have relied on performance ratings by professional colleagues, fellow workers, or superiors. These are frequently unreliable and are based on other factors, such as personal qualities. Use of objective criteria, such as number of scientific papers published, may be criticized as being superficial.

Second, there is the problem of range restriction. Accurate predictions about the relative performance of individuals are easily made where there are sizable differences between individuals; a high degree of variance in the distribution of abilities measured makes prediction easy. However, where differences among members of the group tested are small, it is difficult to predict

---

[2] Numerous studies have examined the effects of "practice" or "coaching," or both, on test scores. Most have found little or no significant effects. A distinction should be made between the effects of specific practice or coaching experiences and the effects of long-term exposure to standardized tests.

[3] For a summary of research on the prediction of academic performance, see Lavin, D. E. *The prediction of academic performance.* New York: Russell Sage Foundation, 1965.

later performance of the members of the group relative to one another. Thus, predictions in a homogeneous group, such as college graduates, are risky. The phenomenon of range restriction accounts in large part for the lack of correlation between either test scores or academic performance and occupational success among able students.

Third, one should not assume that there is a linear relation between qualities measured by a standardized test and occupational success. The assumption that intelligence alone determines success is superficial. In fact, many studies have revealed that the relation between intellectual abilities and success in our society is very complicated. For example, although Terman demonstrated clearly that his gifted group as a whole was more successful than less intellectually able groups, he found no relationship between intelligence and later performance within the gifted group. (Terman, 1959).

These findings are corroborated by the previously noted lack of correlation between college performance and subsequent nonacademic success and suggest that intellectual abilities may function as a threshold variable in relation to occupational advancement. A minimum level of intelligence is obviously required for most occupations, but once at or above this threshold, individual achievement relative to others in the same field is determined by qualities not measured by tests of intellectual abilities.

It should be noted that fields of endeavor differ not only in basic requirements of intelligence, but also with respect to the amount of difference made by increments over this level in one's chances of achieving success. In other words, qualities other than basic intelligence are more important in some fields than in others. [Incidentally, this does not have to be the case; it just happens that our society works this way at present. One could, for example, imagine a society in which a perfect correlation between intelligence and success could be achieved by assigning all jobs and status in the society on the sole basis of intelligence.[4]]

There is some controversy about whether ability tests measure innate capabilities (presumed unchangeable) or learning. Few people with any sophistication in psychometrics believe that even intelligence tests measure only innate capabilities. However, there are significant differences in opinion about whether the qualities measured by intelligence tests are more or less influenced by learning than by inherent potential. Assumptions about exactly what the test measures are likely to have an important effect on how test scores are used. If one interprets a child's performance as an indication of what he has learned (as opposed to a result of innate capability), then one is

[4] Such a society is envisioned by Michael Young in his book *The rise of the meritocracy* (London: Thames & Hudson, 1958).

less likely to make long-run predictions about the child's ultimate success on the basis of his test scores (for example, his motivation might increase, and he might do better next time).

One of the most important criticisms of tests is that they contribute to their own validity by functioning as self-fulfilling prophecies. Hypothetically, a child who does well on a test, and, as a consequence of his performance, is placed in an advanced class, or receives special attention from his teachers, or who is admitted to a good university, is more likely to do well than the one whose score was lower. The likelihood that the optimistic prediction made on the basis of a high test score will be fulfilled is therefore increased because the person who scores high receives special advantages, whereas the individual who does poorly is often denied opportunities.

Experimental data from a recent study by Rosenthal and Jacobson (1968) confirm this hypothesis. They gave all of the children in one California elementary school an ordinary intelligence test at the beginning of the school year. They informed the teachers that the test they had given was specially designed to identify children who could be expected to show substantial I.Q. gains during the coming year. In each class, they then selected at random ten children and informed the teachers that these children had done particularly well on the test. This group in each class formed the experimental group, and the remainder of the children in each class served as the control group. An intelligence test given at the end of the school year showed that the experimental groups in grades kindergarten, one, two, and three had made significant gains in I.Q. when compared to the children in the control groups. In addition, teachers rated children in the experimental groups as being superior to those in the control groups in personal qualities, such as cooperativeness, interest in school affairs, and social adjustment. These data reveal that teachers' expectations contributed substantially to the increased test scores of the children in the experimental groups. Here the first test score reported to the teachers became a self-fulfilling prophecy. The implications of this point are far-reaching, especially for policies concerning the use of standardized intelligence tests in the elementary grades.

Criticisms Independent of the Validity of Tests

The following criticisms may be hypothesized to hold, whether one argues that tests are valid measures of ability or not. In some cases, the force of the criticism is increased if one assumes tests to be highly valid predictors. These criticisms, therefore, stem from the potential social effects of testing, rather than from questions regarding the accuracy of tests.

Standardized ability tests are used throughout the educational system, and children take such tests at periodic intervals. In addition, the spread of the technology of standardized test construction has led many teachers to make use of objective questions in tests they construct. It has been suggested that continual exposure to multiple-choice items during the elementary and secondary grades tends to result in constriction of children's ability to reason. In particular, it is claimed that emphasis on evaluation techniques in which there is always a right and wrong answer makes it difficult for children to deal with issues on which there is no clear right or wrong answer.[5] Children, it is claimed, are therefore handicapped when they attempt to work through questions involving ethical or philosophical judgments, or when arriving at a decision depends upon identifying the assumptions one is going to begin with.

There is no proof that this is a valid criticism. Colleges claim that incoming students do not write as well as formerly, but there is no way of knowing if the older generation is just complaining about the new one, or, if true, whether it is because proportionally more people are going to college today. Lack of a suitable control group (that is, college students who have not taken standardized tests) makes research on this topic difficult.

When a student takes a college entrance examination or almost any standardized test, not only he, but also his teachers and his school, are being tested, since his performance reflects his training. As a consequence, tests have a potentially significant impact on subject matter and teaching methods. Only a very minority of teachers interviewed in a recent study (Goslin *et al.*, 1965) claimed to spend much time preparing students for standardized tests or indicated that they have ever altered a course because the subject matter covered by a standardized test was different from what they normally taught. Nevertheless, there is some evidence that in many situations standardized tests do exert an influence on what is taught. The well-known New York Regents' examination program is pertinent here. Since both teachers and schools were being evaluated along with students, there was, and still is, considerable pressure to prepare students to take the Regents' achievement examinations. Reports of students being drilled on old copies of the Regents' examinations were common. That tests have had an impact on the curricula in this case cannot be disputed (Brickell, 1962).

Whether or not teachers make special efforts to prepare students for taking particular standardized tests, such tests can have a more general impact

---

[5] Often, multiple choice tests require that the "best" answer from the alternatives provided be selected. This choice is, by definition, the "right" answer. Although such tests may measure judgment effectively, they still may cause the person who takes tests to see the world in "right" or "wrong" terms.

on curricula. For example, widely used external examinations, like the College Board achievements tests, may result in pressure on a school system to adopt a new curriculum if the school perceives that the content covered by the test differs significantly from that which is being presented in the school. Thus, standardized tests based on the new mathematics curriculum can be expected to speed the adoption of this curriculum in schools.

It should be noted that such an effect is not necessarily deleterious. Standardized tests may raise school standards as often as they limit innovation and experimentation. This, of course, was the idea behind the Regents' examination program when it was initiated. The problem is striking a balance between raising standards and setting arbitrary limits.

More and more schools, colleges, and testing agencies are giving individuals either their specific score or percentile rank, or a general idea of how they did on standardized tests. Regardless of how such information is transmitted to the examinee, it may be hypothesized that it will affect self-image, motivation, and aspirations in some cases. Users of tests have alternately been criticized for withholding test scores and for indiscriminately giving results. The effect of receiving information about one's abilities will depend on the perceived legitimacy of the source of the information (for example, the pupil's counselor), the perceived accuracy of the test, and the degree to which the test score confirms one's own estimate, including how threatening or rewarding it is. Obviously, individuals make use of many different types of information in arriving at an estimate of their abilities; standardized test scores are only one of many ways in which individuals get information about their capabilities. Data from a national sample of high school students (Brim *et al.,* 1964) indicate that test scores are of relatively minor importance in shaping self-estimates of ability, in comparison with such things as school grades, comments of peers and parents, and contact with teachers.

Test scores do have a potentially great impact when the individual's self-estimate varies considerably from his test score and when he cannot rationalize his poor performance, or when the score is substantially higher than his estimate. Under such conditions we may expect a shift in self-estimate of ability to affect the individual's aspirations, his motivation, and, secondarily, future personal decisions. We should also consider the consequences for overall aspiration levels in the society of a system in which individuals are classified very early with respect to their abilities and available opportunities for the future.

The use of any single criterion or set of criteria to sort individuals into groups or to decide which individuals will be admitted to a group affects the structure and characteristics of groups so formed. These implications may be examined under the following headings: (i) social structure within groups, (ii) tendencies toward uniformity in the characteristics of group members, and (iii) implications for the society as a whole.

With regard to (i), the current widespread use of standardized tests to allocate students to instructional groups or to tracks within schools causes social differentiation within schools based on qualities measured by standardized tests. Ability groupings reduce social contact between pupils of differing levels of ability (as measured by standardized tests). Research indicates that such differentiation may affect performance levels of low-ability pupils negatively, while not significantly facilitating the performance of high-ability pupils (Yates, 1966). In addition, it is clear that ability grouping impedes the process of acculturation of members of culturally deprived groups, who tend to end up together in the low-ability groups.

As for (ii), the use of any single criterion for forming groups produces a strong tendency toward uniformity in the members of the group. Our elite colleges and universities, for example, have difficulty achieving diversity in the student body while admitting only students of exceptional ability. The problem becomes more acute when standardized tests are heavily relied upon as a measure of intellectual ability.

Concerning (iii), Wolfle has pointed out that the success of modern, complex societies depends in large part on the availability of a talent pool in which a great diversity of abilities and skills is represented (Wolfle, 1960). To create such a talent pool, rewards of social status, prestige, and economic returns must be provided for individuals possessing many different talents. A tendency to rely heavily on standardized tests of a limited set of intellectual skills in the allocation of opportunities for achievement must necessarily reduce the diversity of talent available. Here, we might consider testing more abilities than those measured by current tests. We must also ensure adequate rewards for individuals possessing abilities not measured by tests, but which are important for the successful functioning of the society.

Do Tests Invade Privacy?

A test is a potential invasion of privacy because personal information is made available to others. Very important values in American society suggest that individuals have the right to decide to whom and under what conditions they will make available to others information about themselves. Correlative to this point, however, is the fact that participation in the society carries with it certain obligations and responsibilities. Further, certain groups clearly have the right to demand information from those who want the privileges of group membership. Thus, no one is likely to object to being given a driving test before being permitted to operate a motor vehicle. Similarly, few people object to the requirement that they must take an entrance test in order to gain admission to a university or college. In each case, the right of a group to information that is relevant to the stated objectives and goals of the group has been established.

Two important questions remain, however. First, under what conditions does a group have the right to ask aspiring members for information that is irrelevant to the purposes and goals of the group? In order to answer this question, it is probably necessary to make a distinction between public and private groups. A private group usually has the right to ask of applicants for membership anything, whether relevant or irrelevant. The applicant then decides whether he wishes to reveal this information. In the case of a group supported by the society as a whole, including all of the potential applicants to the group, the situation is more difficult. Would it be, for example, legitimate for the state to ask individuals to reveal information about their sexual behavior as a requirement for obtaining a driver's license? Most of us would, I think, object to such a requirement on the grounds that it represents an invasion of our privacy that is not justified by the service being rendered. The issue is one of relevance: must the school have such information in order to do its job?

There is, however, a second and more difficult problem in the case of school testing. In each of the cases presented above, the individual retains a choice as to whether he will submit himself to the test or not. Thus, if an individual does not want to take the College Board Scholastic Aptitude Test (SAT), he does not have to. Nor does he have to submit to a driver's test. As a result of his decision, he may have to give up his chances of attending certain colleges or driving an automobile, but the choice in each case is his. But, for the most part, a child does not have a choice about whether he will take tests or not, including standardized tests. A parent might move to another community, in which the school system did not use standardized tests (if he could find one), or he might send his children to a private school that did not administer tests (if he could afford one). For most parents these are not realistic alternatives.

Does this constitute an invasion of privacy? Carried to its extreme, an affirmative answer leads one to the conclusion that children should be permitted to refuse to take all tests, even those given by their teachers in class. Although this sounds absurd, it is not an unreasonable claim. If a child refused to participate in classroom tests, he would fail his courses and would not be promoted, but this would be his (or his parents') decision. The school clearly does have a right to require pupils to demonstrate their proficiency in school subjects before according them advanced status. But does the school also have the right to require pupils to demonstrate their general intellectual ability apart from their proficiency in specific subjects? If a child refused to take an I.Q. test given in school, would he fail his course? Does a school need such information in order to decide whether or not a child should be promoted?

If one concludes that a school has the right to collect information about intellectual abilities of its pupils, does the school also have the right to withhold this information from the pupil and his parents? Conversely, what right do parents and pupils have to know what information the school possesses about them? In at least one case (in New York State), the courts ruled that parents do have the right of access to information on the pupil's permanent record card maintained by the school (Van Allen vs. McCleary, 1961).

Summary and Conclusions

At the outset a distinction was made between criticisms directed at the validity of tests and criticisms not affected by the validity of the tests. It was noted further that all criticisms of tests must take into consideration the type of test and the use to which the test is put.

Criticisms of the validity of tests involved the following issues: i)tests may be unfair to certain groups and individuals, including the extremely gifted, the culturally disadvantaged, and those who lack experience in taking tests; ii) tests are not perfect predictors of subsequent performance; iii) tests may be used in overly rigid ways; iv) tests may not measure inherent qualities of individuals; and v) tests may contribute to their own predictive validity by serving as self-fulfilling prophecies.

Criticisms that are more or less independent of test validity included the effects of tests on i) thinking patterns of those tested frequently; ii) school curricula; iii) self-image, motivation, and aspirations; iv) groups using tests as a criterion for selection or allocation, or both; and v) privacy. Several concluding remarks are in order:

1) This paper has focused almost entirely on *criticisms* of tests. However, the positive value of standardized tests should not be ignored. Here we must keep in mind what possible alternative measures would be used if standardized tests were abandoned.

2) We must begin thinking about tests in a much broader perspec-

tive—one that includes consideration of the social effects of tests as well as their validity and reliability.

3) Finally, an effort should be made to develop rational and systematic policies on the use of tests with the culturally disadvantaged, the dissemination of test results, and the problem of invasion of privacy. Such policies can be formulated only if we are willing to take a long hard look at the role we want testing to play in the society. Standardized tests currently are a cornerstone in the edifice of stratification in American society. It is up to the social scientist to conduct research that will enable policy makers in education, business and industry, and government to determine in a consistent and rational way the ultimate shape of this edifice.

37 | A Customer Counsels the Testers*

Sidney P. Marland, Jr.

The institution of testing has become an Establishment. As such, it has become a victim of its own success. Even as the Vatican. And the Pope. The Supreme Court, boards of education, universities, school administrators, the Democratic Party—these are other establishments.

To be an Establishment nowadays is to invite the wrath of a fair portion of our society on almost any issue. Dr. John Gardner has reflected on this matter of the Establishment. In an address he gave at Cornell University this past June (I hesitate to paraphrase Gardner with his Churchillian prose), Dr. Gardner said that if an observer could take a pill that would thrust him ahead 300 years from now and permit him to look back upon the history of the latter half of the twentieth century in America, he would find that this was a time when all of our established institutions came under great challenge because of the unloving critics of institutions and the uncritical lovers within the institutions. The critics not responsible for their institutions began to tear them down, and those who loved their institutions so dearly as to be uncritical of them did indeed allow them to languish. As this pill continued to work, it was observed that the wise people in the latter part of the twentieth century began to change: The unloving critics became somewhat loving and concerned, and those who were the uncritical lovers of their establishments became critical and constructively set about corrective action.

Today, I would say that the testers are becoming their own loving critics, and this is as it should be. For example, the College Entrance Examination Board will soon publish a very candid and thorough assessment of all the current criticisms of testing. Here is a passage from the report:

> Standardized tests have been a course of considerable controversy over recent years. Growing competition for jobs, for admission to college and for educational opportunities in general has led to an intensified search for better ways of evaluating capabilities and aptitudes for identifying intellectual potential at earlier ages.
>
> This great reliance on standardized tests has led a number of scholars and others to

raise important questions about the validity of tests being used, about their effects on those who take them and on the society that uses them to differentiate among human beings. . . .

Three years ago, the College Board established a major commission to investigate itself—if you will, to be a critical lover of this Establishment. Richard Pearson, President of the College Board, in initiating the commission, said that the commission members "should undertake a thoroughgoing appraisal of existing tests . . . and in light of the future needs of admissions." This independent twenty-one member commission is now hard at work, having drawn upon the counsel of the most earnest critics in pursuit of its broad mandate from the College Board.[1]

In my approach to the task that has been put to me today, I should like to make it clear that I do not pretend to have competence in the field of testing and all of its many ramifications. I do hope to present the useful observations of a school administrator who has been a customer of the test makers for a long time, who has had to defend budgets calling for hundreds and hundreds of thousands of dollars' worth of tests as well as salaries of staffs to administer those tests, and psychologists and counselors to interpret them and use them wisely with young people and parents. It has also been my task to persuade boards of education as to the usefulness, importance, and the need for a testing program in school systems. Thus, as a consumer of test products, I am in a position to offer some insight as to those criticisms that now surround the Establishment of Testing. In this paper, I will cite some of these criticisms and respond to them as a person claiming competence only as an administrator and a consumer.

Excessive Testing

A criticism that I would offer, and one that is on the lips of many of our critics, is redundancy—the multiplicity and excessive amount of testing that goes on in our schools. I think there is a great deal more testing going on now than there was perhaps even five or six years ago, but I am not sure that there is any evidence to show that it is all happening to the same child! I think that institutions, schools, industries, government, and other consumers of tests are testing more. I think the schools—broadly speaking—are consuming more tests, and more testing and measurement is going on. I think this is probably a product of government intervention, the encouragement of the National Defense Education Act, and increasing respect for some of the applications of testing. At any rate, testing is reaching young people it has not reached before.

---

[1] *Report of the Commission on Tests* (1971), published by the College Entrance Examination Board. [Editor's note]

I feel that there is not an increase in testing in a given school that has been testing for some time; there may indeed be some decrease in testing as teachers and administrators and counselors become more sophisticated in using test information. I think, for example, that I could predict with some confidence that over the next two or three years the duplication between the National Merit Scholarship Testing Program and the Preliminary Scholastic Aptitude Test will be eliminated. Since it is clear that a very high correlation exists between these tests, I believe that they very likely will soon be one and the same, and that educators will agree that they can get the same kind of information from one test instead of two. As we become more certain of what tests can and cannot do, there will be an increased efficiency in their uses. I am speaking as a school administrator who has to justify these things in his budget and justify teacher time and pupil time.

Another point that is noteworthy among the current criticisms of testing is that the test users—namely, those of us in the schools—have extended the function or the implied function of tests beyond the intent of the test makers. This should not be a criticism of the test makers. David Goslin[2] has done some very useful investigating into this whole business of the changing world of testing. According to Goslin a great deal of the criticism surrounding tests relates to those concerned with college entrance selection and prediction, and yet, "considering only school testing, a very strong case can be made for the fact that standardized tests given in elementary schools have a potentially greater impact on both pupils and schools than do college admission tests.

"The tests are used for many purposes (by the schools), even though they may be primarily called the College Entrance Examination Board's Scholastic Aptitude Test, scholastic aptitude being all the the test makers intended this test to be."

Goslin discovered that principals acknowledge using these tests for a great many others things, such as the following:

1. the grouping of students according to some kind of homogeneity in classification within schools;
2. a basis for determining pupil strength and weaknesses for remedial purposes;
3. a basis for providing the pupil with information about his abilities as a guidance function;
4. a basis for evaluating effectiveness of teachers (unfortunate, but in many cases probably true);
5. a basis for evaluating the appropriateness of the curriculum as it relates to overall school system plans and effectiveness.

[2] See Goslin (1967) and Goslin *et al.* (1965). [Editor's note]

Some of these are probably not appropriate uses for test materials. Moreover, if the test is being used for other purposes, it should be known and should not be charged against the test makers. These uses should be optional functions within a given school system.

Another criticism is the one that says standardized ability tests measure only a few of the characteristics of the human beings under instruction; creativity, social responsibility, motivation, physical effectiveness, and many other characteristics are untouched. To give concentrated attention to the early intellectual or academic measures, these critics charge, is to distort the evaluation of any human being.

I happen to feel in full accord with those who make this observation, but I know that the test makers themselves are very much aware of this problem, and I know that they are going about the business of trying to solve it.

One of the dilemmas facing the test makers, I am sure, is that as they try to expand the test to take on qualities beyond the academic or intellectual, they have to deal more and more with some order of subjectivity in a value system of some kind. The paradox is that if we are searching for ways to provide equality of opportunity, especially for our services to the deprived child, the more objective our measures are, presumably the more honest our appraisal. This puts us in the dilemma of relying perhaps more and more on measures of finite things such as measurable achievement and measurable intelligence as distinct from the more subjective values such as attitudes and social responsibility and creativity and the things that make up this human being, quite apart from academic learning.

In our search for sound and thoughtful criticism of present testing, the Commission on Tests of the College Entrance Examination Board has sought the counsel of many outspoken scholars on the subject. Kenneth Clark was among those who contributed to their deliberations on this concern for a wider spectrum of human qualities than our present pattern allows. He calls for a new approach to testing—one that will allow for experimenting with the testing of social values. "These are legitimate components of the education process," says Clark.

The Question of Testing Intelligence

Intelligence testing, I am sure, is one of the great concerns of many scholars. Alexander Wesman, writing in *American Psychologist* last April, said,[3] "There appears to be no more general agreement as to the nature of intelligence or the most valid means of measuring intelligence than was the case fifty years ago. Concepts of intelligence and the definitions constructed

[3] See article no. 23, p. 203. [Editor's note]

to enunciate these concepts abound by the dozens, if not indeed by the hundreds. With so many diverse definitions of intelligence, it is perhaps not surprising that we cannot agree on how to measure intelligence."

Formalization and overemphasis on a numerical or quantitative score is another criticism. Test makers and test users continue to wrestle with this question. If the IQ score is, to those in the field of testing and measurement, a rather unreliable figure (and I think you will say it is), then let us stop using it and let scholars and social scientists, psychologists, psychometricians, and others deal with this in their own privy councils and research. But let *us* stop attaching dubious exactness to an unreliable measure that sounds very reliable to people like teachers and parents and children and school superintendents.

The users of the tests, the translators of the test, the teacher, the parent, are given to feel that the IQ is something exact when no one claims it to be exact. Therefore, have we thought of setting it wholly aside and perhaps confining ourselves to the use of profiles or stanines in the placing of the child for a more easily translated and more comprehensible description of his characteristics and his needs? Quoting again from Wesman in the *American Psychologist:*[4]

> All ability tests—intelligence, aptitude, and achievement—measure what the individual *has* learned—and they often measure with similar content and similar process.

Doesn't this again suggest there could be some kind of a composite measure surrounding the child—again with the increased flexibility that we derived from data processing—so that we could set aside the apparent exactness of finite figures in describing human beings and maybe come up with a profile that could, perhaps with a stanine format, provide some sort of a card-punch expression of each child's characteristics?

It may all be in one category—intelligence, aptitude, and performance—if, as Wesman says, they are so much alike and they merely measure what the human being has learned as a result of systematic and nonsystematic experiences.

It would also be useful if on this same stanine there were modes or norms, norms of the universe, and perhaps norms for the kind of subcommunity in which the child lives, the kind of people with whom he relates, and the kind of environment in which he finds himself. It is desirable that he and the teachers have some idea of how he relates broadly to the immediate and the larger population, without trying to impose an exaggerated exactness in which none of us has confidence, especially those of you engaged in constructing the measuring device.

I would underscore this topic as an important part of this paper. I would

[4]Article no. 23, p. 206. [Editor's note]

emphasize the need for inventing a new way of providing a profile of the child's ability and performance against the environment in which he is living and working. This new device should be so constructed that it can be easily communicated to counselors and teachers, allowing for varying degrees of expertise. It must be so designed that it can be fully comprehended by them and, in turn, readily translated to parents and children.

Moving to another criticism of testing, there is the charge that testing is a mechanism for the self-fulfilling prophecy—that a test score earned at an early age or, indeed, at any age, is such a monumental piece of evidence that it cannot be overcome either by the child or teacher.

I am not so sure that this criticism is valid, I don't think that our teachers are that poor. I don't think that teachers use the test with such vehemence that, indeed, it becomes a self-fulfilling prophecy. I am aware of some of the experiments that have shown teachers to respond in this way, but I would say this is a matter of in-service training of the teacher rather than a fault of the test. It is a matter of administrative management in the school system to determine how tests should be used and how their meaning should be translated to positive and constructive uses. Teachers need much help in using test results, and school leaders should be responsible for insuring such help.

Most of us are familiar with criticism of multiple-choice tests. The charge is usually that the child is dehumanized by standardized testing, that we remove from him the opportunities for creativity, for critical thinking, and for imaginative response to questions by limiting him to the little marks within the constraints of multiple choice. This is probably a good scholarly criticism from the viewpoint of various academic disciplines. But I would say again that the critic may not know what else is going on in the schoolhouse.

The use of standardized tests is a small part of the teaching system. Teachers search constantly for opportunities to release creativity in children, to provide challenging teaching and learning environments in which children can practice critical thinking. In any reasonable schoolroom there are a great many other opportunities for a child to be treated as a lively and distinctive human being, apart from the infrequent constraints of the multiple-choice experience.

Do Tests Test the School?

There is a constant anxiety and concern that tests also test the school system and the teacher. This is probably true to some degree. We evaluate ourselves; we match ourselves, individually or corporately, with some kind of norm and say "We didn't come off so well" or "Aren't we good?" Many teachers—especially young teachers and sometimes not-so-young teachers—fear the results when their children are tested.

We know the unhappy instances of fraudulence in testing in one form or another, reflecting the anxiety of teachers. Grooming for tests, manipulating results, and even making false reports are occasional products of this unhealthy anxiety. This is completely wrong, but it is not a fault of the test itself. It is a fault of the system of teacher management. This is a dilemma that the test makers may wish to consider as a new challenge. We do indeed have a need in education for assessing the effectiveness of teachers. The pupil test is a shabby and unworthy alternative to the assessment of teachers. But we have never faced up to systematic and objective teacher evaluation. I suppose we don't have any valid way of doing it.

Almost any scholar of testing and measurement probably would agree that this is a dangerous thing even to consider, but I would ask that the test makers think of some ways to test the effectiveness of teaching. This is part of education's job. We are trying to increase greatly the effectiveness of teachers. We must discover ways for increasing the productivity of teachers. We must provide for teachers increased means to pour out their professional talents and power, and we need some valid way of calculating benchmarks in this process. This is not for reasons of ranking or dismissing or rewarding or punishing; these are not appropriate purposes for measurement. What we need is a set of measures that can identify superior teaching so that its characteristics can be identified and replicated in others. Until we have some design for measuring effective teaching other than the feelings of a distant and occasional supervisor who says she is a great teacher, or a group of parents who say she is splendid or awful, we don't have very much. I would ask you to ponder this subject as a very real need in education at a time when accountability is more and more a mandate upon the schools.

This raises another question, which concerns the differences in types of groups tested. The teacher in a ghetto may be doing a far better job of teaching if you have some god-like way of assessing what that teacher is doing. The class may be performing two years below normal on the average, with some as many as four years below norm, say, at fifth grade, yet you and I, as experienced observers, might say the teacher is doing a superior job of teaching. In some other community, with a very favored population, there could be a pitiful job of teaching going on yet with children performing two or three grades above norm.

Getting back to my point about the different kinds of communities, I wish that we could have some better measurement tools from those people who analyze tests. We need help comparing like things when we deal with norms. For example, let us say in Pittsburgh we are dealing with a ghetto-school community. I should like to know how those children in that school community, a subcommunity within a large city, compare with the same kinds of children in the same kinds of subcommunities in Chicago, Milwaukee, Cleveland, and Cincinnati. And I would want the same unit of comparative data for favored communities as well as for the total population!

Some tests, particularly the personality test, are considered invasions of privacy. Perhaps they are. I think we are in a time when we are going to have to accept the invasion of privacy. I think that when, for good reasons, all of us at one time or another get around to having our fingerprints taken and recorded somewhere, that is invasion of privacy. And I think that when the credit rating of 120 million Americans is programmed into a computer with an access code available to 27,000 different establishments that can learn about our buying habits and our paying habits—that, too, is an invasion of privacy. But I don't hear anybody rising up and shouting about that.

We might as well decide to live with conditions of data gathering and data retrieval that are presumed to be of sufficient value to offset the discomfort of being "invaded." As a school administrator and parent, I am ready to accept the advancements of science as a resource to the schools provided useful ends are served by the data scientifically gathered.

A critical problem for school administrators has to do with ways in which test results are reported. We are going to go through a period of considerable debate in our country over the publication of test results by schools or by individuals or by neighborhoods. I think it is a wasteful, undesirable, and unethical practice to disseminate test results by schools or neighborhoods. I don't think it accomplishes a thing. But we are going to go through that debate, and we ought to have some ground rules for guiding school policy makers in this difficult field.

There are those who fear the control of the curriculum through testing. A study recently made by Ronald Campbell of Chicago with Roderick McPhee has shown that, indeed, those national symbols of power, prestige, and authority such as the College Entrance Examination Board, the National Merit Scholarship Corporation, and the National Science Foundation have indeed influenced curriculum. I do not think this is necessarily bad. I think that we are living in a time when there have to be some central standards, expectations, and goals that give uniformity and consistency to all the things we are doing in the schools without necessarily being dominated by these external standards. But I think that it is unfortunate that we have to leave everything to be determined at the local level.

I think it is doubtful that the expectations and mandates of our people can be met in a reasonable period of time if we continually have to reinvent curriculum at every crossroads. If the prestige of the College Boards, the Merit Scholarship Program, and similar universal instruments tend to establish an order of excellence that can be translated to all schools as a guide or standard, there is more good than bad in the process. This assumes that local faculties retain the freedom to use the national standards judiciously.

Testing and Vocational Education

So far in this paper, I have sought to review some of the criticisms of testing as I see them. I have tried to respond briefly as a practitioner in the craft of school management to the product that you as test makers have created. At this point I should like to discuss one topic that I have never heard anything about from the critics. It is the whole question of the function of testing in occupational, vocational, and technical education.

One of the enduring curses in our elementary and secondary schools has been the low esteem attached to vocational-technical education. The prestige of the college preparatory program, with its historic aura of excellence by definition, has implied wrongly that the noncollege student is engaged in something that is less than excellent. I ask that those of you who are concerned with the social responsibilities of testing look upon this as a challenge to your ingenuity.

In the minds of young people, the lack of *relevance* now prevailing in much of our high school curriculum is, in part, a source of the discontent and turbulence in big city schools. A child who has little prospect for college sees little reason to apply himself with diligence to an irrelevant and ill-concealed adaptation of a college-entrance spectrum of courses. On the other hand, he could be engaged enthusiastically and relevantly in preparing directly for the world of work. Relatively few young people are so engaged. There was a time, even a few years ago, when there was a place in our society for the unschooled and the unskilled. This time has passed. And society, including parents and some teachers, tends to stigmatize the young person who enters the traditional vocational school, even though he clearly will not be a likely college candidate. We need to make the vocational program important.

There should be a counterpart to the College Entrance Examination Board, with its prestige, motivation, and universality of standards, for that other 50 percent of young people in middle schools and high schools who probably will not enter college—at least without first having earned a living for a time. A culminating examination should be created with all the strength and quality and prestige that now characterize the College Board examinations. This examination should include, in part, the appropriate academics of a liberalizing curriculum, but it should have as its principal message a measure of the quality of skilled performance in a given occupation that may be expected of the examinee. This would suggest a whole range of crafts, such as plumbing, carpentry, or electricity, and it would necessarily reach into the exciting new opportunities for young people in the swiftly emerging technologies—electronics, the health sciences, the computer, performing arts and fine arts, chemistry, aviation, and many other fields. Given a goal culminating in a rigorous test of his competencies, the reluctant student of today could find a new relevance in school tomorrow.

The program should have very substantial participation from industry and labor to include lively and visible local councils participating in the performance evaluation. Work-study relationships between the young person and certain industries, trades, and commercial enterprises in his immediate environment would be increased and would add to the relevance of his learning.

Upon completion of his in-school curriculum, the student would be awarded a certificate, which because of the universality of the examination's influence and respectability, would give him the freedom to move into appropriate job categories anywhere. Trading upon the illustrious name of CEEB, we might call this new dimension of testing the JEEP (Job Entry Examination Program). The name is not important, but the function is long overdue.

A Decade of Criticism

In summary, we have had now for the past 10 years a lively and healthy condition of responsible criticism. Perhaps Professor Banesh Hoffmann is a good example of the critic—earnest, scholarly, and respected. He says that there does not presently exist any generally satisfactory method for evaluating human abilities, that "objective tests are not worthy of a first rate mind." That was in '67.

As early as 1962 in his book, *The Tyranny of Testing,* he strongly recommended the creation of a national committee to examine this whole business of testing, and as I have mentioned two or three times, there is now such a group at work, and its members have interviewed Mr. Hoffmann, along with other distinguished critics.

On the other hand, in this debate about testing are the views of the practitioner, some of which I have mentioned. For example, John Gardner, in his book, *Excellence. Can We Be Equal and Excellent Too?*, says that:

Tests are designed to do an unpopular job. It happens that tests are excellent when limited to the uses for which they were designed. Development of standardized tests is one of the great success stories in the objective study of human behavior, although it is now said that tests give an unfair advantage to the privileged individual.

Before tests, says Gardner, many people seriously believed that the less-educated segments of our society were not capable of being educated. He concludes that anyone who attacks the usefulness of tests must suggest workable alternatives.

In preparing my thoughts for this paper, I talked with Lloyd Michaels, who is viewed by most of us in education as the dean of secondary school leaders in America, and who has a distinguished record of leadership at Evanston Township High School in Illinois. When asked about the critics' claims of over-competitive conditions, exaggeration of testing importance, validity, predictability, and so on, Lloyd has this to say: "I do not believe that undue weight is now attached to the testing surrounding college admissions. The test is simply one of several criteria, albeit an important one. School people and admissions officers have learned to use the test with good sense."

This is an important observation from a man whose school possesses all the conditions of a highly competitive population, including racial and socio-economic differences, and who has been responsible for getting thousands into college over the past 20 or 30 years.

In conclusion, I suppose one might say that testing is something like garbage collection. It finds itself at the mercy of an infinite array of expert observers, as it seeks to serve all the people. It tends to discriminate between the haves and the have-nots. It invades privacy. It rewards conformity—the same size can, keep it in the right place—and it is expected to take on more than was intended—brush, clippings, old mattresses. It is unreliable, unpredictable, and it fails to reach the poor. But if it should stop all of a sudden, there would be the dickens to pay!

Theodore R. Sizer

My central thesis, very simply stated, is that America's greatest crisis rises from persistent inequities among races, ethnic groups, and social classes; that the formal education system must play a significant role in erasing these inequities; and that the testing fraternity has a significant role to play in this process. While I am aware that this analysis marks me as an old style liberal, quite out of fashion, I persist in the belief that a good society is one which, while respecting actual diversity, is open. Within the limits of their talents, individuals should be able to choose their life style and careers—to enjoy rock and roll or Beethoven quartets, as Fritz Machlup differentiates. It is the responsibility of education to make those talents as broad and deep as possible. Testing must identify and record talent, but always with a minimum of group bias. This latter task alone is a difficult one—and, as a look at the recent history of the testing movement suggests, one that too long has been slighted.

The stereotypical twentieth-century American is the engineer. A spiritual descendent of Benjamin Franklin, he is the compleat tinkerer, the man who takes someone else's theories and puts them to constructive use. He is a builder—of railroads, bridges, rockets, moon capsules, and mass education systems. His approach starts from technology—the way things work or can be made to work—rather than from pure, or speculative, science. He spends far more time and resources on developing and marketing Kleenex than on discovering the fundamental biochemistry of nasal drip. He finds ideas and concentrates on putting them to use: the internal combustion engine, pasteurization, atomic fission. And mental testing.

The American mental testing movement is largely a series of variations on the speculations and experiments of Alfred Binet, a Frenchman. At the simplest level, Binet was experimenting with techniques of sorting children. On certain supposedly status-free measures, youngsters might be separated out by

*From *Proceedings of the 1970 Invitational Conference on Testing Problems—The Promise and Perils of Educational Information Systems.* Copyright © 1971 by Educational Testing Service. All rights reserved. Reprinted by permission.

mental abilities, and classified not only in terms of their current achievement, but, more importantly, in terms of their likely future competence. By the turn of the century, America was deep in the first stages of mass education and desperately needed a device for sorting children that was consistent with the movement's egalitarian ideology. Sorting by income, or accent, or conduct, while practiced, could not be publicly defended by the elected schoolman or even the appointed superintendent. Some more politic device was needed, and two emerged— and both are yet very much with us.

The first was the local control of schools, a device for a drastically decentralized school system, which wrapped strict class and ethnic segregation in a mantle of liberal political ideology. The schools must be close to the people, it was argued, and "the people" in this instance were those who lived in a limited geographical area. Control by "the people"—good egalitarian ideology—was in this instance used to defend ethnic group and class ghettoization. Americans added to this insult by then preaching that these school districts, many of which were gerrymandered enclaves, were some sort of classless melting pot. The fact that there were several prominent communities where useful mixing did in fact take place gave credence to the notion that this was the common American way.

The second device for sorting came from the clever mind of Alfred Binet: mental testing. In a democracy, Americans thought that if there should be any hierarchy at all, it should be a hierarchy of talent. Tests were needed to "prove" the existence (or nonexistence) of such talent. Not surprisingly, then, Americans engineered the idea of mental testing and adapted late nineteenth-century European theories to the realities of a more modern America. Terman, Thorndike, and the rest were pioneers, but more as engineers than as theoreticians. Terman's variations on Binet put the Frenchman's work into American terms. His writings were explanations of a method rather than expositions of the basic theoretical underpinnings of the ideas of mental testing. American experimental psychology was lively and productive, but used the basic laboratory approaches that had been accepted earlier in Europe.

The tests so developed were seized by schoolmen and the public to help sort people. World War I gave a massive fillip to the movement: our government had a real, and instant, need to fill round holes with round pegs and to identify potential leaders. American scholars interested in testing were drawn into these massive War Department "sorting" projects. By 1920, we were a nation that fully believed that every man had native intelligence of a certain power; that this power remained relatively constant during an individual's lifetime; and that the power could be measured, even in childhood. The "intelligence quotient" had been popularized. Democracy had a replacement for hereditary distinctions; we would be a nation with an aristocracy of God-given talents rather than an aristocracy of birth. If the mental testing movement had not emerged from Binet's laboratory, it would have had to be invented. Americans, committed politically as they were to a vague sort of egalitarianism, *needed* testing.

The movement, so popularized, quickly became distorted. Before tests were fully reliable, they were accepted as panaceas. While the scholars at the head of the movement were aware of this, public demand still ran ahead of research and development—a state of affairs, one must say, all too character-istic of American educational history. The zenith of the popularization of mental testing is distilled in a remarkable address by G. B. Cutten on the occasion of his inauguration as President of Colgate University in 1922. Cutten devoted his remarks to an analysis of "Democracy." "Let us look the question of democracy fairly in the face and be honest with ourselves," he asserted. "We are ruled in industry, in commerce, in professions, in govern-ment by an intellectual aristocracy. We have never had a true democracy, and the low level of the intelligence of the people will not permit of our having one. We can not conceive of any worse form of chaos than a real democracy in a population of an average intelligence of a little over thirteen years." He went on: "There must be some solution to the problem of government, and we must find it. What is it? We must first recognize that we are and have been, since the revolt against autocracy, ruled by the intelligentsia; more than ever the rule must be by an aristocracy, i.e., a rule by the best. . . . . This aristocracy must inevitably be the most intelligent, but it must also be well trained, benevolently inclined, and willing to admit any others to its member-ship who are fitted to belong. Democracy then comes to be a government of the people, for the people, by all those of their number fitted by intellectual ability, moral ideals, and careful training. The ruling has always been by the few intelligent members of the community or the nation, and in America the aristocracy has always had the 'open shop.' The training has also been a factor, even if an accidental factor, but the element most lacking has been the moral ideals. Government for the people, instead of for the governors, must be the keynote of the future, and the task of the colleges and the universities is the training of this aristocracy.

"It may be interesting to speculate concerning the effect of mental tests upon the problem of democracy. If the present hopes and expectations are realized, they will result in a caste system as rigid as that of India, but on a rational and just basis. We are now examining children in the public schools, and find all ranges of intelligence from imbecility to genius. We are told that the intelligence quotient of a child rarely changes, so that we are enabled to tell early in his life what the limit of intelligence of any person will be, and in a general way to what class of vocation he is best fitted, and, to a certain extent, destined. When the tests for vocational guidance are completed and developed, each boy and girl in school will be assigned to the vocation for which he is fitted, and, presuming that the tests are really efficient, he will in the future not attempt any work too advanced for his ability and hence make a failure of it, neither will he be found in an occupation too elementary for his ability and hence be dissatisfied. Economically nothing could be more desirable. All differences in accomplishments or results from that which the intelligence quotients would indicate would be due to certain traits of character which intelligence tests do not measure, viz.: industry, perseverance, thoroughness, honesty.

"One's intelligence quotient will eventually be known and persons will be classed thereby. Those of high intelligence will be directed into lines of occupation which call for leadership. Those persons will naturally be placed in the professions, and in leading positions in industry, commerce, and politics. Each person will then be directed on a scale of intelligence down to those whose work is of the most routine character of which an imbecile is capable. But what effect will this have on our so-called democracy? It must inevitably destroy universal adult suffrage, by cutting off at least 25 percent of the adults, those whose intelligence is so low as to be incapable of comprehending the significance of a ballot. On the other hand, it will throw the burden and responsibility of government where it belongs, on those of high intelligence, and we come back again to the rule of the aristocracy—this time the real and total aristocracy. For its own salvation the state must assume the obligation and responsibility of selecting this intellectual aristocracy, and having selected it see that it is properly trained" (Cutten, 1922).

Such was the optimism about mental testing in the Age of Warren Harding—and before George Orwell and Michael Young. There were balloon prickers even then, of course, and none more caustic than Walter Lippmann. Writing a series of articles on testing in the *New Republic* during 1922, Lippmann made much of the lack of congruity between the Terman-Stanford-Binet formulas and those that emerged from Yerkes' work with Army recruits during World War I. He was scornful of the gullibility of many concerning the general validity of supposedly standardized measures that had evolved from tests of very small numbers of very homogeneous children. "The real promise and the value of the investigation which Binet started." Lippmann wrote, "is in danger of gross perversion by *muddleheaded and dangerous men*" (Lippmann, 1922).

Lippmann, however, was a cranky exception. Optimistic Americans preferred to believe in the existence of measurable, innate intelligence. To this day, mothers weep over the results of I.Q. tests—and teachers assign their children to categories with the arbitrariness of medieval jailers. And to this day, Americans like to believe that while all of us are created equal, some are more "intelligent" than others, and measurably so. Americans avoid defining this condition they call intelligence; but the layman still believes, as did President Cutten of Colgate, that it is real and fixed. And if some groups appear from tests to be less "intelligent," too many of us still say that they, alas, are congenitally stupid.

In sum, Americans needed mental testing to help classify children in school. They rushed this process into use before sophisticated and broad-scale research could properly be completed. In their haste for a system to cope with the large numbers of children, they brushed aside some glaring inconsistencies—the lack of congruence between Terman's and Yerkes' findings, for example—and supported the system with rhetorical hyperbole. If one is in a cynical mood, one can further speculate that many Americans quietly applauded the finding that proportionally more children from well-to-do families scored well—that is, were considered of innately higher intelligence—than those from low income families. It reinforced the smug belief that those running the country were, in fact, by natural selection the most intelligent. Mental testing for all produced a classification that roughly followed class lines. Local control further provided for safe class and racial enclaves. Together these two pillars of egalitarian idealism—mental testing and localism—largely guaranteed antiseptic and segregated classrooms for the upper middle class. Even the Lynds' study in the mid-1920s of "Middletown," a community of varied social classes but with a single "melting pot" high school, revealed the actuality of class segregated education. The youngsters were classified by supposedly "objective" mental tests—and ended largely in socially homogenous classroom enclaves. To be fair, one cannot suggest there was—or is—a conspiracy to use tests to keep poor people down. One can ask, however, why scholars in the measurement field were incapable of preventing the distortion of their ideas as these were popularized and put to use. Three explanations are plausible. First, and most obvious, is that so many of the leading scholars in the field were involved principally in the engineering aspects of it—developing minimally satisfactory tests for use by the schoolmen who were frantically demanding them—that they lost sight of the forest for the trees. One need only look at our own pell-mell rush in the last decade to computer-aided instruction to see how easily perspective is lost among the ablest of men.

A second reason is equally obvious: the country found mental tests so compatible with its ideals and its practices that it deliberately closed its collective ears to the counsel of scholars. Even Lippmann caused only a ripple. His reasonable critique, ironically, stung the experts more than it educated the general public. Perhaps their sensitivity is a measure of the misgivings that they preferred to keep smothered. The tests did reinforce class bias. But America did not want to lose its faith in a system that filled a needed role so satisfactorily.

A third, and less obvious, reason may be found in the narrow outlook of the leaders of the American movement. Mental testing in the United States came substantially out of the traditions of experimental psychology and statistical measurement. The laboratory approach was nonhistorical; it called for a careful study of a few phenomena at a particular time. Great attention was paid to the subtleties of activities of a relatively few subjects, and statistical analysis was expected. As a result, most research involved few subjects, most often drawn from a narrow social class group. Significantly, the only broad survey undertaken, the Armed Forces study, was headed by a psychobiologist, Robert Yerkes, a man notably skeptical of the statistical approach to mental testing and a critic of Thorndike.

The laboratory approach taken by Thorndike and others was not necessarily unwise; it was, rather, incomplete. The *developmental* aspects of intelligence were slighted. Insufficient attention was given to how "intelligence" (however defined and measured) appeared to change over time, and what caused this change. Sociological and anthropological issues were neglected, and fundamental issues such as the effects of heredity and environment on intelligence either ignored or sloppily treated.

Save for Yerkes—who, after arriving at Yale in 1924, spent most of his research effort on animal psychology—the mental testing field was dominated by a group of scholars who had similar training. A striking number were trained at Columbia by James Cattell—Thorndike, Woodworth, Kelley, Dearborn, and others. This group served as an "invisible college" and dominated the field because, for the consumer, there were no alternatives. The questions of environmental influence, of the effects of social class, ethnicity and race, and of developmental patterns of change on an individual's measured intelligence have had to wait for a group of scholars trained in more diverse ways and sensitive to a broader social experience than were Thorndike and Terman.

Americans used mental testing to give their schools, all too often, more the appearance than the substance of democracy. Characteristically, they oversold the virtues of this convenient, scientific, egalitarian system; they liked what it produced and so marketed it with enthusiasm. Again character-istically, the experts in the field were either unable or unwilling to check or moderate its popularization. And so the mental test became a well-established educational panacea.

How can we use it today? As 70 years ago, we need a device that can democratically predict the achievement of children in a variety of skills, some intellectual, others vocational and affective. Above all, we need a system that both accommodates the effects of the environment and points the way to lessening its effect.

It is no longer hyperbole to note that this country is in the midst of a social revolution, and perhaps on the brink of a violent one. The facts of the matter can be boldly stated: one-twentieth of Americans control one-fifth of the wealth and one-fifth of Americans make do on one-twentieth of the wealth—and this reality has not changed, relatively, since 1945. Both liberal and conservative, if with different rhetoric, now applaud segregation; we are once again hearing justifications for a nation of enclaves from liberal spokes-men. They properly urge cultural diversity, but they fail to face the fact that freedom within diversity requires *understanding* and *toleration* among groups. Equally important, it implies *openness* among groups; a free, if diverse culture must allow individuals to move from group to group. Enclaves may give us diversity, but enclaves without open doors will stifle freedom. The educa-tional system carries a special burden both of encouraging those attitudes of tolerance and justice among youngsters and of teaching skills that allow indi-viduals to move from one group to another. We need tests to show the *development* of an individual's capacities and attitudes, tests that carry as little class bias as possible. Tests of varied qualities must be developed. We need not only "intelligence quotients," but also "bigotry quotients"—and remedial work for youngsters who are excessively bigoted. I am not being facetious here; the moral development of a youngster—his sense of justice and his use of justice—is perhaps more important than his cognitive development. This country has suffered excessively already from intellectually able, but morally stunted people.

Put in a different way, the testing fraternity needs to concentrate on the effects of class, race, and ethnicity on the development of skills and attitudes. It needs to help us understand how these factors influence human develop-ment over time. It needs to suggest ways of lessening those influences that narrow a youngster's options, and ways of measuring the child's progress in increasing his options.

Testing must not in a benign way serve as a device to preserve the social status quo. On the contrary, it must be used to illumine current social rigid-ities—and to help us finally break out of them.

Computers, Criterion-Referenced Measurement and Performance Contracting

Although the origins of psychological and educational testing are to be found in antiquity (see DuBois, 1970), substantial beginnings on a scientific approach to testing were not made until the first quarter of the twentieth century. Two world wars, industrial and educational expansion, and increased professional and societal efforts on behalf of the mentally ill, the mentally retarded and the socially disadvantaged are some of the factors related to the growth of testing during this century. Since 1950 the rate of this growth has accelerated to such an extent that today there is scarcely a school child, job applicant, military inductee or recipient of educational, vocational or personality counseling whose life has not been affected to some degree by tests. And many of the current developments in the field indicate that testing will have an even greater social influence during the last quarter of this century.

In a chapter devoted to a "look at the state of the art," Thorndike (1970) has listed a number of dramatic developments in the field of testing, the majority of them stemming from technological improvements and inventions such as computers and optical scanners. He also refers to several conceptual developments (construct validity, domain and item sampling, response styles), many of which are discussed in the present volume. In a third category, Thorndike cites developments of a more sociopolitical nature—the impact of testing on education, invasion of privacy, and fairness of tests to minorities and underprivileged groups. These last matters are discussed extensively in the articles in Section VIII of this book.

As noted by Thorndike (1970), the digital computer has had an enormous impact on testing, not only in terms of the vast quantities of tests that are scored, item analyzed, factor analyzed and standardized, but also on the design, administration and interpretation of tests. For example, computer programs of a preliminary sort have been constructed to write objective test items (Richards, 1967), interpret personality test profiles (Pearson & Swenson, 1967) and even do counseling (Cassel & Blum, 1970). Conceptual developments in testing, such as domain and item sampling, have also been greatly affected by the speed and versatility of computers. To be sure, new types of test items (tab, interlinear and in-basket items) have been introduced in recent years, and psychometricians are still doing a great deal of paper-and-pencil theoretical work. But the increasing number of references to computer-assisted instruction, sequential testing, data banks, censuses of abilities, item sampling and related topics attests to the growing importance of computers in this field.

The first article in this section, by Wayne Holtzman, continues Thorndike's stress on the importance of computers to educational and psychological measurement. After briefly tracing the history of mental testing, Holtzman surveys new educational technologies (Project PLAN, LR&D Center programs) and measurement techniques. Referring to the concern over the ethics of testing, he maintains that centralization of information by data banks will entail increased vigilance against possible invasion of privacy. The *Link file,* a complex procedure for safeguarding privacy, is described in some detail. Also considered are new methodological techniques and the growing recognition of sociocultural and linguistic variables in the design and interpretation of tests. In summary, Holtzman gives a brief survey of the past and present and highlights certain developments that appear to portend what mental measurement will be like in the last quarter of the twentieth century.

Although the style of the second article, by A. N. Hieronymus, is somewhat terse, and despite the fact that it was written primarily for an audience of professionals in educational measurement, it should serve to give the general reader an introduction to the major areas of progress in the field of testing. Four areas—definition of constructs, use of technology, development of instruments to serve a variety of purposes, and the use of measurement in accountability—are touched upon. After briefly referring to studies concerned with refining psychological constructs and interrelating them with other constructs, Hieronymus considers the various uses of computers: in developing, assembling and printing tests; in preparing norms and reports to teachers, counselors and administrators; in testing applications in instructional systems; in practical and theoretical psychometric applications.

A third area of activity discussed by Hieronymous—contemporary efforts to make testing serve a variety of purposes—has produced some new terminology, e.g., *formative* vs. *summative* evaluation, and *norm-referenced* vs. *criterion-referenced* measurements. Traditional achievement testing has been "summative," in that tests have been administered at the end of an instructional unit or course of study as a "sum total" measure of achievement. In contrast, the philosophy that has spurred the movement toward "formative" measurement is that evaluation and instruction should be inseparable; testing and other means of evaluating progress should occur constantly during the ongoing learning process. Unfortunately, there is no universally agreed-upon definition of the term "criterion-referenced" (see articles no. 41 and no. 42). Generally speaking, however, a score on a criterion-referenced test is evaluated by comparing it to some standard of mastery or desirable level of performance, rather than to a group of averages or "norms." Also highly controversial is the final topic discussed by Hieronymus, and also by Robert Stake in the last article of this section—the use of tests in *accountability*. These two writers concur that when used for purposes of accountability, that is, in determining the extent to which teachers have been successful in teaching students what the teachers contracted to teach them, tests have definite limitations.

The next two articles, by Robert Ebel and James Block, should be read as a pair, since they consider, in turn, the limitations and potentialities of criterion-referenced measurements.[1] Ebel points out that criterion-referenced testing is not a completely new development; it has much in common with the Morrison method of the 1920s and 1930s. As was the case with the Morrison method, Ebel maintains that criterion-referenced measurements will not greatly improve the measurement of educational achievement. The reasons for his belief are summarized in terms of three limitations of criterion-referenced measurements: 1) they do not tell us all that we need to know about educational achievement; 2) there is considerable difficulty in obtaining good criterion-referenced measurements; 3) the tests measure only a fraction of important educational achievements. Ebel believes in attaching content meaning as well as relative meaning to test scores, but he is not very optimistic about the potential contribution of criterion-referenced measurements to education.

Block attempts to counter Ebel's "pessimism" with regard to criterion-referenced measurements by pointing out that they do not purport to measure "how much," but rather "what," the student has learned. Thus, Block maintains that criterion-referenced measurements provide relevant information on excellence or deficiency in learning. Concerning Ebel's assertion that good criterion-referenced measurements are difficult to obtain, Block argues that the stating of instructional objectives, an initial step in designing a crite-

---

[1] The extent of interest in this topic is revealed by a recent book of readings (Popham, 1971), which the interested reader should consult for more details.

rion-referenced test, need not entail a high degree of specificity or an inordinate amount of time by the teacher. Nor does it need to interfere with effective teaching. Also, since a criterion-referenced test supposedly measures a representative sample of skills which students are expected to learn, this type of measurement is more meaningful than norm-referenced measurement. Finally, with regard to Ebel's assertion that criterion-referenced measurements "are necessary for only a small fraction of important educational achievements," Block states that this fraction is much larger than suggested and involves the learning of important skills.

The implication of one of Block's closing remarks is that criterion-referenced tests are potentially more useful than norm-referenced tests in situations where teachers contract to perform certain instructional services and are held accountable for their degree of success. The relationships between achievement testing and performance contracting are considered more extensively in the last article in this book.[2] In this article, Robert Stake discusses some of the curricular, psychometric, and social/humanistic hazards of specific performance testing and performance contracting. He describes various sources of difficulty, including errors in testing, the question of what test items to use, and several problems associated with the interpretation of test scores. These problems, which cannot be ignored if test scores are to be meaningfully interpreted, include the matter of practice effects due to pretesting with the same or a similar test as the posttest, the shortcomings of the popular "grade equivalent" scores, the fact that rate of learning varies with the time of year, the unreliability of posttest minus pretest gain scores, and regression effects on posttest scores. Since unreliable gain scores tend to promote false conclusions concerning amount learned, raw gains in achievement cannot serve as a satisfactory criterion of teacher effectiveness or as an equitable basis for teacher reimbursement. An alternative suggested by Stake is that gains be calculated as discrepancies between actual performance and performance that is predicted by means of a regression equation involving pretest scores. Unfortunately, regressed gain scores do not solve the problem of the "regression effect." A *regression effect,* which occurs whenever pretest and posttest scores are imperfectly correlated, refers to the fact that posttest scores will be less extreme than pretest scores. This is important to consider in performance contracting, because students who score quite low on the pretest may, because of the regression effect and regardless of how much they have learned during the pretest-posttest interval, score significantly higher on the posttest. As Stake suggests, the regression effect should be taken into

[2] The reader is also referred to the collection of articles on accountability and related topics in the book of readings by Sciara and Jantz (1972).

account by reimbursing instructors only when gains in achievement are greater that those explicable on the basis of the regression effect. Furthermore, Stake's conclusions that performance testing alone cannot serve as an adequate basis for evaluating teaching, and that the success of the accountability movement will be affected more by social and political factors than by curricular and psychometric ones, have the ring of truth.

39 | The Changing World of Mental Measurement and Its Social Significance*

Wayne H. Holtzman

One of the great success stories of modern psychology is the development of objective tests for measuring human abilities that are of importance to society. During the past half century, the standardized mental test with nationally based norms has proven to be a highly effective instrument for selection and classification of men in the armed forces; for evaluation of educational progress within our school systems; for selective admission of college students; for selection of employees within government, business, and industry; and for clinical assessment of individuals in need of psychological services. It is estimated that within American schools alone, over 250 million standardized tests of ability are administered each year (Brim, Glass, Neulinger, Firestone, & Lerner, 1969). It is a rare individual indeed, especially among children and young adults, who has not been evaluated by a standardized mental test, a test that has played a significant role in determining his place in society.

From World War I until the late 1950s, the testing movement enjoyed a degree of public acceptance it is unlikely to see again. Judging each person on the basis of his measured performance rather than on his family background, social status, or political connections has been a powerful agent of social change. Assuming unbiased, reliable measurement, what could be more just within the American concept of an egalitarian society than recognizing merit by objective tests of ability? Even today, college entrance examinations have made it possible for able but financially poor students to obtain scholarships in the best private colleges.

Criticisms of Testing

By the late 1950s, it became generally apparent that the large-scale normative use of objective tests for rewarding selected individuals among many

*From Holtzman, W. H. The changing world of mental measurement. *American Psychologist,* 1971, **26**, 546-553. Copyright 1971 by the American Psychological Association, and reproduced by permission.

in competition has serious social consequences of debatable value. The testing movement has always had its critics, but they failed to gain a foothold until the impact of adverse decisions based on tests had been felt by millions of individuals. In the post-Sputnik period, a growing number of critics have claimed that mental tests are unfair to the bright but unorthodox person, to the culturally disadvantaged, and to the naive individual who lacks experience in taking standardized-tests (Anastasi, 1967; Commission on Tests, 1970).

The growing controversies surrounding mental tests have become especially acute within educational institutions. It is generally recognized that the educated person enjoys the riches of society as well as enhanced self-esteem and personal development, while the person who prematurely drops out of school is cast into an inferior role. It is not surprising that the angry cries of black students are directed at normative tests that deprive them of entrance to the better colleges, jobs, and social positions.

A major dilemma arises in attempting to meet these criticisms. The traditional academic curricula of our schools and colleges are becoming increasingly dependent on verbal communication, verbal memory, and the same kind of abstract reasoning as measured by scholastic aptitude tests. Therefore, sufficiently high correlations arise between standardized multiple-choice aptitude tests and course examinations to justify the use of tests for prediction of academic achievement and selective admissions. The rapid growth of higher education and the greatly increased number of students per course have forced more and more instructors to employ mutliple-choice objective examinations for grading students. As a result, the relevance of scholastic aptitude tests for prediction of academic grades has increased, rather than decreased, in recent years. The compelling economics of mass education and objective normative testing are exceedingly difficult to resist in a rapidly expanding system of higher education. Tests that are designed for normative use, whether for college admissions or course examinations, discriminate against those who are culturally different from the majority.

Such incidental discrimination might be more justifiable if there were a close correspondence between success in school and subsequent occupational success. But for a number of reasons, the correlation between grades and later success is too low to argue generally that measured performance in the traditional academic curriculum is that critical. The issue is made more complex by the fact that entry to many occupations is denied an individual who fails to complete the prescribed academic program, regardless of the program's relevance. The growing meritocracy built around traditional curricula that are uniformly prescribed, normative tests that are competitively graded, and restrictive credentials for job entry may be efficient means of building a technological society, but it does so by exacting a heavy toll on those members of society who fail to conform to the majority. The more tightly the meritocracy is drawn, the more self-fulfilling the prophecies.

Educational Reform and the New Technologies

A way out of this dilemma may be closer at hand than many realize. The number of pressures within American society and new developments in measurement and instruction are moving in the same general direction. Led by students, spokesmen for minority rights, and concerned academicians, the general public is becoming increasingly aware of serious inequities within our educational system. As higher education becomes more essential to vocational advancement and personal fulfillment, the fruits of education cannot be denied to anyone who is motivated and capable of profiting from it.

The growing attacks on normative testing for college admission and course grading are having an impact as more and more individuals call for less emphasis on scholastic aptitude measures and more on other abilities and new forms of instruction. The kinds and variety of curricula recognized as appropriate for various forms of education are increasing markedly. Courses aimed at social problems and individual self-development are eroding the traditional, discipline-oriented curricula in many colleges. This new thrust may involve individual competencies in such things as social leadership, self-awareness, regard for human rights and social responsibilities, or other aspects of behavior that typically have not been important in traditional academic pursuits. As the curriculum moves through reform, there will be opportunities for new kinds of measurement as well.

Emphasis is being given in many circles to the idea of individualized instruction in which the learner moves at his own pace and at a time and place that is appropriate for him as an individual. The units of instruction emphasize self-paced learning with regular social reinforcement to maintain a high degree of motivation and relevance, coupled with the concept of continuous progress from one unit to the next. These "microcurriculum units" or modules have fairly well-defined behavioral objectives or performance criteria by which mastery can be recognized. The curriculum itself is viewed in a more global manner as consisting of strings of modules arranged according to an explicit hierarchy of values that are in harmony with the future goals of individual development. In many fields of learning, these specific modules involve training objectives where criterion testing for standardized mastery is employed rather than normative testing for measuring individual differences. Much of what goes on in education is susceptible to treatment in this form. The broader educational objectives differ considerably from one individual to the next in order to maximize potentiality for individual development.

A major force for social change in educational reform is the emergence of new educational technology and related techniques of measurement. Keeping track of a person moving at his own pace in a continuous progress environment, where the particular branching of the curriculum is tailor-made for the student's own learning aptitudes and level, requires a computer to manage the curriculum and assist with the instruction (Holtzman, 1970). In a traditional setting, the instructor keeps a record of how well each student does on each achievement test for the course, while the periodically collected scores from standardized normative tests are stored centrally. When instruction is individualized, testing must be done more frequently and at different times for each student. In many cases, performance testing and instruction are so closely interwoven that they appear as one integrated learning activity. Except for periodic testing at a later date to determine how much a person has retained, even the conceptual nature of measurement shifts from a normative basis, where each person is compared with a general population, to a criterion-referenced basis, where the only decision made is whether or not the student has achieved the desired objective for a specific instructional module. Not only are more short tests given, but many more have to be constructed, again requiring a computer for generating tests from item pools as well as scoring and storing them for each student.

Several large-scale programs of individualized instruction are sufficiently advanced to demonstrate the feasibility and power of this approach to educational reform. Now in its fourth year of operation under the leadership of John Flanagan, and jointly developed by the American Institutes for Research and Westinghouse Learning Corporation, Project PLAN consists of over 1,000 modules divided across nine operating grades and four subject-matter areas (Dunn, 1969). Each teaching unit is coded as to reading difficulty, required teacher supervision, media richness, required social involvement, and a number of other characteristics. A profile is prepared for each student containing measures of abilities, interests, aspirations, and background data for use by the computer in matching the curriculum to the student. The combination of normative measurement on nationally standardized tests for initial guidance and placement of the student and criterion-referenced tests for assessing progress in mastering the curriculum modules is especially noteworthy. Experience to date with over 10,000 students indicates that most individuals like the new freedom provided by PLAN, and that learning proceeds at a faster pace.

A still more detailed form of individualized instruction can be found in the program of individually prescribed instruction developed by Glaser and associates at the University of Pittsburgh's Learning Research and Development Center (Cooley & Glaser, 1969). A specific lesson plan is prescribed individually for each child every day, depending on his performance and desires of the previous day. Thousands of curriculum modules are stored and retrieved manually by clerks at the end of each day until the experimental system can be perfected and stored electronically in computers. Interwoven with each module is a criterion-referenced achievement test that provides a basis for decision making in selecting the next module.

A recent study by Ferguson (1969) serves to illustrate computer-assisted branched testing with elementary arithmetic materials in the Pittsburgh individually prescribed instruction program. A model was developed and tested in which terms are selected on the basis of previous responses and are thus tailored to the competencies of the student. A learning hierarchy of prerequisite relationships among 18 objectives in addition and subtraction was formulated on the basis of previous studies. Two major sequences emerged as dominant in the hierarchy, one involving only addition skills and the other exclusively concerned with subtraction. A third sequence integrated both addition and subtraction. Initially, an examinee was presented with a randomly generated item for the specific objective being tested. The computer scored his response as correct or incorrect and generated another item. The process continued until a sufficient number of items had been answered for the computer to make a decision regarding the individual's proficiency on the objective. The decision model involved assigning a priori probability values to the two types of error constituting incorrect decisions and applying Wald's sequential probability ratio test to terminate the testing on the objective in question. Selection of the next objective to be tested depended on the examinee's proficiency on the first objective as well as the proposed learning hierarchy. When given to 75 students in Grades 1-6 at the Oakleaf Elementary School, Pittsburgh, Pennsylvania, the sequential branched testing method proved to be three times as efficient as a fixed-length conventional test, requiring, on the average, only 52 items instead of 150.

A sequential branched testing procedure proves far superior to conventional testing when one has a computer for generating and scoring items, a suitable communication terminal for interaction of computer and examinee, and a good basis for arranging the skills to be tested in a learning hierarchy. The procedure is ideally suited to criterion-referenced testing but is of questionable value where normative testing is employed. As Lord (1970) has demonstrated, little is to be gained by the use of tailored testing with conventional items for normative measurement except in the case of best and worst students.

Integrating the elements of programmed learning and sequential branched testing into a single curriculum requires a computer for electronic storage and retrieval of the material to be learned, the test items for measuring mastery, and the instructional branching strategy for both the curriculum and the tests. Suitable multimedia teaching terminals with visual display devices, light pens, audio units, and typewriters under either student or computer control, depending on the nature of the curriculum and purpose of the student, must be provided in large numbers at reasonable cost before computer-assisted instruction, testing, and guidance can become operational. Several major companies are now designing hardware configurations that will soon have the required functional capabilities for fully implementing computer-assisted instruction. It is now fairly certain that the cost of such a system can be sharply reduced by mass production to the point where it is economically feasible to think of large-scale implementation (Alpert & Bitzer, 1970). Psychological laboratories for computer-assisted instruction at Stanford University, the University of Texas, the University of Illinois, Florida State University, System Development Corporation, the Mitre Corporation, and a dozen other universities and research institutes have already demonstrated the feasibility of this new technology as well as its dramatic impact on individual learning in many areas.

Such new technologies as Project PLAN, individually prescribed instruction, and computer-assisted instruction are highly promising in their eventual impact on educational practices and the concomitant measurement of standardized mastery using criterion-referenced tests instead of normative testing for competitive selection. Successful prototypes have been developed, but these represent only a small beginning compared to what must be done in the way of research and development before individualized instruction in the true sense of the term can be properly implemented on a large scale.

National Assessment of Educational Change

Still another important departure from standardized normative measurement of individual differences in mental abilities grows out of the increased concern for developing a national system of social indicators, measures that reflect the quality of life, the rate of educational progress, and the value of human resources for the nation as a whole as well as for different regional, ethnic, and socioeconomic groups. A recent report of the Behavioral and Social Sciences Survey Committee (1969) has recommended the establishment of a system of social indicators by the federal government that would lead to an annual social report for measuring changes in many aspects of society. A step in this direction has already been taken by the National Assessment of Educational Progress, a project of the Education Commission of the States (Womer, 1970).

Under the leadership of Ralph Tyler and support from the Carnegie Corporation, the Exploratory Committee on Assessing the Progress of Education began in 1964 to collect information about the knowledge and skills held by 9-year-olds, 13-year-olds, and 17-year-olds and of young adults in 10 subject areas taught in schools. After five years of planning and public debate as to the merits of the project, National Assessment launched its first annual survey for all four age levels in three subject areas—citizenship, science, and writing. The national sample contained a total of approximately 100,000 persons carefully chosen on a stratified random basis involving 52 sampling units from each of four geographic regions.

The first step in preparing materials for National Assessment was to determine a list of educational objectives for each subject. Using these objectives as guides, various measurement research organizations took responsibility for preparing exercises designed to assess what young people actually know. A variety of approaches—questionnaires, interviews, observations, and performance tasks—were employed in addition to traditional multiple-choice and short-answer questions similar to those used in standardized mental tests.

Five important distinctions can be made between the National Assessment exercises and multiple-choice items employed in normative tests. First, the assessment exercises are designed to discover what defined segments of the nation's population can do or what they know, rather than to distribute people normatively according to measured individual differences. For example, what percentage of the 9-year-olds in the country know that most plants get most of their water directly from the soil? Or know how to report a fire? Or report that they had ever taken part in some organized civic project to help other people? Does this percentage shift significantly across different segments of the population or over time?

Second, while items in a test are summed to give a score for each individual, exercises in National Assessment are each analyzed in their own right by pooling data across individuals. For this reason, it is particularly important that the exercises be meaningful to specialist and layman alike, that they be directly related to the stated objectives, and that they have high content validity. Extensive review sessions involving a variety of judges were held for every exercise retained for National Assessment.

Third, the exercises are designed for a broad range of difficulty in order to report to the American public examples of knowledges, skills, and understandings that are common to almost all American youth of a given age, examples that are common to a typical or average American youth, and examples that are common to only the most knowledgeable youth. Ideally, one-third of the exercises should be passed by most of the population, one-third by about half, and one-third by only a small percentage. By contrast, item difficulty level in the typical normative test is likely to hover near the 50% level or to be evenly distributed throughout the range.

Fourth, all exercises, except those in reading, are presented aurally as well as visually, so that no one is severely penalized in responding, say, to citizenship or science questions.

And fifth, the exercises are assembled in heterogeneous packages with different sets of exercises given to different individuals on a sampling basis. A package for 17-year-olds last year, for example, contained seven multiple-choice science exercises, three free-response citizenship exercises, and one essay exercise for writing. Exercises are packaged in any convenient fashion that adds up to no more than 50 minutes of assessment time for each person. Items in a normative test, on the other hand, are assembled in relatively homogeneous scales so that they can be added together to give a reliable score.

Unlike most measurement applications in psychology and education, in National Assessment a person is never asked to record his name. Responses are clustered and analyzed by sex, age, race, region, community, and family characteristics in order to obtain censuslike information about the educational progress of various segments of the population. Repeated applications in the years ahead will provide a wealth of data dealing with change over time—data that should be useful in national planning, particularly when examined together with other social indicators.

Individuals and schools approached by National Assessment were given the option of declining to participate in order to respect their rights to privacy. Exceedingly few refused to participate under these permissive conditions, testifying to the wisdom of this policy. My own experience in soliciting the cooperation of 13,000 high school students in a probability statewide sample (Moore & Holtzman, 1965) and in asking for the continued participation of 420 families in a longitudinal study of personality development (Holtzman, Diaz-Guerrero, Swartz, & Lara Tapia, 1968) has been similarly favorable. Unbiased samples can be obtained in most measurement studies without coercion of even a mild sort. National Assessment provides an exemplary model of how one should proceed in order to protect the privacy of individual participants and their freedom to decline.

Preserving the confidentiality of data is a related problem that continues to worry many thoughtful individuals. As we move into large-scale programs with extensive, centralized data banks stored in computers, the possibility of harm to an individual cannot yet be completely eliminated. The files that may do greatest damage to the individual are those that are kept secret from him but not from those who can take action affecting him. While much of the national concern expressed in recent congressional hearings deals with personal information that psychologists are unlikely to find interesting, specific attention has been directed at potential abuses of individual privacy involving psychological test data, biographical information, and social attitudinal data typically employed in psychological research. The proper balance between protecting the individual against the misuse of information about himself and collating data to help solve major social, economic, and educational problems has not yet been achieved. On the other hand, continuation of the present highly decentralized systems will not cure present abuses of individual privacy, although it will prevent the integration of information required for future social development. As Ruggles (1969) has pointed out, the key to the problem of protecting privacy is not to depend blindly on the inefficiency that accompanies the present situation. Properly developed centralized data banks can eventually assure greater protection for the individual while also providing essential information for basic research as well as future national planning.

One interesting solution to the problem of protecting the confidentiality of data from individual respondents is the Link system that has been devised for the national study of college student characteristics by the American Council on Education's Cooperation Institutional Research Program (Astin & Boruch, 1969). Measurement data and biographical information on several hundred thousand college freshmen are collected each year as part of an ongoing educational data bank. Initially, a more or less traditional system was instituted. Two physically separate tape files were created, one containing the student's answers to research questions together with an arbitrary identification number, and a second containing only the student's name and address and the same arbitrary number. The first tape with the research data file was openly accessible for analysis. The second tape with the name and address file was locked in a vault and used only to print labels for follow-up mailings. The original questionnaires and punched cards were then destroyed.

Good as it may seem, this system still did not offer complete protection against government subpoena or unauthorized disclosure by staff members with access to both files. A third file, the Link file, was created which contained two sets of numbers—the original arbitrary identification numbers from the research data file, and a completely new set of random numbers which were substituted for the original identification numbers in the second file. The final step in establishing the new system was to deposit the new Link file at a computer facility in a foreign country with a firm agreement that the foreign facility would never release it to anyone, including the American Council on Education. Follow-up mailing tapes now have to be prepared by the foreign facility. There is no way that anyone can identify individual responses in the research file.

Such elaborate steps to guarantee the complete confidentiality of personal information in research files may seem far too expensive. Why go to this extreme when the chances are exceedingly remote that any harm could be done to an individual by using a more traditional system? The reason for foolproof data files is that the public demands it. However unlikely, there does exist the possibility of court subpoena or improper invasion of privacy when the data files and decoding files are under the control of the same organization.

Recognition of Social, Cultural, and Linguistic Variability

One of the most important changes of the past decade in the field of mental measurement as well as in society as a whole is the greatly increased respect for social, cultural, and linguistic variability among different kinds of people. Until recently, the "American way of life" was defined almost entirely by middle-class values of white, English-speaking people of largely western-European origin. In general, school curricula, symbols of social status and privilege, occupations, the more highly valued life styles, and to some extent even suggested definitions of intelligence, all conformed to the dominant values of which most Americans were proud. The forgotten minorities were expected to adjust to these values if they were to enjoy the fruits of the nation. As recently as 10 years ago, school principals in the Southwest often pointed proudly to the fact that the speaking of Spanish by Mexican-American children was prohibited on their school grounds, English being the only permissible language in which to receive an education.

The emergence of black culture, the Chicano movement, and the stirring of the American Indian as well as other forgotten groups in the wake of desegregation and civil rights legislation have forced white America to reexamine its soul. The result in the field of mental measurement has been a recognition and acceptance of cultural variability, a search for new kinds of cognitive, perceptual, and affective measures by which to gauge mental development, and a renewed determination to contribute significantly to the task of overcoming educational and intellectual deprivation.

A generation ago, the typical study involving mental measurement and social variability consisted of giving tests, standardized largely on middle-class whites, to people of other ethnic, linguistic, and socioeconomic backgrounds. Countless individual and group differences were observed and classified in a descriptive manner. Today, more attention is given to devising procedures for measurement and evaluation which are indigenous to the culture under study. Illustrative of this new approach is the work of Freeberg (1970) who developed a test battery specifically tailored in content, format, and administration to disadvantaged adolescents drawn largely from the black and Puerto Rican ghettos of New York. The extensive six-year longitudinal study of 2,000 Headstart children undertaken last year by the Educational Testing Service also contains a large variety of new measures that are specifically designed for culturally disadvantaged children (Anderson, 1969). The problem with most such tailored procedures is that they may be just as ill-suited for use with other markedly different individuals as are tests standardized on middle-class whites when employed for assessing educationally disadvantaged children.

The most difficult methodological problems arise in cross-cultural research where two or more distinctly different cultures are compared systematically (Holtzman, 1968). The translation, calibration, and administration of psychological measures across cultures require close and continual collaboration of specialists from each culture who have learned to trust each other fully. In a similar manner, measurement across subcultures within a given nation requires the full participation of representatives from each subculture, a condition that is met by all too few investigators thus far. In spite of such problems, studies dealing systematically with cultural, social, and linguistic variability are growing rapidly in number while also increasing greatly in the power of their research designs. Is it too much to hope that by the end of the coming decade the lingering ethnocentrism of the testing movement will disappear?

In the short span of this article, it has been possible to highlight only selected topics within the broad field of mental measurement. It should be obvious to even the casual observer of trends in the field that other areas also deserve attention. It is worth noting that every one of the new advances reviewed is heavily dependent on the modern electronic computer for its implementation. Fundamental to the changing world of mental measurement is the rapid growth in power, versatility, and accessibility of high-speed computers. Large-scale testing; new educational technology such as individually prescribed instruction, sequential branched testing within the curriculum,

Project PLAN, and computer-assisted instruction; national assessment of educational change and the development of a system of social indicators; new techniques for preserving the confidentiality of personal data; and even new programs for assessing the mental development of culturally different people—all require a computer for implementation.

In focusing primarily on the social implications of new advances, it is easy to overlook the numerous theoretical and methodological contributions to the field of measurement and evaluation that have been made in the past few years. New techniques of scaling, test theory, factor analysis, and multivariate experimental designs are being produced and extended in a lively manner. The immediate social significance of these developments may not be readily apparent because of their indirect, long-range nature as basic research contributions. And yet, without the continued, vigorous support of such theoretical and methodological advances, the truly great potentiality of the changing world of measurement would fail to materialize. Each of the promising new developments surveyed above is heavily dependent on the solution of difficult basic research problems before it can be fully realized to the benefit of society. There is every reason to be optimistic about the next 10 years in the field of mental measurement, given the recognized social significance of new developments and the rapid rate at which basic work is advancing.

40 | Today's Testing: What Do We Know How to Do?*

A. N. Hieronymus

What do we know how to do—at least reasonably well? This is the basic question of accountability: accountability of the profession of educational and psychological measurement to pupils, parents, other educators, and the general public.

Testing has always been a subject for lively debate and a popular target of critics. While we have profited greatly from dialog with well-informed, perceptive critics, it is doubtful that there is another profession that is as prone to, and capable of self-criticism. In fact, at times the rhetoric might be aptly described as intolerant, destructive, or even masochistic.

What do we know how to do? Everything and nothing. Everything in the sense that it is almost inconceivable that anyone can come up with a problem which has not been or is not being researched. The quantity of the output is overwhelming. A cursory skimming of research publications in measurement and related journals, the tests, the manuals, the position papers, and speeches published in a single year constitutes a formidable assignment; mastery an impossible one. The massive *Research at ETS: Projects and Publications* contains 501 entries; the latest edition of Buros, nearly 1800.

On the other hand, it is doubtful that there are any among us who would claim to have a final, absolute solution to any of the problems that challenge us. Next year always holds the promise of improvement if not of breakthrough, whether the problem is one of conceptualization, implementation, technology, or interpretation.

What criteria can we employ in determining what we do relatively well and relatively poorly? The *APA Standards for Educational and Psychological Tests and Manuals* are relatively adequate as a guide to the design and interpretation of validation research of the more traditional measurement activities. Similar "standards" are often proposed as an inherent part of the

*From *Proceedings of the 1971 Invitational Conference on Testing Problems—Educational Change: Implications for Measurement.* Copyright © 1972 by Educational Testing Service. All rights reserved. Reprinted by permission.

presentation of innovative programs. It is possible that additional *external* standards are needed which apply more directly to measurement designed to *compare* the effectiveness of instructional programs, although it is difficult to conceive of any aspect of validation research which Cronbach (1970) did not include in his chapter in *Educational Measurement*. It would seem appropriate to repeat his statement that "validation is the task of the . . . interpreter. Others can do no more than offer him material to incorporate into his thinking [p. 36] ."

I have arbitrarily classified the major areas of progress under four headings: Definition of Constructs, Use of Technology, Development of Instruments to Serve a Variety of Purposes, and Use of Measurement in Accountability.

Definition of Constructs

One of the things we know how to do is to look for, operationally define, and experiment with newly conceived variables or old variables renamed or redefined. Most of these would fall into the general classification of interacting independent variables. Precision in defining and measuring situational and interpersonal variables has resulted in slow but steady progress in the explanation and prediction of behavior. Many able researchers are devoting their professional careers to relatively isolated and independent activity with a minimum of institutional or financial support. It is not surprising, therefore, that the list of such variables is long, diffuse, and for the most part unorganized.

The list includes constructs related to achievement motivation, anxiety, aspiration, attention span, creativity, perseverance, parental attitudes, and dimensions of musical aptitude, to name but a few. It includes concepts from Piaget's theories of cognitive development, the variables corresponding to the cells in Guilford's model of intellect, variables in perceptual or cognitive style, and the cognitive, psychomotor, and interest variables in aptitude batteries for specific occupations.

The constructs of today are constantly being refined, interrelated, and incorporated into educational and psychological theory. More and more research is designed to investigate aptitude-situation-treatment-outcome interactions. However, the results of such studies have not been very productive to date, and even the most optimistic appraisal cannot help revealing how much is still to be learned.

Use of Technology

A good many of the things we know how to do have been a direct result of technological developments in optical scanners and computers. These are well-known and need only be summarized briefly.

1. There has been considerable impact on test development. Very complete, complex, and inexpensive analyses of tryout data are almost routinely available to the test constructor. The development of machine-scorable test booklets has opened up possibilities for item types previously regarded as impracticable because of scoring problems (Lindquist, 1968). Technology has also made it possible to process items in which responses are differentially weighted or which require other complex scoring procedures.

2. Entire tests can be assembled and even printed by computer from item banks. The image this procedure conjures up is disturbing to most of us; yet the computer can do many of the routine sorting and screening tasks of a clerical nature. Computer-stored item banks also provide the possibility of better "teacher-made" tests, and a sharing of items for use in various instructional systems.

3. The use of computers makes feasible more efficient standardizations and the preparation of multiple norms. Data on school characteristics stored in the computer memory provide a basis for selecting accurate, efficient samples. Some nationally standardized batteries now make routinely available the choice of such norms as national, regional, Catholic, large city, and local. The possibilities of pupil, school, and item norms is almost unlimited.

Similarly, in programs such as those of the College Entrance Examination Board and the American College Testing Program, equations developed from applications of multivariate analysis provide differential prediction of success which can be used in selection and placement in a wide variety of institutions, subject areas, and circumstances. Particularly intriguing are Novick's (1971) applications of Bayesian methods to prediction. This technology is also appropriate for occupational selection, placement, and training.

4. The use of computers for test processing makes possible the production of an almost unlimited quantity of reports to teachers, counselors, and administrators. In fact, the test user is deluged with information, much of which he may not be in a position to interpret wisely.

What would seem to be crucial in future computer applications are systems of data reduction related to various decision-making processes. Beginnings have already been made in identifying profile discrepancies, but such applications are still in their infancy.

5. Computer technology has also found its way into testing applications in instructional systems. The uses in computer-assisted instruction and in computer-managed instruction are well known. In such systems the computer is used for test processing, record keeping, and in decision making, and may be used directly in the instructional process.

6. The computer has also aided in a wide variety of psychometric applications, both practical and theoretical. The factor analysis of large matrices is routine and economical. Monte Carlo studies have contributed to understanding of sampling distributions. The computer has also made feasible large-scale psychometric research projects such as Project Talent, National Assessment, and the International Project for the Evaluation of Educational Achievement.

Development of Instruments to Serve a Variety of Purposes

Possibly the greatest improvement in measurement practice has come about through the awareness of the need for instruments which are specifically designed to accomplish a single purpose, or at least a limited number of well-defined purposes.

Many nationally standardized tests of achievement are designed, advertised, sold, purchased, and used to serve multiple purposes. It should be added that they have been used for purposes for which they were never intended.

In looking over the current crop of achievement tests, one notices considerable improvement over those in the past, especially in terms of the relevance of content and in the ingenuity of item writers in getting at higher order mental processes. But even a greater improvement would seem to lie in the use of the tests. A large proportion of standardized achievement tests are now administered early in the school year to serve as a guide to the planning of instructional activities. They are thus being used more for formative than for summative evaluation purposes. Tests used this way can reveal strengths and weaknesses or unevenness of development, may lead to further, more specific, diagnostic testing, and hopefully will result in more appropriate educational programming for individual pupils.

Another important emerging development is that of individualized testing. Branching tests, tab tests, and applications of computer-mediated sequential testing are finding their way into practice in a growing number of applications. There are a few instances in which a short screening test is used to assign Ss to test levels. (In a way this has been done for many years in the administration of the Stanford-Binet.)

Flexibility is also being introduced into the administration of nationally distributed standardized tests. Newer tests reflect the gradual movement of school practices and textbooks away from a strictly graded program in the direction of the implementation of a continuous progress philosophy. It is not unusual to find tests being administered "out-of-level" in EMR[1] classes, in Title I evaluation projects, or in schools whose average level of performance differs markedly from the norm. Such adaptations as have been used to date are far from ideal, but they are more appropriate than the administration of levels without regard to pupil characteristics. The current edition of the *Iowa Tests of Basic Skills* makes provision for the administration of different levels of the tests to different pupils in the same classroom (Hieronymus & Lindquist, 1971). The hoped-for advantage is that each pupil will be provided with a test which is less frustrating, more challenging, more accurate, and more appropriate. There are all sorts of problems in assignment of levels, interpretation, scaling, norming, and communication, but they are not insurmountable. This is just a beginning. The next step is to individualize by subtest and then to build different tests for different subpopulations with different needs. This is something we know how to do. It is time we quit explaining why it cannot be done, and do it.

Perhaps the most spectacular of the changes, at least in terms of activity, is in the development of tests to monitor, modify, and evaluate the effectiveness of certain types of instructional procedures. The procedures tend to be very specific and limited to a narrow range of educational objectives. This implies the use of instruments which a) are built to very carefully prescribed behavioral objectives, b) are sensitive to change *via* intervention, and c) *may* constitute an operational definition of "success" or "mastery."

In general, tests which have been designed with very restricted content specifications to serve a very limited range of highly specific purposes have been referred to as criterion-referenced tests. (Similar tests proposed for use with somewhat different instructional models have been generally known as "mastery" tests.) There are a number of bothersome semantic problems which attend the use of the term "criterion-referenced." The term, "criterion-referenced test," as Glaser & Nitko (1971) point out, "has a somewhat different meaning from the two more prevalent uses of the terms criterion or criterion tests in educational and pscyhological measurement literature [p. 653]." Indeed, this use of the term is about as far as it can be from the use of the term "criterion-related validation" as is used in the *APA Standards* which implies correlation and prediction. There is also the question of whether the adjective "criterion-referenced" applies to tests, purposes, or interpretations.

[1] Educable mentally retarded. [Editor's note]

Popham & Husek (1969) have indicated that a criterion-referenced test cannot be distinguished from the other type by simple inspection; that such tests are distinguished by purpose, construction procedures, specificity of information, generalizability of test performance to domain and use. All of these distinctions are obviously a matter of degree. Furthermore, the construction model for the "other type" starts with the same procedures, the sampling of test tasks from a universe of relevant tasks. Thus, both types could be designated as criterion-referenced in this sense.

Tests of the "other type" to which I have been referring are generally labeled "traditional tests" or "norm-referenced" tests. Contrasting criterion-referenced with norm-referenced tests would seem to imply a critical distinction in terms of interpretation, i.e., a norm-referenced interpretation *vs.* a non-norm-referenced interpretation. The latter is presumably a direct interpretation of some type of raw score, often in relation to a more-or-less subjectively determined raw score cutting point which may be described as passing, acceptable performance, or mastery. Of course, the same types of interpretations may be made of raw scores from the so-called norm-referenced tests, but these interpretations are not often advocated or encouraged. And, as Klein (1970) suggests, norms may be derived from tests labeled as criterion-referenced, to aid in interpretation.

The tests employed in the National Assessment Program, also frequently referred to as criterion-referenced tests, seem to differ substantially from the criterion-referenced tests used primarily for program evaluation. These are not "tests" in the usual sense in that the analyses have been focused on group performance on individual items. Even in national assessment, crude norms are implied, in that comparisons of item ps[2] are made between different groups; the performance of a given group is placed in relation to other groups. It would be a small step to deriving norms for states or local systems. For that matter, indices of group performance for individual items have been provided as routine service to schools for a long time for many of the nationally standardized test batteries. Two different kinds of interpretations are generally suggested (Hieronymus & Lindquist, 1971). The first is a comparison with item norms; the second is a comparison of performance with a subjective judgment of how a particular group "should" perform, to which the phrase "criterion-referenced interpretation" might be considered appropriate.

It is realized that the focus on the semantic aspects of terms constitutes nit-picking to a large degree. On the other hand, confusion in terminology and concept appears to be rampant among teachers and administrators, if not among measurement specialists.

[2] p = item difficulty index, i.e., the proportion of examinees who answer an item correctly. [Editor's note]

It has not been my intention to put down the appropriate use of any of the variations of criterion-referenced tests. Glaser & Nitko (1971), Bloom (1971), Merwin & Womer (1969), and others have presented very thorough and convincing rationales for the need and use of such tests to serve a variety of purposes. The criterion-referenced approach is probably making its greatest contribution in the monitoring and assessment of instructional strategies and outcomes. Applications range from programs such as the IPI project (Lindvall & Bolvin, 1967) and Project PLAN (Flanagan, 1969), which focus on instructional procedures, to National Assessment, which is concerned with description and the relatively long-range monitoring of outcomes.

This approach to evaluation would also seem to have an important place in communication and accountability at the local level. Even in situations in which direct accountability benefits may be questionable, there is the potential for improved communication through the involvement of the lay public and educators in the process of thinking through and operationally defining behavioral objectives.

Use of Measurement in Accountability

If we were to adopt a theme song for 1971 it would likely be entitled, "Accountability—That's Where It's At."

There have been innumerable conferences, speeches, and papers on the subject. Especially recommended are the papers by Lennon (1971), Dyer (1970a), Barro (1970), Innes (1971), Stake (1971), the American Institutes for Research volume, *Evaluative Research* (1970), and the papers in the ETS *Proceedings of the Conference on Educational Accountability* (1971). With minor exceptions, my views are congruent with those of Lennon.

The common element in most of these papers is a statement that accountability means different things to different people, and that the basic questions are: Who should be accountable? To whom? For what? And by what procedures is accountability to be determined?

Here are some rather imprecisely stated generalizations which imply some of the issues.

1. Accountability in *some* form is generally acceptable to all parties concerned. As Lennon (1971) said, "Accountability . . . is an idea whose time has come—again, or perhaps an idea whose time is always." School personnel have always regarded accountability as an important responsibility. Most objections are not to accountability *per se* but to some of the instructional and evaluation procedures designed to implement it.

2. The optimum evaluation design for accountability purposes is not

often the best design for differentiating instruction and stimulating creative teaching. For years we have been trying to convince teachers that they have nothing to fear from tests, that tests are for their use as aids to better instruction. Emphasis on tests for accountability purposes will almost inevitably contribute to misinterpretation and misuse of tests.

3. An important distinction can be made between group accountability and individual accountability. In its extreme form, group accountability refers to the *joint* accountability of *all* concerned to the *group* of pupils who attend a particular school in attaining a *uniform* set of objectives. For group accountability, the use of existing tests and those under development are probably relatively adequate for the limited objectives they represent, provided an appropriate design is employed to relate performance to independent variables.

Individual accountability is another story. By this I mean the responsibilities a teacher, counselor, psychologist, and so on, has to an individual pupil on a one-to-one basis to help him to develop his uniqueness. Here the objectives vary and are likely to be long-range. Tests which maximize individual differences both qualitatively and quantitatively are at least partially appropriate, particularly when they are used for formative purposes. This is not to say that the measurement of mastery outcomes is unimportant. Bloom (1971), in particular, has written about the potential contribution which mastery learning may make to self-actualization. But it should be recognized that the contribution of mastery tests to total individual accountability is limited.

4. There is also an important distinction between accountability in terms of product and process. In evaluating product we may employ a fairly straightforward input-output model. But as Wallace (American Institutes for Research, 1970) points out, in evaluating process the basic accountability question is "What happened?", and the focus of attention is on ". . . . what helps, how it helps, and when and where it succeeds or fails [p. v] ." This variety of accountability requires assessment by instruments sensitive to short-range change which are used for continuous monitoring. Its basic purpose is to establish cause and effect as directly as possible.

5. In performance contracting a distinction can be made between a "service contract" and a contract for the development of procedures which can be turned over to the school system (the so-called "turn-key" provision). The latter type of contract, which calls for installation and evaluation, should be conceived of and designed in exactly the same way as any other "methods" study, which in fact it is.

There are a great many accomplishments I have not mentioned: better test manuals, better aids to interpretation and use, considerable work in scaling, recognition of social, cultural, and linguistic variability (Holtzman, 1971), among others. If the endeavor to which you are devoting your professional career is among these, please consider it as an accomplishment so well known that its mention is unnecessary.

Summary

In closing, I will try to answer the four questions posed in the program as directly and tersely as possible.

Q: Has the attempt to have testing serve multiple functions with the same test been productive or counter-productive?

A: Productive—if only in the sense that inadequacies in traditional tests have led to the development of tests which will serve the functions for which traditional tests have been ineffective.

Q: Are norm-referenced tests different from criterion-referenced tests?

A: Yes, and speaking for both sides, *vive la différence.*

Q: Should today's standardized tests be used to hold schools accountable for meeting their objectives?

A: The appropriateness of today's tests for the multiplicity of accountability applications is limited. It is hoped that tomorrow's tests will better serve these important functions, but let's not cop out on our obligations to students in order to find something we can objectively account for.

Q: Are there some things we have been doing right?

A: Not in an absolute sense; we have not yet achieved a final mastery criterion.

41 | Criterion-referenced Measurements: Limitations*

Robert L. Ebel

Every mental test is intended to indicate how much of a particular characteristic an individual can demonstrate. To determine and express "how
much," one needs a quantitative scale. Even those tests used primarily for
categorical pass-fail decisions almost always involve a quantitative scale on
which a critical "passing" score has been defined. Because the human characteristics that mental tests seek to measure are often complex and hard to
define, appropriate quantitative scales are not easy to establish. Some of the
most difficult problems of mental measurements arise in the process of getting a useful scale.

The essential difference between norm-referenced and criterion-
referenced measurements is in the quantitative scales used to express how
much the individual can do. In norm-referenced measurement the scale is
usually anchored in the middle on an average level of performance for a
particular group of individuals. The units on the scale are usually a function
of the distribution of performances above and below the average level. In
criterion-referenced measurement the scale is usually anchored at the extremities—a score at the top of the scale indicating complete or perfect mastery of
some defined abilities; one at the bottom indicating complete absence of
those abilities. The scale units consist of subdivisions of this total scale range.

It is interesting to note that the percent grades which were used almost
universally in schools and colleges in this country up to about 1920 represent
one type of criterion-referenced measurement. True, the extremities of the
scales used for percent grades in most courses were very loosely anchored in
very poorly defined specifications of what would constitute perfect mastery.
But this lack was more a consequence of the great difficulty in developing
such definitions than of failure to appreciate their importance. Little has
happened to the subject matter of education since 1920 that would make the
task of defining complete mastery any easier. If anything, as the scope of our

*From *School Review*, 1971, 79(2), 282-288. Copyright 1971 by The University of
Chicago. Reproduced by permission of the author and publisher.

educational content and objectives has broadened, the task has probably become more difficult.

The replacement of norm-referenced measures by criterion-referenced measures in education is not likely to be easy. If it were to happen in the next decade, as some seem to advocate, educational measurement would have come full circle. Those who accept the half-truth that there is nothing new under the sun would have another example to cite. More important, the difficulties and limitations of criterion-referenced measures, which half a century ago led to their virtual abandonment, would once again become apparent and would, in all probability, start the pendulum swinging back toward norm-referenced measures.

This is not to say that there is no value in criterion-referenced measurements, or no possibility of using them effectively. They have a kind of meaning, a very useful kind, that norm-referenced measurements lack. In some instances good criterion-referenced measures can be obtained (Ebel, 1962). But it is to say that the idea of criterion-referenced measurement is not new, that recent emphasis on norm-referenced measurements has not been misplaced, and that good criterion-referenced measures may be practically unobtainable in many important areas of educational achievement.

Criterion-referenced measures of educational achievement, when valid ones can be obtained, tell us in meaningful terms what a man knows or can do. They do not tell us how good or how poor his level of knowledge or ability may be. Excellence or deficiency are necessarily relative concepts. They cannot be defined in absolute terms. The four-minute mile represents excellence in distance running not in terms of any absolute standards for human speed, but because so few are able to run that fast for that long.

In many areas of education we do pursue excellence; in many areas we are concerned with deficiency. For these purposes we need norm-referenced measures. To say that such measures leave us in the dark about *what* the student is good at doing or poor at doing is seldom a reasonable approximation of the true situation. Usually our knowledge of typical test or course content gives us at least a rough idea of amount of knowledge or degree of ability.

Limitations of Criterion-referenced Measures

One limitation of criterion-referenced measures, then, is that they do not tell us all, or even the most important part, of what we need to know about educational achievement. Another is, as we have already suggested, that good criterion-referenced measures are often difficult to obtain. They require a degree of detail in the specification of objectives or outcomes that is quite unrealistic to expect and impractical to use, except at the most elementary levels of education.

The argument that effective teaching begins with a specification of objectives seems logical enough. If we will settle for statements of general objectives, unencumbered with the details of what is to be taught, how it is to be taught, or what elements of knowledge or ability are to be tested, it is practically useful. But general objectives will not suffice as a basis for criterion-referenced tests. And the formulation of specific objectives which would suffice costs more in time and effort than they are worth in most cases. Furthermore, if they are really used, they are more likely to suppress than to stimulate effective teaching.

The good teacher knows and is able to do thousands of things that he hopes to teach his students. Some of them are recorded in the readings he assigns or in the lecture notes he uses. Others are stored in his memory bank for ready recall when the occasion arises. Why should he labor to translate all these detailed elements of achievement into statements of objectives? If he should do so, how could he actually keep such a detailed array of statements in mind while teaching? And if he were to manage such a tour de force, how formal, rigid and dull his teaching would become.

There is obvious logic in the argument that teachers need to think hard about their objectives in teaching. But when the argument is extended to call for specific statements of objectives, written before the teaching begins, it involves assumptions and implications that are open to question. One is that instructional efforts are guided more effectively by explicit statements of objectives than by implicit perceptions of those objectives. Another is that the effectiveness of a teacher's efforts depends more on the explicitness than on the quality of his objectives, or that explicitness means quality where objectives are concerned. The implication is that programmed teaching which has been carefully planned in detail is likely to be better than more flexible, opportunistic teaching.

Have you ever seen a statement of objectives for educational achievement (not just an outline of learning tasks to be performed) which did justice to all the instructor actually taught in the course and which therefore provided a solid foundation for criterion-referenced measurements of achievement in the course? If you have, did you not find that these objectives substantially duplicated the instructional materials used in the course?

Criterion-referenced measurement may be practical in those few areas of achievement which focus on cultivation of a high degree of skill in the exercise of a limited number of abilities. In areas where the emphasis is on knowledge and understanding, the effective use of criterion-referenced measurements seems much less likely. For knowledge and understanding consist of a complex fabric which owes its strength and beauty to an infinity of tiny fibers of relationship. Knowledge does not come in discrete chunks that can be defined and identified separately.

Another difficulty in the way of establishing meaningful criteria of achievement is that to be generally meaningful they must not be idiosyncratic. They must not represent the interests, values, and standards of just one teacher. This calls for committees, meetings, and long struggles to reach at least a verbal consensus, which in some cases serves only to conceal the unresolved disagreements in perceptions, values, and standards. These processes involve so much time and trouble that most criterion-referenced type measurements are idiosyncratic. Is this not what was mainly responsible for the great disagreements Starch and Elliott (1912) found in their classic studies of the grading of examination papers? To the extent that criteria of achievement are idiosyncratic, they lack validity and useful meaning.

So a second limitation of criterion-referenced measurement is the difficulty of basing such measurement soundly on adequate criteria of achievement. The third and final limitation to be discussed here is less a limitation of the method of measurement itself than of one of the principal justifications that has been offered for its use. This justification argues that when the goal of teaching and learning is mastery, criterion-referenced measurements are essential, since only they are capable of indicating whether or not the mastery has been attained.

Given the assumption of mastery as a goal, this justification is logically unassailable. But should mastery be the goal? At first glance it is most attractive. Partial learning cannot possibly be as good as complete learning. Only a goal that is fully attained can be fully satisfying.

The Morrison Method

More than forty years ago Prof. H. C. Morrison, at the University of Chicago, developed and popularized a method of teaching based on the mastery of "adaptations" of understanding, appreciation, or ability (Morrison, 1926). These, unlike skills, seemed to him not to be matters of degree. "The pupil has either attained it or he has not." To achieve such an adaptation the instructor should organize his materials into units, each focused on a particular adaptation. He should then follow a systematic teaching routine: pretest, teach, test, reteach, retest, to the point of actual mastery.

For a time Morrison's ideas were popular and influential. Around 1930, the *Education Index* listed about fourteen articles per year on applications of the system he had advocated. By 1950 the rate had fallen to about five articles per year. The *Education Index* volume for the 1967-68 academic year lists not a single article on this subject.

Recently the concept of mastery has been reintroduced into educational discussions as a corrollary of various systems of individually prescribed instruction and as a solution to the problem of individual differences in learning ability. Several authorities have pointed out, quite correctly, that these differences can be expressed either in terms of how much a student can learn in a set time or in terms of how long it takes him to learn a set amount (Adkins, 1958; Glaser, 1963; Carroll, 1963; Gagné, 1965; Bloom, 1968). Why, they ask, should we not let time be the variable instead of amount learned?

Their arguments have great force when applied to basic intellectual skills that everyone needs to exercise almost flawlessly in order to live effectively in modern society. But these basic skills make up only a small fraction of what the schools teach and of what various people are interested in learning. Look about you at the various talents and interests that different people have developed. See how these differences complement each other in accomplishing the diverse jobs that need doing in our society. Then ask why we should expect or require a student of a subject to achieve the same level of mastery as every other student of that subject.

Ernest E. Bayles (1934) made this point in his criticism of the Morrison method. He made another to which we have already alluded. Abilities, understandings, and appreciations are, in the experience of almost everyone, not all-or-none adaptations. They are matters of degree. None but the simplest of them can ever be mastered completely by anyone. Hence any criterion of mastery is likely to be quite imperfect and arbitrary. To the extent that it is, our criterion-referenced measurements will also be imperfect and arbitrary, as were the percent grades that norm-referenced measurements replaced fifty years ago.

Summary

To summarize, the major limitations of criterion-referenced measurements are these:

1. They do not tell us all we need to know about achievement.
2. They are difficult to obtain on any sound basis.
3. They are necessary for only a small fraction of important educational achievements.

Contrary to the impression that exists in some quarters, criterion-referenced measurements are not a recent development that modern technology has made possible and that effective education requires. The use of criterion-referenced measurements cannot be expected to improve significantly our evaluations of educational achievement.

It is true of course that norm-referenced measurements of educational achievement need to have content meaning as well as relative meaning. We need to understand not just that a student excels or is deficient, but what it is that he does well or poorly. But these meanings and understandings are seldom wholly absent when norm-referenced measures are used. They can be made more obviously present and useful if we choose to do so.

42 | Criterion-referenced Measurements: Potential*

James H. Block

At a time when the criterion-referenced testing movement has just begun to gather steam, Professor Ebel's paper comes as something of a surprise. He was one of the first educators to call attention to the need for criterion-referenced, what he termed "content meaningful," measurements (Ebel, 1962). Yet now, when research is producing such measurements, he pessimistically concludes their use cannot "be expected to improve significantly our evaluations of educational achievement." Fortunately, his pessimism is unjustified.

Before examining each of the alleged flaws of the criterion-referenced measurements, it is necessary to point out that the measurements defended here are those currently being developed and advocated, not those briefly defined in Ebel's opening remarks. The defended measurements are *absolute* indices designed to indicate *what* the pupil has or has not learned from a given instructional segment. The measurements are absolute in that they are interpretable solely vis-à-vis a fixed performance standard or criterion and need not be interpreted relative to other measurements. They indicate what the student has or has not learned because they are taken on a fully representative sample of skills (content and behaviors) drawn from those he was expected to learn (Bormuth, 1970; Glaser & Nitko, 1970).

The current criterion-referenced measurements differ from those defined by Ebel in two major respects. First, they are intended to measure what, not how much, the student has or has not learned. Measures that indicate what will also indicate how much, but the converse need not hold. For example, the percent grades of the past indicated how much of the tested material the learner had acquired. However, since the tested material was not fully representative of the skills taught, no sound inferences could be drawn from a student's measurement regarding what had or had not been learned. Second, the current measurements are much more complex. In particular, they cannot be distinguished from normative measurements simply by their scale properties.

The purposes for which they are made, the manner in which they are obtained, the specificity of information they provide regarding student learning, and the purposes for which they are used all serve to distinguish criterion-referenced from norm-referenced measurements (Popham & Husek, 1969; Glaser & Nitko, 1970).

Given the preceding definition, let us now consider each of the limitations Ebel assigns to criterion-referenced measurements.

Limitation One

First he argues that criterion-referenced measurements do not tell us all we need to know about student achievement. Nowhere does the argument detail what we do need to know, but it suggests that knowledge of pupil learning excellence or deficiency is crucial. Excellence and deficiency are asserted to be "necessarily" relative concepts and, thus, can only be measured normatively.

It is true that criterion-referenced measurements do not tell us all we need to know about student learning. The major point, however, is that for much school learning, they can provide the only relevant information on pupil learning excellence or deficiency.

Most school learning is sequential especially at the elementary level; one course or topic builds upon and assumes the learning of previous courses or topics. For example, a second arithmetic course builds upon the first, and a third builds upon the second and the first. In such learning, if at each stage the student acquires those skills prerequisite to the learning of skills at the next stage, he is likely to acquire the subsequent skills. If, however, he fails to learn the prerequisite skills, he is likely to fail to learn skills at not only the next, but at all subsequent stages. In sequential learning, therefore, excellence and deficiency can be viewed as absolute simply because the pupil's learning success or failure throughout the sequence is contingent upon his learning of certain skills at each stage within the sequence.

If pupil learning success throughout the sequence is to be promoted, specific evidence must be gathered at each stage regarding what the student has not yet learned. Given this information, steps can be taken to insure that each student completes his learning before moving on to the learning of related skills at later points. A "rough idea," provided by norm-referenced measurements, of what each pupil has not learned will not suffice. Only criterion-referenced measurements can provide the required information.

Limitation Two

Ebel's second stated limitation of criterion-referenced measurements is the difficulty of obtaining good measuring instruments. It is argued that their construction requires too much specificity in the statement of instructional objectives. This specificity is too costly in terms of teacher time and effort. Further, even if the objectives are specified, they will suppress rather than stimulate effective instruction. Finally, it is suggested that the achievement criteria will be chosen arbitrarily; hence, the measurements will be invalid and meaningless.

The argument is weak in several respects. First, the amount of specificity needed to state the objectives has been greatly exaggerated. Objectives are prespecified primarily to guide the instruction and not to facilitate instrument construction. They represent the instructional goals—the minimal set of skills it is hoped the student will obtain. Objectives stated in great enough detail to guide the teaching-learning process will provide an adequate base for the construction of sound criterion-referenced measuring instruments. These objectives should be stated specifically enough so that the teacher has a definite idea of what must be taught and the students of what must be learned. But the objectives should not be delineated in such great detail that they are limited to trivial, easily specified skills. They should also not be stated so specifically that they cannot be refined and redefined in the constant interaction between goals and the exigencies of day-to-day instructional practices.

Second, the formulation of objectives is not as costly in terms of teacher time and effort as Ebel suggests. In work with formative testing (a type of criterion-referenced testing), it has been found that the objectives, as well as evaluation instruments, for each chapter in typical algebra, chemistry, and biology textbooks can be constructed by groups of three to four teachers working approximately two hours a day in less than ten weeks (Airasian, 1969). While Ebel is correct that objectives derived solely from the learning materials may not do justice to all that is taught, our work suggests that in many cases they provide a very close approximation to teachers' minimal instructional goals. Instructors do teach more than the learning materials, but they typically hold students accountable primarily for the skills embodied in the materials.

Two developments have been proposed which might cut to almost nothing the amount of teacher time and effort necessary to construct good criterion-referenced tests. Publishers of textbooks and other instructional materials might provide component or task-analytic descriptions of their materials and criterion-referenced tests constructed from these descriptions. For example, a textbook chapter description would include the new content introduced, the cognitive behavioral level intended for the material's learning, and the relevance, if any, of each content-behavior element's learning to the learning of other skills in the chapter and subsequent chapters. The teacher could use the test provided or use the unit descriptions to differentiate his objectives from those of the textbook and adapt or reconstruct the test accordingly. The tremendous capacity of the computer might also be used to construct tailor-made instruments. Item banks might be constructed and stored, especially for subjects taught repeatedly and not likely to change in content for some time (Husek & Sirotnik, 1967). The teacher might then construct a test quickly by specifying his instructional goals in the appropriate computer terms.

Third, the prespecification of instructional objectives need not suppress effective teaching. In fact, if used correctly, it can help transform group-based instruction of any initial quality into instruction of optimal quality for each learner.

Ebel is correct in saying that good teachers know and are able to do many things to help their students learn. Unfortunately, even the best teachers may not provide instruction of optimal quality for each of their students because of the group-based instructional situation. There is typically only one teacher for twenty or more learners. For some learners the instructional cues will not be clear or appropriate. Aptitude-Instructional Treatment Interaction research, for example, indicates that one mode of instruction may be optimal for some students and nonoptimal for others, depending on their aptitude patterns (Cronbach & Snow, 1969). Some pupils will also not be allowed the active involvement in and practice of the learning they require. One student may learn best through lectures and independent study; another through classroom discussion and drill. Finally, some learners will not receive either the amounts or types of reinforcements to which they best respond. One student might work best for an *A* and another for the teacher's smiles.

Need for Feedback/Correction

Recent research begins to suggest that classroom instruction of any initial quality can be transformed into instruction of optimal quality if the original instruction is supplemented by simple and inexpensive feedback/correction procedures. Essentially, these procedures make the same kind of instructional adjustments, based on each pupil's initial learning, as would a well-trained tutor. When the tutor finds his initial instruction is ineffective at certain points, he immediately presents new instructional cues, or allows the tutee more active involvement in or practice of the learning, or alters the quantity and type of his reinforcements. Feedback/corrective procedures systematize these same kinds of adjustments for classroom use.

The key to the procedures' effectiveness is the criterion-referenced measurements, derived from prespecified instructional objectives, which form the feedback system. Throughout the instruction, brief, diagnostic, criterion-referenced progress tests are administered to check the quality of the teaching-learning process. On the basis of this information, it is possible to determine what the student failed to learn from a given instructional segment. Corrective devices are then used to help the pupil complete his learning. The correctives may involve reteaching the class, individualized tutoring by other students, directing the learner to alternative instructional materials, or small group problem sessions. The correctives are designed to provide each learner the cues, participation-practice, and reinforcement lacking in the original instruction. Thus they fill in the learning gaps left by the original instruction and help make the large, original instructional investment fully pay off per student.

The powerful effect of supplementary feedback/correction on student learning has been demonstrated in studies by Kim and by me (Kim et al., 1969; Block, 1970). In my research, suburban eight graders were taught three sequential units of elementary matrix arithmetic. Students were randomly assigned to five groups. One group, the control ($N = 27$), learned the arithmetic solely through the original instruction. The remaining groups ($N = 16$ each) each received different amounts of supplementary feedback/correction. On measures of achievement, transfer, retention, and short- and long-term interest in and attitude toward the arithmetic, the findings revealed significant and substantial differences between the groups who received optimal and near optimal feedback/correction and the group who received none. In particular, optimal feedback/correction produced maximal average student achievement and minimal achievement variability, while no feedback/correction produced minimal student achievement and maximal variability. Most students who received optimal feedback/correction, despite individual differences in skills, scored within a few points of the same high level. As the amount of feedback/correction per group became progressively less optimal, average achievement decreased and achievement variability increased, eventually approaching that found for the control group.

Kim reported similar findings under a one teacher to approximately seventy students group-based instructional situation. Seventh graders ($N =$

272) were taught a unit on "Simple Geometric Figures" for eight classroom sessions. Half were randomly assigned to learn with supplemental feedback/ correction and half without. Almost twice as many of the former students (74 percent) attained high levels of mastery as did the latter (40 percent). Thus, even under these poor instructional conditions, a large majority of students with instruction supplemented by feedback/correction achieved to the same high level.

Much more work is needed on the role of feedback/correction procedures in instruction. The findings to date, however, suggest that prespecified instructional objectives provide a key to maximally effective classroom instruction when put into operation in the form of criterion-referenced measurements for use in a feedback/correction system.

Fourth, and finally, the selection of the test tasks for the measuring instruments is not arbitrary, and, hence, the measurements need not be invalid and meaningless. As mentioned previously, a criterion-referenced measurement is taken on a fully representative sample of skills drawn from those which students are expected to learn. Since the instructional objectives define what pupils are expected to learn, once the objectives are set, the achievement criteria are set. True, the goals may be idiosyncratic. What teacher would not resist being told what his goals should be? The derivation of sample test items from these goals, however, is carried out systematically, replicably, and hence, objectively (Bormuth, 1970). As Ebel once wrote, a test produced by explicitly defined and replicable processes may take more time to construct and may "lack some kinds of excellence which a creatively artistic test constructor might achieve, but the increase in *objective meaningfulness and reproducibility* could more than offset the cost" (Ebel, 1962).

Limitation Three

Ebel's final alleged limitation of criterion-referenced measurements is that they are necessary for only a small fraction of what students learn. His argument acknowledges that they are appropriate for "the few basic intellectual skills that everyone needs to exercise almost flawlessly in order to live effectively." But it suggests they are not appropriate for measuring the diverse talents and interests that keep our society functioning or for those "abilities, understandings, and appreciations" possessed in varying degrees by all.

The measurements are appropriate for only a fraction of what students learn, although the fraction is much larger than suggested. The major problem with this argument is that it overlooks the great importance of the learning of these few skills for the fullest development of each pupil's talents, interest, understandings, and appreciations.

For at least ten years, American children are legally compelled to attend school. Especially at the elementary level, they spend a good portion of their time learning the basic intellectual skills. Due to the usual organizational characteristics of schools and their curricula, the students' learning of these skills differs in several major respects from the learning of most other skills. First, the learning of skills forms the bulk of each child's initial school experiences. Second, the skills are learned sequentially over several years. Third, their learning is required of all students. Finally, the pupil's learning of these skills is continually graded. In fact, perhaps at no other time will students' learning be judged more frequently.

Suppose a student encounters problems early in the learning of any basic skill. Since the skill is learned sequentially, his failure to learn may, if not corrected, doom him to continual failure throughout the remainder of the sequence. Regardless of how humiliating and/or frustrating these subsequent learning attempts may be, he cannot escape. The learning of the skill is required; hence, the pupil must serve his time until the sequence terminates. Further, because his learning is so frequently judged, he must submit to a bombardment of negative evaluations of his academic worth. Thus in failing to learn the skill, he will acquire a long history of painful learning encounters and negative evaluations of his learning ability. The student's initial school learning experiences are likely to be neither pleasant nor rewarding.

Both his failure to learn the skill and his long history of frustration are likely to have major negative consequences for his future development. His failure to acquire the basic skill may block his learning of related skills and, hence, the development of any talent or interests dependent on those skills. This is especially likely as a society becomes increasingly specialized. For example, the young man who desires to become a journeyman mechanic or machinist must acquire certain fundamental skills as an apprentice. Increasingly, the acquisition of these skills has come to depend on the apprentice's reading ability. Thus, if the youth cannot read, he may not be able to become a journeyman.

The student's long history of painful and unsuccessful learning experiences is likely to be an even greater block to his development. Research evidence suggests that a pupil's history of academic success or failure is instrumental in the formation of his interest in and attitude not only toward school and school learning, but also toward extracurricular and postschool learning. It also suggests a strong, perhaps casual, link between the learner's perceived academic success and his personality development. In particular, consistent evidence of adequate or inadequate learning shapes the pupil's academic and, under some conditions, general self-concept and influences his susceptibility to mental and emotional health problems (Bloom, 1971). Hence, a student's failure to acquire a skill may impair not only his future learning ability, but also his desire for further learning and his general psychological well being. In so far as the fullest development of his talents, interests, abilities, understandings, and appreciations rests upon his desire to learn and his psychological health, failure in learning the basic skills may block this development.

This is the plight of at least 20 percent of our elementary school students. If these students are to be given the fullest opportunity for self-development under our present school system, each must be assured success in learning the basic required skills. This will not insure that they will realize their full potential, but it will insure that they possess at least a positive cognitive-affective base from which they can develop in any chosen direction. The key to providing this base is the pinpointing and correcting of deficiencies in each student's skill learning before related learning is impaired. Norm-referenced measurements do not provide sufficient information on what the student has not learned to fulfill this function. Only criterion-referenced measurements will suffice.

Conclusion

Perhaps at no time in the history of American education have our schools faced greater pressure to produce more and better educated students. Teachers are increasingly deluged with demands that they assume more responsibility, even accountability, for all students' learning. In the face of these demands we cannot continue to use measurements which simply assess the outcomes of the teaching-learning process when measurements exist which can not only assess, but positively shape these outcomes for each learner. The potential of criterion-referenced measurements lies in their ability to promote the learning of all.

43 | Testing Hazards in Performance Contracting*

Robert E. Stake

In the first federally sponsored example of performance contracting for the public schools, Dorsett Educational Systems of Norman, Oklahoma, contracted to teach reading, mathematics, and study skills to over 200 poor-performance junior and senior high school students in Texarkana. Commercially available, standardized, general-achievement tests were used to measure performance gains.

Are such tests suitable for measuring specific learnings? To the person little acquainted with educational testing, it appears that performance testing is what educational tests are for. The testing specialist knows better. General achievement tests have been developed to measure correlates of learning, not learning itself.

Such tests are indirect measures of educational gains. They provide correlates of achievement rather than direct evidence of achievement. Correlation of these test scores with general learning is often high, but such scores correlate only moderately with performance on many specific educational tasks. Tests can be built to measure specific competence, but there is relatively little demand for them. Many of those tests (often called criterion-referenced tests) do a poor job of predicting later performance of either a specific or a general nature. General achievement tests predict better. The test developer's basis for improving tests has been to work toward better prediction of later performance rather than better measurement of present performance. Assessment of what a student is now capable of doing is not the purpose of most standardized tests. Errors and hazards abound, especially when these general achievement tests are used for performance contracting. Many of the hazards remain even with the use of criterion-referenced tests or any other performance observation procedures.

One of the hazards in performance contracting is that many high-priority educational objectives—for various reasons and in various ways—will be cast

*From *Phi Delta Kappan*, 1971, **53**, 583-589. Copyright 1971 by Phi Delta Kappa, Inc. Reproduced by permission of the author and publisher.

aside while massive attention is given to other high-priority objectives. This hazard is not unrelated to testing but will not be discussed here. This article will identify the major obstacles to gathering direct evidence of performance gain on targeted objectives.

Errors of Testing

Answering a *National School Board Journal* (November, 1970) questionnaire on performance contracting, a New Jersey Board member said:

> Objectives must be stated in simple, understandable terms. No jargon will do and no subjective goals can be tolerated. Neither can the nonsense about there being some mystique that prohibits objective measurement of the educational endeavor.

Would that our problems withered before stern resolve. But neither wishing nor blustering rids educational testing of its errors.

Just as the population census and the bathroom scales have their errors, educational tests have theirs. The technology and theory of testing are highly sophisticated; the sources of error are well known (Lord & Novick, 1968). Looking into the psychometrist's meaning of a theory of testing, one finds a consideration of ways to analyze and label the inaccuracies in test scores. There is a mystique, but there is also simple fact: No one can eliminate test errors. Unfortunately, some errors are large enough to cause wrong decisions about individual children or school district policy.

Some educators and social critics consider the whole idea of educational testing to be a mistake (Hoffmann, 1962; Sizer, 1970). Unfortunate social consequences of testing, such as the perpetuation of racial discrimination (Goslin, 1970) and pressures to cheat (McGhan, 1970), continue to be discussed. But, as expected, most test specialists believe that the promise in testing outweighs these perils. They refuse responsibility for gross misuse of their instruments and findings and concentrate on reducing the errors in tests and test programs.

Some technical errors in test scores are small and tolerable. But some testing errors are intolerably large. Today's tests can, for example, measure vocabulary word-recognition skills with sufficient accuracy. They cannot, however, adequately measure listening comprehension or the ability to analyze the opposing sides of an argument.

Contemporary test technology is not refined enough to meet all the demands. In performance contracting the first demand is for assessment of performance. Tests do their job well when the performance is highly specific—when, for example, the student is to add two numbers, recognize a misspelled word, or identify the parts of a hydraulic lift. When a teacher wants to measure performances that require more demanding mental processes, such as conceptualizing a writing principle or synthesizing a political argument, performance tests give us less dependable scores (Bloom *et al.*, 1956).

Unreached potentials. Many educators believe that the most human of human gifts—the emotions, the higher thought processes, interpersonal sensitivity, moral sense—are beyond the reach of psychometric testing. Most test specialists disagree. While recognizing an ever-present error component, they believe that anything can be measured. The credo was framed by E. L. Thorndike in 1918: "Whatever exists at all exists in some amount." Testing men believe it still. They are not so naive as to think that any human gift will manifest itself in a 45-minute paper-and-pencil test. They do believe that, given ample opportunity to activate and observe the examinee, any trait, talent, or learning that manifests itself in behavior can be measured with reasonable accuracy. The total cost of measuring may be 100 times that of administering the usual tests, but they believe it can be done. The final observations may rely on professional judgment, but this could be reliable and validated judgment. A question for most test specialists, then, is not "Can complex educational outcomes be measured?" but "Can complex education outcomes be measured with the time and personnel and facilities available?"

When it is most important to know whether or not a child is reading at age-level, we call in a reading specialist, who observes his reading habits. She might test him with word recognition, syntactic decoding, and paragraph-comprehension exercises. She would retest where evidence was inconclusive. She would talk to his teachers and his parents. She would arrive at a clinical description—which might be reducible to a statement such as "Yes, Johnny is reading at or above age-level."

The scores we get from group reading tests can be considered estimates of such an expert judgment. These objective test scores correlate positively with the more valid expert judgments. Such estimates are not direct measurements of what teachers or laymen mean by "ability to read," nor are they suitably accurate for diagnostic purposes. Achievement gains for a sizable number of students will be poorly estimated. It is possible that the errors in group testing are so extensive that—when fully known—businessmen and educators will refuse to accept them as bases for contract reimbursement.

Professional awareness. Classroom teachers and school principals have tolerated standardized test errors because they have not been obligated to make crucial decisions on the basis of test scores. Actually, in day-to-day practice they seldom use test scores (Hastings, Runkel, & Damrin, 1961). When they do, they combine them with other knowledge to estimate a child's progress in school and to guide him into an appropriate learning experience. They do not use tests as a basis for assessing the quality of their own teaching.

In performance contracting, the situation is drastically changed; tests are honored as the sole basis for contract reimbursement. The district will pay the contractor for performance improvement. An error in testing means money misspent. Course completion and reimbursement decisions are to be made without reliance on the knowledge and judgment of a professional observer, without asking persons who are closest to the learning (the teacher, the contractor, and the student) whether or not they *see* evidence of learning. Decisions are to be made entirely by objective and independent testing. Numerous human errors and technical misrepresentations will occur.

Which Test Items?

It is often unrealistic to expect a project director to either find or create paper-and-pencil test items, administrable in an hour to large numbers of students by persons untrained in psychometric observation and standardized diagnostics, objectively scorable, valid for purposes of the performance contract, and readily interpretable. The more complex the training, the more unrealistic the expectation. One compromise is to substitute criterion test items measuring simple behaviors for those measuring the complex behaviors targeted by the training. For example, the director may substitute vocabulary-recognition test items for reading-comprehension items or knowledge of components for the actual dismantling of an engine. The substitution may be reasonable, but the criterion test should be validated against performances directly indicated by the objectives. It almost never has been. Without the validation the educator should be skeptical about what the test measures.

It always is unrealistic to expect that the payoff from instruction will be apparent in the performances of learners at test-taking time (Broudy, 1970). Most tests evoke relatively simple behavior. Ebel wrote:

> ... most achievement tests ... consist primarily of items testing specific elements of knowledge, facts, ideas, explanations, meanings, processes, procedures, relations, consequences, and so on (Ebel, 1971).

He went on to point out that more than simple recall is involved in answering even the simplest vocabulary item.

Much more complex behavior is needed for answering a reading-comprehension item. These items clearly call for more than the literal meanings of the words read. The student must paraphrase and interpret—what we expect readers to be able to do.

These items and ones for problem solving and the higher mental processes do measure high-priority school goals—but growth in such areas is relatively slow. Most contractors will not risk basing reimbursement on the small chance that evidence of growth will be revealed by *these* criterion tests. Some of the complex objectives of instruction will be underemphasized in the typical performance-contract testing plan.

The success of Texarkana's first performance-contract year is still being debated. Late winter (1969-70) test results looked good, but spring test results were disappointing (Andrew & Roberts, 1970; Dyer, 1970b; Lennon, 1971). Relatively simple performance items had been used. But the "debate" did not get into that. It started when the project's "outside evaluator" ruled that there had been direct coaching on most, if not all, of the criterion test items, which were known by the contractor during the school year. Critics claimed unethical "teaching for the test." The contractor claimed that both teaching and testing had been directed toward the same specific goals, as should be the case in a good performance contract. The issue is not only test choice and ethics; it includes the ultimate purpose of teaching.

Teaching for the test. Educators recognize an important difference between preparation for testing and direct coaching for a test. To prepare an examinee, the teacher teaches within the designated knowledge-skill domain and has the examinee practice good test-taking behavior (for example, don't spend too much time on overly difficult items; guess when you have an inkling though not full knowledge; organize your answer before writing an essay) so that relevant knowledge-skill is not obscured. Direct coaching teaches the examinees how to make correct responses to specific items on the criterion test.

This is an important difference when test items cover only a small sample of the universe of what has been taught or when test scores are correlates, rather than direct measurements, of criterion behavior. It ceases to be important when the test is set up to measure directly and thoroughly that which has been taught. In this case, teaching for the test is exactly what is wanted.

Joselyn pointed out that the performance contractor and the school should agree in advance on the criterion procedure, though not necessarily on the specific items (Joselyn, 1971). To be fair to the contractor, the testing needs to be reasonably close to the teaching. To be fair to parents, the testing needs to be representative of the domain of abilities *they* are concerned about. A contract to develop reading skills would not be satisfied adequately by gains on a vocabulary test, according to the expectations of most teachers. All parties need to know how similar the testing will be to the actual teaching.

A dissimilarity scale. Unfortunately, as Anderson observed (Anderson, 1970), the test specialist has not developed scales for describing the similarity between teaching and testing. This is a grievous failing. Educators have no good way to indicate how closely the tests match the instruction.

There are many ways for criterion questions to be dissimilar. They can depart from the information taught by: 1) syntactic transformation; 2) semantic transformation; 3) change in content or medium; 4) application, considering the particular instance; 5) inference, generalizing from learned instances; and 6) implication, adding last-taught information to generally known information. For examples of some of these transformations, see Table I. Hively, Patterson, and Page (1968), Bormuth (1970), and Jackson (1970), discussed procedures for using some of these transformations to generate test items.

For any student the appropriateness of these items depends on prior and subsequent learning as well as on the thoroughness of teaching. Which items are appropriate will have to be decided at the scene. The least and most dissimilar items might be quite different in their appropriateness. The reading-comprehension items of any standardized achievement battery are likely to be more dissimilar to the teaching of reading than any of the "dissimilarities" shown in Table I. Immediate instruction is not properly evaluated by highly dissimilar items, nor is scholarship properly evaluated by highly similar items. Even within the confines of performance contracting, both evaluations are needed.

TABLE I   *An example of transformations of information taught into test questions.*

Information taught:	Pt. Barrow is the northernmost town in Alaska.
Minimum transformation question:	What is the northernmost town in Alaska?
Semantic-syntactic transformation question:	What distinction does Pt. Barrow have among Alaskan villages?
Context-medium transformation question:	The dots on the adjacent map represent Alaskan cities and towns. One represents Pt. Barrow. Which one?
Implication question:	What would be unusual about summer sunsets in Pt. Barrow, Alaska?

For the evaluation of instruction, a large number of test items are needed for each objective that—in the opinion of the teachers—directly measure increase in skill or understanding. Items from standardized tests, if used, would be included item by item. For each objective, the item pool would cover all aspects of the objective. A separate sample of items would be drawn for the pretest and posttest for each student, and instruction success would be based on the collective gain of all students.

Creating such a pool of relevant, psychometrically sound test items is a major—but necessary—undertaking[1] It is a partial safeguard against teaching for the test and against the use of inappropriate criteria to evaluate the success of instruction.

What the Scores Mean

At first, performance contracting seemed almost a haven for the misinterpretation of scores. Contracts have ignored 1) the practice effect of pretesting,[2] 2) the origins of grade equivalents, 3) the "learning calendar," 4) the unreliability of gain scores, and 5) regression effects. Achievement may be spurious. Ignoring any one of these five is an invitation to misjudge the worth of the instruction.

Grade-equivalent scores. Standardized achievement tests have the appealing feature of yielding grade-equivalent scores. Each raw score, usually the number of items right, has been translated into a score indicating (for a student population forming a national reference group) the average grade placement of all students who got this raw score. These new scores are called "grade equivalents." Raw scores are not very meaningful to people unacquainted with the particular test; the grade equivalents are widely accepted by teachers and parents. Grade equivalents are common terminology in performance contracts.

Unfortunately, grade equivalents are available from most publishers only for tests, not for test items. Thus the whole test needs to be used, in the way prescribed in its manual, if the grade equivalents are to mean what they are supposed to mean. One problem of using whole tests was discussed in the previous section. Another problem is that the average annual "growth" on most standardized tests is only a few raw-score points. Consider in Table II the difference between a grade equivalent of 5.0 and 6.0 within four of the most popular test batteries.

---

[1] Dorsett indicated the desirability of such an item pool in the original Texarkana proposal.
[2] Not discussed here because of space limitations.

TABLE II   *Gain in items right needed to advance one grade equivalent on four typical achievement tests.*

	Grade equivalent		Needed for an improvement of one grade equivalent
	5.0	6.0	
Comprehensive Test of Basic Skills, Level 3: Reading Comprehension	20	23	3 items
Metropolitan Achievement Test, Intermediate Form B: Spelling	24	31	7 items
Iowa Tests of Basic Skills, Test A1: Arithmetic Concepts	10	14	4 items
Stanford Achievement Test, Form W, Intermediate II: Word Meaning	18	26	8 items

Most teachers do not like to have their year's work summarized by so little change in performance. Schools writing performance contracts perhaps should be reluctant to sign contracts for which the distinction between success and failure is so small. But to do so requires the abandonment of grade equivalents.

The learning calendar. For most special instructional programs, criterion tests will be administered at the beginning of and immediately following instruction, often in the first and last weeks of school. A great deal of distraction occurs during those weeks, but other times for pretesting and posttesting have their hazards, too. Recording progress every few weeks during the year is psychometrically preferred, but most teachers are opposed to "all that testing."

Children learn year-round, but the evidence of learning that gets inked on pupil records comes in irregular increments from season to season. Winter is the time of most rapid advancement, summer the least. Summer, in fact, is a period of setback for many youngsters. Beggs and Hieronymus found punctuation scores to spurt more than a year between October and April but to drop almost half a year between May and September (Beggs & Hieronymus, 1968). Discussing their reading test, Gates and MacGinitie (1965, p. 5) wrote:

> . . . in most cases, scores will be higher at the end of one grade than at the beginning of the next. That is, there is typically some loss of reading skill during the summer, especially in the lower grades.

The first month or two after students return to school in the fall is the time for getting things organized and restoring scholastic abilities lost during the summer. According to some records, spring instruction competes poorly

TABLE III   *Learning calendar for a typical fifth-grade class.*

			Month					
	S	O	N	D J	F	M	A	M
Mean achievement score	5.0	5.3	5.6	5.9		6.2		6.3

with other attractions. Thus, the learning year is a lopsided year, a basis sometimes for miscalculation. Consider the results of testing shown in Table III.

The six-week averages in Table III are fictitious, but they represent test performance in many classrooms. The mean growth for the year appears to be 1.3 grade equivalents. No acknowledgement is made that standardized test results in early September were poorer than those for the previous spring. For this example, the previous May mean (not shown) was 5.2. The real gain, then, for the year is 1.1 grade equivalents rather than the apparent 1.3. It would be inappropriate to pay the contractor for a mean gain of 1.3.

Another possible overpayment on the contract can result by holding final testing early and extrapolating the previous per-week growth to the weeks or months that follow. In Texarkana, as in most schools, spring progress was not as good as winter. If an accurate evaluation of contract instructional services is to be made, repeated testing, perhaps a month-by-month record of learning performances, needs to be considered (Wrightman & Gorth, 1969).

Unreliable gain scores. Most performance contracts pay off on an individual student basis. The contractor may be paid for each student who gains more than an otherwise expected amount. This practice is commendable in that it emphasizes the importance of each individual learner and makes the contract easier to understand, but it bases payment on a precarious mark: the gain score.

Just how unreliable is the performance-test gain score? For a typical standardized achievement test with two parallel forms, A and B, we might find the following characteristics reported in the test's technical manual:

Reliability of Test A = +.84.
Reliability of Test B = +.84.
Correlation of Test A with Test B = +.81.

Almost all standardized tests have reliability coefficients at this level. Using the standard formula (Thorndike & Hagen, 1969, p. 197), one finds a disappointing level of reliability for the measurement of improvement:

Reliability of gain scores (A-B or B-A) = +.16.

The test manual indicates the raw score and grade-equivalent standard deviations. For one widely used test, they are 9.5 items and 2.7 years, respectively. Using these values we can calculate the errors to be expected. *On the average,* a student's raw score would be in error by 2.5 items, grade equivalent would be in error by 0.72 years, and grade-equivalent *gain score* would be in error by 1.01 years. The error is indeed large.

Consider what this means for the not unusual contract whereby the student is graduated from the program, and the contractor is paid for his instruction, on any occasion that his performance score rises above a set value. Suppose—with the figures above—the student exits when his improvement is one grade equivalent or more. Suppose also, to make this situation simpler, that there is *no* intervening training and that the student is not influenced by previous testing. Here are three ways of looking at the same situation:

> Suppose that a contract student takes a different parallel form of the criterion test on three successive days immediately following the pretest. The chances are better than 50-50 that on *one* of these tests the student will gain a year or more in performance and appear to be ready to graduate from the program.
>
> Suppose that three students are tested with a parallel form immediately after the pretest. The chances are better than 50-50 that one of the three students—entirely due to errors of measurement—will gain a year or more and appear ready to graduate.
>
> Suppose that 100 students are admitted to contract instruction and pretested. After a period of time involving no training, they are tested again, and the students gaining a year are graduated. After another period of time, another test and another graduation. After the fourth terminal testing, even though no instruction has occurred, the chances are better than 50-50 that two-thirds of the students will be graduated.

In other words, owing to unreliability, gain scores can appear to reflect learning that actually does not occur.

The unreliability will give an equal number of false impressions of deteriorating performance. These errors (false gains and false losses) will balance out for a large group of students. If penalties for losses are paid by the contractor at the rate bonuses are paid for gains, the contractor will not be overpaid. But according to the way contracts are being written, typified in the examples above, the error in the gain scores does not balance out; it works in favor of the contractor. Measurement errors could be capitalized upon by unscrupulous promoters. Appropriate checks against these errors are built into the better contracts.

Errors in individual gain scores can be reduced by using longer tests. A better way to indicate true gain is to calculate the discrepancy between actual and expected final performances (Tucker, Damarin, & Messick, 1965). Expectations can be based on the group as a whole or on an outside control group. Another way is to write the contract on the basis of mean scores for the group of students.[3] Corrections for the unreliability of gain scores are possible, but they are not likely to be considered if the educators and contractors are statistically naive.

Regression effects. Probably the source of the greatest misinterpretation of the effects of remedial instruction is regression effects. Regression effects are easily overlooked but need not be; they are correctable. For any pretest score, the expected regression effect can be calculated. Regression effects make the poorest scorers look better the next time tested. Whether measurements are error-laden or error-free, meaningful or meaningless, when there is differential change between one measurement occasion and another (when there is less-than-perfect correlation), the lowest original scorers will make the greatest gains and the highest original scorers will make the least. On the average, posttest scores will, relative to their corresponding pretest scores, lie in the direction of the mean. This is the regression effect. Lord discussed this universal phenomenon and various ways to correct for it (Lord, 1963).

The demand for performance contracts has occurred where conventional instructional programs fail to develop—for a sizable number of students—minimum competence in basic skills. Given a distribution of skill test scores, the lowest-scoring students—the ones most needing assistance—are identified. It is reasonable to suppose that under unchanged instructional programs they would drop even farther behind the high-scoring students. If a retest is given, however, after any period of instruction (conventional or special) or of no instruction, these students will no longer be the poorest performers. Some of them will be replaced by others who appear to be most in need of special instruction. Instruction is not the obvious influence here—regression is. The regression effect is not due to test unreliability, but it causes some of the same misinterpretations. The contract should read that instruction will be reimbursed when gain exceeds that attributable to regression effects. The preferred evaluation design would call for control group(s) of similar students

---

[3] This would have the increased advantage of discouraging the contractor from giving preferential treatment within the project to students who are in a position to make high payoff gains.

to provide a good estimate of the progress the contract students would have made in the absence of the special instruction.

The Social Process

The hazards of specific performance testing and performance contracting are more than curricular and psychometric. Social and humanistic challenges should be raised, too. The teacher has a special opportunity and obligation to observe the influence of testing on social behavior.

Performance contracting has the unique ability to put the student in a position of administrative influence. He can make the instruction appear better or worse than it actually is by his performance on tests. Even if he is quite young, the student will know that his good work will benefit the contractor. Sooner or later he is going to know that, if he tests poorly at the beginning, he can benefit himself and the contractor through his later achievement. Bad performances are in his repertoire, and he may be more anxious to make the contractor look bad than to make himself look good. Or he may be under undue pressure to do well on the posttests. These are pupil-teacher interactions that should be watched carefully. More responsibility for school control possibly should accrue to students, but performance contracts seem a devious way to give it.

To motivate the student to learn and to make him want more contract instruction, many contractors use material or opportunity-to-play rewards. (Dorsett used such merchandise as transistor radios.) Other behavior modification strategies are common. The proponents of such strategies argue that, once behavior has been oriented to appropriate tasks, the students can gradually be shifted from extrinsic rewards to intrinsic. That they *can* be shifted is probably true; that it will happen without careful, deliberate work by the instructional staff is unlikely. It is not difficult to imagine a performance-contract situation in which the students become even less responsive to the rewards of conventional instruction.

In mid-1971, performance contracting appears to be popular with the current administration in Washington because it encourages private businesses to participate in a traditionally public responsibility. It is popular among some school administrators because it affords new access to federal funds, because it is a way to get new talent working on old problems, and because the administrator can easily blame the outside agency and the government if the contract instruction is unsuccessful. It is unpopular with the American Federation of Teachers because it reduces the control the union has over school operations, and it reduces the teacher's role as a chooser of what learning students need most. Performance contracting is popular among most instructional technologists because it is based on well-researched principles of teaching and because it enhances their role in school operations.

The accountability movement as a whole is likely to be a success or failure on such sociopolitical items. The measurement of the performance of performance contracting is an even more hazardous procedure than the measurement of student performances.

Summary

Without yielding to the temptation to undercut new efforts to provide instruction, educators should continue to be apprehensive about evaluating teaching on the basis of performance testing alone. They should know how difficult it is to represent educational goals with statements of objectives and how costly it is to provide suitable criterion testing. They should know that the common-sense interpretation of these results is frequently wrong. Still, many members of the profession think that evaluation controls are extravagant and mystical.

Performance contracting has emerged because people inside and outside the schools are dissatisfied with the instruction some children are getting. Implicit in the contracts is the expectation that available tests can measure the newly promised learning. The standardized test alone cannot measure the specific outcomes of an individual student with sufficient precision.

Bibliography

Adkins, D. C. Measurement in relation to the educational process. *Educational and Psychological Measurement,* 1958, **18**, 221-240.

Adler, A. Characteristics of the first, second, third child. *Children,* 1928, 3(5), 14, 52.

Aiken, L. R. *Psychological and educational testing.* Boston: Allyn and Bacon, Inc., 1971.

Airasian, P. W. Formative evaluation instruments: A construction and validation of tests to evaluate learning over short time periods. Unpublished doctoral dissertation, University of Chicago, 1969.

Allport, G. W. *Personality: A psychological interpretation.* New York: Holt, 1937.

Allport, G. W. The use of personal documents in psychological science. *Social Science Research Council Bulletin,* No. 49, 1942.

Alpert, D., & Bitzer, D. L. Advances in computer-based education. *Science,* 1970, **167,** 1582-1590.

Altus, W. D. Sibling order and scholastic aptitude. *American Psychologist,* 1962, **17,** 304.

Altus, W. D. Some birth-order parameters related to verbal and quantitative aptitude for 1,120 college students with one sibling. *American Psychologist,* 1963, **18**, 361.

Altus, W. D. Birth order and a brief (ten-point) measure of aptitude. *American Psychologist,* 1964, **19,** 506.

Altus, W. D. Birth order and academic primogeniture. *Journal of Personality and Social Psychology,* 1965, **2**, 872-876. (a)

Altus, W. D. Birth order and scholastic aptitude. *Journal of Consulting Psychology,* 1965, **29**, 202-205. (b)

American Council on Education: The Cooperative Test Service. *A booklet on norms.* New York: Author, 1938.

American Educational Research Association, Committee on Test Standards. *Technical recommendations for achievement tests.* Washington, D.C.: AERA, 1955.

American Institutes for Research. *Evaluative research: Strategies and methods.* Pittsburgh: American Institutes for Research, 1970.

American Psychological Association. *Technical recommendations for psychological tests and diagnostic techniques.* Washington, D.C.: Author, 1954.

American Psychological Association. *Standards for educational and psychological tests and manuals.* Washington, D.C.: Author, 1966.

Anastasi, A. The influence of specific experience upon mental organization. *Genetic Psychology Monographs,* 1936, **18**, 245-355.

Anastasi, A. The nature of psychological "traits." *Psychological Review,* 1948, **55**, 127-138.

Anastasi, A. *Psychological Testing.* New York: Macmillan, 1954, 1961, 1968.

Anastasi, A. *Differential psychology.* (3rd ed.) New York: Macmillan, 1958.

Anastasi, A. Culture-fair testing. *Educational Horizons,* 1964, **43**, 26-30.

Anastasi, A. Psychology, psychologists, and psychological testing. *American Psychologist,* 1967, **22**, 297-306.

Anastasi, A. *Psychological testing.* New York: Macmillan, 1954, 1961, 1968.

Anastasi, A., & D'Angelo, R. Y. A comparison of Negro and white preschool children in language development and Goodenough Draw-A-Man IQ. *Journal of Genetic Psychology,* 1952, **81**, 147-165.

Anastasi, A., Fuller, J. L., Scott, J. P., & Schmitt, J. R. A factor analysis of the performance of dogs on certain learning tests. *Zoologica,* 1955, **40**, 33-46.

Anderson, R. C. Comments on Professor Gagné's paper. In M. C. Wittrock & D. E. Wiley (Eds.), *The evaluation of instruction.* New York: Holt, Rinehart & Winston, 1970. Pp. 126-133.

Anderson, S. B. Estimating grade reliability. *Journal of Applied Psychology,* 1953, **37,** 461-464.

Anderson, S. B. The ETS-OEO longitudinal study of disadvantaged children. *Untangling the tangled web of education.* Princeton, N.J.: Educational Testing Service, 1969.

Andrew, D. C., & Roberts, L. H. Final evaluation report on the Texarkana dropout prevention program. Magnolia, Ark.: Region VIII. Education Service Center, July 20, 1970 (mimeo).

Apperly, F. L. A study of American Rhodes scholars. *Journal of Heredity,* 1939, **30,** 493-495.

Asch, M. J. Negative response bias and personality adjustment. *Journal of Counseling Psychology,* 1958, **5,** 206-210.

Astin, A. W. Racial considerations in admissions. In D. C. Nichols & O. Mills (Eds.), *The campus and the racial crisis.* Washington, D.C.: American Council on Education, 1970. Pp. 113-141.

Astin, A. W., & Boruch, R. E. A "Link" system for measuring confidentiality of research data in longitudinal studies. *ACE Research Reports,* 1969, **5**(3).

Astin, H. *Educational progress of disadvantaged students.* Washington, D.C.: Human Service Press, 1970.

Avakian, S. A. An investigation of trait relationships among six-year-old children. *Genetic Psychology Monographs,* 1961, **63,** 339-394.

Balinsky, B. An analysis of the mental factors of various age groups from nine to sixty. *Genetic Psychology Monographs,* 1941, **23,** 191-234.

Balma, M. J., Ghiselli, E. E., McCormick, E. J., Primoff, E. S., & Griffin, C. H. The development of processes for indirect or synthetic validity—A symposium. *Personnel Psychology,* 1959, **12,** 395-420.

Barber, T. X., *et al.* Five attempts to replicate the experimenter bias effect. *Journal of Consulting and Clinical Psychology,* 1969, **33**(1), 1-14.

Barber, T. X., & Silver, M. Fact, fiction and the experimenter bias effect. *Psychological Bulletin,* 1968, **70** (6, Pt. 2).

Barro, S. M. An approach to developing accountability measures. *Phi Delta Kappan,* 1970, **52,** 196-205.

Bass, B. M. Authoritarianism or acquiescence? *Journal of Abnormal and Social Psychology,* 1955, **51,** 616-623.

Bayles, E. R. Limitations of the Morrison unit. *Science Education,* 1934, **18,** 203-207.

Bechtoldt, H. P. Construct validity: A critique. *American Psychologist,* 1959, **14,** 619-629.

Beez, W. Influence of biased psychological reports on teacher behavior and pupil performance. *Proceedings of the 76th Annual Convention of the American Psychological Association,* 1968, **3,** 605-606.

Beggs, D. L., & Hieronymus, A. N. Uniformity of growth in the basic skills throughout the school year and during the summer. *Journal of Educational Measurement,* 1968, **5,** 91-97.

Behavioral and Social Sciences Survey Committee. *The behavioral and social sciences: Outlook and needs.* Washington, D.C.: National Academy of Sciences, 1969.

Bender, I. E. Ascendance-submission in relation to certain other factors in personality. *Journal of Abnormal and Social Psychology,* 1928, **23,** 137-143.

Bendig, A. W. The reliability of letter grades. *Educational and Psychological Measurement,* 1953, **13,** 311-321.

Berdie, R. F. Intra-individual variability and predictability. *Educational and Psychological Measurement,* 1961, **21,** 663-676.

Berne, E. The nature of intuition. *Psychiatric Quarterly*, 1949, **23**, 203-226.

Black, H. *They shall not pass*. New York: Morrow, 1963.

Black, J. D. To interested parties. Mimeographed memorandum. Stanford University Counseling and Testing Center, Nov. 6, 1970.

Block, J. *The challenge of response sets: Unconfounding meaning, acquiescence, and social desirability in the MMPI*. New York: Appleton-Century-Crofts, 1965.

Block, J. H. The effects of various levels of performance on selected cognitive, affective, and time variables. Unpublished doctoral dissertation, University of Chicago, 1970.

Bloom, B. S. Learning for mastery. UCLA CSEIP *Evaluation Comment*, 1968, **1**, No. 2 (May).

Bloom, B. S. Affective consequences of school achievement. In J. H. Block (Ed.), *Mastery learning: Theory and practice*, New York: Holt, Rinehart & Winston, 1971.

Bloom, B. S., *et al. A taxonomy of educational objectives: Handbook I. The cognitive domain.* New York: David McKay, 1956.

Bloom, B. S., Hastings, J. T., & Madaus, G. F. *Handbook of formative and summative evaluation of student learning*. New York: McGraw-Hill, 1971.

Borgen, F. H. *Research Reports of the National Merit Scholarship Corporation*, 1970, **6**, 2.

Boring, E. G. The logic of the normal law of error in mental measurement. *American Journal of Psychology*, 1920, **31**, 1-33.

Bormuth, J. *On the theory of achievement test items*. Chicago: University of Chicago Press, 1970.

Bowers, J. Factor structures and predictive validities of college ability tests for regularly admitted and disadvantaged beginning freshmen at the university of Illinois. Paper presented at the annual convention of the American Educational Research Association, Minneapolis, March, 1970.

Brickell, H. M. *Organizing New York State for educational change: A report to the state commissioner of education*. Albany, N.Y.: State Department of Education, 1962.

Bridgman, P. W. *The logic of modern physics*. New York: Macmillan, 1927.

Brim, O. G., Jr., Glass, D. C., Neulinger, J., Firestone, I. J., & Lerner, S. C. *American beliefs and attitudes about intelligence*. New York: Russell Sage Foundation, 1969.

Brim, O. G., Jr., Goslin, D. A., Glass, D. C., & Goldberg, I. *The use of standardized ability tests in American secondary schools*. New York: Russell Sage Foundation, 1964.

Brogden, H. E. On the interpretation of the correlation coefficient as a measure of predictive efficiency. *Journal of Educational Psychology*, 1946, **37**, 65-76.

Broudy, H. S. Can research escape the dogma of behavioral objectives? *School Review*, 1970, **79**(1), 43-56.

Brown, C. W., & Ghiselli, E. E. Per cent increase in proficiency resulting from use of selective devices. *Journal of Applied Psychology*, 1953, **37**, 341-344.

Brown, F. G. *Principles of educational and psychological testing*. Hinsdale, Ill.: Dryden, 1970.

Bruce, M. Factors affecting intelligence test performance of whites and Negroes in the rural South. *Archives of Psychology of New York*, 1940, No. 252.

Bunderson, C. V. Transfer functions and learning curves: The use of ability constructs in the study of human learning. *Educational Testing Service Research Bulletin*, RB-64-62, 1964.

Buros, O. K. (Ed.) *The fifth mental measurements yearbook*. Highland Park, N.J.: Gryphon Press, 1959.

Buros, O. K. *Summary of definitions, basic concepts, and formulas in the schematization of test reliability*. Highland Park, N.J.: Gryphon Press, 1963. (hectographed)

Burt, C. *The factors of the mind: An introduction to factor-analysis in psychology*. New York: Macmillan, 1941.

Burt, C. The structure of the mind: A review of the results of factor-analysis. *British Journal of educational Psychology*, 1949, **19**, 100-114, 176-199.

Burt, C. The differentiation of intellectual ability. *British Journal of Educational Psychology*, 1954, **24**, 76-90.

Campbell, D. P. The vocational interests of APA presidents. *American Psychologist,* 1965, **20,** 636-644.

Campbell, D. P. Stability of interests within an occupation over thirty years. *Journal of Applied Psychology,* 1966, **50,** 51-56.

Campbell, D. T. Recommendations for APA test standards regarding construct, trait, or discriminant validity. *American Psychologist,* 1960, **15,** 546-553.

Campbell, D. T. Reforms as experiments. *American Psychologist,* 1969, **24,** 409-429.

Campbell, D. T., & Fiske, D. W. Convergent and discriminant validation by the multi-trait-multimethod matrix. *Psychological Bulletin,* 1959, **56,** 81-105.

Campbell, N. R. *Physics, the elements.* London: Cambridge University Press, 1920.

Campbell, N. R. *An account of the principles of measurement and calculation.* London: Longmans, Green and Company, Ltd., 1928.

Campbell, N. R. *Foundations of science.* New York: Dover, 1957.

Capra, P. C., & Dittes, J. E. Birth order as a selective factor among volunteer subjects. *Journal of Abnormal and Social Psychology,* 1962, **64,** 302.

Carmichael, O. Television program of Sept. 13, 1959. Atlanta: Southern Regional Council, Dec. 15, 1959.

Carroll, J. A model for school learning. *Teachers College Record,* 1963, **64,** 723-733.

Carroll, J. B. Factors of verbal achievement. In A. Anastasi (Ed.), *Testing problems in perspective.* Washington, D.C.: American Council on Education, 1966.

Cassel, R. N., & Blum, L. P. Computer Assist Counseling (COASCON) for the prevention of delinquent behavior among teenagers and youth. Unpublished paper, Department of Educational Psychology, University of Wisconsin-Milwaukee, 1970.

Cattell, J. M. Families of American men of science, III. *Scientific Monthly,* 1917, **5,** 368-377.

Cattell, R. B. A culture-free intelligence test, I. *Journal of Educational Psychology,* 1940, **31,** 161-179.

Cattell, R. B. Some theoretical issues in adult intelligence testing. *Psychological Bulletin,* 1941, **38,** 592.

Cattell, R. B. Personality structure and measurement: I. The operational determination of trait unities. *British Journal of Psychology,* 1946, **36,** 88-103.

Cattell, R. B. *IPAT Culture-Fair Intelligence Test Scales 1, 2, & 3.* (Revised) Champaign, Ill.: Institute for Personality and Ability Testing, 1960.

Cattell, R. B. Theory of fluid and crystallized intelligence: A critical experiment. *Journal of Educational Psychology,* 1963, **54,** 1-22.

Cattell, R., Feingold, S., & Sarason, S. A culture-free intelligence test, II. *Journal of Educational Psychology,* 1941, **32,** 81-100.

Chall, J. S. *Learning to read: The great debate.* New York: McGraw-Hill, 1967.

Chant, S. N. F., & Freedman, S. S. A quantitative comparison of the nationality preferences of two groups. *Journal of Social Psychology,* 1934, **5,** 116-120.

Chauncey, H., & Dobbin, J. E. *Testing: Its place in education today.* New York: Harper & Row, 1963.

Claiborn, W. *An investigation of the relationship between teacher expectancy, teacher behavior and pupil performance.* (Doctoral dissertation, Syracuse University.) Ann Arbor, Mich.: University Microfilms, 1968, No. 69-8619.

Clark, K. B., & Plotkin, L. *The Negro student at integrated colleges.* New York: National Scholarship Service and Fund for Negro Students, 1963.

Clark, K. E. *Vocational interests of non-professional men.* Minneapolis: University of Minnesota Press, 1961.

Clark, W. W. Los Angeles Negro children. *Educational Research Bulletin, Los Angeles,* 1923, 3(2), 1-2.

Clarke, E. L. *American men of letters, their nature and nurture.* New York: Columbia University Press, 1916.

Claudy, J. C. Educational outcomes five years after high school. Paper presented at the annual meeting of the American Educational Research Association. New York, February, 1971.

Cleary, T. A. Test bias: Prediction of grades of Negro and white students in integrated colleges. *Journal of Educational Measurement,* 1968, **5,** 115-124.

Cleary, T. A., & Hilton, T. L. An investigation of item bias. *Educational and Psychological Measurement,* 1968, **28,** 61-75.

Coleman, J. S., Campbell, E. Q., Hobson, C. J., McPartland, J., Mood, A. M., Weinfeld, F. D., & York, R. L. *Equality of educational opportunities.* Washington, D.C.: U.S. Government Printing Office, 1966.

Commission on Tests. *Report of Commission on Tests: I. Righting the balance.* New York: College Entrance Examination Board, 1970.

Committee on Special Educational Projects, Cornell University. *Expanding opportunities for minority groups.* Ithaca, N.Y.: Author, no date, circa 1968 (table 2).

Comrey, A. L. An operational approach to some problems in psychological measurement. *Psychological Review,* 1950, **57,** 217-228.

Conn, L., Edwards, C., Rosenthal, R., & Crowne, D. Perception of emotion and response to teacher expectancy in elementary school children. *Psychological Reports,* 1968, **22,** 27-34.

Conrad, H. Information which should be provided by test publishers and testing agencies on the validity and use of their tests. In *Proceedings of the 1949 Invitational Conference on Testing Problems.* Princeton, N.J.: Educational Testing Service, 1950. Pp. 63-68.

Cooley, W. W., & Glaser, R. The computer and individualized instruction. *Science,* 1969, **166,** 574-582.

Cooley, W., & Lohnes, P. *Multivariate procedures for the behavioral sciences.* New York: Wiley, 1962.

Couch, A., & Keniston, K. Yeasayers and naysayers: Agreeing response set as a personality variable. *Journal of Abnormal and Social Psychology,* 1960, **60,** 151-174.

Cronbach, L. J. Coefficient alpha and the internal structure of tests. *Psychometrika,* 1951, **16,** 297-334.

Cronbach, L. J. Assessment of individual differences. In P. R. Farnsworth and Q. McNemar (Eds.), *Annual Review of Psychology,* Vol. 7. Stanford, Calif.: Annual Reviews, 1956. Pp. 173-196.

Cronbach, L. J. *Essentials of psychological testing.* New York: Harper, 1960, 1970.

Cronbach, L. J. How can instruction be adapted to invividual differences? In R. M. Gagné (Ed.), *Learning and individual differences.* Columbus, Ohio: Merrill, 1967. Pp. 23-39.

Cronbach, L. J. Validation of educational measures. In *Proceedings of the 1969 Invitational Conference on Testing Problems.* Princeton, N.J.: Educational Testing Service, 1970, Pp. 35-52. (b)

Cronbach, L. J., & Gleser, G. C. *Psychological tests and personnel decisions.* Urbana, Ill.: University of Illinois Press, 1957, 1965.

Cronbach, L. J., Gleser, G. C., Nanda, H., & Rajaratnam, N. *The dependability of behavioral measurements.* New York: Wiley, 1970.

Cronbach, L. J., & Meehl, P. E. Construct validity in psychological tests. *Psychological Bulletin,* 1955, **52,** 281-302.

Cronbach, L. J., Rajaratnam, N., & Gleser, G. C. Theory of generalizability: A liberalization of reliability theory. *British Journal of Statistical Psychology,* 1963, **16,** 137-163.

Cronbach, L. J., & Snow, R. E. *Individual differences in learning ability as a function of instructional variables.* (Final Report, USOE, contract No. OEC-4-6-061269-1217.) Stanford, Calif.: Stanford University, School of Education, 1969.

Cureton, E. E. Validity. In E. F. Lindquist (Ed.), *Educational measurement*. Washington, D.C.: American Council on Education, 1951. Pp. 621-694.

Cutten, G. B. The reconstruction of democracy. *School and Society*, 1922, **16**, 409, 479-481.

Das, R. S. Analysis of the components of reasoning in nonverbal tests and the structure of reasoning in a bilingual population. *Archiv für die gesamte Psychologie*, 1963, **115**, 217-229.

Davids, A., Joelson, M., & McArthur, C. Rorschach and TAT indices of homosexuality in overt homosexuals, neurotics, and normal males. *Journal of Abnormal and Social Psychology*, 1956, **53**, 161-172.

Dean, D. A. The relation of ordinal position to personality in young children. Unpublished master's thesis, State University of Iowa, 1947.

Dockrell, W. B. Cultural and educational influences on the differentiation of ability. In *Proceedings of the 73rd Annual Convention of the American Psychological Association*. Washington, D.C.: APA, 1965. (Summary)

Dreger, R. M., & Miller, K. S. Comparative psychological studies of Negroes and whites in the United States. *Psychological Bulletin*, 1960, **57**, 361-402.

DuBois, Ph. H. *The history of psychological testing*. Boston: Allyn and Bacon, Inc., 1970.

Duncan, O D. Ability and achievement. *Eugenics Quarterly*, 1968, **15**(1), 1-11.

Dunham, J. L., Guiltord, J. P., & Hoepfner, R. Abilities pertaining to classes and the learning of concepts. *Reports from the Psychological Laboratory, University of Southern California*, No. 39, 1966.

Dunn, J. A. The accommodation of individual differences in the development of personal programs of study. In J. C. Flanagan (Chm.), Project PLAN: A computer-supported individualized education program. Symposium presented at the meeting of the American Psychological Association, Washington, D.C., Sept., 1969.

Dye, N. W., & Very, P. S. Growth changes in factorial structure by age and sex. *Genetic Psychology Monographs*, 1968, **78**, 55-58.

Dyer, H. S. Toward objective criteria of professional accountability in the schools of New York City. *Phi Delta Kappan*, 1970, **52**, 206-211. (a)

Dyer, H. S. Performance contracting: Too simple a solution for difficult problems. *The United Teacher*, 1970 (Nov. 29), 19-22. (b)

Ebel, R. L. Estimation of the reliability of ratings. *Psychometrika*, 1951, **16**, 407-424.

Ebel, R. L. Content standard test scores. *Educational and Psychological Measurement*, 1962, **22**, 15-25.

Ebel, R. L. *Measuring educational achievement*. Englewood Cliffs, N.J.: Prentice-Hall, 1965.

Ebel, R. L. When information becomes knowledge. *Science*, 1971, **71**, 130-131.

Eckland, B. K. College dropouts who came back. *Harvard Educational Review*, 1964, **34**, 402-420. (a)

Eckland, B. K. Social class and college graduation: Some misconceptions corrected. *American Journal of Sociology*, 1964, **70**, 36-50. (b)

Educational Testing Service. *Proceedings of the Conferences on Educational Accountability*. Princeton, N.J.: Educational Testing Service, 1971.

Edwards, A. L. *The social desirability variable in personality assessment and research*. New York: Dryden, 1957.

Edwards, A. L., & Diers, C. J. Social desirability and the factorial interpretation of the MMPI. *Educational and Psychological Measurement*, 1962, **12**, 501-509.

Edwards, A. L., Diers, C. J., & Walker, J. N. Response sets and factor loadings on sixty-one personality scales. *Journal of Applied Psychology*, 1962, **46**, 220-225.

Edwards, A. L., & Heathers, L. B. The first factor of the MMPI: Social desirability or ego strength? *Journal of Consulting Psychology*, 1962, **26**, 99-100.

Eells, K., Davis, A., & Havighurst, R. J., *et al. Intelligence and cultural differences.* Chicago: University of Chicago Press, 1951.

Elashaff, J. D., & Snow, R. E. *A case study in statistical inference: Reconsideration of the Rosenthal-Jacobson data on teacher expectancy.* Technical Report No. 15, Stanford Center for Research and Development in Teaching, 1970.

Ellis, H. *A study of British genius.* Boston: Houghton Mifflin, 1926.

Englehart, M. D. A comparison of several item discrimination indices. *Journal of Educational Measurement,* 1965, **2,** 69-76.

Evans, S., & Anastasio, E. Misuse of analysis of convariance when treatment effect and covariate are confounded. *Psychological Bulletin,* 1968, **69,** 225-234.

Ferguson, A., *et al.* Quantitative estimates of sensory events. *Report of the British Association for the Advancement of Science,* 1938, **108,** 277-334.

Ferguson, G. A. On learning and human ability. *Canadian Journal of Psychology.* 1954, **8,** 95-112.

Ferguson, G. A. On transfer and the abilities of man. *Canadian Journal of Psychology,* 1956, **10,** 121-131.

Ferguson, L. W. Life insurance interest, ability and termination of employment. *Life Insurance Agency Management Association Personnel Journal,* 1958, **11,** 189-193.

Ferguson, L. W. Ability, interest, and aptitude. *Journal of Applied Psychology,* 1960, **44,** 126-131.

Ferguson, R. L. *Computer-assisted criterion-referenced testing.* Working Paper No. 49, Learning Research and Development Center, University of Pittsburgh, 1969.

Filella, J. F. Educational and sex differences in the organization of abilities in technical and academic students in Colombia, South America. *Genetic Psychology Monographs,* 1960, **61,** 115-163.

Findley, W. G. A rationale for evaluation of item discrimination statistics. *Educational and Psychological Measurement,* 1956, **16,** 175-180.

Fishman, J. A., Deutsch, M., Kogan, L., North, R., & Whiteman, M. Guidelines for testing minority group children. *Journal of Social Issues,* 1964, **20,** 129-145.

Flanagan, J. C. *Factor analysis in the study of personality.* Stanford University, Calif.: Stanford University Press, 1935.

Flanagan, J. C. A short method for selecting the best combination of test items for a particular purpose. *Psychological Bulletin,* 1936, **33,** 603-604.

Flanagan, J. C. A proposed procedure for increasing the efficiency of objective tests. *Journal of Educational Psychology,* 1937, **28,** 17-21.

Flanagan, J. C. *Scaled scores.* The Cooperative Test Service of the American Council on Education, 1939.

Flanagan, J. C. Units, scores, and norms. In E. F. Lindquist (Ed.), *Educational measurement.* Washington, D.C.: American Council on Education, 1951. Pp. 695-763.

Flanagan, J. C. *Tests of general ability: Technical report.* Chicago: Science Research Associates, 1960.

Flanagan, J. C. Program for learning in accordance with needs. *Psychology in the Schools,* 1969, **6,** 133-136.

Fleishman, E. A., & Bartlett, C. J. Human abilities. *Annual Review of Psychology,* 1969, **20,** 349-380.

Fleishman, E. A., & Fruchter, B. Factor structure and predictability of successive stages of learning Morse code. *Journal of Applied Psychology,* 1960, **44,** 97-101.

Fleishman, E. A., & Hempel, W. E., Jr. Changes in factor structure of a complex psychomotor test as a function of practice. *Psychometrika,* 1954, **19,** 239-252.

Fleishman, E. A., & Rich, S. Role of kinesthetic and spatial-visual abilities in perceptual-motor learning. *Journal of Experimental Psychology,* 1963, **66,** 6-11.

Ford, A. H. Prediction of academic success in three schools of nursing. *Journal of Applied Psychology,* 1950, **34,** 186-189.

Frederiksen, C. H. Abilities, transfer, and information retrieval in verbal learning. *Multivariate Behavioral Research Monographs,* No. 69-2, 1969.

Freeberg, N. E. Assessment of disadvantaged adolescents: A different approach to research and evaluation measures. *Journal of Educational Psychology,* 1970, **61,** 229-240.

French, J. W. The relationship of problem-solving styles to the factor composition of tests. *Educational and Psychological Measurement,* 1965, **25,** 9-28.

Fulkerson, S. C. Individual differences in response validity. *Journal of Clinical Psychology,* 1959, **15,** 169-173.

Gage, F. H. An experimental investigation of the measurability of auditory sensation. *Proceedings of the Royal Society of London* (Series B), 1934, **116,** 103-122.

Gage, N. L., Leavitt, G. S., & Stone, G. C. The psychological meaning of acquiescence set for authoritarianism. *Journal of Abnormal and Social Psychology,* 1957, **55,** 98-103.

Gagné, R. *The conditions of learning.* New York: Holt, Rinehart & Winston, 1965.

Games, P. A. A factorial analysis of verbal learning tasks. *Journal of Experimental Psychology,* 1962, **63,** 1-11.

Gardner, E. F. Comments on selected scaling techniques with a description of a new type of scale. *Journal of Clinical Psychology,* 1950, **6,** 38-42.

Gardner, E. F. The importance of reference groups in scaling procedure. *Proceedings of the 1952 Invitational Conference on Testing Problems.* Princeton, N.J.: Educational Testing Service, 1953. Pp. 13-21.

Gardner, J. *Excellence. Can we be equal and excellent too?* New York: Harper, 1961.

Garrett, H. E. A developmental theory of intelligence. *American Psychologist,* 1946, **1,** 372-378.

Garrett, H. E., & Schneck, M. R. *Psychological tests, methods, and results.* New York: Harper's, 1933.

Gates, A. I., & MacGinitie, W. H. *Technical manual for the Gates-MacGinitie Reading Tests.* New York: Teachers College Press, Columbia University, 1965.

Getzels, J. W., & Jackson, P. W. *Creativity and intelligence: Explorations with gifted students.* New York: Wiley, 1962.

Ghiselli, E. E. Differentiation of individuals in terms of their predictability. *Journal of Applied Psychology,* 1956, **40,** 374-377.

Ghiselli, E. E. The prediction of predictability. *Educational and Psychological Measurement,* 1960, **20,** 3-8. (a)

Ghiselli, E. E. Differentiation of tests in terms of the accuracy with which they predict for a given individual. *Educational and Psychological Measurement,* 1960, **20,** 675-684. (b)

Ghiselli, E. E. Moderating effects and differential reliability and validity. *Journal of Applied Psychology,* 1963, **47,** 81-86.

Gilliland, A. R. Socioeconomic status and race as factors in infant intelligence test scores. *Child Development,* 1951, **22,** 271-273.

Gini, C. Superiority of the eldest. *Journal of Heredity,* 1915, **6,** 37-39.

Girshick, M. A. An elementary survey of statistical decision theory. *Review of Educational Research,* 1954, **24,** 448-466.

Glaser, R. Instructional technology and the measurement of learning outcomes. *American Psychologist,* 1963, **18,** 519-521.

Glaser, R., & Nitko, A. J. *Measurement in learning and instruction.* Pittsburgh: University of Pittsburgh, Research and Development Center, 1970.

Glaser, R. & Nitko, A. J. Measurement in learning and instruction. In R. L. Thorndike (Ed.), *Educational measurement.* Washington, D.C.: American Council on Education, 1971. Pp. 625-670.

Gleser, G. C. Projective methodologies. In P. B. Farnsworth (Ed.), *Annual Review of Psychology.* Vol. 14. Palo Alto, Calif.: Annual Reviews, 1963. Pp. 391-422.

Goodenough, F. L. *Mental testing.* New York: Rinehart, 1949.

Goslin, D. A. *Teachers and testing.* New York: Russell Sage Foundation, 1967.

Goslin, D. A. Ethical and legal aspects of the collection and use of educational information. Paper presented at the Invitational Conference on Testing Problems, New York, October, 1970.

Goslin, D. A., Edstein, R. R., & Hallock, B. *Testing in elementary schools.* New York: Russell Sage Foundation, 1965.

Gough, H. G. Clinical versus statistical prediction in psychology. In L. Postman (Ed.), *Psychology in the making.* New York: Knopf, 1962. Pp. 526-584.

Green, R. F., & Berkowitz, B. Changes in intellect with age: II. Factorial analysis of Wechsler-Bellevue scores. *Journal of Genetic Psychology,* 1964, **104**, 3-18.

Green, R. L., & Farquhar, W. W. Negro academic motivation and scholastic achievement. *Journal of educational Psychology,* 1965, **56**, 241-243.

Greene, E. B. An analysis of random and systematic changes with practice. *Psychometrika,* 1943, **8**, 37-52.

Gross, M. L. *The brain watchers.* New York: Random House, 1962.

Guertin, W. H., Rabin, A. I., Frank, G. H., & Ladd, C. E. Research with the Wechsler intelligence scales for adults: 1955-60. *Psychological Bulletin,* 1962, **59**, 1-26.

Guilford, J. P. The structure of intellect. *Psychological Bulletin,* 1956, **53**, 267-293.

Guilford, J. P. Three faces of intellect. *American Psychologist,* 1959, **14**, 469-479.

Guilford, J. P. Zero intercorrelations among tests of intellectual abilities. *Psychological Bulletin,* 1964, **61**, 401-404.

Guilford, J. P. *The nature of human intelligence.* New York: McGraw-Hill, 1967.

Guilford, J. P., & Hoepfner, R. Sixteen divergent-production abilities at the ninth-grade level. *Multivariate Behavior Research,* 1966, **1**, 43-66.

Guilford, J. P., & Lacey, J. I. (Eds.) *Printed Classification Tests.* Washington, D.C.: Government Printing Office, 1947.

Gulliksen, H. *Theory of mental tests.* New York: Wiley, 1950.

Guthrie, G. M. Structure of abilities in a non-Western culture. *Journal of Educational Psychology,* 1963, **54**, 94-103.

Guttman, R., & Guttman, L. Cross-cultural stability of an intercorrelation pattern of abilities: A possible test for a biological basis. *Human Biology,* 1963, **35**, 53-60.

Hall, C. S., & Lindzey, G. *Theories of personality.* New York: Wiley, 1957, 1970.

Harlow, H. F. The formation of learning sets. *Psychological Review,* 1949, **56**, 51-65.

Harlow, H. F. Learning set and error factor theory. In S. Koch (Ed.), *Psychology: A study of a science,* Vol. 2. New York: McGraw-Hill, 1960.

Harman, H. H. *Modern factor analysis.* Chicago: University of Chicago Press, 1967.

Harrington, A. *Life in the crystal palace.* New York: Knopf, 1959.

Hastings, T., Runkel, P. J., & Damrin, D. E. *Effects on use of tests by teachers trained in a summer institute.* Cooperative Research Project No. 702. Urbana, Ill.: Research Project No. 702. Urbana, Ill.: Bureau of Educational Research, College of Education, University of Illinois, 1961.

Heinonon, V. A factor analytic study of transfer of training. *Scandinavian Journal of Psychology,* 1962, **3**, 177-188.

Herrnstein, R. I.Q. *The Atlantic,* 1971, **228**(3), 43-58, 63-64.

Hieronymus, A. N., & Lindquist, E. F. *Teacher's guide for administration, interpretation, and use: Iowa Tests of Basic Skills.* Boston: Houghton Mifflin, 1971.

Hirsch, J., & Tryon, R. C. Mass screening and reliable individual measurement in the experimental behavior genetics of lower organisms. *Psychological Bulletin,* 1956, **53**, 402-410.

Hively, W. II., Patterson, H. L., & Page, S. H. A "universe-defined" system of arithmetic achievement tests. *Journal of Educational Measurement,* 1968, **5**, 126-133.

Hoffmann, B. *The tyranny of testing.* New York: Crowell-Collier, 1962.

Holt, R. R. Clinical and statistical prediction: A reformulation and some new data. *Journal of Abnormal and Social Psychology*, 1958, **56**, 1-12.

Holtzman, W. H. Statistical models for the study of change in the single case. In C. Harris (Ed.), *Problems in measuring change*. Madison: University of Wisconsin Press, 1963. (a)

Holtzman, W. H. The robot personality—static or dynamic? In S. S. Tomkins & S. Messick (Eds.), *Computer simulation of personality*. New York: Wiley, 1963. (b)

Holtzman, W. H. Cross-cultural studies in psychology. *International Journal of Psychology*, 1968, **3**, 83-91.

Holtzman, W. H. Computers in education. In W. H. Holtzman (Ed.), *Computer-assisted instruction, testing, and guidance*. New York: Harper & Row, 1970.

Holtzman, W. H. The changing world of mental measurement and its social significance. *American Psychologist*, 1971, **26**, 546-553.

Holtzman, W. H., Diaz-Guerrero, R., Swartz, J. D., & Lara Tapia, L. Cross-cultural longitudinal research on child development: Studies of American and Mexican school children. In J. P. Hill (Ed.), *Minnesota Symposia on Child Psychology*, Vol. 2. Minneapolis: University of Minnesota Press, 1968.

Holtzman, W. H., Thorpe, J. S., Swartz, J. D., & Herron, E. W. *Inkblot perception and personality*. Austin: The University of Texas Press, 1961.

Horst, P. A generalized expression for the reliability of measures. *Psychometrika*, 1949, **14**, 21-31.

Humphreys, L. G. Racial differences: Dilemma of college admissions. *Science*, 1969, **166**, 167.

Hunt, J. McV. *Intelligence and experience*. New York: Ronald Press, 1961.

Huntington, E. *Season of birth*. New York: Wiley, 1938.

Husek, T. R., & Sirotnik, K. *Item sampling in educational research*. (Occasional Rep. No. 2) Los Angeles: University of California at Los Angeles, Center for the Study of Evaluation of Instructional Programs, 1967.

Innes, T. C. Measurement, accountability, and humaneness. *Measurement and Evaluation in Guidance*, 1971, **4**, 90-98.

Irvine, S. H. Factor analysis of African abilities and attainments: Constructs across cultures. *Psychological Bulletin*, 1969, **71**, 20-32.

Jackson, D. N., & Messick, S. Content and style in personality assessment. *Psychological Bulletin*, 1958, **55**, 243-252.

Jackson, D. N., & Messick, S. (Eds.) *Problems in human assessment*. New York: McGraw-Hill, 1967.

Jackson, R. *Developing criterion-referenced tests*. Princeton, N.J.: ERIC Clearing House on Tests, Measurement, and Evaluation. Educational Testing Service, June, 1970.

Jarett, R. F. Percent increase in output of selected personnel as an index of test efficiency. *Journal of Applied Psychology*, 1948, **32**, 135-145.

Jenkins, M. D. *The Morgan State College Program—An adventure in higher education*. Baltimore, Md.: Morgan State College Press, 1964.

Jensen, A. R. How much can we boost I.Q. and scholastic achievement? *Harvard Educational Review*, 1969, **39**, 1-123.

Jessor, R., & Hammond, K. R. Construct validity and Taylor anxiety scale. *Psychological Bulletin*, 1957, **54**, 161-170.

Johnson, H. M. Pseudo-mathematics in the mental and social sciences. *American Journal of Psychology*, 1936, **48**, 342-351.

Jones, H. E. The environment and mental development. In L. Carmichael (Ed.), *Manual of child psychology*. New York: Wiley, 1954.

Joselyn, E. G. Performance contracting: What it's all about. Paper presented at the Truth and Soul in Teaching Conference of the American Federation of Teachers, Chicago, Janaury, 1971.

Joseph, G., & Newsom, B. *Cornell Alumni News*, 1968, **70**, No. 8 (June), p. 10.

Karmel, L. J. *Measurement and evaluation in the schools.* Toronto: Macmillan, 1970.

Katz, M. R. *Selecting an achievement test.* E. & A. Series, No. 3 (p. 26). Princeton, N.J.: Educational Testing Service, 1958.

Kelley, T. L. *Interpretation of educational measurements.* New York: World Book Company, 1927.

Kelley, T. L. The selection of upper and lower groups for the validation of test items. *Journal of Educational Psychology,* 1939, **30**, 17-24.

Kendrick, S. A. The coming segregation of our selective colleges. *College Board Review,* No. 66 (Winter 1967-68), pp. 6-13.

Kenny, D. T. Transcendence indices, extent of personality factors in fantasy responses, and the ambiguity of TAT cards. *Journal of Consulting Psychology,* 1954, **18**, 345-348.

Kenny, D. T. A theoretical and research reappraisal of stimulus factors in the TAT. In J. Kagan and G. Lesser (Eds.), *Contemporary issues in thematic apperceptive methods.* Springfield, Ill.: Thomas, 1961. Pp. 288-310.

Kim, H., *et al. A study of the Bloom strategies for mastery learning.* Seoul: Korean Institute for Research in the Behavioral Sciences, 1969. (In Korean)

Klein, S. Evaluating tests in terms of the information they provide. *UCLA Evaluation Comment,* 1970, **2**, 1-6.

Klineberg, O. *Negro intelligence and selective migration.* New York: Columbia University Press, 1935.

Klineberg, O. (Ed.) *Characteristics of the American Negro.* New York: Harper, 1944.

Knobloch, H., & Pasamanick, B. Further observations of the behavioral development of Negro children. *Journal of Genetic Psychology,* 1953, **83**, 137-157.

Koch, H. L. The relation of "primary mental abilities" in five- and six-year-olds to sex of child and characteristics of his siblings. *Child Development,* 1954, **25**, 209-223.

Koch, H. L. Sissiness and tomboyishness in relation to sibling characteristics. *Journal of Genetic Psychology,* 1956, **88**, 231-244.

Kohfeld, D. L. The prediction of perceptual-motor learning from independent verbal and motor measures. *Psychonomic Science,* 1966, **4**, 413-414.

Kostlan, A. A method for the empirical study of psychodiagnosis. *Journal of Consulting Psychology,* 1954, **18**, 83-88.

Kreidt, P. H. Vocational interests of psychologists. *Journal of Applied Psychology,* 1949, **33**, 482-488.

Kriedt, P. H., Stone, C. H., & Paterson, D. G. Vocational interests of industrial relations personnel. *Journal of Applied Psychology,* 1952, **36**, 174-179.

Kuder, G. F. Identifying the faker. *Personnel Psychology,* 1950, **3**, 156-167.

Kuder, G. F. *Preference Record, Occupational Form D, manual.* Chicago: Science Research Associates, 1956. (a)

Kuder, G. F. *Preference Record, Occupational Form D, research handbook.* Chicago: Science Research Associates, 1956. (b)

Kuder, G. F. A comparative study of some methods of developing occupational keys. *Educational and Psychological Measurement,* 1957, **17**, 105-114.

Kuder, G., & Richardson, M. W. The theory of the estimation of test reliability. *Psychometrika,* 1937, **2**, 151-160.

Lasko, J. R. Parent behavior toward first and second children. *Genetic Psychology Monographs,* 1954, **49**, 97-137.

Lawshe, C. H., & Steinberg, M. D. Studies in synthetic validity. 1. An exploratory investigation of clerical jobs. *Personnel Psychology,* 1955, **8**, 291-301.

Lee, E. S. Negro intelligence and selective migration: A Philadelphia test of Klineberg's hypothesis. *American Sociological Review,* 1951, **61**, 227-233.

Lennon, R. T. Accountability and performance contracting. Invited address to the American Educational Research Association, New York City, 1971.

Lesser, G. S., Fifer, G., & Clock, D. H. Mental abilities of children from different social-class and cultural groups. *Monographs of the Society for Research in Child Development,* 1965, **30**(4), 1-115.

Lienert, G. A. *Belastung und Regression: Versuch einer Theorie der systematischen Beeintrachtigung der intellektuellen Leisungs-fähigkeit.* Meisenheim am Glan: Hain, 1964.

Lienert, G. A., & Crott, H. W. Studies on the factor structure of intelligence in children, adolescents, and adults. *Vita Humana,* 1964, **7**, 147-163.

Lindgren, H. C. College grades—success in life. *Science,* 1971, **171**, 232, 234.

Lindquist, E. F. *The impact of machines on educational measurement.* Bloomington, Ind.: Phi Delta Kappa International, 1968.

Lindsey, J. M. *The factorial organization of intelligence in children as related to the variables of age, sex, and subculture.* (Doctoral dissertation, University of Georgia) Ann Arbor, Mich.: University Microfilms, 1966. No. 67-3567.

Lindvall, C. M., & Bolvin, J. O. Programmed instruction in the schools: An application of programming principles in "Individually Prescribed Instruction." In P. Lange (Ed.), *Programmed instruction.* 66th Yearbook, Part II. Chicago: National Society for the Study of Education, 1967. Pp. 217-254.

Lindzey, G. Thematic Apperception Test: Interpretive assumptions and related empirical evidence. *Psychological Bulletin,* 1952, **49**, 1-25.

Lindzey, G. *Projective techniques and cross-cultural research.* New York: Appleton-Century-Crofts, 1961.

Lindzey, G., Bradford, J., Tejessy, C., & Davids, A. Thematic Apperception Test: An interpretive lexicon for clinician and investigator. *Journal of Clinical Psychology, Monograph Supplement,* 1959, No. 12.

Lindzey, G., & Newburg, A. S. Thematic Apperception Test: A tentative appraisal of some "signs" of anxiety. *Journal of Consulting Psychology,* 1954, **18**, 389-395.

Lindzey, G., & Silverman, M. Thematic Apperception Test: Techniques of group administration, sex differences and the role of verbal productivity. *Journal of Personality,* 1959, **27**, 311-323.

Lindzey, G., & Tejessy, C. Thematic Apperception Test: Indices of aggression in relation to measures of overt and covert behavior. *American Journal of Orthopsychiatry,* 1956, **26**, 557-576.

Lindzey, G., Tejessy, C., & Zamansky, H. Thematic Apperception Test: An empirical examination of some indices of homosexuality. *Journal of Abnormal and Social Psychology,* 1958, **57**, 67-75.

Lippmann, W. The mental age of Americans. *New Republic,* Oct. 25, 1922, 412, 415.

Loehlin, J. C. A computer program that simulates personality. In Tomkins, S. S., & Messick, S. (Eds.), *Computer simulation of personality.* New York: Wiley, 1963.

Loevinger, J. Objective tests as instruments of psychological theory. *Psychological Reports,* 1957, **3**, 635-694.

Loevinger, J. A theory of test response. *Proceedings of the 1958 Invitational Conference on Testing Problems.* Princeton, N.J.: Educational Testing Service, 1959. Pp. 36-47.

Loevinger, J. Person and population as psychometric concepts. Presidential address to Division 5, American Psychological Association, September, 1963.

Loevinger, J., & Ossorio, A. G. Evaluation of therapy by self-report: A paradox. *Journal of Abnormal and Social Psychology,* 1959, **58**, 392-394.

Lord, F. M. Elementary models for measuring change. In C. Harris (Ed.), *Problems in measuring change.* Madison: University of Wisconsin Press, 1963. Pp. 21-38.

Lord, F. M. Some test theory for tailored testing. In W. H. Holtzman (Ed.), *Computer-assisted instruction, testing, and guidance.* New York: Harper & Row, 1970.

Lord, F. M., & Novick, M. *Statistical theories of mental test scores.* Reading, Mass.: Addison-Wesley, 1968.

Ludlow, H. G. Some recent research on the Davis-Eells Games. *School and Society,* 1956, **84**, 146-148.

Lykken, D. T. A method of actuarial pattern analysis. *Psychological Bulletin,* 1956, **53,** 102-107.

Lykken, D. T., & Rose, R. Psychological prediction from actuarial tables. *Journal of Clinical Psychology,* 1963, **19,** 139-151.

MacKinney, A. C. The assessment of performance change: An inductive example. *Organizational Behavior and Human Performance,* 1967, **2,** 56-72.

Manley, M. B. A factor-analytic study of three types of concept attainment tasks. *Educational Testing Service Research Bulletin,* RB-65-31, 1965.

Masling, J. The influence of situational and interpersonal variables in projective testing. *Psychological Bulletin,* 1960, **57,** 65-85.

Matarazzo, J. D., Allen, B. V., Saslow, G., & Wiens, A. N. Characteristics of successful policemen and firemen applicants. *Journal of Applied Psychology,* 1964, **48,** 123-133.

McArthur, C. Clinical versus actuarial prediction. In *Proceedings of the 1955 Invitational Conference on Testing Problems.* Princeton, N.J.: Educational Testing Service, 1956. Pp. 99-106.

McArthur, R. T., & Elley, W. B. The reduction of socio-economic bias in intelligence testing. *British Journal of Educational Psychology,* 1963, **33,** 107-119.

McClelland, D. C. *The achieving society.* New York: Van Nostrand, 1961. p. 345.

McCornack, R. L. Vocational interests of male and female social workers. *Journal of Applied Psychology,* 1956, **40,** 11-13.

McGhan, B. R. Accountability as a negative reinforcer. *American Teacher,* 1970, **54,** 13 (Nov.).

McGraw, M. B. A comparative study of a group of southern white and Negro infants. *Genetic Psychology Monographs,* 1931, **10,** 1-105.

McGurk, F. C. J. *Comparison of the performance of Negro and white high school seniors on cultural and non-cultural psychological test questions.* Washington, D.C.: Catholic University of America Press, 1951.

McNemar, Q. Lost: Our intelligence? Why? *American Psychologist,* 1964, **19,** 871-882.

McPartland, J. *Johns Hopkins Magazine,* 1970, **21,** No. 20 (April).

Meehl, P. E. *Clinical versus statistical prediction: A theoretical analysis and a review of the evidence.* Minneapolis: University of Minnesota Press, 1954.

Meehl, P. E. Clinical versus actuarial prediction. In *Proceedings of the 1955 Invitational Conference on Testing Problems.* Princeton, N.J.: Educational Testing Service, 1956. Pp. 136-141.

Meehl, P. E. When shall we use our heads instead of the formula? *Journal of Counseling Psychology,* 1957, **4,** 268-273.

Meehl, P. E. A comparison of clinicians with five statistical methods of identifying psychotic MMPI profiles. *Journal of Counseling Psychology,* 1959, **6,** 102-109.

Meehl, P. E., & Rosen, A. Antecedent probability and the efficiency of psychometric signs, patterns, or cutting scores. *Psychological Bulletin,* 1955, **52,** 194-216.

Mefferd, R. B., Jr., Moran, L. J., & Kimble, J. P., Jr. Chlorpromazine-induced changes in blood constituents in schizophrenia. *Transactions of the Fourth Research Conference on Chemotherapy and Psychiatry.* Washington, D.C.: Veterans Administration, 1960. Pp. 241-245.

Mehrens, W. A., & Ebel, R. L. (Eds.) *Principles of educational and psychological measurement.* Chicago: Rand McNally, 1967.

Melametsa, L. The influence of training on the level of test performance and the factor structure of intelligence tests. *Scandinavian Journal of Psychology,* 1965, **6,** 19-25.

Merwin, J. C., & Womer, F. B. Evaluation in assessing the progress of education to provide bases of public understanding and public policy. In R. W. Tyler (Ed.), *Educational evaluation: New roles, new means.* 68th Yearbook, Part II. Chicago: National Society for the Study of Education, 1969. Pp. 305-334.

Mischel, W. *Personality and assessment.* New York: Wiley, 1968.

Mitchell, J. V., Jr. A comparison of the factorial structure of cognitive functions for a high and low status group. *Journal of Educational Psychology*, 1956, **47**, 397-414.

Moore, B. M., & Holtzman, W. H. *Tomorrow's parents*. Austin: University of Texas Press, 1965.

Morrison, H. C. *The practice of teaching in the secondary school*. Chicago: University of Chicago Press, 1926.

Mukherjee, B. N. The factorial structure of aptitude tests at successive grade levels. *British Journal of Statistical Psychology*, 1962, **15**, 59-65.

Murray, H. A. *Explorations in personality*. New York: Oxford University Press, 1938.

Murray, H. A., *et al. Assessment of man*. New York: Rinehart, 1948.

Myers, C. E., Orpet, R. E., Attwell, A. A., & Dingman, H. F. Primary mental abilities at mental age six. *Monographs of the Society for Research in Child Development*, 1962, **27**, No. 1.

Nicholson, E. *Final report* (to the Ford Foundation) *of the study of success and admission criteria for potentially successful risks*. Brown University, 1970.

Novick, M. R., *et al. Applications of Bayesian methods to the prediction of educational performance*. ACT Research Report No. 42. Iowa City: The American College Testing Program, 1971.

Nunnally, J. C. *Introduction to psychological measurement*. New York: McGraw-Hill, 1970.

Oden, M. H. The fulfillment of promise: 40-year follow-up of the Terman gifted group. *Genetic Psychology Monographs*, 1968, **77**, No. 1, 3-93.

Osborne, R. T., & Lindsey, J. M. A longitudinal investigation of change in the factorial composition of intelligence with age in young children. *Journal of Genetic Psychology*, 1967, **110**, 49-58.

Owen, J. D. *Towards a more consistent socially relevant college scholarships policy*. Report No. 61 of the Center for Social Organization of Schools, Johns Hopkins University, Baltimore, Md., 1970.

Pasamanick, B. A comparative study of the educational development of Negro infants. *Journal of Genetic Psychology*, 1946, **69**, 3-44.

Pasamanick, B., & Knobloch, H. Early language behavior in Negro children and the testing of intelligence. *Journal of Abnormal and Social Psychology*, 1955, **50**, 401-402.

Pearson, J. S., & Swenson, W. M. *A user's guide to the Mayo Clinic automated MMPI program*. New York: The Psychological Corporation, 1967.

Peck, R., & Diaz-Guerrero, R. Two core-culture patterns and the diffusion of values across their border. *Proceedings of the VIIth Inter-American Congress of Psychology*. Mexico City: Sociedad Interamericana de Psicologia, 1963.

Popham, W. J. (Ed.) *Criterion-referenced measurement*. Englewood Cliffs, N.J.: Educational Technology Publications, 1971.

Popham, W. J., & Husek, T. R. Implications of criterion-referenced measurement. *Journal of Educational Measurement*, 1969, **6**, 1-9.

Primoff, E. S. The J-coefficient approach to jobs and tests. *Personnel Administration*, 1957, **20**, 34-40.

Quereshi, M. Y. Patterns of psycholinguistic development during early and middle childhood. *Educational and Psychological Measurement*, 1967, **27**, 353-365.

Reese, T. W. The application of the theory of physical measurement to the measurement of psychological magnitudes, with three experimental examples. *Psychological Monographs*, 1943, **15**, No. 3.

Richards, J. M. Can computers write college admissions tests? *Journal of Applied Psychology*, 1967, **51**, 211-215.

Richardson, M. W. The relation between the difficulty and the differential validity of a test. *Psychometrika*, 1936, **1**, 33-49.

Rodd, W. G. A cross-cultural study of Taiwan's schools. *Journal of Social Psychology*, 1959, **50**, 3-36.

Roe, A. A psychological study of eminent psychologists and anthropologists, and a comparison with biological and physical scientists. *Psychological Monographs*, 1953, **67**, No. 2, 1-55.

Rosenthal, R. The effect of the experimenter on the results of psychological research. In B. Maher (Ed.), *Progress in experimental personality research*. I. New York: Academic Press, 1964.

Rosenthal, R. *Experimenter effects in behavioral research*. New York: Appleton-Century-Crofts, 1966.

Rosenthal, R. Teacher expectation and pupil competence: Studies in the social psychology of self-fulfilling prophecies. Paper presented at the meeting of the American Association for the Advancement of Science, New York, Dec., 1967.

Rosenthal, R. Interpersonal expectations: Effects of the experimenter's hypothesis. In R. Rosenthal & R. L. Rosnow (Eds.), *Artifact in behavioral research*. New York: Academic Press, 1969.

Rosenthal, R., & Jacobson, L. *Pygmalion in the classroom*. New York: Holt, Rinehart & Winston, 1968.

Ruggles, R. How a data bank might operate. *Think*, 1969, **35**(3) 22-23.

Sabine, G. A. Michigan State's search for more Negro students. *College Board Review*, 1968, No. 69 (Fall), pp. 11-14.

Sarbin, T. R. Clinical psychology—art or science? *Psychometrika*, 1941, **6**, 391-400.

Sarbin, T. R. A contribution to the study of actuarial and individual methods of prediction. *American Journal of Sociology*, 1942, **48**, 593-602.

Saunders, D. R. Moderator variables in prediction. *Educational and Psychological Measurement*, 1956, **16**, 209-222.

Schachter, S. *The psychology of affiliation*. Stanford, Calif.: Stanford University Press, 1959.

Schachter, S. Birth order, eminence and higher education. *American Sociological Review*, 1963, **28**, 757-768.

Schachter, S. Birth order and sociometric choice. *Journal of Abnormal and Social Psychology*, 1964, **68**, 453-458.

Schooler, C. Birth order and schizophrenia. *Archives of General Psychiatry*, 1961, **4**, 91-97.

Schooler, C. Birth order and hospitalization for schizophrenia. *Journal of Abnormal and Social Psychology*, 1964, **69**, 574-579.

Sciara, F. F., & Jantz, R. K. *Accountability In American education*. Boston: Allyn and Bacon, Inc., 1972.

Sears, R. R., Maccoby, E., & Levin, H. *Patterns of child rearing*. Evanston, Ill.: Row Peterson, 1957. p. 418.

Segel, D. Intellectual abilities in the adolescent period. *Bulletin No. 6*, United States Office of Education, 1948.

Shaffer, L. Information which should be provided by test publishers and testing agencies on the validity and use of their tests. Personality tests. In *Proceedings of the 1949 Invitational Conference on Testing Problems*. Princeton, N.J.: Educational Testing Service, 1950.

Shames, M., & Adair, J. Experimenter bias as a function of the type and structure of the task. Paper presented at the meeting of the Canadian Psychological Association, Ottawa, May, 1967.

Sherman, M., & Key, C. B. The intelligence of isolated mountain children. *Child Development,* 1932, **3,** 279-290.

Shuey, A. M. *The testing of Negro intelligence.* Lynchburgh, Va.: J. P. Bell, 1958.

Sines, L. K. The relative contribution of four kinds of data to accuracy in personality assessment. *Journal of Consulting Psychology,* 1959, **23,** 483-492.

Sizer, T. R. Social change and the uses of educational testing: An historical view. Paper presented at the Invitational Conference on Testing Problems, New York, October, 1970.

Smith, B. O. *Logical aspects of educational measurement.* New York: Columbia University Press, 1938.

Somerville, B. Can selective colleges accommodate the disadvantaged? *College Board Review,* 1967, No. 65 (Fall), p. 5.

Sowell, T. Colleges are skipping over competent blacks to admit "authentic" ghetto types. *New York Times Magazine,* Dec. 13, 1970, pp. 36-52.

Spearman, C. "General intelligence" objectively determined and measured. *American Journal of Psychology,* 1904, **15,** 201-293.

Spearman, C. *The abilities of man.* New York: Macmillan, 1927.

Stake, R. E. Testing hazards in performance contracting. *Phi Delta Kappan,* 1971, **53,** 583-589.

Stallings, F. H. *Atlanta and Washington: Racial differences in academic achievement.* (Report No. L-16) Atlanta: Southern Regional Council, Feb., 1960.

Stanley, J. C. Predicting occupational success. *Science,* 1968, **160,** 139.

Stanley, J. C. Plotting ANOVA interactions for ease of visual interpretation. *Educational and Psychological Measurement,* 1969, **29,** 793-797.

Stanley, J. C., & Porter, A. C. Correlation of Scholastic Aptitude Test scores with college grades for Negroes versus whites. *Journal of Educational Measurement,* 1967, **4,** 199-218.

Stanley, J. C., & Wang, M. D. Weighting test items and test-item options: An overview of the analytical and empirical literature. *Educational and Psychological Measurement,* 1970, **30,** 21-35.

Starch, D., & Elliott, E. C. Reliability of grading high school work in English. *School Review,* 1912, **20,** 442-457.

Stewart, M. *The success of the first born child.* London: Workers Educational Association, 1962.

Stodolsky, S. S., & Lesser, G. S. Learning patterns in the disadvantaged. *Harvard Educational Review,* 1967, **37,** 546-593.

Strong, E. K., Jr. Vocational interests of accountants. *Journal of Applied Psychology,* 1949, **33,** 474-481.

Strong, E. K., Jr. *Vocational interests 18 years after college.* Minneapolis: University of Minnesota Press, 1955.

Strong, E. K., Jr., & Tucker, A. C. The use of vocational interest scales in planning a medical career. *Psychological Monographs,* 1952, 66(9), 1-61.

Sutherland, T. *The effect of school departmentalization on the organization of certain mental abilities.* (Doctoral dissertation, University of Kentucky) Ann Arbor, Mich.: University Microfilms, 1960. No. 60-708.

Tanser, H. A. *The settlement of Negroes in Kent County, Ontario, and a study of the mental capacity of their descendants.* Chatham, Ont.: Shepherd, 1939.

Taylor, H. C., & Russell, J. T. The relationship of validity coefficients to the practical effectiveness of tests in selection: Discussion and tables. *Journal of Applied Psychology,* 1939, **23,** 565-578.

Terman, L. M. Genetic studies of genius. Vol. 1. *The mental and physical traits of a thousand gifted children.* Stanford, Calif.: Stanford University Press, 1925, p. 121.

Terman, L. M. *The gifted group at mid-life.* Stanford, Calif.: Stanford University Press, 1959.

Terman, L. M., & Oden, M. H. The gifted child grows up. *Genetic studies of genius,* IV. Stanford, Calif.: Stanford University Press, 1947.

Tetlow, W. L., Jr. The official weekly record for Cornell University. *Cornell Chronicle,* 1969, **1** (Oct. 16), 6.

Thomas, C. L., & Stanley, J. C. Effectiveness of high school grades for predicting college grades of black students: A review and discussion. *Journal of Educational Measurement,* 1969, **6,** 203-215.

Thomas, L. G. Mental tests as instruments of science. *Psychological Monographs,* 1942, **54,** No. 3, 1-87.

Thomson, G. H. A hierarchy without a general factor. *British Journal of Psychology,* 1916, **8,** 271-281.

Thomson, G. H. *The factorial analysis of human ability.* (3rd ed.) Boston: Houghton Mifflin, 1948.

Thorndike, E. L. Intelligence and its uses. *Harper's Magazine,* 1920, **140,** 227-235.

Thorndike, R. L. Some methodological issues in the study of creativity. In *Proceedings of the 1962 Invitational Conference on Testing Problems.* Princeton, N.J.: Educational Testing Service, 1963, Pp. 40-54.

Thorndike, R. L. Review of *Pygmalion in the Classroom. American Educational Research Journal,* 1968, **5,** 709-711.

Thorndike, R. L. Educational measurement in the seventies. In R. L. Thorndike (Ed.), *Educational measurement.* (2nd ed.) Washington, D.C.: American Council on Education, 1970. Chapt. 1.

Thorndike, R. L., & Hagan, E. *Measurement and evaluation in psychology and education.* (3rd ed.) New York: Wiley, 1969.

Thrush, R. S., & King, P. T. Strong Vocational Interest Blank profiles for third year medical students. *Testing and Counseling Service Report,* University of Missouri, 1964. No. 18.

Thurstone, L. L. *The vectors of mind.* Chicago: University of Chicago Press, 1935.

Thurstone, L. L. Primary mental abilities. *Psychometric Monographs,* 1938, No. 1.

Thurstone, L. L. Current issues in factor analysis. *Psychological Bulletin,* 1940, **37,** 189-236.

Tryon, R. C. A theory of psychological components—an alternative to "mathematical factors." *Psychological Review,* 1935, **42,** 425-454.

Tryon, R. C. *Cluster analysis.* Ann Arbor, Mich.: Edwards, 1939.

Tryon, R. C. Genetic differences in maze-learning ability in rats. *Thirty-ninth Yearbook, National Society for the Study of Education,* 1940, Part I, 111-119.

Tryon, R. C. Identification of social areas by cluster analysis. *University of California Publications in Psychology,* 1955, 8(1), 1-100.

Tryon, R. C. Reliability and behavior domain validity: Reformulation and historical critique. *Psychological Bulletin,* 1957, **54,** 229-240.

Tryon, R. C. Experimental behavior genetics of maze ability and a sufficient polygenic theory. Paper presented at the meeting of the American Psychological Association, Philadelphia, September, 1963.

Tryon, R. C. Person-clusters on intellectual abilities and on MMPI attributes. *Multivariate Behavioral Research,* 1967, **2,** 5-34.

Tryon, R. C. Comparative cluster analysis of social areas. *Multivariate Behavioral Research,* 1968, **3,** 213-232.

Tucker, L. R., Damarin, F., & Messick, S. *A base-free measure of change.* Research Bulletin RB-65-16. Princeton, N.J.: Educational Testing Service, 1965.

Tyler, L. E. The relationship of interests to abilities and reputation among first-grade children. *Educational and Psychological Measurement,* 1951, **11,** 255-264.

Van Allen v. McCleary 27 Misc 2d 81, 211 NYS 2d 501 (Superior Court, Nassau County, 1961).

Vandenberg, S. G. The primary mental abilities of Chinese students: A comparative study of the stability of a factor structure. *Annals of the New York Academy of Science,* 1959, **79**, 257-304.

Vandenberg, S. G. The primary mental abilities of South American students. *Research Reports, Louisville Twin Study* (University of Louisville, Louisville, Ky.), Report No. 9, 1966.

Vernon, P. E. *The structure of human abilities.* London: Methuen, 1950, 1961.

Vernon, P. E. Ability factors and environmental influences. *American Psychologist,* 1965, **20**, 723-733.

Vernon, P. E. *Intelligence and cultural environment.* London: Methuen, 1969.

Very, P. S. Differential factor structures in mathematical ability. *Genetic Psychology Monographs,* 1967, **75**, 169-207.

Wald, A. *Statistical decision functions.* New York: Wiley, 1950.

Wallace, W. L. The prediction of grades in specific college courses. *Journal of Educational Research,* 1951, **54**, 587-595.

Watley, D. J., & Vance, F. L. *Clinical versus actuarial prediction of college achievement and leadership activity.* U.S. Office of Education Cooperative Research Project No. 2202. Minneapolis: University of Minnesota, 1964.

Weiner, M. Organization of mental abilities from ages 14 to 54. *Educational and Psychological Measurement,* 1964, **24**, 573-587.

Whimbey, A. E., & Denenberg, V. H. Programming life histories: Creating individual differences by the experimental control of early experiences. *Multivariate Behavioral Research,* 1966, **1**, 279-286.

Whiteman, M. Intelligence and learning. *Merrill-Palmer Quarterly,* 1964, **10**, 297-309.

Wiggins, J. S. Strategic, method, and stylistic variance in the MMPI. *Psychological Bulletin,* 1962, **59**, 224-242.

Winch, R. F., & More, D. M. Does TAT add information to interviews? Statistical analysis of the increments. *Journal of Clinical Psychology,* 1956, **12**, 316-321.

Witmer, D. R. Economic benefits of college education. *Review of Educational Research,* 1970, **40**, 511-523.

Wolfle, D. L. Diversity of talent. *American Psychologist,* 1960, **15**, 535-545.

Womer, F. G. *What is National Assessment?* Denver, Colo.: Education Commission of the States, 1970.

Woodrow, H. The relation between abilities and improvement with practice. *Journal of Educational Psychology,* 1938, **29**, 215-230.

Woodrow, H. Factors in improvement with practice. *Journal of Psychology,* 1939, **7**, 55-70.

Woodworth, R. S. *Psychology.* (Rev. ed.) New York: Holt, 1929.

Wrightman, L., & Gorth, W. P. CAM: The new look in classroom testing. *Trend,* 1969, Spring, 56-57.

Yates, A. *Grouping in education.* New York: Wiley, 1966.

Yoder, A. H. The study of the boyhood of great men. Pedagogical Seminary, 1894, **3**, 134-156.

Zimmerman, W. S. Hypotheses concerning the nature of the spatial factors. *Educational and Psychological Measurement,* 1954, **14**, 396-400.

Zubin, V. Clinical versus actuarial prediction. In *Proceedings of the 1955 Invitational Conference on Testing Problems.* Princeton, N.J.: Educational Testing Service, 1956. Pp. 107-128.

Zwicky, F. *Morphological analysis.* Berlin: Springer, 1957.

Index of Terms